RAISING CAIN

The Life and Politics of Senator Harry P. Cain

What Others Are Saying about *Raising Cain*...

"Harry Cain was Tacoma's first modern mayor. He was also Tacoma's most famous mayor, running as his party's nominee for the U.S. Senate while still on General Dwight Eisenhower's staff in London, being elected to the Senate when he returned home from the war and, finally, serving on the Subversive Activities Control Board during the height of the McCarthy era. Harry Cain was always colorful, controversial, and unpredictable. C. Mark Smith, who knew Cain as a young man, captures it all in *Raising Cain*. A "must read" for Washington State political history lovers!"

Dr. Bill Baarsma
Professor Emeritus, University of Puget Sound
Mayor of Tacoma
2002-2010

"Mark Smith has given us a thorough and fascinating account of the life and complex career of Harry Cain. A soldier and a politician, he was a significant and somewhat puzzling participant in the flow of American history from the 1930s to the 1970s. Smith's book provides many insights and anecdotes about the man and his politics previously unavailable to historians of this period."

Dr. Richard Kirkendall
The Scott and Dorothy Bullitt Professor Emeritus
University of Washington

"Former U.S. Senator Harry Cain of Washington State truly left his mark on the many institutions in which he served—among them the mayoralty of Tacoma, the Supreme Allied Command under Gen. Eisenhower during World War II, the United States Senate, the Subversive Activities Control Board, and the Miami-Dade County Commission. Today Cain is largely forgotten, but this is truly an unjust fate and legacy, as he was a fascinating and courageous (if sometimes puzzling) character and, especially, as he played a key role in helping to discredit some of the worst aspects of the post-World War II American Red Scare, even though he had for years been viewed as a hard-core "McCarthyite." In this exhaustively researched and well-written book, C. Mark Smith takes us a long way in bringing Cain back from obscurity and putting him in the spotlight which he both loved and, often, deserved."

Robert Justin Goldstein
Professor Emeritus of Political Science, Oakland University
Author of American Blacklist: The Attorney General's List of Subversive
Organizations
(University Press of Kansas, 2008)

RAISING CAIN

The Life and Politics of Senator Harry P. Cain

C. Mark Smith

BOOK PUBLISHERS NETWORK

Book Publishers Network
P. O. Box 2256, Bothell, WA 98041
(425) 483-3040
www.bookpublishersnetwork.com

10 9 8 7 6 5 4 3 2 1

LCCN: 2010913494
ISBN13: 978-1-935359-65-4
ISBN10: 1-935359-65-7

Smith, C. Mark.

Raising Cain : the life and politics of Senator Harry P. Cain / C. Mark Smith. -- Bothell, WA : Book Publishers Network, c2011.
p. ; cm.

ISBN: 978-1-935359-65-4
Includes bibliographical references and index.

1. Cain, Harry P. (Harry Pulliam), 1906-1979. 2. Legislators--United States--Biography. 3. Washington (State)--Politics and government--20th century. 4. Internal security--United States--History--20th century. 5. Subversive activities--United States--Prevention--History--20th century. I. Title.
E748.C185 S65 2011 2010913494
973.92/0924--dc22 1101

Manufactured in the United States of America

A portion of the proceeds from the sale of this book will go to the Harry P. Cain Memorial Scholarship Fund at the University of Puget Sound.

Cover and book designed by Chuck Luce.
Edited by Julie Scandora.
Composed by Stephanie Martindale.
Printed and bound by Bang Printing, Brainard, Minnesota.

*This book is dedicated to the many people
who helped make it possible.*

*It is also dedicated to my family for putting up with me
while I spent more time with Harry Cain than
I did with them.*

Contents

Acknowledgments

The African proverb, "It takes a whole village . . ." is overused, I think, but in the case of this project it's apt. This book would not have been possible without the help of many people, most of whom were unknown to me when I started this project. Indeed, there have been so many people who have helped me that I am almost certain to overlook someone. I apologize for that and any other oversights in advance.

I probably would not have undertaken this project without the encouragement of a group of my former classmates at the University of Puget Sound who knew of my love of history and convinced me to proceed. Likewise, this book would not have been possible without the full and enthusiastic cooperation of Harry Cain's children. I would like to thank each of them for their friendship and for their generous help. One of my primary motivations in writing this book has been to help them better understand and remember the remarkable man they never had a chance to know well enough. Each of them has provided me with valuable insights and memories. Their attics and closets have yielded a treasure trove of documents, often original, that include scrapbooks, letters, photographs, invitations, event programs, journals, speeches, and other mementos.

There was a time in high school when I thought I wanted to be a librarian. In the process of writing and researching this book, I have come to understand just how valuable good research librarians *really are* and how thankful I am that I chose a less-demanding profession. I want to thank two that have been particularly helpful to me. Jean Fisher is a research librarian at the Tacoma (Washington) Public Library's fabulous Northwest Room—a facility that serves as home away from home for many historians and researchers. I'm sure that I have imposed upon her patience and skill far more than the library's administrative procedures allow. In retrospect, I don't believe I could have completed this book without her help and that of the rest of the Northwest Room staff. Connie Farr is the research librarian at the wonderful Richland (Washington) Public Library. She has helped me find many out-of-print books and articles with understanding and good cheer.

In addition, I want to recognize the following: Deborah May of the Nashville (Tennessee) Public Library; Joe Hardesty of the Louisville (Kentucky) Free Public Library; John Tilford, archivist at the Jesse Ball duPont Library of the University of the South; Ken Despertt at the Washingtoniana Room of the District of Columbia Public Library; Gary Lundell, Special Collections Reference Specialist, at the University of Washington Library; Jennifer Manning, Gary Johnson, and Jonathan Eaker at the Library of Congress; John Shipley, manager of the Florida Room at the Miami-Dade County Public Library System; Peggy Firman and Andrea Kueter at the Collins Memorial Library at the University of Puget Sound; and Harvey Gover at the Max E. Benitz Memorial Library at Washington State University Tri-Cities. Mary Baumann and Amy Camilleri of the U.S. Senate Historical Office and Heather Moor, photo historian of the U.S. Senate, have also been quite helpful. I would particularly like to mention the assistance of David Clark at the Harry S. Truman Library and Museum in Independence, Missouri, and of Jim Leyerzapf and Mary Burtzloff at the Dwight D. Eisenhower Presidential Library & Museum in Abilene, Kansas.

I also need to mention David Nicandri and Joy Werlink of the Washington State Historical Society. David is the Society's executive director. David and I served together on the Washington State Centennial Commission in the 1980s. His exceptional leadership has made the Society, its museums and archives, into one of the best organizations of its kind in America. Joy is an archivist at the Society's Washington State Historical Research Center who has shepherded me through the Cain papers there and assisted me in many other ways. I should also like to acknowledge the assistance of Scott Daniels, research librarian at the Oregon Historical Society, for his assistance with photos and material from the 1924 Hill Military Academy yearbook and of photos and other materials made available by Hugh Dawn at the Historical Museum of Southern Florida in Miami.

Acknowledgments

For assistance related to Cain's military service, I would like to thank several military historians, notably Synthia Santos, I Corps and Fort Lewis historian at the Fort Lewis Military Museum, and Donna Tabor and John W. Aarsen, division historian and curator, respectively, of the 82d Airborne Division Memorial Museum, Fort Bragg, North Carolina.

I would also like to thank all of those who have generously given their time to read and comment on all, or portions of, this book. They include Cain's son and daughter; my longtime friend Elaine Bolton of Griffin, Georgia, who undertook the genealogical research into the remote complexities of the Cain and Pulliam families; Dr. Caroline Gallacci and Dr. Ronald Magden, both authors, teachers, and historians, who have provided me with excellent advice in many areas, but particularly with regard to Tacoma's early history; another friend, Thomas Moak—Tacoma native, librarian, historian, and until recently, mayor of Kennewick, Washington; and, finally, Dale and Marlene Wirsing. Dale and I went to high school and college together. He is a former copy desk chief and news editor for the *Tacoma News Tribune* and past president of the Tacoma Historical Society. I also cannot fail to recognize the support of Dr. Bill Baarsma, who had established the public administration program at the University of Puget Sound prior to the Harry Cain Scholarship being established. Bill then went on to be elected to the Tacoma City Council and to serve as mayor of Tacoma from 2002 to 2010. He was instrumental in helping to create the Harry P. Cain Promenade in downtown Tacoma. Bill has been a tremendous help in a great many ways, but none more important than his continuing friendship.

In addition to the above, three other prominent academicians read the entire book and, apart from their commitment of time—for which I am deeply appreciative, their comments and suggestions have improved my manuscript in innumerable ways. Most important, they have kept me from making many errors of fact and misinterpreting sometimes arcane events and activities that otherwise would have gone unnoticed.

Professor John Pierce is the former executive director of the Oregon Historical Society and vice chancellor emeritus at the University of Colorado at Colorado Springs, now teaching at the University of Kansas. John and I share a common affiliation with the University of Puget Sound.

Professor Richard Kirkendall is a noted Truman historian and author and the Scott and Dorothy Bullitt Professor Emeritus at the University of Washington. He has been generous beyond measure with his time and advice, including several delightful lunches together at the University of Washington Faculty Club. He has guided many talented students through their doctoral dissertations, and I am honored that he has similarly helped me through this project.

I am indebted to Professor Robert Justin Goldstein, research associate at the Center for Russian and East European Studies at the University of Michigan at Ann Arbor and emeritus professor of Political Science at Oakland University in Rochester, Michigan, not only for his help and advice in trying to understand better the arcane world of the government's loyalty-security programs but also for his objective view of Cain's role in trying to change the Eisenhower Administration's policy during the 1950s. His 2008 book, *American Blacklist*, is the first in-depth look at the Attorney General's List of Subversive Organizations. His article in the Spring 2007 issue of *Pacific Northwest Quarterly*, "Raising Cain: Senator Harry Cain and His Attack on the Attorney General's List of Subversive Organizations," discusses Cain's efforts in more detail.

Each of these individuals helped me in one way or another to write the book. Publishing it, however, was another matter. When all looked bleak, Sheryn Hara and her wonderful team at Book Publishers Network stepped up and helped me make the project a reality. I owe her, and each of them, a deep debt of gratitude.

Finally, I need to thank my family—Elsa, Scot, and Todd—who accepted, even if they did not completely understand, my need to undertake this project. Their patience and understanding of the countless hours I spent behind the closed doors of my office and the unanticipated expenditures associated with my periodic trips in pursuit of research information are deeply appreciated.

So, as you can see, many people have been responsible for what is good about this book. I, alone, am responsible for what is not.

Raising Cain

The Life and Politics of Senator Harry P. Cain

Introduction

On November 12, 1940, during the dark days of the London Blitz, Prime Minister Winston Churchill spoke in the House of Commons, delivering a powerful eulogy to the memory of his political adversary, Neville Chamberlain, who had died three days earlier of cancer. "History with its flickering lamp stumbles along the trail of the past, trying to reconstruct its scenes, to revive its echoes, and kindle with pale gleams the passion of former days. What is the worth of all this? The only guide to a man is his conscience; the only shield to his memory is the rectitude and sincerity of his actions."[1] Churchill was speaking of Chamberlain, but his comments applied equally to himself. His observations also applied to another controversial politician half a world away who, like Churchill, experienced both the highs and lows of public life during his career but survived them to provide an invaluable service at a crucial time in his nation's history.

Most Americans have probably never heard of Harry Pulliam Cain. Even for those who have, he is, today, little more than a footnote on the pages of Washington State history—a colorful, complicated, and controversial man whose public career spanned four decades of the mid-twentieth century and whose actions helped change the course of civil liberties in America.

Cain was a progressive mayor, a highly decorated army officer, U.S. Senator, member of the Subversive Activities Control Board during the Eisenhower Administration, a commercial banker, community leader, and civil libertarian. In the ultimate controversy of his career, Cain defied both his party and his president to protect the freedom of thousands of Americans during the post-war Red Scare.

Regardless of where he was or what he was doing, Harry Cain was likely to be at the center of whatever was going on around him. For nearly forty years in public life, he offered his leadership, contributed his time and effort, and participated in the public debate. Indeed, he was often responsible for *creating* the debate in which he participated. Some part of this was just in the nature of the man. More often, it was the result of his evolving politics and viewpoints. Cain admitted as much when he once told a reporter, "From time to time and for different reasons, [I have] been a conservative, a militant, a liberal, a moderate, a purist, a radical, and now and again, a populist . . . who has simply done the best I could when confronted with situations demanding action."[2]

During the 1940s and 1950s, Cain's career had blazed across the public sky like a spectacular shooting star. But having at one time or another infuriated both of America's major political parties, Cain spent the final twenty-three years of his life in Florida where most of his many accomplishments there remained unnoticed by the rest of the country. Even before his death in 1979, the nation had largely forgotten about Harry Cain. America was moving on to embrace new leaders and new issues. The country's focus on internal security—arguably the most important legacy of Cain's public service—changed in its emphasis. While the threat of subversion remained, in the public's mind, it became a sub-plot in the larger, worldwide conflict between the United States and the Soviet Union as they battled for dominance over the rest of the world. In the aftermath of the Cold War, scholars of the period reassessed the legacy of the post-war Red Scare and, in doing so, rediscovered Harry Cain.

The period of the "Second Red Scare," also commonly, if too broadly, known as the McCarthy era, was not the first time that Americans like Harry Cain have had to confront the fine balance between protecting the internal security of the nation and defending the civil liberties of its citizens, and unfortunately, it will not be the last. The issue has been with us since the founding of our Republic and remains with us today. It is not hard to substitute today's "War on Terror" for the "Red Scare" of Cain's time. Cain spoke knowingly of these concerns when he noted, "We can be safe and free at one and the same time, but it is possible to become so safe that nobody can be free."[3] Cain knew what he was talking about. He had seen the internal fear and repression of Nazi Germany firsthand. Cain understood that the United States, in its short history, had not only tried but could certainly succeed in making itself much safer, but that would mean many more restrictions on the freedoms of its citizens.

ANY STUDY OF Harry Cain's life and public career is bound to be filled with "why" questions. Why did Cain oppose the detention and internment of the Japanese during World War II when most elected public officials either supported the action or remained silent? Once considered a progressive mayor of Tacoma—and a Democrat—why did he, once he was elected to the U.S. Senate as a Republican, align himself with the most conservative elements of the Republican Party? Once there, why were so many of his votes on key issues so out-of-step with the views of the majority of his constituents—even those who had originally supported him? Finally, after his public career had been redeemed by the Eisenhower Administration, why did he so publicly oppose the administration's loyalty-security program; why didn't he resign and continue his opposition from the outside?

At the time, and later, his unpredictability and contradictory politics confounded and amazed both his friends and foes alike. Cain took a certain perverse pleasure in this, but over the course of his career, few understood that many of his more controversial actions were based on a set of personal core beliefs, which were rooted in the conservative-libertarian philosophy he had embraced as a young man and which were expanded by the experiences he went through during the Second World War. Cain believed in constitutional rights, as little government as necessary, individual freedom and personal liberty, free markets, an adequate national defense, a limited role in foreign affairs, and defending both the security of the nation and the civil liberties of its citizens.

Like many others, before and since, Cain found that acting on his core beliefs made for difficult and often self-destructive politics. Because of his newspaper training, Cain was very good at researching and understanding a problem—at least from his point of view—but he was much less effective when it came to the art of compromise or negotiation. As a result, Cain was unable or unwilling to practice successfully the art of partisan politics. It has been said that politics is "the art of the possible," and Harry Cain showed very little inclination in a partisan setting to search for what was possible.

In spite of his shortcomings, many of the core issues that Cain believed in and acted upon remain at the forefront of American political debate. How he dealt with them is not only a fascinating story but an instructive one as well. As Churchill said of Chamberlain on that bleak and rainy November day in 1940, "In one phase men seem to have been right, in another they seem to have been wrong. Then again, a few years later, when the perspective of time has lengthened, all stands in a different setting. There is a new proportion. There is another scale of values."[4] That's why I decided to write this book.

THE DEFINITIVE BIOGRAPHY about Harry Cain should have been written by longtime Tacoma and Washington, DC, newspaper reporter and columnist—and former Cain staffer—Emily Walker. She understood Cain better than most (see Chapter 8). Over the years, Walker exhibited both the critical eye and personal affection that would have resulted in an unvarnished evaluation of the man. I can imagine Cain reading her account and commenting to her with a wry smile on his face, "You really skewered me!" In the 1990s, a Tacoma historian, Jess Giessel, become interested in Cain's career and developed an extensive Website about him (now, unfortunately, gone) with the intent of some day writing a book about Cain. Unfortunately, health issues intervened for Giessel, and that project was never completed.

The fact that there is no contemporary biography of Cain is probably due to several factors. By the time Cain left the national stage, he had largely burned his own political bridges in both major political parties, so the market for such a project would have been severely limited. The passage of time and a growing interest in his terms as mayor of Tacoma and his battles with the Eisenhower Administration have generated new interest. Another problem is that most of Cain's personal and political papers as mayor, senator, and member of the SACB are missing. Fortunately, a number of Cain's letters and portions of some of his journals survive, as well as the extensive press coverage he generated for most of his public life. We know that Cain's SACB papers existed into the 1960s because he used them to help both his son and me to write about his "mutiny" in school papers at the time.

This project began with a simple e-mail. Following Cain's death in 1979, I created the Harry P. Cain Public Administration Memorial Scholarship at my alma mater, the University of Puget Sound in Tacoma, Washington. The scholarship was expanded in 1995 because of the generosity of Cain's children, Harry Cain II and Marlyce "Candy" Cain Tingstad. From time to time, Candy, who lives in Tacoma, and I would correspond about the high quality of recipients of the Cain Scholarship. During an exchange of e-mails in June 2008, Candy commented to me that she had never really known her father as she was born a month after Cain left for World War II and he was frequently gone during her childhood. Candy observed that I probably knew more about some aspects of her father's life than she did. Her off-hand comment led me to write a magazine article about Cain's term as mayor of Tacoma for *Columbia,* the journal of the Washington State Historical Society, which then became the primary motivation for writing this book.

Growing up in Tacoma as the son of a successful mortgage banker who was a close friend and political supporter of Cain's, I was somewhat acquainted with his children, seeing them mostly during their summer vacations in Tacoma. Occasionally, Harry himself would stay at our home. As a teenager, I thought that he was larger than life itself. Harry had a penchant for nicknames, and my two years of obligatory military service in the army during the mid-1950s resulted in my being forevermore called "General" by this highly decorated airborne infantry colonel.

In 1963, during a quick visit to Tacoma, Cain asked me to accompany him on a secretive trip to remote Okanagan, Washington, where he was to be a surprise witness at the John Goldmark libel trial (see Chapter 11). Cain loved the secrecy and the irony of the occasion as the defendants had all been former supporters of his, and he thought it would be a good "civics lesson" for me. Over the years, I came to understand and embrace the value that Cain placed on individual freedom and public service. I owe much of the success that I have enjoyed over my own long career, and certainly my longstanding interest in government, politics, and public service, to Harry Cain. It is a debt for which I was never fully able to thank him in person. I hope that this telling of his remarkable story helps to express the debt of gratitude I feel.

FINALLY, I SHOULD comment on a decision I made when writing this book, which might be confusing without further explanation, that deals with the description of military rank and organizational nomenclature used in the book. Until Chapter 4, such designations are exclusively American. But Harry Cain's war service is somewhat unusual in that he spent much of his time in the service either working with or for British officers. In the Mediterranean theater, military government was almost exclusively a British responsibility. The Americans came late to the game and generally reported to their British counterparts. To avoid confusion, I have used the same written form of referring to military rank and organizations that was employed by each country's military. At first, this may seem overly technical to the average reader, but we will later be dealing with situations in which both British and American officers and units of the same rank and numerical designation will appear at the same time. Thus, at SHAEF (Supreme Headquarters Allied Expeditionary Force) headquarters in London, Cain worked for and, ultimately, reported directly to a British Lieutenant-General—the future Sir Arthur Edward Grassett, who served as Eisenhower's top civil affairs and military government advisor and Assistant Chief of Staff. The British form of referring to a Lieutenant-General employs a hyphen, whereas the form employed by the U.S. Army does not. British unit designations are normally rendered by a cardinal number followed by the type of unit, i.e. 10 Corps, 1 Airborne Division, or 5 Para (Parachute Brigade), while the corresponding American unit designations use Roman numerals or ordinal numbers, i.e., XVIII Corps (Airborne), 82nd Airborne Division, or 504th PIR (Parachute Infantry Regiment). I hope this helps more than it confuses.

1

Beginnings

NASHVILLE, TENNESSEE, WAS a city of nearly 81,000 in 1900, the state's capital, and the center of transportation, finance, wholesale trade, and manufacturing for the Upper South. Like many other Southern cities, Nashville had been devastated by the Civil War but recovered more rapidly than most because of its progressive leadership and its location as a key transportation hub on the Tennessee River. By the turn of the century, it boasted a growing, modern downtown and a series of new neighborhoods served by an expanding system of streetcar lines. However, while the city's wealth and status made it unusual, Nashville was—like the rest of the state—racially segregated, politically conservative, and solidly Democratic.

It was into this environment that twin boys were born on January 10, 1906, to George William Cain, Jr., and his wife, Grace Elizabeth Pulliam Cain in their large, brick Victorian home on Seymour Avenue in a newly fashionable neighborhood in East Nashville. Harry was named for his mother's favorite brother, Harry Clay Pulliam, who had been the former editor of the *Louisville Commercial* newspaper and, in 1906, the president of the National Baseball League. Harry's twin brother, William—known as Bill—was named for their father and grandfather. An older sister had died in infancy. Their father could trace his family roots at least as far back as 1768 to Sussex County, Virginia. In 1822, his family joined the migration of Virginians from that area to Limestone County, Alabama, just below the Alabama-Tennessee line. In 1827, Allison Chappell Cain married Mary Green Malone, the daughter of a local plantation owner. The couple prospered, and by 1850, they owned a 1,025-acre plantation called Dover, which was worked by fifty slaves. In May 1862, Allison Cain died, defending his plantation from federal soldiers commanded by Colonel John Basil Turchin, a former Russian army officer, who became notorious as one of the earliest proponents of a "scorched earth" policy against Southern noncombatants.

The couple had seven children, the third of whom, the first George William Cain—known as George—was born on March 28, 1833. After serving with the Confederate army during the Civil War, George Cain returned home to Athens, Alabama, and married Susan Stith Malone in 1866. At least three generations of Cains and Malones were intermarried, and apparently, two adult Malone women lived with Cain prior to his marriage to Susan. The 1870 census shows him engaged in the dry goods business in Athens, and the 1880 census lists Cain as the Athens postmaster, indicating that he probably operated the post office out of his dry goods store. He died on January 16, 1892, at the age of fifty-nine.

The second George William Cain, Jr.—known as Will or Billy—was Harry Cain's father. He was born in Athens on August 28, 1871, the second of four children. The Cains were devout Methodists, and Will followed his older brother, Stith Malone Cain, to Nashville in August 1888 to "commence life's battles." Stith Cain was a successful attorney and future judge, socially prominent, and an avid sportsman, serving as president of both the Nashville Tennis Club and the Nashville Golf and Country Club. Will Cain shared his brother's interest in all sports but particularly in golf.

Will Cain was employed by the publications branch of the Board of Missions of the Methodist-Episcopal Church South at its headquarters at 346 Public Square in Nashville. In 1896, he married Agnes Stratton, the eighteen-year-old daughter of wealthy parents who also lived in Athens. There were no children from this union, and she died of tuberculosis following a trip to New York City in 1899.

In August 1902, Will Cain married Elizabeth Grace Pulliam—"Gracie" to her family—in Louisville, Kentucky, where her parents were well known in both business and society. A graduate of Potter College in Bowling Green, Kentucky, Gracie had by the time of her marriage already published several short stories written while she vacationed at Mapledale, her family's large farm in Allen County, Kentucky. The announcement of their wedding in the *Louisville Courier-Journal* noted that she was active in Louisville society and called her family "one of the oldest and most prominent families of the South."[1]

Will Cain advanced steadily through various management positions at the Board of Missions, becoming treasurer in 1897, chief clerk by 1901, and manager by 1904. That same year, he joined businessman John Early's successful equestrian tack and leather goods business as vice president while still retaining his position at the Board of Missions. Early was a prominent entrepreneur and civic leader, who originally made his mark with a successful patent medicine company and served as president of Nashville's United Charities. By 1910, Cain appears to have left the Board of Missions to work for the company full-time because its name was changed from the Early-Mack Company to the Early-Cain Company. The *Nashville City Directory* lists Cain as an owner of the Early-Cain Company until 1912, although by that time he had moved to Tacoma, Washington. Harry Cain later remembered his father as a "big personage" in the harness and leather goods business in Nashville.[2]

Grace Pulliam's family can be traced back to Yorkshire, England, as early as 1520. Members of the family had immigrated to Culpeper County, Virginia, by 1744. Grace's great-grandfather Benjamin Pulliam served as a soldier from Virginia in the later years of the Revolutionary War and then moved his family west to Warren County, Kentucky, near Bowling Green, before 1800. Her grandfather, Robert Ficklin Pulliam, was born in nearby Scottsville in 1805. Robert was a farmer who was elected as the county's sheriff for fourteen years and then served as the clerk of the circuit court for another twelve years.

Grace's father, Henry Clay Pulliam, was also born in Scottsville, in 1830, one of eleven children of Robert and Eveline Ellis Pulliam. He married Mary Thomas Page in Barren, Kentucky, on January 13, 1856. Henry became a successful businessman, operating a cotton commission business in Arkansas during the Civil War and, then by 1865, moving to Louisville, where he eventually joined his father-in-law, John Hudson Page, in managing the Farmer's Old Tobacco Warehouse, one of the first tobacco warehouses in Louisville. After Page died in 1878, Pulliam continued to manage the business under the name of Page and Pulliam until he retired in 1903. Henry and Mary Pulliam were wealthy and active in Louisville society. Elizabeth Grace Pulliam, born in 1877, was the youngest of the couple's six children.

Her favorite older brother, Harry Clay Pulliam, for whom young Harry was named, was a sports writer who covered baseball for the *Louisville Commercial* and, at the time, was considered one of the leading authorities on the game. Soon after becoming the paper's city editor, Harry Pulliam was hired away by the owner of the Louisville Colonels baseball team, eventually becoming the club's president. Pulliam was so successful with the Colonels that, after a reorganization of the league in 1902, he was unanimously chosen by the rest of the club owners to serve as president of the National Baseball League. In addition to being the league's president, Pulliam also served as its secretary and treasurer until 1907. Apparently, the accumulated stress of all three jobs finally was too much for Pulliam, who committed suicide in his room at the New York Athletic Club in 1909.[3] As an indication of the close relationship that existed between Grace Cain and her older brother, it was Grace's husband, Will, who was sent to New York to accompany Pulliam's remains back to Nashville.

BY THE TURN of the century, Tacoma, Washington, was beginning to recover from the deep financial depression that had stifled its growth for most of the previous decade. Its population had grown to nearly 38,000, but only 1,700 of the residents had arrived during the past ten years. Almost half of the city's residents were foreign born, mostly immigrants from England, Canada, Sweden, Germany, Italy, Croatia, and Japan who had lived in Tacoma for less than five years.[4]

Tacoma's history had been defined by the Northern Pacific Railroad. After a series of fits and starts, its rails had finally reached Puget Sound at Commencement Bay on December 16, 1873, where its real estate subsidiary, the Tacoma Land Company, began to build a town. That work had hardly started when it was nearly forced to stop as a result of the financial Panic of 1873. The company's partially logged town site existed two miles away from another small village that had been platted in anticipation of the arrival of the railroad. The two towns operated independently of each other and in open competition until they were forced to merge in 1884. By the following year, both the native Puyallup Indians and former Chinese railroad laborers had been forcibly removed from the fledgling community as detriments to its future development.

The young city was a very lively place. Bars and brothels flourished to such a degree that the town's main street was called "Whiskey Row." Although the railroad had constructed the elegant new Tacoma Hotel in 1884, so many other hotels—of a decidedly less elegant nature—were built that one civic booster suggested that they call the new town the "City of Hotels." Tacoma's well-deserved reputation as a wide-open town would extend well into the mid-twentieth century. Then, renewed efforts to eliminate vice and another effort to remove an ethnic minority population would play prominent roles in Harry Cain's future political career.

By 1900, Tacoma, while still heavily dependent on timber, wood products, and the railroad, was finally becoming more diversified. The Tacoma smelter was the largest on the West Coast, processing up to 700 tons of copper ore in one day. The Northern Pacific Railroad's shops in South Tacoma provided the largest foundry in the West for forging iron wheels and repairing rail cars. The city's flourmills were also the largest in the West. Tacoma boosters were exhorting anyone who would listen, to "Watch Tacoma Grow!"

Between 1900 and 1910, the city's population grew by 122 percent, to more than 83,000. In 1904, the federal government ended the Northern Pacific's rail monopoly in Tacoma. According to historian Herbert Hunt, one of the major contributors to Tacoma's growth during this time may have been the rumor that the Union Pacific Railroad was also considering moving its western terminus from Portland to Tacoma.[5] Also in 1904, Congress finally agreed to allow the Puyallup Indians to sell their reservation lands legally to non-Indians, a practice that had been common but camouflaged from official view for many years. This finally opened up the tide flats of the Puyallup River delta for port and industrial development.[6]

By 1910, Tacoma's voters agreed to change the city's government from the then-current mayor-council form to the commission model, which was then in great vogue around the country. Under the commission form of government, voters elected a number of nominally equal commissioners (normally five or seven) one of whom was elected to the largely honorary title of mayor. Each assumed responsibility for a portion of the city government, thus reducing the power of an elected mayor. It was felt that non-partisan, civic-minded commissioners, committed to running the city like a business, would end the patronage and corruption that had characterized the previous government. The new charter also included Progressive Party-inspired provisions that allowed for initiative and referendum petitions, as well as the means to recall an elected official.

The proposed new charter represented a "win-win" situation for almost everyone: labor liked the decentralization of power; minority Democrats felt that they might fare better under the proposal; majority Republicans supported it because most of the reformers came from their ranks; the police department had some concerns but came to the conclusion that they were better off having to deal with only a single commissioner rather than with the mayor and the full council; and, finally, the criminal element liked it because if they could control the mayor and the public safety commissioner, they could control the whole city with just one more vote.[7] The new charter was approved by a vote of three to one in 1910, but only 39 percent of the voters took the trouble to vote. It was this form of government that Harry Cain would inherit when he became mayor in 1940.

WHILE HE RETAINED his ownership position in the Early-Cain Company until 1912, Will Cain decided to move his family to Tacoma in 1910.[8] The Cains were accompanied by their African-American handyman, Tony McChristian, who had been with the family in Nashville. In the twin's baby book, Gracie Cain referred to McChristian as their "tried and true friend."[9] The reasons for the move are not well understood. Harry always contended that the move was the result of his father's recurring malaria. Malaria was endemic to the southeastern United States at this time, and its causes were often associated with "bad air." Perhaps Will felt that Tacoma's maritime climate was the solution to his problem.[10] In any event, no member of the family had ever before lived above the Mason-Dixon Line. Life in Tacoma was a far cry from the established society of a Louisville or Nashville, but it was young and vibrant and full of economic opportunity. By the time the Cains arrived, Tacoma had been incorporated as a city for only twenty-six years, and Washington had been a state for even less time than that.

Upon his arrival, Cain rented a recently renovated flat at 708 North Fourth Street in a large, three-story Victorian apartment building with a corner turret and a commanding view overlooking Commencement Bay. The family moved three more times in the next seven years, renting various single-family homes in the same generally up-scale neighborhood near Wright Park and the growing commercial area that had evolved around First Street and Division Avenue. The boys attended Tacoma's Lowell School, located within convenient walking distance of their various residences.

It is unknown whether Will Cain knew anyone in Tacoma before moving there, but it seems likely that he either knew someone already in Tacoma—probably an associate at the Methodist Publishing House in Nashville—or had learned of a business opportunity in Tacoma. In any event, Cain quickly joined the staff of the *West Coast Lumberman*, a respected lumber industry trade publication, as a traveling sales representative. By 1914, the *Tacoma City Directory* listed Cain as the publication's president and, by 1924, as its manager. Its offices were located on the seventh floor of the Tacoma Building at Eleventh and A Streets in the heart of the city—the same building occupied by the Weyerhaeuser Timber Company and the Tacoma Chamber of Commerce.

The Cains, although still relatively young, soon became well known in Tacoma's social and literary circles. Both were writers. Of course, Will made his living as one, and after her marriage, Gracie had continued to publish her work in such publications as the *Southern Woman's Magazine* and poetry in a Tacoma newspaper under an assumed name. An example of Gracie's work survives in an article she wrote in 1915 about an effort to build a "Great Columbus Light" tower and beacon at Santo Domingo in the Dominican Republic—an effort that was being orchestrated by one of her brothers, William Ellis Pulliam, who lived there and was interested in the project as a means of recognizing the final resting place of Christopher Columbus's remains.[11] Gracie was a member of the Aloha Club, a ladies' study club that worked to provide public art to Tacoma schools, and was involved in both the Lowell School Parent-Teacher Association and the regional Congress of Mother's and Parent-Teacher Associations. After America's entry into World War I, Gracie became active in local Red Cross work. Harry remembered that his mother had been responsible for starting the school lunch program in the Tacoma public schools. She was a "talented, imaginative and lovely woman, a writer of stories for children, and an entertainer."[12]

Both the Cain and Pulliam families were particularly proud of their Southern heritage, and both parents passed that pride on to their boys. In keeping with family tradition, the Cains were "conservative Democrats." Grace had belonged to the Kate Littleton Chapter of the United Daughters of the Confederacy (UDC) in Nashville and joined Tacoma's Dixie Chapter after she moved to Tacoma. Grace was an active member of the Tacoma group and reported on a tea she hosted at her home for other chapter members in the November 17, 1912, issue of the *Confederate Journal*, the organization's publication. Gracie's membership in the UDC was based on the service of her uncle, William W. Page, who had been a member of the famous "Orphan" Brigade of the Confederate Army of

Tennessee. Organized in the summer of 1861, the brigade consisted of six regiments of Kentucky infantry who were forced to retreat to Tennessee when Union troops occupied Kentucky. The brigade fought with distinction in many of the fiercest battles of the Civil War. Only 500 of the original 4,000 volunteers remained to surrender in May 1865.[13]

Will was mentioned frequently in the *Confederate Journal* as a donor to numerous Confederate war memorials. In 1862, his father had enlisted in the Confederate army at Corinth, Mississippi, as a private in Company E, 26th Alabama Infantry (later the 50th), known as the "Limestone Rebels." The regiment fought at Shiloh, Murfreesboro, Chickamauga, Atlanta, and Franklin. Few of the regiment survived long enough to surrender in 1865, but Cain was one of them.[14]

One of George Cain's fellow officers in the Limestone Rebels was Nicholas Davis, Jr., who had represented Limestone County in the Alabama Legislature and had been a delegate to both the Alabama secession convention and the Confederate Provisional Congress in 1861. His father, Nicholas Davis, was a War of 1812 veteran, member of the Alabama State Senate, and the Whig Party candidate for governor in 1831. The younger Nicholas Davis was Harry Cain's great-great-grandfather. Given these affiliations, it is almost certain that the boys were aware of the stories about their family members' political and military service prior to and during the Civil War.

Even with her varied interests, Grace did not adapt well to life on Puget Sound. She had difficulty adjusting to the maritime climate, and the quality of life to be found in early Tacoma was not equal to what she had known in Nashville. She had mentioned the frequent rain in a one of the reports she wrote for the *Confederate Journal*.[15] Harry later remembered that his mother also suffered from a nearly constant pain in one of her legs that caused her great difficulty.[16] Whatever the reason—the weather, the pain, or a combination of the two—Grace became increasingly depressed and, in February 1917, left Tacoma with her twin sons for an eight-month trip to Tennessee and California to visit her relatives. On October 22, shortly after she returned home and without the knowledge of her maid or her children, she went to her room, locked the door, and turned on the gas. Her body was discovered by her husband when he returned from work.[17]

Grace's suicide, following that of her favorite brother, Harry, only eight years before, raises an obvious question about a potential genetic predisposition for depression within the Pulliam family. We now have circumstantial evidence that this was, indeed, the case. In 2009, a great-granddaughter of Grace's only sister, Mary Page Pulliam, confirmed a family pattern of depression and suspected suicide in subsequent generations.[18]

His mother's death devastated Harry. He had been devoted to his mother, while his twin brother had tended to gravitate toward their father. After he was in the U.S. Senate, Harry told an interviewer that he had not been able to accept the reality of his mother's death for many years. "I went out walking alone looking for her, and at times expected to see her come smiling toward me. She was that close and real to me; even after she had gone . . . . I still have her picture here on my desk. And I still hope that maybe, somehow, she gets a kick out of some of the things I do."[19]

Sometime prior to 1920, young Harry was stricken with an attack of Bell's palsy, which left him with partially paralyzed facial muscles. The disease is a form of paralysis that results in an inability to control the facial muscles on the affected side of the face. The onset of the paralysis can take place in a single day. Although unknown at the time, Bell's palsy can be caused by Lyme disease. For months, young Harry could not speak at all and, then for many more months, could not speak clearly. The experience caused him to withdraw from his friends and associates. At some point, the lack of socialization created in him an overwhelming determination to recover his speech. As he later related in an interview, he drove himself "relentlessly—speaking with pebbles in my mouth, practicing in front of mirrors to control my facial muscles, going off where I could talk loudly and shout." Cain must have been familiar with the story of Demosthenes, reputed to be the greatest orator of ancient Greece, who also used pebbles and a mirror to overcome a serious speech impediment. Like Demosthenes, Cain went on to become one of the best public speakers of his era.

Will Cain assumed the full responsibility for raising his eleven-year-old twins after his wife's death. Both boys were excellent students and, like their father, loved sports. Both became excellent golfers, and Harry played to a four handicap for most of his adult life. It was important to Will that the boys remained conscious of their family roots and Southern heritage, that they not be reared entirely in an all-male atmosphere, and that they enjoy a well-rounded family life. For all of those reasons, he arranged to spend Christmas 1918, and each of the next seven Christmases, until the boys went away to college, with his sister, Mary Eliza, along with her husband, Ben G. Mason, and a large number of Tennessee and Alabama relatives at Seven Oaks, a large, pillared, frame house on a steep hill overlooking 2,500 acres of rich cotton bottom-land along the Elk River in Prospect Station, Tennessee, about twenty miles north of the Alabama-Tennessee border.

Harry remembered those annual visits with great fondness. The boys and their father would board a train in Tacoma and travel for four days and three nights, each way—changing trains three times along the way—to get there. "There was no electricity then at the house. We lit oil paper tapers in jars on every mantelpiece. There was a fireplace in every room, and we slept under big comforters. By the time everyone arrived, there were twenty to thirty-five, and a huge sideboard in the dining room was kept full of food for eating all during the holidays. Christmas Eve was a great time. That was when we put up the tree. With needle and thread, we would put endless yards of popcorn together. Someone always brought along a star for the top. Even the candles were made in the kitchen. It was a wonderful holiday and one which set my whole appreciation [of Christmas] for the rest of my life. The value is not in any kind of gift, it's the joy of sharing each other's company in a room with a tree."

Cain appreciated his father's efforts. "I have never known anyone who worked so hard and so long as my father to provide an identification of the family from which one came. And in so doing, he also gave me an appreciation of two different areas of life: the Pacific Northwest and Tennessee, the South."[20]

Harry and his twin brother, Bill, had a complicated relationship. They were very competitive with each other and loyal, if need be, but were very different in their interests and circles of friends. When the time came to consider high school, the decision was made that both boys would attend the Hill Military Academy in Portland, Oregon, where they enrolled in the fall of 1920. Why Hill was selected among other possibilities is unknown. Perhaps a friend of Will Cain's had recommended it.

Located in Portland's Pearl District, Hill Military Academy consisted of a number of individual houses that served as offices and classrooms and of athletic fields that saw double duty as a drill grounds. In keeping with their family's military heritage, both brothers excelled at Hill and served as presidents of their class. Harry was the better athlete, although his brother Bill was a very "stubborn and determined" competitor, particularly against his brother.[21] Bill was considered the class brain and made the school's Honor Roll each year. Harry never did, a point not ignored by his father in a 1924 letter, but he earned nine varsity letters in athletics. In his senior year, he achieved the rank of Cadet Captain and president of the "H" Club for student athletes, but Bill was named Cadet Major, the highest honor at the academy.[22]

In 1940, during a visit to Portland for a National League of Cities meeting, Cain was honored by the school. In comments made during a visit to the academy's new campus, Cain remembered living in wooden barracks at NW 23rd and Marshall "that weren't very beautiful, substantial or fireproof, but those who managed and peopled the school were ranked high by any standard." Even later, he remembered being taught by "an unusually fine set of professors, all of whom were retired persons of great age." He credited them with helping to form his future values and attitudes toward life.[23]

For two years Cain served as the associate editor of the *Adjutant*, the school's yearbook, and editor of the *Hill Cadet*, the school's student newspaper. [24] The school's 1924 yearbook included an interesting "class prophecy" in which a former student imagines that he is writing to his alma mater in 1940, having just returned from a trip around the world—during which he happened to meet each of his old mates from the class of 1924. When in England, the imaginary world traveler says that he went to Oxford University and "nearly collapsed in my surprise," when he discovered that the headmaster was "none other than Bill Cain!" Further along in the prophecy he wrote, "I went on to Calcutta, India, and as it was a warm day I dropped in at a little shop for refreshment. I was looking through the window of the shop when a large, good-looking fellow in a symphony of white walked leisurely by. I recognized him immediately as Harry Cain. . . . He is a 'soldier of fortune' and is having a great time!"[25] With the passage of time, both descriptions were plausible. After graduation, Harry remained at Hill to take post-graduate courses in English and Spanish and to study practical journalism as a police reporter for the now-defunct *Portland News-Telegram*. Bill went on to Oregon Agricultural College, the predecessor of Oregon State University, where he graduated with honors in electrical engineering and was actively recruited to work for General Electric.[26]

As Harry considered college, he found himself "drawn more and more to the traditions and to the heritages of the area from which I had come, and this led me to the University of the South."[27] The prestigious, liberal arts-oriented university and its Episcopal seminary were, and are, universally known as Sewanee, after its location in remote Sewanee, Tennessee. Perched on top of the western face of the Cumberland Plateau, more than 900 feet above the valley floor below, the campus was built on one of the highest points of land between Chattanooga and Nashville. The campus and adjacent village occupy 13,000 wooded acres, known as the Domain, with all of the land owned by the Episcopal Church. Its traditional Gothic architecture was borrowed from Oxford and Cambridge in England. So too was the tradition of wearing academic gowns on campus. The lofty location of the campus—sometimes literally in the clouds—added to its remoteness, and this, along with its sometimes quaint traditions and personal honor code, provided an ideal opportunity for students to become fully immersed in academic and campus social life. When Cain attended the school, there were approximately 300 students there, not including seminarians preparing for the Episcopal priesthood.

At Sewanee, Cain studied history, literature, and German, as well as classical languages, lettered in four sports, was a member of the school's drama society, was a varsity debater for four years and editor of the school's newspaper for two, and was a member of numerous honor and scholastic societies. Cain was influenced by his study of classical philosophy, particularly the Stoics, whose emphasis on universal reason had influenced America's founding fathers. Cain appreciated the importance that the Stoics placed on politics and engagement in the broader world and the idea that a good life involves doing what you believe is right, even if that view is not shared by others. The Greeks and Romans also placed great value on oratory, which Harry Cain also shared. Burke correctly predicted the failure of the French Revolution because he believed that it tried to restructure society based on abstract principles. He believed, rather, that society develops as a result of well-defined duties and precedents and that liberty is an inheritance passed down from our forefathers to be transmitted to all who follow. In addition to Burke, Cain was further influenced by the writings of philosopher Herbert Spencer and the British cleric John Cardinal Newman.

Cain organized his fellow students to fight the longstanding practice of hazing underclassman on campus and chafed at the region's pervasive Jim Crow laws. Both practices clashed with his concept of individual freedom and human dignity. Indeed, Cain so admired the African-American head trainer of Sewanee's football team, Willie Six, that he included extensive remarks about him in *The Congressional Record* on the occasion of Six's death in 1950. In a 1962 speech to the National Institute on Police-Community Relations at Michigan State University, Cain again remembered Willie Six's perennial optimism about the future. When asked about the prospects of Sewanee's football team for the upcoming season, the then-elderly Six would always say, "Why, the best team that Sewanee's ever had is the team that's coming up."[28] A knee injury in his sophomore year ended Cain's football career but not his life-long interest in sports.

Not all of the education Cain received at Sewanee was in the classroom or on the playing field. Cain, like his brother Bill at Oregon Agricultural College, joined Phi Delta Theta Fraternity and remained active in it for the rest of his life. His ambition was to become a writer like his father. In 1950, a retired local newspaperman, John Sutherland, called Cain the best editor the school paper, *The Purple*, ever had.[29] It is believed that either Sutherland or Coleman Harwell, the executive editor of the *Nashville Tennessean*, or both, may have used their contacts to secure an offer of employment for Harry from the *New York Times* upon his graduation from Sewanee. Harry P. Cain graduated from the University of the South on June 11, 1929, in a class of forty-three with a Bachelor of Arts degree in classical literature and languages. For the rest of his life, Cain never failed to refer to his alma mater as that "wonderful institution of liberal learning, the University of the South at Sewanee."

Now a young man, Harry Cain was ready to make his mark on the world. Influenced by the memory of his young mother and the varied interests of his father, deeply aware of his Southern heritage, strengthened by the discipline and rigorous standards of his military high school and his classical, liberal arts education at Sewanee, and bolstered by his success in the classroom and on the athletic field, Cain already held most of the core convictions that would influence him for the rest of his life. They included a passionate belief in individual rights, limited government, and the primacy of the American Constitution. To these he added his own competitive will to win, his desire to succeed, and an unquenchable enthusiasm for life as he looked forward to his future.

After graduation, Cain headed home to Tacoma for a quick visit with his father, an offer of employment from the *New York Times* in his hand, and visions of a career in journalism in his head.[30]

2

"Hurry" Cain

WHEN HE RETURNED home to Tacoma, Harry Cain assumed it would be for a quick visit with his father and friends and, perhaps, a few rounds of golf before moving on to New York to accept the offer from the *New York Times*. Instead, Harry learned that his father had developed some serious health problems that had been kept from him while he was away at school. It is not now completely clear what those problems were, but it is known that Will Cain suffered increasingly from hypertension during his later life. Whatever the problem, the diagnosis was serious enough for his doctor to recommend that he step down from the day-to-day management of the *West Coast Lumberman,* a decision he now discussed with his son.

With Harry's twin brother, Bill, unavailable—at first because he was in graduate school and then, upon graduation, because he was immediately hired as an engineer by the General Electric company in Fort Wayne, Indiana—Harry decided that he needed to remain in Tacoma, at least until his father's medical problems were stabilized or resolved. The unexpected turn of events was a disappointment to him, but not a major problem. Since the death of his mother in 1917, Harry had grown increasingly close to his father, and the two men shared many common interests, including writing and sports, but particularly, golf. His father was well connected with local timber and lumber company executives, so finding employment for a bright, articulate young college graduate would not be too difficult. If all else failed, there might be a job opening with one of the local newspapers.

Perhaps as a result of a referral from his father, Harry was interviewed and hired in September 1929 by George H. "Herb" Raleigh, manager of the Tacoma office of the Bank of California and a good friend of Will Cain's. Raleigh had a well-deserved reputation as something of a talent scout in the banking business, hiring promising young men and training them for future banking careers. Under his tutelage, several of his protégés rose to top leadership positions within the bank, both in Tacoma and San Francisco.

Cain was hired for one year as a self-described "gofer," with a salary of one hundred dollars a month, "several notches up, because I was a college graduate, the first they had ever hired."[1] Harry's timing could have been better, however, because within a month of being hired, the stock market crashed. Cain determined that the calamity might, in some ways, present him with an opportunity. He approached Raleigh and told him that he wanted to become a bank messenger. Raleigh asked him, "How much money are you making now?" Cain replied, "A hundred dollars a month." Raleigh asked, "Do you know what bank messengers make?" "Yes sir," Cain replied, "they make $60 a month. But that's where you have to start if you ever want to be a manager." Cain remembered that, for the next year, "I ran from bank to bank, with checks that were by that time no good, and I learned an awful lot about the personalities of those in the banking business and the misery and sorrow that was so much a part of the business in 1929."[2]

Hard times came to the Pacific Northwest not simply as a result of the stock market crash. Rather, they had begun a decade earlier as a result of the sharp recession that followed World War I. However, once the Great Depression *did* arrive, it made conditions much, much worse.[3] The Depression unfolded in roughly three phases: the critical transition period between the Hoover and Roosevelt administrations in 1932–1933, underscored by the state and federal bank holidays; the excitement of the New Deal, highlighted by the First Hundred Days and the more controversial Second New Deal of 1935–1937; and a final phase beginning in 1937 that included premature efforts to balance the budget, the unsuccessful effort to enlarge the Supreme Court, and a new recession.

Harry Cain was lucky enough to have a job during the Depression, but many others didn't. Tacoma had its own shantytown, called "Hollywood on the Tide Flats," built of whatever materials were available and located out on the tide flats between a commercial waterway and a meat packing plant—no potable water, electricity, or any other utilities. After he became the city's mayor, Cain had the shantytown declared a health hazard and burned down.

2. "Hurry" Cain

The Great Depression affected everyone: the bankers and business-men with whom Harry Cain worked and socialized; the Japanese and Filipino truck farmers and other small-business owners who banked with him; but most of all, the unemployed and those who knew that they could become unemployed at any time. As cultural historian Morris Dickstein notes, the Great Depression didn't depress the conditions of those already poor, it merely publicized them.[4] By 1933, Washington's unemployment rate had officially climbed to 24.9 percent and never fell below 10 percent again until 1941. However, some estimates of the unemployment rate in the Seattle-Tacoma area were said to be even higher—perhaps more than 40 percent. What was even worse was the widely held fear that the Depression seemed to have no visible end. Tacoma attorney Joe Gordon, Sr., remembered walking for many blocks to find a grocery store that sold meat for eighteen cents a pound instead of the twenty-one cents a pound it cost at the store nearer to his apartment. "Business was pretty good, but people just didn't pay their bills."[5]

AFTER THE STOCK market crash and near-collapse of the economy, Cain, like many others, began to search for answers. Some found them in radical or leftist politics. Cain followed a more conventional approach. In 1931, he helped to organize, and then became president of, the Pierce County Young Democrats Club. The following year, he "worked like a demon" for the election of Franklin Roosevelt but gradually lost confidence in economic policies of the New Deal, concluding that they represented a growing pattern of intrusion by the government into the daily lives of its citizens and their businesses.[6] While Cain remained "in awe" of the President, he later said that he came to the view that "Roosevelt was a man who had gone too far, too quickly." He once told the author that he believed that Roosevelt and Henry VIII were much the same: both had accomplished much during their early years in power but had "stayed too long."[7] Cain later remembered that he relinquished his position due to "a growing disenchantment" with the Democratic Party.[8] He believed that Roosevelt's support for legislation, such as the Wagner Act that promoted unionization and the proposed Judicial Reorganization Act that would allow the President to pack the Supreme Court were efforts to change fundamentally the distribution of power and resources in America. Cain must have managed his separation with some skill because a decade later many in Tacoma still thought of him as a Democrat.

Cain likewise became increasingly concerned about the growing influence of left-wing radicalism on the labor movement in Washington State. In May and June 1935, Cain witnessed a series of increasingly violent clashes between the striking workers of the Sawmill and Timber Workers Union (and their supporters and the local "Committee of Two Hundred," led by local attorney and brother of a future President of the United States, Edgar Eisenhower).[9] Cain was on hand when local police, along with the Washington State Patrol and the Washington National Guard, successfully blocked strikers from access to the tide flats on the other side of the City Waterway where their former employers had hired non-union replacement workers in a series of bloody confrontations known as the "Battle of the 11th Street Bridge." Of course, not all of the radicals in Washington State were to be found in its labor unions. Socialism and communism held out a promise of change to many who were concerned that the existing free market economic system could not, or would not, care for those in need. The left-leaning Washington Commonwealth Federation and Washington Pension Union represented a powerful faction within the state's Democratic Party, and the two organizations would play a recurring role in Harry Cain's future.

WASHINGTON, LIKE THE rest of the nation, voted overwhelmingly Democratic in 1932. One of President Roosevelt's first acts after being inaugurated on March 6, 1933, was to declare a bank holiday. When the surviving banks finally reopened, there were far fewer of them. The Bank of California, with its unique charter, was not affected. Within the year, Harry Cain was promoted to clerk and, by 1934, moved to the bank's trust department, a position normally reserved for older men and individuals with the personality and communication skills needed to interact with wealthy clients.

By the mid-1930s, Harry was increasingly involved in the bank's business development activities, expanding his business and social contacts in the community and using the many organizations to which he belonged to promote both the bank and himself. Cain's choice of the Bank of California would later prove to have important consequences because many of his customers were farmers and small-business owners who came to know and trust him. He also became increasingly involved in the Washington Bankers Association, serving as the chair of its Public Relations and Education Committee from 1937 to 1939. Promoting the commercial banking industry during this period must have been a challenge. In a 1938 report to his Public Relations Committee, Cain noted the difficulty in trying to find organizations willing to listen to bankers "at a time when clubs without number burden their members with weekly speakers . . . the subject of banking is a deep mystery and they conceive the banker to be as bloodless as a ghost and as passionless as a handful of dust."[10]

For a banker, Cain had some unusual talents. He was outgoing and gregarious with an easy ability to strike up a conversation with just about anyone he met, whether on the street, in the bar at the golf club, or with perfect strangers on a train or an airplane. Cain would engage them directly and ask questions—and it was clear that he was actually interested in what they had to say. He also developed a well-deserved reputation as a wit, a gifted speaker, and the life of the party. Already a member of Phi Delta Theta Fraternity from his days at Sewanee, Cain was an active joiner. At one time or another, he belonged to the University-Union Club, the Young Men's Business Club (YMBC), the Eagles and the Elks Lodges, and the Advertising and Sales Club. Later he joined the Tacoma Kiwanis Club and the local chapters of the American Legion, the Veterans of Foreign Wars, and the AMVETS. As mayor, Cain would later help to found the Tacoma Athletic Club. He was active in the Tacoma Chamber of Commerce, serving on its Golden Jubilee, Civil Affairs, and Forum Program Committees. He was also a gifted amateur golfer who played to a four handicap for most of his adult life. He played at all of the local courses but most often joined his father at the Tacoma Country and Golf Club.

The two also shared a fondness for the theater. By the time he attended Hill Military Academy, Harry had already developed a sense of personal style and a flair for the dramatic. He had been a member of the Purple Masque dramatic club at Sewanee, and his interest in theater continued after he moved back to Tacoma. By 1934, Cain had appeared in several performances, including *Engaged* and *The Ghost of Yankee Doodle* and had served as the president of the Tacoma Drama League. His sense of drama would become a staple of his future political life. Later, during his senate term, it would be claimed that Cain performed on the Senate Floor or in the committee room like an actor on a large stage.[11]

One night Cain happened to visit the rival Civic Arts Theater with the scene designer from their current production. Harry was introduced to the theater's new director, Marjorie Dils—tall, classically beautiful, and a recent graduate of the University of Washington's drama department. The three went out for coffee. "We just fell into love," she told a reporter during World War II. "We'd both been looking the field over for a long time, we decided this was it. Why wait any longer?"[12]

They waited for ten days and then were married at Plymouth Congregational Church in Seattle on Saturday, September 22, 1934. There wasn't time for formal invitations or many arrangements. Harry just mentioned his upcoming wedding when talking to friends on the telephone. Hundreds of people showed up. Marjorie wore a tailored suit. Harry arrived in an old blue shirt with a frayed collar. Marj winced. She remembered that he told her that "this is my lucky shirt. I won an oratorical contest at college in it." After a weekend honeymoon, the Cains returned to Tacoma to collaborate on several plays, including *The Three Cornered Hat* and *The Animal Kingdom,* in which, according to one account, Marjorie directed her new husband "as impersonally as she would manipulate a puppet."[13]

The new Mrs. Cain had been born on December 26, 1908, in Shelbyville, Indiana. She had lived in Gary, Indiana, for nine years with her parents, Hugh and Mary, and her five other siblings before the family moved to Whidbey Island in Puget Sound. Hugh started a new venture growing loganberries on the island, but his financial backing dried up during the Depression, and he took a job with the *Seattle Star* newspaper.

Marjorie attended Lincoln High School in Seattle, Washington State College, and the University of Washington, where she majored in drama. She was a schoolteacher for two years and was studying for her master's degree in theater arts when she was hired to come to Tacoma to direct the productions of the Civic Arts Theater in the summer of 1934.

Marjorie Dils Cain—"Marj" to her friends but "Bunny," "Bushy Head," or "Mop Head" to Harry—is described by her daughter as a Renaissance woman. Marj had many interests: she directed theater productions on both coasts, encouraged talented artists, loved fashion, and worked as an interior designer. She was fond of hats—then very much in vogue for women—and wore them with style. Marjorie was an accomplished hostess and enjoyed entertaining. Her daughter later remembered that "she had an aura about her of drama and elegance, but in many ways she was down to earth and practical."[14] Every home dinner party began with her trademark canapés. She played the piano, and Harry would join in, but for all his speaking ability and acting skills, he could not carry a tune. The one song he knew the words to was "Home on the Range."

Marjorie was frugal, but Harry could better be described as being downright miserly. As a mid-level employee of a commercial bank in the 1930s, he never had much money. The couple lived in the same apartment building and shared a car with Harry's father. Later, when they finally owned their own home, Harry was not above questioning her interior decorating or entertainment expenses, but he always managed to afford his golf hobby. By the same token, she found a way to buy the piano that was thereafter a fixture in their home. Sometimes their interests could converge in interesting ways. Harry loved cats. He invariably played with them on the furniture. When the furniture became unsightly, it served as the justification Marj had been looking for to re-decorate the room.[15] His daughter remembers that the family owned two Siamese cats when her father served in the U.S. Senate. He would shave in the morning with the two cats looking on, one on each shoulder. On another occasion, she remembered that he flew home from Washington, DC, with both cats. "For some reason we could not keep them anymore (I think it was the reelection year and the family was all in limbo) and my uncle and his wife agreed to take them. Dad stopped at the Davenport Hotel in Spokane and somehow the cats got out on the roof. He had to get a bellman to go after them."[16]

Marj had her hands full with her new husband. For one thing, he was (to put it mildly) "sartorially challenged." His unruly hair was only partially controlled by the beat-up, shapeless fedora habitually perched on the back of his head. A rumpled shirt, a shapeless, only partially pressed suit, mismatched socks, a casually knotted tie, and well-worn shoes often completed the picture. His casual clothing was something else again. It could be anything but tended toward old golf sweaters and shapeless trousers. He looked presentable in photographs or in public only because Marj helped him buy his clothes, then helped him select what to wear in the morning. His daughter said of him, "He couldn't match a tie with a white shirt." He had fifteen pairs of shoes that he refused to wear because he claimed that the leather was "cold." He once dyed a pair of white summer shoes so that they had a mottled, Easter-egg look. He wore them for a year because they were "warm."[17]

If Marj tended to be a little formal, Harry was just the opposite. If he was tired, he would simply go to sleep, often in the most unlikely situations. One night, he came home late from the office to find that Marj had guests in the living room. He went around the outside of the house, pried the screen off his bedroom window, climbed into the room, and went to bed. About three o'clock in the morning, convinced that something had happened to him, she decided to go looking for him. Entering the bedroom to get her coat, Marj found him smiling in his sleep.[18] He pulled the same stunt at the home of some friends they were visiting for dinner. He got tired of the conversation, excused himself, went upstairs where he found a likely bench under a dormer window, and curled up and went to sleep. The others hardly noticed. They thought he had just gone to the restroom. They finally found him some hours later.

In spite of his quirks, or maybe because of them, women found Cain attractive. He had the physical features—trim, athletic, and ruggedly handsome—but they also admired his informal manner, his enthusiasm, and his eloquence. In a superficial way, he returned their admiration. Cain was universally polite: he opened doors for the ladies and called them "ma'am." They thought of him as "courtly," and a real "Southern gentleman." But on an emotional level, deep relationships with women were difficult for him. His daughter later referred to him as "essentially clueless." She never once heard him argue with her mother, and yet he could be hugely insensitive. While they enjoyed each other and were an effective team, they were both independent personalities whose relationship was based as much on their own separate needs as it was on each other's.

Cain's relationships with men were very different. At one level they were based on a kind of fraternal camaraderie, the love of sport, a shared drink, a conversation about politics, or the competition of a golf match. Ultimately, however, relationships were governed by an unwritten code of conduct that could influence Harry's opinion of a man for life. By his definition of personal honor, any hint of dishonesty, a broken promise, or an unpaid debt was enough to earn his undying contempt.

Another of Harry's more engaging eccentricities was his total unpredictability. One day, about a year after their marriage, Harry and Marj were driving out to the Tacoma Country and Golf Club when he turned to her and asked nonchalantly, "How would you like to go to Europe?" She said, "Fine. When do we start?" With what was probably a wry smile, he replied, "Today." They scraped together what money they could find, borrowed some more from his father, and packed their bags.

Amid shouts of "fair weather" and "happy days" from friends and family, Harry and Marj boarded the Northern Pacific's *North Coast Limited* at Tacoma's Union Station on the evening of September 4, 1935, and began what would be one of the great adventures of their life. They carried with them a couple of bags, a portable typewriter that at least on one occasion served as a pillow, and a box of sandwiches intended to reduce the need to eat in the dining car. At night, the two wedged themselves into a lower berth of their sleeper, holding on to the window and to each other for dear life in order to keep from falling out into the aisle.

Harry immediately used the typewriter to begin a daily journal. His entries—often one or more typed, single-spaced pages—chronicled who they met, what they saw, what they experienced, and often what they thought in wonderful prose and clear detail. The vivid, colorful, and witty descriptions display his well-developed powers of observation, his curiosity and varied interests, and a reporter's keen investigative instincts. The journal entries served as letters to his father and friends, like Herb Raleigh at the bank, but they also served as a record of what they did and saw so they could share their experiences with friends when they returned home.

The portion of Cain's European journal that remains was written between September 4 and November 17, 1935, and covers the early portion of their trip to Great Britain. The entries for the next ten months—four more in England, and then six in which they toured the Continent, including Nazi Germany—have been lost. It is possible that these notes were used as the basis of the many speeches Cain made after he returned to Tacoma, warning all who would listen about the threat of Nazi Germany and the need to prepare for the coming war.

While en route from Chicago to New York, the couple took a side trip to Fort Wayne, Indiana, to visit his brother Bill and his wife, Lea, and their nineteen-month-old daughter. Bill was by this time carving out a highly successful career as a senior engineer with the steam turbine division of General Electric. The two brothers managed to play four rounds of golf in two days. Harry wrote in his journal, "Just the two of us tramped around, and what was lacking in golf was more than offset by the unspoken feeling that it was very good to be together once again. We worked out the holes all even, but the young man was as bad as ever with the dice and the beers were on him. Dad's absence was all that was lacking to make complete the unity of years gone by."[19] It was the last quality time Cain would spend with his brother.

A day later they were in New York City, a first for Marj, where they attended a performance of Erskine Caldwell's *Tobacco Road* with friends from Tacoma. On September 11, they boarded the 24,000-ton SS *Manhattan*, the pride of the United States Line then sailing on the New York-to-Hamburg route. Once on board, they found their third-class cabin among "every human being and quality known to man . . . good blood and bad, peasants and intellectuals, students and spongers, seekers of adventure and seekers of old homes."[20]

The voyage was smooth, and Harry readily engaged in his habit of striking up extensive conversations with total strangers in order to find out about them and what they were thinking. It was not long before he engaged a young German woman who was returning home after a visit to the United States. Not surprisingly, he questioned her about free speech in Nazi Germany. "We had our fill of that," she responded. "Everyone talked at once and did nothing. Hitler does all the talking now and we are getting somewhere."[21] He also talked to a businessman who had traveled to Germany and who held similar positive views about what was happening there. The man lauded the efficiency and progress of the German state, saying that the United States would benefit from "Hitlerism." He urged Cain not just to take his word for it but to go and see for himself. Harry had already decided to do just that.

Arriving in Ireland and then traveling on to Scotland, the couple headed for St. Andrews, the birthplace of golf. Located on the North Sea, roughly between Dundee and Edinburgh, the four courses of St. Andrews stretch out across a peninsula jutting north into the sea from the historic small village of the same name. St. Andrews, particularly its Old Course and the Royal and Ancient Golf Club, were considered the mecca of golf. Cain was in his element. It was probably the high point of the entire trip, so much so that he filled sixteen pages of his journal with vivid descriptions of the week they spent there between September 19 and 26—the golf courses, the people, the town, technical notes regarding the game, and the full range of their experiences.[22] From St. Andrews, the couple made their way to Edinburgh, and then on to London by bus, in order to save two pounds over the cost of the train. They had developed a list of plays and theaters they wanted to attend and a list of tourist attractions they wanted to see.

Harry had justified his request for a leave of absence from the bank by suggesting that he could study British banking methods while in London and during the rest of their trip. It was the depth of the Great Depression, and his absence from the bank was, in all probability, not seriously missed. As a way of keeping a promising employee, Herb Raleigh recommended to the bank's management in San Francisco that Harry be allowed to take a year's leave of absence and even provided him with a letter of introduction to their correspondent bank in London, the Guaranty Trust Company. He also arranged a letter of introduction to the London bureau of the Associated Press.

But first they had to find a place to live. After several false starts, they finally found two single rooms—one on the fourth floor, sixty-four steps up from the ground floor, and one on the fifth floor, seventy-nine steps up—at 197 Gloucester Terrace, conveniently located near Regents Park, for thirty-four shillings a week (approximately $6.80). A bath was located on the landing between the floors. One of the rooms had a shilling meter to monitor electricity use, and both had shilling meters to monitor their consumption of gas. Coal for their small grated fireplaces cost a shilling (twenty cents) per fire. Keeping warm and dry was a constant struggle in what was one of the wettest winters in London history. They ate one main meal a day at one of the nearby restaurants and supplemented that with tea or light meals taken in their rooms, and more tea taken at theater cafes.

Their daily schedule generally included one or more tourist attractions in the London area and one—sometimes two—theater performances a day. By bus or subway, they made the rounds of the obvious and not so obvious attractions: Westminster Abbey, Whitehall and Trafalgar Square on Remembrance Day, the numerous book stores, the House of Commons, the Tower of London, Kew Gardens, the London Zoo, Madam Tussauds Wax Museum, the British Museum, and Hampton Court, near where Harry would work in London during the approaching war.

Another place that fascinated Harry was Hyde Park Corner, located not far from where they were staying. Lines of speakers were perched on ladders, most with signs or flags. Their audiences were not afraid to try to shout them down, and Harry was amazed at their skill, their conviction, and the fact that many of them were not hauled away to jail. "England is known as a nation of excellent orators. Hyde Park will show you where a good many of them must have gotten their start or finished their careers," he wrote.[23]

They discovered soccer and rugby and attended several matches. With his interest in sports, Harry concluded that "American football is a spectacle, British football is a game," and repeated a saying he had picked up: "Soccer is a gentleman's game played by hooligans; rugby is a hooligan's game, played by gentlemen."[24]

They turned theater-going into an art form. They would queue up to buy the theater's cheap tickets, sometimes waiting for several hours in the rain to do so, but it was worth it. Cain's journal is filled with reviews of twenty or more productions they saw, including their comments on the acting, the technical aspects of the productions, and the theaters themselves. The only thing missing from the experience was Harry's father, Will, who was also a huge fan of the theater.

Cain's journal is filled with his keen observations and vivid descriptions of the detail of everyday life in pre-war England: men in kilts, bowler hats, wing-collared shirts, and jackets with tails; others in military uniform or wearing their service medals from the last war; the lack of coat hooks in restaurants; how to tell the age of a building from the size of the locks and keyholes in the front doors; the omnipresence of church bells and chimes; the fact that there were few shoe-shining establishments on the street because men's shoes were shined when left outside their hotel rooms at night; some very detailed descriptions of the large public buildings and castles they visited; audiences standing and singing "God Save the King" after theater performances; and of not being able to smoke after a dinner with bank officials until the King's health had been toasted.

The couple's visit to England also happened to coincide with several of the dramatic events leading up to the war. Harry's journal provides a running commentary on what he was hearing from friends and on the street. In October 1935, Italy's dictator, Benito Mussolini, sent his forces into Ethiopia. The League of Nations in Geneva imposed economic sanctions on Italy a month later, essentially paving the way for Italy to become economically dependent on Germany, when France—Italy's largest trading partner—decided to impose the sanctions. The ground floor windows of downtown newspaper offices were filled with large maps of the Ethiopian war zone, and headlines were full of Mussolini's threats of future war in response to the League's sanctions.

2. "Hurry" Cain

Cain's journal entries clearly indicate that he believed that some action by the League was better than none but that he also had little confidence in the result. "If present efforts don't prevail, there will be but small hope for anyone or any country."[25] From his conversations with the people he met on the street, in cafes, or at the bank, it was obvious that England had little stomach for a confrontation with either Italy or Germany. He wrote, "Thus far you can't tell by mingling with those in front of the maps what they think. They stand silently, perhaps too full of thoughts of the last war to express themselves on what may come. It won't be long, however, before they start to speak their minds, and I imagine that anyone who wants to rush them into conflict had better look to their safety."[26]

Parliamentary elections in Great Britain took place on November 14, 1935. British voters didn't know it at the time, but the result of these elections would determine the makeup of the British Parliament until after World War II. Harry devoted several pages of his journal to detailed descriptions of the political situation and election results. The National Government, a coalition of the Conservatives and National Liberals, led by Prime Minister Stanley Baldwin, won enough seats to remain in office but with a much-reduced majority. The British Labour Party, whose members Cain characterized as Socialists in his journal, picked up 102 seats, mostly at the expense of the Conservatives. Harry correctly predicted that the newly elected government would find some way to compromise with Mussolini (they withdrew their sanctions over the invasion of Ethiopia in 1936). Cain's time in England and his familiarity with the British people would later prove to be invaluable to him when he would serve under various British commanders during World War II.

In February 1936, Harry and Marj left London for a six-month tour of the Continent—another goal of their trip. They visited France, Holland, Germany, Austria, and Switzerland, traveling mostly on bicycles and staying in student hostels and other low-cost accommodations. Harry would talk with common people he met on the street or in restaurants to find out what they thought, just as he had in Tacoma and London. In a Personnel Placement Questionnaire he filled out prior to entering the army in 1943, Cain said that the purpose of their trip to Europe was to contrast the "economic structures of the countries in question" and to "watch Germany prepare for the coming conflict."[27] Unfortunately, this portion of Cain's journal is lost, so we don't know the specific dates that the couple was present in Germany or what they did there beyond the later anecdotal references he made about listening to Hitler during an indoor rally, falling asleep during a performance of Wagner, and talking with Western newspapermen and privately with German bankers about their perception of the Third Reich. As it was, the couple was in Europe, and probably in Germany, during the German occupation of the Rhineland in March 1936 and for the Summer Olympic Games held in Berlin in August.

Remembering his experiences years later, Cain told an interviewer that "He [Hitler] was wiping out all human rights. [We] lived in an international house where students from all over Europe talked about the terror he was imposing. When I called on German bankers, they waited until their secretaries had left the room before they spoke, in whispers, about the government."[28] He was fascinated, but thoroughly chilled, by his impression of the Nazi dictator. Speaking to a meeting of the American Municipal Association in October 1942, he recalled Hitler vividly: "I listened to him on more than one occasion and once I sat not twenty feet from him when he said, in a crowded hall, 'The time is soon to come when we will take this world, America included, and mould it to our own liking.' I knew that he meant what he said and the 25,000 Germans who sat before him and listened with me [also] knew what he meant and they believed it."[29] Two months later, he told a Spokane Chamber of Commerce audience that "Hitler's fanaticism had brought about the blind following of his leadership by a herd of people who submitted like sheep until they were under his iron rule."[30]

While his journal from this part of the trip is missing, we do have several revealing letters that his father sent to both Harry and Marj, obviously responding to letters he had already received from them. How they managed to return and survive is unknown. On November 18, 1935, Will wrote to Harry, wondering "whether you have gone to Berlin. I will be glad when you get out of there. In fact, I will be glad when you get back to England for two reasons. You will be nearer to home, and if trouble should come over there, it will be easier for you to get out."[31]

Returning home in September 1936, Harry couldn't wait to tell others about what he had seen and heard in Germany. Over the next year and a half, he gave at least 150 talks on the European situation to local civic and service groups, first in Tacoma and then across the state. His audiences listened attentively but were somewhat incredulous. Some felt that he was an alarmist, even a warmonger, but none could deny that he was certainly entertaining.[32] Later Cain would remember, "In my opinion, Hitler by 1936 had decided upon war as an instrument of his policy. Unless he was stopped in the beginning we would certainly become involved."[33] Adolf Hitler and his Nazi state—with its glorification of the supremacy of the state and its suppression of individual liberty and freedom—was the antithesis of everything Harry Cain believed in. Those speeches were the beginning of his preparation for public life.

It was not so much *what* Harry Cain said, but *how* he said it. He was a hypnotic, dynamic, and dramatic speaker. His appearance gripped his audiences as much as his rhetoric did. His hair would be tousled, his shirt collar open, his tie loosened, his hands gesturing with the rhythm of his phrases. His speech pattern utilized the full range of emotion, dramatic pauses, and a complicated, ornate sentence structure that generated an almost endless avalanche of words. Cain's use of the English language was not unlike how Lord Moran, Winston Churchill's personal physician, once described his friend and patient. "Winston feasts on the sound of his adjectives. He likes to use four or five words all with the same meaning as an old man shows you his orchids; not to show them off, but just because he loves them."[34] The resulting impression was of a man who was spontaneous, friendly, and well informed but driven by some internal dynamo that marked him for greater things in the future.

He was also not averse to a little self-promotion along the way. One example was his flirtation with radio. Because of his avid interest in sports, he was occasionally asked to provide commentary during radio broadcasts of local sporting events. Once, in June 1937, during a golf tournament he was attending, the announcer who was supposed to broadcast the event didn't show up. Without missing a beat, Cain picked up the microphone and gave a two-hour, stroke-by-stroke account of the matches over the radio.[35] Not long afterward, he received a letter from the station's news editor, telling him that the station had received many telephone calls from listeners asking, "Who was that fine and amusing announcer?" The station executive, Roscoe Smith, concluded by asking, "Would you be interested in working out a program which would bring back to the air that inimitable voice of yours? I believe we could work up a fine program which would secure a large following in Tacoma and in the Northwest."[36] It was the start of a long professional relationship between the two men.

Intrigued by radio's possibilities, Cain tried to accelerate the process. Harry knew of another Sewanee graduate who had become a vice president of the National Broadcasting Company in Chicago. Cain began an intense correspondence with him, suggesting that he be hired as a radio commentator and offering to come to Chicago for an audition. Instead, it was suggested that he make a demonstration recording at the network's then-local Seattle affiliate, KIRO. After several months of correspondence in which the NBC executive tried to let Harry down gracefully, an assistant finally sent him a letter in May, thanking him for his interest.[37]

By 1937, Cain's personal life was also changing. Marj was pregnant with their first child, a boy born on September 26, 1937, and christened Harry Pulliam Cain II but known within the family and to close childhood friends as "Buzz" or "Buzzy." Since the couple's marriage, they had lived in the same fashionable apartment building as his father on North Third Street. Later in 1937, the couple rented a small but attractive house at 606 North G Street and then, in July 1938, with the help of a $1,500-promissory note from Will, purchased a secluded red brick home at the end of what was little more than a two-block-long alley at 415 North Tenth Street next door to Annie Wright Seminary, a prestigious girls' finishing school.

Will's medical problems were also becoming more serious. He had been splitting his time between Tacoma and long visits to Tennessee, but in May 1937, he suffered what may have been a slight stroke that necessitated a lengthy hospital stay.[38] A year later, now clearly in failing health, he moved in with Harry and Marj until his death a year later. There were also growing concerns about his brother, who was still working in Fort Wayne but was beginning to suffer from symptoms of schizophrenia or bi-polar disorder.[39] He became increasingly withdrawn from his job and his family, and in June 1937—a month after his father's possible stroke—Bill wired to ask whether it would be convenient and advisable for him and his family to join Harry and Marj in Tacoma. On his doctor's advice, Bill had taken a leave of absence for a complete change and rest.[40] With all of their other distractions in Tacoma, Harry and Marj were in no position to accommodate Bill's request, and the family moved to Portland, Oregon, instead.

Despite the challenges he faced with his extended family, Harry Cain was becoming well known in the Tacoma community as a result of his speeches and his involvement in numerous organizations and civic affairs. Quietly, he was looking for a bigger opportunity to become known without being too obvious about it. The opportunity presented itself in the early afternoon hours of a January day in 1939 in the form of a summons to appear on short notice before a group of community leaders who were just finishing their after-lunch drinks and cigars at the Tacoma Club.

The idea of staging a celebration to mark the fiftieth anniversary of Washington's statehood had been under consideration for at least thirteen years. The Chamber of Commerce had created a Jubilee Celebration committee, naming a new chairman every year, but accomplished very little else. Reno Odlin, president of the rival Puget Sound National Bank, now held the job. Odlin was a conservative Republican who had been trounced by New Dealer Lewis Schwellenbach in the U.S. Senate race of 1934, but he was politically astute enough to know that the Golden Jubilee idea needed more political and financial help. Through a series of negotiations, Odlin had finally been successful at obtaining both from the state. What the men finishing their lunch needed now was someone to run the event on a day-to-day basis. Someone suggested Harry Cain.

Odlin was already well acquainted with young Cain through the Washington Banker's Association. He made a quick call to Herb Raleigh at the Bank of California, telling him what he had in mind and asking him if he would mind sending Cain over to the Tacoma Club right away. When Harry arrived, the group made its pitch to him. Cain listened, considered the unique opportunity, and quickly made up his mind. "Well, gentlemen," he said, "it seems to me you ought to hire somebody who knows about running such things, but if that's the way you feel about it—I'll take the job."[41] Raleigh provided Cain with another leave of absence and, this time, even paid him.

The thirty-three-year-old Cain gathered together a group of other young businessmen, most of whom had worked with him on YMBC and other projects. They either contributed their time or had it provided by their employers. The whole effort was very much a bootstrap operation. They had hoped to raise $10,000 but ended up securing only $4,575. In the end, some wealthy lumber executives solicited one-hundred-dollar loans from local businessmen, which were ultimately repaid at twenty cents on the dollar at the end of the celebration. Office furniture and other services were donated. Cain, never a spendthrift, purchased a comfortable old chair he found for a dollar and set up his desk right next to his secretary's.

The funding schemes they created to finance the Golden Jubilee were audacious. A carnival raised $2,000. Sale of souvenir programs generated another thousand. Jubilee buttons raised $600. Someone came up with the idea of persuading local haberdashers to stock supplies of ludicrous headgear at reduced prices—top hats, cowboy hats—anything you could wear on your head and tie a streamer around. The sale of the Golden Jubilee commemorative streamers for the hats raised another $1,600 and exhausted every bolt of suitable ribbon on the West Coast. At least one well-known downtown clothier thought that the idea was going to be a complete flop, both from the clothiers' and the public's standpoints. Then they ran out of streamers. More were ordered, and 25,000 were sold, one for every five people in Tacoma. Many merchants failed to order enough hats and ran out. Not only did they lose business, but "they were abused by those who thought them uncooperative."[42] Several weeks before the start of the celebration, the clothier walked up to Cain, shook his hand, and declared, "Mr. Cain, you are a man of destiny!"[43]

On April 16, 1939, in the midst of the planning for the Golden Jubilee celebration, Cain lost his father to the combined effects of arterial sclerosis and stroke. His passing was not unexpected. But his loss was still a blow. Even so, Cain continued to be fully involved in the planning of the celebration. He assembled a staff—Pearl Rhebock, Emily Walker, and Irving Thomas—who would work for him again as mayor and in the U.S. Senate.

The celebration took shape. It would begin on Sunday, July 16, 1939, and extend through the following Sunday, July 23. There would be an air show, a Mardi Gras-type street celebration, a fourteen-mile-long parade that was watched by an estimated 250,000 people, a water carnival that attracted 30,000 spectators, a rodeo, and a visit from a squadron of U.S. Navy battleships.[44] The high point of the celebration was an extravagant theatrical pageant, "Saga of the West," which involved a cast of 2,000 and told the history of Washington State before a packed crowd in the 15,000-seat Stadium Bowl on the nights of July 20–22, 1939.[45] The *Tacoma Times,* in a backgrounder about Cain printed on June 24, referred to him for the first time in print as "A Human Hurricane," which others shortened to "Hurry" Cain—a nickname that would stick. By the time the Golden Jubilee was over, Harry Cain had lost twenty pounds, but he had made a local name for himself. "I'm telling you," he would say to anyone who would listen, "this has been a great experience."[46]

CAIN RETURNED TO the Bank of California, where he was now on a fast track to be transferred to the bank's home office in San Francisco. But, buoyed by the recent success of the Golden Jubilee and encouraged by many of his admirers, Cain began to think seriously about a future in politics. "Deep inside me, I knew that if I wanted to make an impression with my tongue, I had to have a platform, and the only way to have a platform was to be elected to public office."[47]

The bank offered to give him another leave of absence to run for office, but this time Cain politely refused. He believed—probably correctly—that he couldn't run for mayor of blue-collar Tacoma in 1940 as an employee of a bank and be elected. "If I'm going to do it, I've got to do it my own way."[48] So, on October 24, Cain wrote a letter of resignation to Herb Raleigh. "If future years bring to me any degree of success, I shall always be indebted to my preliminary background and training for making that progress possible." Three days later, his resignation was accepted by the bank. He was probably not aware of a letter that bank president James J. Hunter had sent to Raleigh on the same day they received Cain's resignation letter. "I regret that he has seen fit to leave the bank for the career he has outlined for himself. Maybe he is taking a wise course, for who knows the future of our economic condition. However, the unfortunate thing is that public life is not a particularly good environment for a straight thinking man. God knows that we need straight thinking men in politics and I earnestly hope that he will be able to resist influences which might tie his hands, so that he may enjoy 'the luxury of integrity.'"[49]

On Wednesday, November 1, 1939, Cain announced his candidacy for mayor, the first candidate to announce for the open seat that would be available in the 1940 special election. In his pocket, he carried several five-by-eight-inch index cards with his handwritten notes on them. One of them was titled, "Why Run For Mayor?" on which he had carefully printed the following answers:

1. Because of Definite Desire Based on Developing Talents [followed by sub-points] Articulate, Love of People, Joy of Combat, Support of Many Kinds of People;

2. Because of Belief in Spencer [sub-point] Long Life and Broad One;

3. Because of Faith in Future [sub-points] Past Has Been Tremendous, Future Fulfillment of Promise, Keep Pace with Federal Aid;

4. Because Democracy Starts at Home [sub-point] Leaders Can Be Produced Here, and

5. Because Politics is Important [with sub-point] Better Men May Follow.[50]

On another card he wrote, "Functions of Mayor." Beneath the title, he had written, "To Coordinate, To Sell, To Keep Pace, To Be Aware, and To Remember Newman (see things as they are)."[51] It is most doubtful that Cain's references to Herbert Spencer or John Cardinal Newman were understood or appreciated by many in his audiences, but his listeners must have been impressed by the level of his enthusiasm.

The Tacoma mayor's office hadn't exactly exuded an aura of permanency in recent years. George A. Smitley, elected in 1934, had served one term. The new mayor, J. C. Siegle, who was said to have ruined his health during his campaign, died in office in April 1939. A respected retired furniture merchant, J. J. Kaufman, was appointed by the city commissioners to serve as the interim mayor until a scheduled special election could be held in 1940.

Cain worked with Kaufman as an unofficial advisor and speechwriter, but Kaufman, who had deep concerns about the viability of Tacoma's existing commission form of government, decided not to seek election. Among Cain's papers at the Washington State Historical Society archives is a copy of a speech, obviously written by Cain for Kaufman, announcing that he would not seek re-election as mayor. In it, Kaufman notes a number of problems facing Tacoma, including the need to revise its city charter and the need for new municipal facilities—issues that Cain adopted as his own when he announced that he would run for mayor.[52]

Cain formally kicked off his campaign at an old-time political rally at South Tacoma's Royce Hall on January 11, 1940, before 400 supporters entertained by "Red" Sypher's five-piece orchestra. His eleven-point platform included better civic cooperation, more industrial jobs, better marketing of the city, a new civic auditorium and parks, more cooperation between Tacoma and the state capital in Olympia as well as between

2. *"Hurry" Cain*

Tacoma and Seattle, a more effective planning commission, and more openness in government.[53]

Cain's progressive, "good government" platform owed a great deal to another young political newcomer, Arthur B. Langlie, who had been elected mayor of Seattle in 1938 in spite of entrenched opposition from groups as disparate as "open town" business interests, Dave Beck of the Washington Teamsters Union, and the far-left Washington Commonwealth Federation led by Hugh De Lacy and Howard Costigan.[54] Tacoma faced many of the same problems as its larger neighbor to the north, and Langlie, who had been an announced Republican for only about a year and shared Cain's passion for golf, became something of a role model for Cain. Both men brought the promise of change after the dismal years of the Great Depression. As fellow mayors, the two would cooperate on various issues they faced in office, and that cooperation continued after the politically moderate Langlie was elected as Washington's governor in November 1940.

By the end of January, there were five candidates in the Tacoma mayor's race, but the top three were Cain, who was said to be supported by Tacoma business leaders; a liberal state senator, Dr. G. B. Kerstetter, who was supported by the more liberal elements of organized labor; and the former two-term mayor, Melvin G. Tennent, who was thought to hold the middle ground.

Cain's opponents painted him as a "Chamber of Commerce man," a political lightweight with no prior government experience and—worst of all—a *banker!* Even as a banker, Cain believed he understood the concerns and needs of labor. Personally, he sympathized with many of them. He knew more than a few men who belonged to the unions. By 1940, the percentage of union workers in Washington State had grown to almost 30 percent, and in Tacoma it was much higher than that. It was the beginning of a long and complicated relationship between organized labor and Harry Cain. To make matters worse, in 1938, Cain had publicly supported Initiative 130, an anti-union Prevention of Labor Uprisings measure that was supported by Washington's farmers and business community (including the Bank of California). During the campaign, Cain claimed that he had been representing his bank's views and not his own, but that didn't convince the *Tacoma Labor Advocate,* which on February 23, 1940, published an editorial called "Cain Not Able," claiming that he was unfit to be mayor. "Cain had no part in building up this city, either as a banker or as a supporter of Initiative 130. Cain had no part in securing the shipyards or in building the Narrows Bridge. It is not a question of loving labor unions, but of hating industrial turmoil and commercial chaos which should induce the voting public that they are not able to vote for Cain even if his self-acclaimed genius, his nationality, and his sense of civicism have every basis in fact."[55] Cain didn't publicly respond to labor's criticisms. He knew that there were elements of Tacoma's labor community that had appreciated the way he included them in the Golden Jubilee celebration. His campaign was focused on the future, not the past. He campaigned for his list of needed municipal capital improvements, the need for better planning, and a need to look at a city charter revision.

Cain genuinely liked and appreciated the liberal Kerstetter, but he reviled Tennent. In a 1979 radio interview, Cain remembered him as a "profligate, who had been mayor twice before and had run up bills on everybody all over the West Coast."[56] Dr. Kerstetter won the primary with 12,937 votes, followed by Tennent with 9,342. Cain came in third by less than 1,000 votes. Cain remembered, "I worked so very hard. I was disappointed. I take losses not with any bitterness, but with great disappointment."[57] He remembered, "No one was ever so unhappy. I thought I was one of the best-known young men in the City of Tacoma . . . and of course I *was* . . . by *some* people! There were people up on the hills [Tacoma's largely immigrant, blue-collar, working-class neighborhoods] who had never *heard* of me."[58]

On the Friday before the general election on Tuesday, March 12, 1940, Kerstetter and Tennent squared off for what was to be their final debate at the Young Men's Business Club. "It was painful for me to go. I didn't want to do it, but I did. I couldn't stay away. I didn't want to be seen as a poor loser. Tennent spoke first and just ripped Kerstetter's legislative voting record [apart]. Kerstetter stood up, [spoke], and made no reference to the attack that had been leveled against him. He said 'Thank You' and started to sit down. He never made it. He was dead. I was sitting in the second row and I watched him die. It was very quick, a massive heart attack."[59]

The next day, March 9, Cain's supporters went to court to ask that his name replace Kerstetter's on the ballot. Two days later, Superior Court Judge Ernest Card approved the request. Kerstetter's supporters, angry about Tennent's attack on their candidate just before his death, threw their support to Cain. Responding to charges from the Tennent camp that a deal had been made for their support, Cain made a fifteen-minute radio address on Monday night. He reminded his listeners that Kerstetter had always desired "us to work in the direction of coordinating labor, business and government." He noted that he had met with a number of Kerstetter's labor supporters on Sunday night and he tried to reach out to the rest of the labor community in his radio broadcast. "To those of organized labor, thru its press or person, who have sometimes taken issue with me, I hold no ill will. The solid, fundamental principles, upon which labor has grown to maturity, are impregnable to attack from any individual, be he great or small. . . . Let the chips fall where they will; and win or lose I shall forever cherish as a fond memory the opportunity afforded me of serving your city and mine."[60] Twenty years later, Cain remembered, "The papers ran red headlines noting that, 'Cain is Back,' and probably thinking he's hard to get rid of. I didn't make a speech. I didn't campaign. I was stunned. There were only three days—and I won overwhelmingly."[61]

"Overwhelmingly" turned out to be slightly more than 1,800 of the nearly 36,000 votes cast, but that was not the point. Cain was mayor of Tacoma. "This is the dirtiest deal ever pulled in the City of Tacoma,"[62] declared a bitter Mel Tennent. He filed a legal brief in Pierce County Superior Court, claiming that the action by the election board in placing Cain's name on the ballot was illegal. It was turned down. Tennent then appealed the ruling to the state Supreme Court. He was turned down again. Cain would not comment on the Justices' decision, other than to say, "I've got a job to do" before spending the rest of the afternoon playing golf.[63]

While all this was going on, Harry and Marj Cain took a two-week working holiday in California. Cain met with municipal officials in San Francisco and Berkeley. Marj visited film studios in Los Angeles, and Harry attended a U.S. Conference of Mayors' meeting in Portland, where he met New York's mayor Fiorello LaGuardia. "The man is amazing," Cain said with admiration upon his return. LaGuardia must also have enjoyed the colorful young mayor-elect because he invited Cain to visit him in New York.[64]

Harry Cain was mayor-elect of Tacoma. He held that position as a result of coincidence and chance—and not a little self-assurance. Had his father not been ill, Harry would not have been in Tacoma in the first place. Had he not convinced the bank to let him take a year off in Europe, he would not have been there to observe the events leading up to World War II or to talk about them when he came home. Had he not been selected to direct the Golden Jubilee Celebration, or if the bank had objected to granting him another leave of absence, he would have been transferred to the bank's home office in San Francisco and unable to run for mayor of Tacoma. Had Dr. Kerstetter not dramatically died four days before the general election and his supporters switched their support to Cain, he would not have been elected.

Only one question remained: what he was going to do with his new opportunity?

3

"I've Got a Job to Do!"

HARRY CAIN WAS sworn in as Tacoma's twenty-third mayor (some former mayors had served multiple and non-consecutive terms) in the Tacoma City Council Chambers on June 3, 1940, with City Clerk Genevieve Martin administering the oath of office. The council chambers were packed with friends and family members. Cain's first official action as mayor was to re-appoint former Police Chief Harold Bird as Superintendent of the Garbage Department, and E. M. (Ernie) Wetherell as secretary to the mayor. Both had served under the previous mayor, J. J. Kaufman, were Cain loyalists, and would play important roles in his future political career.

Tacoma was no stranger to high-visibility mayors. John Sprague had been a decorated Civil War general and a former superintendent of the Northern Pacific Railroad. Jacob Weisbach had been a European revolutionary. Angelo V. Fawcett, known as "Turkey Fawcett" for his sponsorship of annual Christmas dinners for underprivileged children in the 1890s and later as "Fighting Fawcett" for his frequent court battles and conflicts with other city officials, dominated Tacoma politics for nearly forty years, serving parts of six terms as mayor, both gaining and losing the office in disputed elections, as well as being recalled once. Fawcett had been elected as both a Democrat and a Republican, and once ran for the U.S. Senate as a Progressive.[1] In this, his career shared many similarities with Harry Cain. But Cain was different. Cain was the first and only Tacoma mayor who would become a nationally recognized political figure.

At thirty-four, Cain was also the youngest mayor in the city's history—at least a decade younger than the other city commissioners with whom he would serve. Unlike most of them, though, Cain had no real background in politics or government and had never been a city hall insider. Cain was, in equal parts, enthusiastic and naïve about what he thought he could accomplish. He had a vision for the future of the city, and with Kaufman's help, he had developed it into a set of goals that he felt his persuasive powers could implement/achieve. Cain's *real* challenge lay in convincing his fellow commissioners to accept his vision. That would turn out to be far more difficult than he had ever imagined.

Cain may have been Tacoma's mayor, but under its commission form of government, his formal responsibilities were limited to being the Commissioner of Public Welfare, Health, and Sanitation. The best known of the other four commissioners was Public Finance Commissioner C. Val Fawcett, son of the controversial former mayor. The younger Fawcett had served from 1921 to 1926 as secretary for his father and was then elected Finance Commissioner in 1930. By 1940, he was a well-entrenched member of the city hall establishment. Public Works Commissioner Abner R. Bergersen had first been elected to his position in 1932 and was re-elected overwhelmingly in 1940. Public Utilities Commissioner R. D. "Bob" O'Neil was an electrical engineer who had been elected along with Cain in 1940 after defeating a man who had served in the job since 1918. Perhaps the most controversial member of the group was Public Safety Commissioner Holmes Eastwood. First elected in 1938, Eastwood had brought his own desk and chair with him, reportedly quipping, "Should I get kicked out of here, they'll have to kick out my desk and chair, too." He exercised his power through his complicit police chief, Einar Langseth.

Generally guarded in their actions, each commissioner was intensely protective of his own sphere of influence and jealously guarded it from both his fellow commissioners and the public, agreeing or disagreeing with them as the situation benefited their own self-interest. Without the votes of at least two of these other men, Cain would have very little real power and even less ability to achieve the success he desired.

Cain determined that he would build his own independent political power base in the way he knew best—by establishing a direct relationship with the people using his powers of self-promotion. Three days after taking office, Cain decided to walk across the nearly completed Tacoma Narrows Bridge. This was no casual walk, taking advantage of the spectacular views, but an *event*—a timed and measured walk replete with starting gun, an official timekeeper, newspaper photographers, and a welcoming committee at the finish line. According to the timekeeper—longtime friend and local photographer Lee Merrill—Cain took 2,026 steps to walk 5,988 feet in 20 minutes and 29 seconds.[2] Of course, it was captured in a top-of-the-page, three-picture, eight-column spread in the June 6 issue of the *Tacoma News Tribune.* The public loved it, but the stunt smacked of political grandstanding to his fellow commissioners.

Cain was like a kid in a candy store. No group was too remote or too unimportant to ignore its request to speak. Each new talk required new ideas, and Cain provided them in abundance. Some were good. Some were bad. But each provided him with something new to talk about—quickly earning him the nickname of "Hairbreadth Harry." Cain personally wrote out or typed all of his speeches, following a practice he began when he returned from Europe in 1936.[3] In the meantime, as thoughts came to him, Cain would jot them down on three-by-five-inch index cards that he kept in his pocket or on any other scrap of paper available. It was not unheard of for the enthusiastic Cain to write his notes on paper tablecloths at luncheons, often spilling over into the space occupied by his tablemates.

Some of his advisors felt that the new Mayor Cain was speaking too often—that he was *too* visible. On February 12, 1941, Cain commented on their concerns in a handwritten journal he had begun to keep. "Sometimes political advisors suggest [that my] speeches are too numerous. What's the answer when groups leave [the] selection [of dates] up to me. My program will be successful [only] to the extent that [the] public believes and approves. A favor by me will bear fruit in support by others. [I] told Ernie [Wetherell] that matters political belong to him and Harold [Bird], but that I will continue to go here, there, and everywhere so long as invitations are written by others. Let the boys worry about politics, whether that means speeches or anything else; the job must be left to me."[4]

Visibility and publicity came naturally to Cain, but these traits were reinforced by his visit with New York Mayor LaGuardia in Portland shortly after Cain's election. The dynamic and colorful LaGuardia had used his talent for publicity to become one of the most visible men in America. He suggested that Cain follow his lead and begin a weekly radio program. With this expert advice, Cain began a fifteen-minute program that aired on radio station KMO at 9:15 on Monday nights and quickly became the second-most popular radio show in the area. Cain personally wrote the scripts for 128 of the regular broadcasts and for a number of special addresses, such as the one he made following the Japanese attack on Pearl Harbor. He began each one with his trademark "Good Evening, Tacoma. This is Harry Cain."[5]

Cain was also able to take advantage of two major opportunities to promote the city early in his term. The first was a three-day community celebration to commemorate the official opening of the Narrows Bridge on July 1, 1940, and the dedication of the new U.S. Army Air Corps base at McChord Field two days later during the Fourth of July holiday. The second was a much-heralded, three-theater premiere in October of the new film *Tugboat Annie Sails Again*, starring Marjorie Rambeau, Ronald Reagan, Donald Crisp, and Alan Hale. The event was held in Tacoma, rather than in Hollywood, because of a personal request that Cain made to Warner Brothers studio mogul Jack Warner.[6] Both events brought credit to Cain and good publicity to his city.

Harry Cain knew that, in order to succeed in his job, he had to do more than just manage a successful public relations effort. He had campaigned for the mayor's job on an eleven-point platform that included more industrial jobs, better marketing of the city, new capital improvements, better cooperation between Tacoma and Seattle, more effective planning, and more openness in government.[7] But, as he became more familiar with his new job, Cain discovered that the city faced some serious problems—both long-standing and immediate—that he had not fully appreciated before his election. Addressing them simply couldn't wait.

By 1940, Tacoma was finally beginning to recover from the Great Depression. Because of reduced tax revenues during those years, the city had neglected and underfunded its basic services and infrastructure. Harry Cain's normal response to a problem was to create a citizen advisory board, or a committee, to study the matter and suggest recommendations that he would then present to the rest of the commission for adoption. He encouraged the use of outside consultants. Invariably, the problem and its solution infringed on the private domain of one or more of his fellow commissioners. Not surprisingly, they were less than enthusiastic about what they perceived as Cain's meddling in their affairs and frustrated by the resulting positive publicity he generally received after doing so. Cain believed that changing the city charter to adopt the council-manager form of government was the only answer to most of these problems, but, not surprisingly, no one else on the commission agreed.

Closely related to the issue of growth was the problem of finding adequate housing for the shipyard workers and military personnel who lived off the nearby military bases. The New Deal, in spite of its huge impact, didn't end the Great Depression; the build-up toward World

3. "I've Got a Job to Do!"

War II did, and Tacoma was one of those cities uniquely positioned to benefit from it. Almost overnight, thousands of new jobs were created in newly reopened shipyards or in other local industries, attracting job-seekers from all over the nation. In 1940, the population of Tacoma had been barely 109,000. It had grown by less than 3,000 since 1930. Now, it seemed the city could grow that much in a single month!

Early efforts during 1940 to obtain federal help for new housing were unsuccessful. Characteristically, Cain decided to act on his own. He recommended to the city commission that a new Tacoma Housing Authority be created and charged with building 250 homes at a cost of more than $1,000,000, if funding could be obtained. The new housing agency would use federal funding, if possible, but it would be authorized to borrow the money and build and manage the new units itself, if necessary.[8] The government's Federal Works Administration (FWA) housing program permitted its funds to be used for the elimination of slums, to provide low-cost housing, and to alleviate unemployment. While everyone agreed on the housing goal, many in Tacoma were concerned about the concept of using the funds to remove slums. As far as the other commissioners were concerned, Tacoma's working-class neighborhoods were not slums, as they understood the term, nor did they even want to *imply* that these neighborhoods were slums. The commissioners announced that they were not interested in using federal money, even if they could get it, for "slum clearance." The Tacoma Board of Realtors agreed but for a different reason.[9] The Realtors were primarily concerned about what they perceived as an unwarranted public sector intervention in what had been, to that point, a private sector activity. By December, the FWA announced that it would build more than 500 new units near McChord Field. While these newly approved units began to address the problem near the military bases, they did nothing to alleviate the overall housing shortage in Tacoma.[10]

By the time Cain took office, many of the closed or barely operating local shipyards were gearing up to produce ships for the U.S. Navy. The largest of these facilities belonged to the Seattle-Tacoma Shipbuilding Company. Located next to the Port of Tacoma on the tide flats, the company was jointly owned by Todd Shipyards and Henry J. Kaiser. Todd had operated the facility during World War I, when it had produced ships for the Emergency Fleet Corporation, but the facility had been mothballed in 1925 due to a lack of business. In August 1940, the yard launched the

Cape Alva, the first of a series of five large freighters constructed for the U.S. Maritime Administration. Cain was on hand as the ship was commissioned by Mrs. John (Anna) Boettiger, wife of the publisher of the *Seattle Post-Intelligencer* newspaper and the only daughter of President Roosevelt. At full production, the yard employed 33,000 and, in addition to the five freighters, would build thirty-seven escort carriers, as well as a number of tankers and destroyer tenders during the war. Eight smaller local yards, which had been building fishing boats and yachts, were now building minesweepers and utility craft for the navy. In December 1941, Cain presided over the launching of four minesweepers at three different local yards in one day.

The situation became even worse when, in October 1940, President Roosevelt signed the Selective Service Act initiating a military draft for all eligible men twenty-one to thirty-six years of age. Within months, thousands of the new draftees were arriving at Fort Lewis, located approximately twelve miles south of Tacoma, increasing its military population from 5,000 to more than 40,000 by March 1941—a number that did not include the rapidly growing number of civilian workers employed there by the military. There was no new or rental housing to be had. The city needed 500 or 600 new housing units almost immediately, just to meet the existing demand.

McChord Field, Tacoma's former municipal airport, had been turned over to the U.S. Army Air Corps in July 1940, and North Fort Lewis, a massive new 2,000-acre complex of wooden barracks that could house an entire additional division, was completed in August 1941. As mayor, Cain had close ties with the senior officers at the facilities, playing golf, and socializing with them. It was there, before the war, that he first met many of the military leaders who would later become famous and with whom he would later serve, including Kenyon Joyce, Mark Clark, and Dwight Eisenhower.

Since his year-long visit to England and Europe in the mid-1930s, Harry Cain believed in the inevitability of a future war and knew that his community needed to prepare itself for the coming emergency. In the summer of 1940, he created a new Home Defense Council of civilian volunteers who would cooperate with the military authorities in all aspects of local defense. The group was organized at the end of July, and the enthusiastic enlistment of volunteers got underway in August. Eventually, the council recruited thousands of local volunteers, most trained as block wardens in case of blackouts or potential bombing, and many more as aircraft spotters. Some received rudimentary military training, including a squadron of horse cavalry, and a fleet of yachts that patrolled Puget Sound's waters for the length of the emergency.[11] Cain's actions attracted national attention, including a front-page story in the *New York World-Telegram* under the headline "Tacoma Forms Model Home Defense Corps; Even Has Civilian Navy for its Harbor."[12]

Hardly a new problem, but one that was rapidly growing out of control with the influx of defense workers and soldiers, was Tacoma's long-standing easy relationship with prostitution, gambling, and unlicensed drinking establishments. These had long been a staple of Tacoma life. In Angelo Fawcett's era and subsequently, vice was tolerated, and even encouraged, by a loose coalition of citizens who profited from it in various ways, so long as it was contained within certain restricted areas and its negative effects were not too obvious to the general public.

That became more and more difficult to accomplish as the massive influx of workers and soldiers arrived in the city during the run-up to World War II. The matter was made public in September 1940 when a citizen watchdog group began appearing at city commission meetings and calling for Commissioner Holmes Eastwood's resignation. With concerns of his own about Eastwood and the police department, but not yet willing to discuss them in public, Cain appeared neutral—even defensive—in response to the charges made by the citizens' group, to the point where members of the group began to make pointed jibes at him during the council meetings. In private, however, Cain forcefully pressed his public safety commissioner and chief of police for answers. In response, Eastwood assured him that the problem was not significant and that, in any event, his department lacked the officers or funding to do more than they were already doing. Cain received a very different perspective from his aide, former Tacoma Police Chief and future Pierce County Sheriff Harold Bird, who knew the inside workings of the police department well, and from his director of public health, Dr. L. E. Powers. They told him that on any "good" night, "there would be as many as three hundred girls, madams, procurers and camp-followers" engaged in commercial prostitution in downtown Tacoma.[13]

It was not long before Cain received a visit from high-ranking officers at Fort Lewis who were concerned about the alarmingly rapid spread of venereal disease among their soldiers. A subsequent private meeting was held in October between Cain, Eastwood, Powers, and the military to explore available options. Essentially, there were two: regulate the brothels through identification and fingerprinting of the girls, combined with weekly health examinations, or suppress the trade altogether through active law enforcement. Eastwood again claimed that the latter course was impossible, given the available level of police resources. Cain and Powers were skeptical, but the decision was made to try regulation. Powers called in the madams and informed them that they were now to be regulated. Their obvious delight at this announcement surprised Cain until he realized that the new policy allowed them both to stay open and to advertise that they were disease-free.[14] Venereal disease rates continued to soar. Regulation didn't regulate.

By December, Tacoma's illicit nightlife was back on the front pages of the local papers when the army threatened to take their knowledge of illegal gambling activities to the state authorities if the city didn't act. When the *Tacoma Times* made the army's threat public, Eastwood threw a couple of punches at the reporter responsible for the story and refused to meet with the media.[15]

In the meantime, housing, civil defense, and vice were not the only issues to occupy the mayor's attention. He was also deeply interested in community planning and had campaigned on the issue in 1940. During the Great Depression, Tacoma had lived from hand to mouth, and there had been little interest in and even less money available for planning. His views on the subject had been encouraged by his new mentor, Fiorello LaGuardia, who had responded enthusiastically to Cain's questions regarding the subject during their meeting in Portland. Cain believed that the region's cities should plan proactively so that they would not be forced to react in inefficient ways to the rapid growth that was occurring.[16] Then, on November 5, 1940, an opportunity presented itself. Tacoma was selected by the National Resources Planning Board as one of only three cities to participate in a special urban planning program to develop new procedures for the "post defense deployment of men and materials in city rebuilding."[17] Cain immediately appointed a new Long-range Planning Council, to be chaired by the noted College of Puget Sound economist and author Dr. Paul R. Fossum. The group was tasked with nothing less than preparing a twenty-year plan for the future development of the city.

Based on his experience with the Golden Jubilee celebration, Cain knew that public involvement was the key to the future success of the effort.

He invited 500 individuals and groups to participate in the community effort. He provided the groups with a list of his pet projects. "If the plan represents what the people of Tacoma really want, ways and means will be found to finance each item."[18] Unfortunately, once the various community clubs and civic organizations got involved, each proceeded to promote its own self-serving proposals and project priorities, and Cain began to lose overall control of the process. There was no effective administrative vehicle for evaluating and prioritizing the community responses. More important, time was running out in the run-up to the war.

The result of the multi-year effort finally made its way to the city commission in 1944 in the form of a report, entitled "Tacoma, the City We Build," published while Cain was absent during the war. An additional report was released at the same time that estimated the costs of the various proposals in order to assist with project prioritization, but little more was done.[19] Compared to the results obtained in the other two federally selected target cities, Corpus Christi, Texas, and Salt Lake City, Tacoma's effort was a relative failure. Cain had been the project's most enthusiastic supporter, but his efforts to involve the community were hampered by a lack of central coordination. In addition, the effort was constantly frustrated by his fellow city commissioners, who disapproved of his very public leadership on the issue and feared that the result might lead to a change in the city's charter and to a new city manager—a job that Cain might well covet himself. The city's public works director, Abner Bergersen, refused to cooperate with National Resource Planning Board's field agent, or even to call a meeting of the planning commission.[20] At least Cain's efforts were recognized by his fellow regional officials who elected him as chairman of the Puget Sound Regional Planning Commission in 1942.

While some problems can be planned for, others can hardly be anticipated. On the morning of November 7, 1940, just five months after it had opened, the Tacoma Narrows Bridge crashed into Puget Sound. Financed by more than $6,000,000 in New Deal Reconstruction Finance Corporation grants and an anticipated $1,600,000 in tolls, the bridge had been built on the cheap. Soon known for its tendency to sway even in gentle winds, the structure was referred to as "Galloping Gertie."

On that morning, the Pacific Northwest was lashed by one of its periodic winter storms. Cars on the bridge immediately sped off as quickly as possible, but one driver, unable to make it across, climbed out of his car and made his way on foot to the east end of the bridge. His dog remained in the car and became the disaster's only fatality. At 10:30 a.m., a large chunk of concrete fell from a section on the west side of the center span. At 11:02, a 600-foot-long section of roadway in the eastern half of the center span broke free and fell into the Tacoma Narrows below. At 11:08 a.m., the final section of roadway came crashing down.

Cain and the few other commissioners who were at city hall dropped everything and made a mad dash to the bridge after the first reports were phoned in that the bridge was breaking up. City engineers later said that there had long been a question about whether the solid concrete slabs that formed the bridge deck would be able to stand the strain of certain types of winds. One pointed out that the roadbed was only forty feet wide with a length of 2,800 feet, making it the narrowest suspension bridge in the world. These objections had been overruled by the designers and the state in order to keep the cost of the structure within budget.[21]

As 1940 TURNED into 1941, prostitution was again back in the headlines with Public Safety Commissioner Eastwood complaining that the military police were failing to cooperate with his officers by refusing to share information with them about illegal activities. The Fort Lewis base commander responded to Eastwood's complaints by again threatening to place Tacoma "off limits" to all military personnel.[22] The *Tacoma Times* called for Eastwood's resignation. By this time, Cain had enough and was ready to dismiss him but was powerless to do so without the support of a majority of his fellow commissioners. Regulation had not worked. The army's latest threat meant that something else had to be tried. Cain and Public Health Director Powers decided to explore repression (or suppression) of the trade altogether.

Powers was aware of a successful repression program that had been carried out in Vancouver, British Columbia. He visited the city, meeting with public health officials, interviewing social workers, and personally observing conditions on the street and in the hotels, bars, and dance halls where prostitution had flourished. He became convinced that suppression would work—at least during the war—but it would certainly require a change in public attitudes. The justification for closing the brothels clearly needed to be based on public health issues and their resulting disease-based social costs, rather than on moral or economic grounds.

Using advice provided by the American Social Hygiene Association, Cain and Powers began a four-month campaign of public information, using the newspapers, distributing 85,000 pamphlets, tucking 25,000 leaflets into utility bills, and talking to any group that would listen. The results were amazing. Within a year, the number of prostitutes infected with syphilis declined 47 percent. The percentage with the harder-to-detect gonorrhea fell 25 percent. In an effort to reduce the number of young freelancers, an ordinance was enacted that prohibited unescorted women from going into taverns. [23]

In the meantime, President Roosevelt signed the May Act, which allowed local base commanders to determine where prostitution was occurring and to declare such communities "off limits" to military personnel. Colonel Ralph Glass, the Fort Lewis base commander, lost no time in sending Cain a letter indicating his willingness to act under the new legislation if Tacoma didn't. Overnight, the issue became an economic problem, not just a moral problem, for Tacoma. We now know that Glass's action was not spontaneous. In a July 22 entry in his journal, Cain described a meeting he had held with officials from Fort Lewis the previous Thursday. "We discussed suppression [of prostitution] and how best to approach the problem. It was agreed by all that direct action was required."[24] A series of frantic meetings with business leaders and his fellow commissioners resulted in a July 24 pledge to the army from Cain that "all discoverable houses of prostitution within the city limits would be closed within two weeks."

The events that followed were the basis of one of Harry Cain's favorite stories. The following version is taken from a taped interview he conducted with Miami public affairs radio personality Charles Kappes in March 1975. Cain called all thirty-one local madams into his office on the morning of July 25, 1941. "I was well prepared and in a good mood. They were all handsomely dressed—they should have been; they were all making a fortune—and I said, 'Ladies, when you leave this office, you'll be on your way back to close up. You're done.' Well, they were indignant, some screamed, some swore, and some threatened to go out into the neighborhoods. I told them, 'If you do that, because of the difficulty in [customers] getting to you, your business is going to decline and your prices increase, and the local housewives are going to know where you are, and they're going to come and complain to me, and I'm going to send the police out there [and] put you in the Bastille.' This closure is for six months. If the venereal disease rate goes up during that time, instead of down, I'll not only allow you to re-open, I'll become a barker at your doors and encourage more trade for you."[25] Cain was so tickled with his success in cleaning up the brothels that he wrote an article about it in the December 1943 issue of the *Journal of Social Hygiene*, called "Blitzing the Brothels." Its publication brought favorable attention to Tacoma and, not coincidentally, to Harry Cain.

Police began raiding the brothels on August 4, and Police Chief Einar Langseth declared that all of the houses were closed up "tight" two days later.[26] Local newspapers reported, however, that Tacoma's night-life was proceeding as usual, and the stories of closings were generally met around town with knowing smiles. By the end of the year, both Eastwood and Chief Langseth had announced that they planned to run for Commissioner of Public Safety in the upcoming 1942 elections. Eastwood announced that he was taking a five-week "fact-finding" trip to look at public safety issues in several Southwestern cities. When he returned, he was greeted by a new eight-member Public Safety Council that had been created by Cain in his absence. Just to be on the safe side, Cain soon announced the appointment of seven more members to the group. Within a year, the venereal disease rate had fallen dramatically. Cain's efforts at suppressing prostitution were recognized by the U S. Army, the U.S. Surgeon General, and the American Social Hygiene Association.

Cain also continued his efforts to obtain more federally funded housing. The need increased, but the obstacles remained, including a battle between conflicting housing agencies in Washington, DC, a lack of broad public support at home, intense competition for available funds, and conflicting motivations between the city and the federal government.[27] The bureaucratic and philosophical clashes between liberals, who saw the issue as being more about the social and economic future of cities than it was about housing defense workers, and conservatives, who were opposed to "socialistic experiments" that might include racial integration of public housing in Southern cities, kept the issue in perpetual turmoil and resulted in unfortunate delays.[28] On March 4, Cain confided to his journal, "Past attempts to secure low cost housing for Tacoma [have been difficult] because [the] feeling has prevailed that [the] need was not here. If people only knew how the other half lived."[29]

In June 1941, it looked as if the city's application for $1,000,000 in federal housing funds might finally be approved, but local interests were still not on the same page. The Board of Realtors organized a mass meeting of the potentially affected property owners and called for a public referendum on the matter. Finally, under public pressure, the Housing Authority voted to withdraw the grant request altogether. By August, the need had become so critical that the mayor's Defense Housing Committee (a different body from the Housing Authority that Cain had earlier created) recommended that the city apply for another federal grant for 300 units for defense worker housing. This time, the city's application was approved in October with money for another 100 units added to the request.[30]

AND THEN, IN the short time it took a radio announcer to read a "flash" bulletin, all of those issues seemed very much less important. On December 7, 1941, Japan attacked the American naval and military bases surrounding Pearl Harbor in the Hawaiian Islands. That evening, in a special Sunday evening radio broadcast, Cain appealed to his citizens to "stay calm" and "not to surrender reason to racial intolerance" as a result of the Japanese attack. He proceeded to detail exactly what steps he would take to mobilize local manpower by creating a Tacoma Municipal Defense Council, which would meet in his office at eight o'clock Monday morning. He concluded by saying, "Let us frown on hysteria! Let us protect the rights of those Japanese who know so well what it means to be an American."[31]

Despite the mayor's admonition, members of the local Japanese community soon began to experience serious acts of discrimination. Local Japanese merchants bought large ads in the local papers reprinting a "Japanese American Creed" defending their loyalty. Mayor Cain responded by seeing that copies of birth certificates were made available to local Nisei (persons of Japanese ancestry born in America) and had signs printed that could be installed in the shop windows of Japanese-owned businesses reading:

THIS BUSINESS IS OPERATED BY AMERICAN-BORN JAPANESE AND IS UNDER THE PROTECTION OF THE MAYOR.[32]

On December 13, only six days after the attack on Pearl Harbor, the First Lady of the United States, Eleanor Roosevelt, arrived at Harry Cain's city hall office on a previously scheduled West Coast tour promoting civil defense. Her visit was followed two days later by that of Fiorello LaGuardia, who had recently been named national director of the Office of Civil Defense by President Roosevelt. LaGuardia had lobbied for the appointment, and Cain had supported him, sending a letter of support to President Roosevelt on May 8, 1941.[33]

Meeting with local civil defense workers in Cain's office and then answering questions that were phoned in on a live radio broadcast, Mrs. Roosevelt assured her listeners that Tacoma was "on the track," and urged them to become engaged in local civil defense activities. "Some of the most courageous people I know have admitted fear. But it is most important to "play the game and never show fear of anything. Calm is the greatest trait we can cultivate at this time."[34] Then she and Cain did something remarkable. Following the meeting with the civil defense workers, they met with four Japanese-American students representing the thirty-six Japanese students then attending the College of Puget Sound. Cain had arranged the meeting after reading that two of the invitees had expressed their loyalty and their fears at the school's regular morning convocation on the Monday following the Pearl Harbor attack. In their meeting with Mrs. Roosevelt, the students expressed their concerns about the negative impact the war would have on both native-born Japanese Americans and loyal Japanese born immigrants. Mrs. Roosevelt said that she would talk with the President about the matter.[35] Cain was later one of only two elected officials on the West Coast to oppose the internment of Japanese-American citizens during the war—the other being Senator Sheridan Downey of California.[36]

IN MID-JANUARY 1942, Cain was again in Washington, DC, for the annual meeting of the U.S. Conference of Mayors. On Saturday, the seventeenth, Cain was asked to have lunch with the First Lady at the White House. In her syndicated newspaper column the following Wednesday, Mrs. Roosevelt wrote of her second meeting with Cain. "Mayor Cain of Tacoma, Wash., lunched with me and I was happy to see him again. I remembered how impressed I was by the way in which he was taking hold of his job in the hectic week after Pearl Harbor."[37] The two would remain friends until her death in 1962.

The next day, Cain announced through his secretary in Tacoma that he would again be a candidate for mayor in the upcoming election, seeking a full four-year term in his own right. "Two absorbing and history-making years have passed since the citizens of Tacoma elected me mayor. I want your votes, but more importantly I want your support, sympathy and willingness to protect what is worthwhile and to try new things necessary during times which, without question, will be most uncertain and will demand the greatest energies and intelligence of all of us."[38] Two days later, the Tacoma Advertising and Sales Club named Cain, a club member of long-standing, its "Man of the Year."

In a reversal of its long-standing policy against early endorsements, the *Tacoma News Tribune* referred to Mrs. Roosevelt's positive comments about Cain in her syndicated column. The paper editorialized that "Harry Cain has made a good mayor for Tacoma. . . . [The city] is indeed fortunate that it has a mayor of this caliber at the helm in these trying times."[39]

The campaign for mayor in 1942 was a low-key affair, and when the final votes were counted in the February 24 primary, Cain won by a landslide, receiving 20,147 votes to his closest opponent's 5,266. It was the largest plurality ever recorded in a Tacoma municipal election, making a general election unnecessary. The *Tacoma Times* editorialized, "Few mayors in the short time available have cut as wide a swath in the administration of city affairs as Harry Cain. None has labored as hard and as long as he in the conduct of affairs. He has traveled extensively in the city's interest; he has publicized the city favorably in a fashion seldom equaled by predecessors. He has been alert and on the job every minute."[40]

But times had changed. The Tacoma in 1942 was not the same city as the Tacoma of 1940 with its movie premieres and street parades, or even of 1941 with its ongoing battles to clean up vice and provide wartime housing. Men were now leaving daily for the training camps, and the Allies were facing the loss of the Philippines, Singapore, and the Dutch East Indies. Germany was on the move in Russia and in North Africa. England's lifeline to America was being threatened by German U-boats.

Life went on, but much more seriously. The war brought badly needed jobs, but with rationing and wage and price controls, it did not bring prosperity. Generally, however, the war was an economically stimulating rather than an economically destructive force. While it brought hardship and tragedy, it created greater confidence and a sense of shared effort. It was a time of scrap-metal drives, war-bond rallies, and hosting servicemen on leave at the local USOs or in private homes. Marj Cain and Irving Thomas produced a two-night *Victory Varieties* show at the large

Temple Theater to raise funds for medical supplies and a badly needed ambulances for the local Red Cross. Harry and Marj were photographed picking raspberries in the Puyallup Valley to publicize the critical short-age of berry pickers.

In January 1942, the federal government began to consider plans to control and perhaps relocate approximately 112,000 Japanese living in the three Pacific states (almost 94,000 of them in California alone). Of these, 40,869 were aliens (known as Issei), ineligible for citizenship through naturalization proceedings, and 71,484 were American-born Nisei and, therefore, United States citizens. There were also about 58,000 Italian and 22,000 German aliens living in the Pacific states. A good many of the German aliens were recent refugees from Nazi Germany. Most of the Germans and a large proportion of the Japanese and Italians lived in or near the principal cities or adjacent to militarily sensitive or strategic areas.

For several decades, and certainly since the attack on Pearl Harbor, the local Japanese population had been the target of growing hostility and restrictive actions. Some, including seventy-three Japanese from the Puget Sound area, were considered security risks and had already been arrested and sent to a camp near Missoula, Montana. The government was coming under increasing pressure to add to that number.

The man who was responsible for the defense of the western United States and who would have to deal with the Japanese issue was Lieutenant General John L. DeWitt, commander of the U.S. Fourth Army. DeWitt, himself the son of an army general, was a short, bald, myopic, and highly excitable career supply officer who suddenly found himself thrust into one of the most complex and unfortunate decisions in American history.[41] DeWitt at first said that the growing call to remove the Japanese from the West Coast was "damn nonsense." He had absolutely no idea of what to do with the 112,000 Japanese under his jurisdiction, but he was intent that his actions would not be found wanting by higher authority as had those of his counterpart in Hawaii after Pearl Harbor.

On January 30, members of Congress from the eight western states met with officials of the U.S. War and Justice Departments to discuss the "Japanese Question." Most wanted the Japanese, both citizens and aliens alike, relocated out of their states. On February 11, over the objection of his Attorney General, Francis Biddle, President Roosevelt approved a secret War Department recommendation, authorizing the wholesale evacuation of Japanese aliens and citizens on the basis of "military necessity." The next day, a congressional committee chaired by Washington Senator Monrad C. Wallgren recommended to Roosevelt that "the immediate evacuation of all persons of Japanese lineage" be undertaken.

DeWitt was observant enough to determine which way the public wind was blowing and, on February 14, warned the Secretary of War, Henry L. Stimson, of an imminent attack on coastal cities, recommending that all "persons of Japanese extraction be removed from 'sensitive areas' of the West Coast. . . . The very fact that no sabotage has taken place to date is a disturbing and confirming indication that such action will be taken."[42] Stimson questioned DeWitt's demands on two levels; first, because he was concerned that DeWitt was given to exaggeration and, second, because he recognized that the forced removal of the Japanese would "make a tremendous hole in our constitutional system. . ." He finally decided that DeWitt's recommendations made "common sense," though on any other grounds "it may be hard to justify it."[43]

On February 18, only six days before Tacoma's primary city elections, Roosevelt signed Executive Order 9066, paving the way for the evacuation and internment of most Japanese-Americans living on the West Coast. A terse announcement appeared in the February 20 issue of the *Tacoma News Tribune:*

PRESIDENT ROOSEVELT HAS AUTHORIZED AND DIRECTED THE SECRETARY OF WAR TO SET UP MILITARY AREAS IN THE COUNTRY FROM WHICH ANY PERSONS, EITHER ALIEN OR CITIZEN, MAY BE BARRED OR REMOVED.[44]

Roosevelt neither discussed the matter in any substantive way with his cabinet nor consulted his military advisors. If he discussed the matter at all with his wife, her views apparently made little difference. His decision was based on DeWitt's recommendation, which essentially said that the government had no reasonable way to distinguish loyal Japanese from disloyal Japanese.[45]

Harry Cain opposed the wholesale relocation of the Japanese. As a banker, he had admired many of his Japanese and Filipino customers. In his mind, the proposed wholesale relocation violated both their civil rights and their property rights. It was being pursued only out of fear and political pandering to a hysterical public. He testified before Wallgren's committee, holding a hearing on the matter in Seattle, saying that for far too long, the term "alien enemy" meant only one race, the Japanese. "I feel it would be preferable to make careful selection of those to be evacuated rather than just say, 'Let's get rid of our problem by the easiest, most obvious way, of moving everybody out.'"[46]

On March 3, the final day of the hearings, General DeWitt announced the imposition of Military Area No.1 in the three Pacific Coast states, which extended inland ninety-five to 250 miles from the Pacific Ocean. By March 11, DeWitt had created the Wartime Civil Control Administration (WCCA) to administer the divestment of the property belonging to voluntary evacuees. A week later, the War Relocation Authority (WRA) was created to supervise the resettlement of more than 112,000 Japanese. In Pierce County, 823 alien Japanese were being evacuated, and all but six of 111 Japanese farmers in Pierce County had registered with the WCCA. However, only twenty-five of these farmers had actually negotiated the lease or sale of their land.[47] Most of the Japanese suffered major financial losses as a result of the evacuation. A national study in 1983 estimated that the Japanese who were forced to evacuate had suffered a cumulative loss of between $810 million and $2 billion. Many never returned to their farms and businesses.

By mid-April, hundreds of Caucasian carpenters and laborers had assembled 380 wooden buildings, under budget and ahead of schedule, at the Puyallup fairgrounds to house 8,000 expected Japanese residents. Each family had a seventeen-by-twenty-foot living space. By the end of the month, the Japanese were ordered to report to what was now being called "Camp Harmony."[48] After two months there, 7,149 Japanese from Seattle and Tacoma were relocated to camps at Minidoka in Central Idaho and Tule Lake, California. Tacoma's Japanese community never forgot Harry Cain's support in their hour of need and would officially honor him for his efforts on their behalf more than thirty years later.

THE CITY'S EFFORTS to increase housing and reduce vice began to pay dividends in 1942. An application to the federal government for more public housing units was approved in April, with federal officials agreeing to fund 1,200 units immediately and 400 more later that year. In October, a massive construction contract was let for Salishan, a massive 1,600-unit housing development to be built on Tacoma's east side. During the year, the city would attempt to obtain 6,500 new government housing units in addition to the 2,000 units that had been built by private contractors over the past two years.

Suppression of prostitution (at least as practiced by professionals) appeared to be working, but organized gambling of all kinds continued to be a problem. Police Chief Einar Langseth had pulled off a somewhat surprising election victory over his old boss, Holmes Eastwood, in the general election held on March 10, 1942, and would become the city's new Public Safety Commissioner. Having tried to deal with Langseth in the past, the army promptly again put Tacoma on notice that if the gambling and illegal drinking establishments were not closed by 9:00 a.m. on Monday, April 21, the city would be placed off-limits to military personnel. Pre-warned by the army officials, Cain had provided a similar warning to the commissioners at their meeting the day before. Having lost the election, Eastwood declined even to attend the meeting. Cain immediately called on Eastwood to take a leave of absence for the remaining six weeks of his term, with the clear implication being that, if he did not do so, formal charges would be brought against him for misconduct in office. The commission was willing to strip Eastwood of his vice-related duties, but it would not agree to relieve him completely. Considering his options, Eastwood grudgingly agreed to turn over his vice-related duties to Cain but said that he would fight any broader effort to oust him from office.[49] Harry P. Cain was now in charge of eradicating vice in Tacoma.

The issue continued to simmer in early summer while Cain and his public health director, Leland Powers, rolled out their public information campaign about the social costs associated with venereal disease. Cain confronted his new Public Safety Commissioner about the army's complaints, but Langseth, like Eastwood, discounted the problem and complained about what he claimed were a lack of available recourses. Cain then decided to address the issue another way. Unknown to anyone, he drove to Olympia and met with his old friend, Arthur Langlie, who was by then Washington's Governor. He asked Langlie if he could borrow the Washington State Patrol. Langlie agreed, and on the night of August 16, 1942, the patrol, without notifying local police, raided two gambling establishments on Pacific Avenue, arrested twenty, and confiscated thousands in cash and gambling paraphernalia. The names of those arrested were printed in the paper. Langseth commented that if his men spent all their time policing occasional card games they wouldn't have any time to control traffic. "I couldn't expect anything else from Mayor Cain. I guess he's just picking up where he left off."[50]

Cain faced other pressing problems. A controversial decision to install downtown parking meters had finally been approved but at the cost of a number of bruised feelings. Plans to provide public bus service for workers at the shipyards and other industries located on the tide flats ran into funding and "turf" problems. Development of the huge Salishan public housing project encountered numerous delays and other frustrations. Cain recommended massive changes to the city charter in his annual report to the commission, but his ideas were quickly rejected. At the time, the city's reformers, who generally agreed with Cain in theory, were otherwise involved and were mindful of the defeats they had suffered in the 1920s.[51] Cain also continued his efforts to build a regional airport, and construction on it began in October 1942. A massive controversy erupted over the cost of two city-owned hydroelectric dams on the Nisqually River, including serious questions involving decisions made by the city's Public Utilities Commissioner, R. D. O'Neil, whose relationship with Cain deteriorated into something just short of open warfare.

And then, on the night of April 17, 1943, the Washington State Patrol struck once more. Again, without notifying Tacoma officials, they raided several Chinese gambling dens on lower Broadway. Eleven Chinese were arrested, and seventy patrons were detained. In order to enter the clubs, the state troopers had to barge past the off-duty Tacoma police officers who were lounging around outside. Langseth released a statement to the press charging that Cain wasn't interested in law enforcement, only in his future political career. Cain had had enough. Two days later, Cain sent a letter to his fellow commissioners, formally asking for Langseth's resignation and charging misconduct and willful neglect of duty.

A formal hearing on Cain's charges against Langseth was held on Friday, May 1, in front of the rest of the commissioners with Cain acting as prosecutor and Langseth defended by his legal counsel, E. K. Murray, a former City Attorney. State patrol witnesses testified that Tacoma police officers were on hand at the time the raid took place. Tacoma officers testified that they knew nothing about the illegal gambling activities being conducted inside the premises. When it was all over, the commissioners voted 3-1 to allow Langseth to remain in office. It was clear that the decision had more to do with their growing opposition to Cain and his management style than with the facts of the case against Langseth.[52] Cain's battles with his public safety commissioners and chiefs of police were reminiscent of similar confrontations between former Mayor Fawcett, his law enforcement officials, and the rest of the commission in 1914–15. The outcome had been the same.[53]

As Tacoma entered its second year of war, rumors began to circulate that its mayor was considering another job. Cain had joined the U.S. Army Reserve upon graduation from Hill Military Academy in 1925 and, at Sewanee, had been impressed by, and identified with, the Athenians' concept of the "citizen-soldier"—the idea that it was every citizen's duty not only to participate in governing of the nation but also to become a soldier and defend it when necessary.[54] Cain had become frustrated with the bureaucratic infighting and the various obstacles created by his fellow commissioners that always seemed to stand in the way of achieving his goals. He increasingly desired to be where the action was.

It's not known exactly when the contacts began, but by early 1943, Cain was quietly being recruited by the army to join its newly formed military government branch. In his application for the job, Cain noted that he would be interested in serving if he could do so overseas.[55] On May 5, 1943, based on his prior service in the U.S. Army Reserve, Cain was sworn in as a major in the U.S. Army with orders to report to the School of Military Government at the University of Virginia for a four-month training course beginning May 14. "I feel this is an opportunity I could not pass up. At this school, I will have as teachers the foremost authorities in government and I hope to return a better mayor."[56] Because he and Marj were expecting their second child later that month, he requested a thirty-day delay in his reporting date. His request was denied.

Many, but far from all, Tacomans were sorry to see Harry go. On May 7, the *Tacoma Times* editorialized, "Tacoma never had a better mayor. The *Tacoma Times* unreservedly stamps with approval the record of Harry Cain as chief executive of this city. We sincerely believe the Cain administration will more than match that of any official in any municipality of the nation. We believe we speak for all Tacoma when we say 'thank you, good luck, God bless you—and a speedy return.'"[57] Regret over his pending departure was not shared by his fellow city commissioners, by the various gambling, bootlegging, and prostitution interests, or even by some citizens who merely needed a rest.

On Monday, May 10, Cain attended his next-to-last commission meeting, during which his fellow commissioners cast a preliminary vote to grant Cain a leave of absence and name Finance Commissioner Fawcett to act as mayor in his absence, but it didn't happen without some last-minute fireworks. As the commission was about to vote on the leave of absence motion, Utility Commissioner O'Neil interrupted, demanding to know if Cain expected "to receive pay from the city and the government at the same time." Cain, plainly flabbergasted, shot back, "No man worthy of the name of gentleman would ever ask such a question." The room sat in stunned silence. "Well," O'Neil retorted, "I want to tell you I'll do everything in my power to keep you from getting pay from the city and the government." Cain started to speak, caught himself, and called for a vote on the motion, which passed, then called for another motion to adjourn, which also passed. Cain was out of his chair in an instant and squarely facing the shorter O'Neil, who had also risen to his feet. Cain started to confront him, "Robert . . .," but then caught himself and left the chambers.[58]

That night he made his last radio address to his Tacoma audience. He thanked KMO, the local press—particularly those who covered city hall, his listeners, his wife, and his staff. "Thus comes to an end the happiest in a long line of conversations. May I wish for you a city with a purpose and good health for each of you individually? So, until the next time at this same time, this is Harry Cain saying Good Night, May God Bless You, and Good Luck."[59]

Two days later, he presided over the last council meeting before he left town in a newly purchased summer khaki uniform. The mood was more reserved as the council took a final vote to approve Cain's leave of absence and approve Val Fawcett as acting mayor. "I've had a constructively fine time in this job," the mayor told his colleagues. "I've learned a lot and there was doggoned little that I did know when I first came in. I want to publicly acknowledge my gratitude for your sympathy, arguments, help and cooperation."[60] From that meeting, he attended a farewell tribute from his local Kiwanis club, and later drove to Seattle's Boeing Field, where he was seen off by his family and a group of close friends. As the silver Northwest Airlines DC-3 taxied onto the runway, the mayor's five-year-old son, Buzzy, called out, "Bye, dad-e-e-e-e. . . ."

Less than a month later, on June 5, the Cains' second child, a girl named Marlyce but quickly known to all as Candy, was born.

3. "I've Got a Job to Do!"

HARRY CAIN PROBABLY didn't realize it at the time, but his tenure as mayor of Tacoma was effectively over. He would re-assume the job briefly after he returned from World War II, but by that time, his sights were already set on higher office.

Harry Cain was Tacoma's first "modern" mayor: the first to understand and use modern communications techniques to project the office and himself, the first to open up the processes of government to the general public and to promote transparency, the first to introduce innovations such as placing covers over the beds of garbage trucks, the first truly to embrace regionalism and to promote better cooperation between Tacoma and Seattle; and the first to promote long-range planning.

By what standard should Cain's time in office be judged? How well did he succeed at what he started out to do? One place to start is with the eleven-point platform Cain announced on the night of his thirty-fourth birthday, January 10, 1940—the night he kicked off his campaign for mayor.[61] His platform called for greater civic cooperation and for the community to "be positive in every action" so as to achieve future success. The community *did* come together during the years that Cain was in office. In his first year in office, Cain led the city both in triumph and tragedy. During the next sixteen months, his leadership was largely driven by efforts to prepare for the war and to deal with problems associated with it.

Cain called for creating more industrial jobs. The city was just beginning to climb out of the Great Depression, and new jobs were needed. Unemployment was still at double-digit levels. The jobs were already on the way by the time he made his announcement, but there was no way to be sure. When it came, the war would only increase the size and diversity of the local economy.

Cain called for "better advertising" of the city and its products. There was no question on this point. Harry Cain was Tacoma's number one promoter. He called for specific capital improvements, such as a new civic auditorium, which was dedicated in February 1941, although many other needed projects, like the new city hall and library, would have to wait until after the war.

Cain called for more unity between Tacoma and the state capitol and between Tacoma and Seattle. Both were achieved with the help of Cain's in-state mentor, Arthur Langlie, who had been elected Seattle's mayor in 1938 and as Washington's Governor in 1940.

Cain called for "better reporting"—today known as more openness and transparency in government. He was the first mayor to make periodic reports directly to the people using his weekly radio program.

Cain called for more authority and funding for the city's struggling planning commission. When, in 1942, the opportunity presented itself, he jumped at the chance to develop a new twenty-year, long-term plan. Most of the ideas it generated were ultimately achieved but not until long after Cain left office. The process of developing the plan was largely ineffectual because of the city's inability to coordinate the process and the lack of cooperation from the rest of the city commission.

Finally, Cain called for tolls to be collected on the new Tacoma Narrows Bridge. Tolls were, indeed, imposed after the bridge opened, but they didn't last for long. Five months later the bridge fell into Puget Sound.

Harry Cain was forced to deal with many issues he hadn't anticipated. He received high marks for creating one of the most effective volunteer civil defense programs in the country. After a slow start, he led an impressive effort to set up a network of USOs to provide off-duty servicemen an alternative to Tacoma's steamy night-life. The USOs ultimately included one for the specific use of African Americans who were otherwise excluded.

Efforts to obtain public housing for defense workers and military personnel living off base were also generally successful. Tacoma applied for more than 6,500 units during the war, most of which were ultimately completed in spite of federal government infighting and local objections. The disposition and use of public housing would become a major cause for U.S. Senator Cain later in his career.

The area in which Cain may have shown his greatest leadership in office was his on-going campaign to reduce, if not wholly eliminate, prostitution, gambling, and bootlegging in Tacoma. Vice was well entrenched when he took office. Had it not been for the build-up to the war, Cain might have been willing to accept some level of continued presence, so long as it didn't interfere with his efforts to market the city. But that was never an option. He faced both the continuing threats of the army to place the city "off limits" and a clear public health emergency were the brothels to remain open. Cain faced delay and opposition from two successive Commissioners of Public Safety, acquiescence on the part of his other city commissioners, and near rebellion from most of his own police department. Ultimately, he had to conspire with the army, with the governor, and with the Washington State Patrol to clean up the problem. Even then, it returned to some degree after he left for the war.

By any objective standard, Harry Cain was successful in dealing with issues. He was less successful in dealing with politics. He was least successful in his interactions with his fellow city commissioners. He was perhaps too young or naïve to recognize that they would resent him and resist his efforts to micro-manage their departments. He did not believe in the form of government that provided them with their source of power, and he did not really respect either the intellect or the ability of most of them. However, until Tacoma's form of government was changed and the commissioners were gone, they represented reality.

Harry Cain was, as he had been since the 1930s, a man in a hurry. When he finally understood that he could not accomplish his goals and ambitions within the environment in which he served, he looked for an opportunity to serve elsewhere.

4

"The Sooner Begun, the Sooner Finished"

HARRY CAIN LEFT the exhilarations and the frustrations of the mayor's office behind to enter a new chapter in his life. He felt that he had accomplished a great deal in Tacoma, but how much more he could accomplish under the circumstances was open to question. Now he had an opportunity to serve his country in another way. Indeed, the army had actively recruited Cain because of his unique background and experiences. Cain was being asked to serve and, as he had in the past, he jumped at the chance.

While some, certainly including some of the other city commissioners, may have felt relief at Cain's pending departure, the general public's view was expressed in a *Tacoma Times* editorial. "Major Cain, as mayor, has been the answer, we believe, to the years-old yearnings of all good citizens. His embarkment on a military career (still in his chosen field of government, however) will represent a distinct loss to this community. That cannot be denied. But we offer him gladly and proudly—although but temporarily, we hope—to our Army and to our nation."[1]

Cain arrived at the historic campus of the University of Virginia at Charlottesville over the weekend of May 13–14, 1943, in time to begin his orientation on the following Monday. Founded by Thomas Jefferson, who designed its first building in 1819, the campus was, and is, a storied and iconic place. In 1943, it still provided a setting that was uniquely appropriate to the interdisciplinary curriculum of the U.S. Army's School of Military Government.

Early recruits to the program had included historians, political scientists, economists, public health experts, and others who might be useful in the administration of occupied territories. In March 1943, the Army decided to recruit some civilians in field grades (major through colonel), and it was at this point that Harry Cain was recruited.[2] He was the first sitting mayor to attend the school. His growing national recognition, his record of accomplishment in Tacoma (particularly his cooperation with local military authorities in cleaning up prostitution), and his military education and his former status as a reserve officer made him an ideal candidate for the job.[3] His unusual status at the school was confirmed when, after spending only two weeks there, he was allowed to fly to Ottawa on May 27 to make a previously scheduled address to the Canadian Federation of Mayors and Municipalities.

In mid-July—halfway through his course of instruction—he finally found time to write to Marj who, through Ernie Wetherell, shared the letter with both Tacoma newspapers. It is not clear whether Cain knew that at least certain parts of his letters would be printed by the local papers and, if so, what the ground rules were, but he probably assumed—even planned—on that being the case. In Cain, the papers had a trained reporter who could help bring the war home to their readers while, at the same time, he succeeded in keeping his name in front of the public.

The daily schedule at Charlottesville began at 6:00 a.m. and often lasted until after midnight. Cain struggled to learn Japanese. Students and faculty lived and studied together. His classmates were "worth knowing as people who have accomplished things," he wrote. "They have been 'doers' for years. . . . I would crawl across the country on my thumbs to listen to the lectures. Both old army men and selected college professors are telling us things we never dreamed of before."[4]

Completing his formal course work on August 4, Cain was allowed to fly home on a forty-eight hour leave to see his two-month-old daughter, Marlyce (already nicknamed Candy), who was born a month after he left for the Army. After an all-night flight, Cain arrived at Boeing Field at 6:18 a.m. He was met by Ernie Wetherell, who had brought along several reporters and staff photographers from the local newspapers. After a side trip to check on the progress of construction on the new Seattle-Tacoma Airport and toting a pith helmet for his son, Buzzy, Cain arrived at the front door of their North 10th Street home. Harry beamed as he saw his new daughter for the first time and exclaimed with a perfect lack of understanding, "Can she talk yet?"[5]

Cain spent the next day at the Tacoma City Hall, where he met with his former colleagues. Knowing of his impending overseas deployment but unable to discuss the details with them, he simply told them, "I think I shall be away for a quite a long time." He raised the question of how they should handle his absence since his term as mayor still had three years to run. No decision was made as the conversation drifted toward his experiences at Charlottesville. The rest of the day was taken up with briefings on the progress of pet projects, including the long-range planning study and the progress of financing and building wartime housing, as well as a review of the city's budget. After an evening with his family and friends, Cain left Tacoma early on the morning of August 7 and arrived back in Charlottesville by air the next day.[6]

By August 13, Cain was in West Palm Beach, Florida, waiting for space on board a plane bound for Brazil, the first leg of his flight to North Africa. Dashing off to Marj an undated V-mail message (single-sided short messages like telegrams, reduced in size to save space on the transport ships that carried them), Cain noted that he had arrived in "a very large, if not fair city," at noon that day. "I will cross the water soon; looks like a full schedule, but one of these days, I will cross the water to you. Small wonder a fellow likes to get on with the job—the sooner begun, the sooner finished."[7]

Approximately sixty of his letters and V-mails, written primarily to Marj between August 1943 and September 1945, survive. All were addressed to "Dearest Bunny" or "Bushy Head" and signed "Harry." Most also included a little cartoon drawing of his head and a series of "X's." While many are thoughtful and introspective, they are somehow strangely impersonal. If he had access to a typewriter, his letters were typed. If not, they were written in longhand on whatever paper was available—a lined tablet or on the stationery of a local hotel or a captured city hall. In addition, there is a portion of another journal (similar to the one he had kept during his European vacation and at the beginning of his first term as mayor), written once or twice a week, between January 6 and May 14, 1944, as conditions permitted. It is not clear what the purpose of the journal was—simply to record his thoughts or for later use, perhaps as notes for future speeches. Cain's journal was much more candid than his letters and would never have passed an Army censor's scrutiny.

On arrival in North Africa, Cain reported to the civil affairs section at the headquarters of the 15th Army Group, commanded by British General Sir Harold R.L.G. Alexander, a genial Irish Guards officer, who was generally considered to be Winston Churchill's favorite general. Alexander had previously commanded a division in the retreat at Dunkirk, then commanded the British retreat from Burma to India, and finally found success in North Africa as Commander-in-Chief, Middle East Command, during the defeat of the Axis forces there. Alexander reported to General Dwight Eisenhower, commanding the Allied Forces Headquarters (AFHQ) in the Mediterranean Theater of Operations, also located in Algiers. His primary combat forces included the British Eighth Army, commanded by Lieutenant-General Bernard Law Montgomery, and the U.S. Seventh Army under the command of Lieutenant General George Patton. Together, they had successfully invaded Sicily in July.

For the next month, Cain served as an unassigned civil affairs officer, undergoing orientation both in Algiers and in Sicily after the fighting there ended. While there is no mention of it in his service records, there is strong circumstantial evidence to suggest that Cain was temporarily assigned to a unit of the 82nd Airborne Division (probably the 325th Glider Infantry Regiment) during his orientation period in Sicily and the impending invasion of the Italian mainland.

The entity created to administer Sicily after it was conquered was AMGOT—the Allied Military Government for Occupied Territories. The organization was patterned on a similar entity that had been created at the end of World War I for the occupation of Germany. The organization's acronym soon came to stand for "Aged Military Gentlemen on Tour." It was also noted that the name approximated a crude, explicit, Turkish term for male genitalia.[8] AMGOT was primarily a British affair. Its titular head was General Alexander, but its functioning chief was an experienced British military administrator, Major-General Lord Rennell of Rodd, who had established the military government of Madagascar in the previous year. Lord Rennell's chief deputy was Brigadier General Frank J. McSherry, an American engineering officer who had served in the Army since 1917. McSherry had developed a well-deserved reputation as sort of "jack of all trades," serving as a War Department liaison officer with various federal agencies in Washington, DC, developing policy and planning manuals, and landing in Sicily to take charge of restoring vital physical infrastructure.

The battle for Sicily was officially over by August 17. Cain missed getting in on it by a matter of days. On the 26th, he sent a V-mail home, mentioning that he had spent several days in Algiers, "a city mostly of white [buildings] and inserted in a high hill—a city of mystery, intrigue and suffering. I had a fine bed in a railroad yard and survived countless swarms of mosquitos [sic]. They are dive bombers with stilettos. The fleas are less sinister. They laugh out loud for numbers are on their side. Sometime I may stay somewhere long enough to learn a language. Am more confused than ever at the moment for what we are trying to master at the moment has nothing to do with Japanese [a reference to his language studies at Charlottesville]."[9]

While there, he lunched with author and war correspondent Quentin Reynolds and with Captain John Boettiger, the publisher of the *Seattle Post-Intelligencer* and President Roosevelt's son-in-law, who was now also assigned to the civil affairs staff. In another letter to Ernie Wetherell, written on August 31, Cain hinted that he had been notified of his future assignment during his trip to Algiers. Cain chose his words carefully, indicating that he would soon be taking a sea trip, "the swimming in this part of the world is superior, especially surf board riding; will try it myself one of these days and expect to have my board on the first wave."[10]

After the invasion of Sicily, British Prime Minister Winston Churchill immediately and characteristically began pushing for an invasion of the Italian mainland directed at Naples and Rome. "Why should we crawl up the leg like a harvest bug, from the ankle upwards? Let us rather strike at the knee."[11] On September 3, Montgomery began the invasion of the Italian mainland, beginning to move his British Eighth and Canadian First Armies across the narrow Strait of Messina to Calabria on the Italian mainland. Although there was little opposition from the retreating Germans, the British commander was irked at having to play a secondary role to Operation AVALANCHE, the upcoming invasion of the Italian mainland at Salerno, south of Naples, to be led by General Mark Clark. Neither Montgomery nor Clark had received much strategic direction from either Eisenhower or Alexander. Monty was told to "help out as you can." There was no consensus about what to do if the Germans actually fought for Italy or whether the operation made sense at all if Italy surrendered.[12]

Operation AVALANCHE was predicated on the belief that Italy would surrender before the Allies invaded. As events transpired, the Italians delayed their planned surrender because they feared German reprisals. Without their surrender, there were potentially thirty-five Axis divisions available to defend the country.[13] Because of the shortage of Allied sealift and landing craft, only three divisions—two British and one American—were available for the Salerno landings, less than half the force that had earlier been available for Sicily. Everything was in short supply—troops, landing craft, bombers, and fighter protection.

An estimated 40,000 Germans faced the landings, but that number was capable of growing to 100,000 within four days. Clark would not have that number of troops available to him until the coming fall.

Realizing that they had finally run out of options, the Italian government accepted unconditional surrender on September 8. The night before, the Germans had assumed responsibility for the defense of the Naples region by shooting the commanding general of the local Italian forces when he failed to surrender to them.[14]

Located forty miles southeast of Naples, Salerno's twenty-two miles of beautiful beaches stretched along the crescent of the Salerno plain, narrow at both ends, approximately ten miles wide at the center, and commanded by a ring of mountains. Mount Eboli divided the plain into a northern half, where the British 10 Corps was to land, and a southern half, assigned to the United States VI Corps. One U.S. Navy officer likened the topography to being in "the inside of a teacup."

There were problems with the invasion from the start. A race began between the Allies, trying to amass enough power to force themselves through the mountains, and the Germans, trying to throw the invaders into the sea. Allied naval forces covering the beachhead were attacked for the first time by German guided missiles, which nearly sank the cruiser USS *Savannah*. A ferocious German counterattack along the Sele River on September 13, carried out by a fresh and newly arrived German division, appeared likely to split the Allied forces in two. Clark cabled Eisenhower that his position had deteriorated from "precarious" to "extremely critical." Montgomery was more than sixty miles away, advancing leisurely up the Italian boot.

Finally, Clark was forced to call on his only available strategic reserve, the 82nd Airborne Division, commanded by Major General Matthew Ridgway and then located in Sicily, to come immediately—that night. The division was available because a planned jump near Rome had been cancelled only days before. There was no time for planning or briefings or preparations. One historian has written that the orders given the paratroopers were simple and in language they understood: "The Krauts are kicking the shit out of our boys at Salerno and we're going to jump into the beachhead tonight and rescue them. Put on your parachutes and get on the plane."[15] The 1st and 2nd Battalions of the 504th Parachute Regiment jumped onto the beachhead on the nights of September 13 and 14, while the Regiment's 3rd Battalion and the 325th Glider Infantry

Regiment landed on the beaches in a conventional seaborne assault the next day. Landing with them was Major Harry P. Cain, assigned to the civil affairs section of the U.S. Fifth Army.

Cain had to leave a hospital bed to do it. It may have been those mosquitoes in the rail yard in Algiers or others he encountered in Sicily, but Cain had contracted malaria (very common among troops in Sicily) earlier that month and was confined to a field hospital in Palermo. In a later interview, he said that he persuaded "friends" to "get him out" of the hospital, carry him to the beach, and place him on a landing craft, "and that's how I got to Salerno. When we arrived, they carried me through the surf, dug a hole on the beach, and stuck me in it. Mortar fire was heavy, but I was too sick to care. After about 36 hours I crawled out of the hole and went about my business."[16] Cain later remembered those first two nights, lying in the cold, "freezing to death" and the kindness of a fellow officer from San Francisco, also sick and lying next to him, who loaned him one of his two blankets so that he could keep warm. Cain learned several months later that the man had subsequently been killed. In a letter received back home on September 24, Cain said that he was writing from a city about the same size as Tacoma (probably Salerno) that "had been shot to shreds. The population of the city must be somewhere in the hills, for the natives are not here."[17]

The weight of Allied reinforcements arriving on the beachhead and the belated arrival of Montgomery's Eighth Army from the east and south finally began to press the German left flank, allowing the Allies to push through the heavily defended mountains on the Sorrento Peninsula. Cain moved north from Vietri sul Mare toward Nocera with elements of the British 7th Armored Division—the famous 'Desert Rats'—hoping to exploit a breakthrough.[18]

Cain's was no comfortable staff job located behind the front lines. He would often move into an area as soon, or even before, it had been cleared of Germans troops in order to see to the immediate needs of the civilian population. "The town I am spending the night in is one I was chased out of three nights in a row while trying to get it running after twenty days of siege and occupation. I actually set up an office and peopled it with officials dragged from the hills, while tanks of both sides rumbled into action not four blocks away. We didn't know who had the place for seventy-two hours or who would take over the management of the city hall the next morning."[19]

Cain's letters to Marj describe his duties and the conditions he was living in (at least as much as he and the censors allowed) during this time. Cain had been given the job of administering the Northwest District of Salerno. In his letter of October 4, he tried to describe it to Marj. "The territory I was given to administer is almost all in our hands and I shall stay behind for a time to help others return things to normal. When we started here there was almost nothing: 50 percent of all the homes uninhabitable; no water, lights or sewage; nothing much to eat and no stores to sell it in. It's miraculous what can take place overnight. Draft 1,000 men as laborers and watch what happens. What appeared to be a mass of rubble and debris became a living form and, presto! You have a city once more with a heart and soul. The one under my feet breathes tonight and a week ago I thought it dead forever."[20]

Continuing the letter the next day, Cain wrote that he had had a magnificent day, "most of which was spent in the mountains looking for a town the Germans had used as a firing base. Quaint and old and over-run with 15,000 people who had lived only on bread for a solid month. It isn't any use trying to tell you what that means because you must see the faces to understand. The Germans left one single cow and that's where all the milk has to come from. Maybe I can get some food in tomorrow and, even at that slim prospect, the people cry with joy and want individually to kiss your hand. Also found time to fall heir to 1,500 mental patients in an asylum. Same story, no food."[21]

Later that week, he wrote again. "[I] spent last night and all of today feeding, nursing, petting and raising hell with several hundred so-called utter strangers. They are the kind of derelicts of this war who have been living in caves and holes in the ground for want of better places to stay. It just isn't possible to describe the indescribable. I wish more people could see what war does to the innocent. I must go through the delouser tomorrow, because of my exposure today but I would do that every day of the week if need be."[22]

By September 18, the German high command in Italy had determined that Salerno could no longer be defended and started to retreat northward, covered by a ferocious rear-guard action. British troops entered a destroyed Naples on October 1. The retreating Germans demolished anything the war had not already destroyed, including every ship in the port, the port facilities, the water system, train tunnels, and ageless antiquities. Allied troops quickly swept northward, along the coast and through the city of

4. "The Sooner Begun, the Sooner Finished"

Caserta (where an immense, ancient castle would become Mark Clark's headquarters) to the Volturno River—200 feet wide, swift, barely fordable, and heavily defended. Matthew Ridgway, observing the area in advance of the Allied offensive, wrote, "It was about as mean a place to try a river crossing as any I saw during the whole war."[23]

By mid-October, the Allies were able to get across the river but with heavy casualties—15,000 between September 3 and October 20.[24] By the second week in November, after advancing only fifty-five miles beyond the Volturno, Clark knew that his offensive had stalled—a victim of the Italian winter and the seemingly endless mountains that lay before him.

In the meantime, Major Harry Cain continued to go about his civil affairs responsibilities. On October 16, he held a meeting of 118 local Italian officials, in theory now Allies, who reported to him, including "distinguished people and others who compare with the greatest and most vicious cutthroats known to man." Cain also courted the hierarchy of the local Catholic Church to help him in organizing the relief efforts and told a story about personally driving the local Catholic archbishop and two other bishops around in his jeep, to the horror of his British colleagues and the delight of the priests and their local parishioners.[25]

Under the terms of Italy's surrender, an Allied Control Commission (ACC) was created to implement its terms, and ultimately it replaced AMGOT in the administration of those parts of Italy that had been liberated. In mid-November, Cain was called from his administrative duties in the field and re-assigned to the skeleton headquarters of the ACC, located alongside the shadow Italian government—which at this time consisted of only the King, his Prime Minister, and some military ministers—in the southeastern port city of Brindisi.

Cain's new responsibilities included the Civil Administration and Personnel branches of the ACC. His new boss was none other than his old friend, Major General Kenyon A. Joyce, a former cavalryman who had joined the Army as a private in the Spanish-American War and rose to command the IX U.S. Corps at Fort Lewis between 1940 and 1942. Joyce served as the Deputy President of the ACC and its day-to-day administrator—appointed by Dwight Eisenhower, who served as its ex-officio President. Joyce was joined by his chief of staff, Brigadier General Maxwell D. Taylor, a small group of British and American staff officers including Cain, representatives of the Free French and the Soviet Union, and such notables as future British Prime Minister Harold MacMillan, future Under Secretary of State Robert Murphy, and future Russian Foreign Minister M. Andrei Vyshinsky.[26] Cain remembered his tour at Brindisi as "cold, cheerless and miserably dreary but . . . filled with conversations which predicted, in remarkably accurate fashion, the pattern of things to come." The members of the Russian mission clearly spelled out "what the Soviets had in mind for the years ahead."[27]

Joyce liked Cain and had recognized his organizational and public relations skills in Tacoma. Joyce had specifically asked for Cain to serve as his "personal representative and public relations chief." However, if Cain thought that working for Joyce was going to consist of sitting at a desk in Brindisi, he was sadly mistaken. Cain accompanied Joyce to meetings and inspection trips and was often tasked with special assignments that put him in close proximity to the front. In a letter written on a Saturday (probably November 20) soon after he joined the ACC, Cain described something of his new assignment, starting out with, "Whoever said my staff job was likely to be a quiet one has my permission to change his mind. I have had enough unexpected items in the last three weeks to last a lifetime."[28]

Cain described some of his recent harrowing experiences, including a flight he took with "his general" from an island (probably Malta) back to the Italian mainland in which they encountered high winds, a low ceiling, and ice on the wings that almost forced their plane to ditch in the Mediterranean. Cain also described being present at a dinner party for high-ranking officials that was interrupted by a German air attack that destroyed the banquet room in which they had been eating just minutes before. As they attempted to evacuate the building, "the front door, near which I was standing, grew tired and fell in, but not on me for I was thrown into a corner across the way. What a way to make a living!"[29] That incident was almost certainly the December 2 surprise German bombing of the port of Bari, about seventy-five miles north of Brindisi, that sank seventeen ships anchored in the harbor, including one that was carrying a cargo of mustard gas, which then dispersed all over the harbor, gassing many soldiers, sailors, and civilians. The incident was not publicly disclosed until many years later.[30]

In another letter written on January 15, 1944, Cain described an incident that had occurred during of the past month, telling Marj that he had been involved in a "convoy crash" that landed him in a British hospital. He characterized his experience as "service excellent, customs amusing, and different. The first night they brought me what I took to be medicine and I hid it. The next morning, as they cleared away the debris, I asked what that vile stuff was and, to my chagrin, amazement, and horror, I was told it was my whiskey ration. 'So sorry you don't like it!' Ho Ho! Ha Ha! Thus an education continues."[31]

Kenyon Joyce announced his retirement at the end of 1943. He was replaced by Lieutenant-General Sir Frank Noel Mason-Macfarlane, the former Governor-General of Gibraltar. Cain had been alerted in late December that he was going to be re-assigned: first to a temporary assignment at Fifth Army headquarters at Caserta and then to Eisenhower's staff in London. Cain recorded in his journal on January 6 that he had orders to leave for England on January 29 and "no joke! Unless somebody wants to fight, and I am not interested at the moment, it looks as though I will be on my way by the 29th."[32]

Cain was formally transferred to the Fifth Army's Rome Area Command on January 17 and arrived at its headquarters at Caserta three days later to await further assignment. It was not long in coming. On the 24th, he was ushered into the office of Major General John A. Crane, who was slated to become the Rome Area Commander under Mark Clark. Crane wanted Cain to do the same job for him as he had done for Kenyon Joyce. Almost immediately, Crane was transferred to a another job, and Cain found himself working for Major General Henry Hubbard Johnson, a National Guard officer and self-proclaimed friend of President Roosevelt's.

His duties for Johnson were similar to those he had performed for Kenyon Joyce and John Crane. His position in the civil affairs section permitted him to attend the intelligence briefings provided to members of the Fifth Army's senior staff in the bowels of the huge Caserta Castle and to observe two of the most difficult battles of the Italian campaign.

Operation SHINGLE, the Allied invasion of Anzio, thirty-eight miles south of Rome, the nearly concurrent assault on the Gustav Line, and the later bombing of the ancient monastery of Monte Cassino, were closely interrelated. As Mark Clark's ground advance slowed to a crawl in the mountains of Italy, the Allies—particularly British Prime Minister Winston Churchill—looked for a way to break the deadlock. He recommended and pushed through another seaborne end-run at Anzio. The Allies landed in January, the Germans responded—once again quickly and powerfully—nearly throwing the Allies back into the sea. Nothing survives that suggests that Cain actually visited the Anzio beachhead, although his journal candidly discusses conditions there (information he could have obtained from the daily intelligence briefings). However, the possibility remains that he was there, however briefly. He received a Battle Star for Rome-Arno when he left Italy.

Just enough pressure was placed on the Germans at Anzio to allow Clark's ground offensive to move forward to the Gustav Line, which was anchored by the ancient monastery of Monte Cassino. Successive waves of Allied soldiers were thrown against the dug-in German defenses there, and it was widely held that the Germans were using the monastery as an observation post to direct fire at the attacking Allied troops. With advance knowledge that Monte Cassino was going to be bombed, Cain went up to the front to view the spectacle.[33] Because of bad weather on one occasion and the presence of Indian troops too close to the target on another, the bombings didn't take place, but Cain's presence attracted the attention of the German gunners anyway. "We didn't get as far as we wanted to for Jerry was banging hell out of the OP [Observation Post] we sought and it wasn't healthy to get within 500 yards—not if you wanted to come back. The fight for Cassino is a month old and we haven't got the place yet. They say it's a war of extermination in the Pacific, but the same is true here."[34] The bombing of Monte Cassino finally took place on the morning of February 15, killing many of the remaining occupants and reducing the ancient abbey to rubble. Even then, the ruin was not finally captured until May.

Harry Cain's last official duty at the Rome Area Command was to write a mission statement that General Johnson had requested. He went on travel status as of March 1, traveling to Naples to say goodbye to good friends with whom he had worked the past nine months. Saturday morning, the 4th of March, dawned under buckets of rain. On the way to the pier, Cain noticed that their baggage had been sitting outside in the rain and mud all night. He boarded his ship, the 14,100-ton former Dutch passenger ship MV *Tegelberg*, which had a Dutch captain and a British crew. The convoy, consisting of twenty-six ships, and protected by nine destroyers, the elderly British battleship, HMS *Warspite*, and two escort carriers, left Naples on Sunday morning.

Cain had served in Italy for slightly less than half a year. It was his introduction to war. From the day he landed on the beach at Salerno until he joined the staff of the Allied Control Commission a month later, Cain was frequently under enemy fire. He had seen death and the suffering of freezing and starving civilians who had nowhere to hide. He had successfully tested his leadership skills and his capacity for innovation and leadership. He had impressed all of his commanding officers and was now being summoned by one of them to England. General Johnson awarded Cain with a Bronze Star Medal "for meritorious achievement in connection with military operations" for his efforts on behalf of the Rome Area Command during his short tenure there. He earned two Battle Stars (Naples-Foggia and Rome-Arno), and an assault arrowhead for his European-African-Middle Eastern Service Medal as a result of his landing on the beachhead at Salerno.

After a mostly uneventful voyage, Ireland appeared out of the mist on Monday, March 20, 1944, and by that night, the convoy was anchored at the mouth of the Clyde in Scotland. The next morning, Cain disembarked and rode thirty minutes up the Clyde to the town of Grenock, where, after being served hot coffee and warm doughnuts by Red Cross workers, Cain boarded a train for the village of Shrivenham, located in Oxfordshire, and the temporary headquarters of American civil affairs personnel in England.[35]

5

"Who Are These Republican Leaders?"

THE TRIP THROUGH wartime Scotland and England was a delightful and fascinating experience for Cain after months of witnessing the poverty and destruction in Italy. Beautiful spring weather, railway station masters in their bowler hats, young women working in the fields, lots of cattle and sheep with hair in their eyes, people waving from the window of their homes to the soldiers on the train—Cain took it all in as he fondly remembered his previous extended visit to Britain almost a decade before.

In the early pre-dawn hours of March 23, 1944, he arrived at the sprawling former Royal Artillery training base at Shrivenham, Oxfordshire, which now served as the gathering point for nearly 800 American civil affairs officers awaiting assignment. More were expected to arrive within the month. About 40 percent of them had been civilians recruited for their various specialties. The rest had transferred in from other branches of the service.[1]

Cain expected that Shrivenham would be just a way-stop to his next assignment to the field—which is where he very much wanted and *expected* to be. Instead, it quickly became apparent that no one knew where any of those assembled were headed. He had known many of these men at Charlottesville or in Italy, and they were utterly bored, discouraged by a perceived lack of interest in them by the army's top brass and what seemed to be a series of constant reorganizations. Characteristically, lacking any direction from above, Cain decided to act on his own. On a tip, he wrote to Lieutenant General Troy Middleton, whom he had met in Italy and who was now scheduled to command the VIII Corps, applying for a job.

Once the word of his contact with Middleton got out, Cain was quickly told by the chief of staff of the civil affairs division to forget any thought of a transfer. "There aren't enough officers [here] now, and those that are trained aren't going to get away."[2] Cain settled in to the same routine that was frustrating everyone else at Shrivenham: repetitive classroom training, language instruction, and outdoor exercise—including instruction on how to ford a rushing river or disassemble a Jeep—all while the reorganization continued.

Cain decided he would try again to get things moving by laying out his plight to Brigadier General Frank J. McSherry, the ranking American civil affairs officer in COSSAC (Chief of Staff to Supreme Allied Commander) and Cain's former commanding officer in the Naples area. McSherry had been called to London six months earlier by Supreme Allied Commander Dwight D. Eisenhower to share the responsibility with Major-General L. R. Lumley (the former Governor of Bombay), as they transitioned the civil affairs functions of COSSAC to SHAEF (Supreme Headquarters Allied Expeditionary Force). It was this process that was creating the confusion and delay that was so frustrating to the men awaiting assignment at Shrivenham.

The transition was made even more difficult by the fact that there were deep disagreements between officials in Washington and London and those who had run civil affairs in the Mediterranean Theater about how civil affairs should be organized at SHAEF. Ultimately, Eisenhower's chief of staff, Lieutenant General Walter Bedell Smith, decided that the civil affairs functions should be separated into two divisions: Policy and Operations. Policy would be subdivided into functional branches and would report to Lumley. McSherry would head Operations, supervising plans and their execution but without exercising direct command authority. As these various negotiations proceeded, Smith lost confidence in Lumley. Smith wanted to replace him with an American, but Eisenhower, deciding that the position should go to a British military officer, selected Lieutenant-General Arthur Edward Grassett to be his G-5 (Assistant Chief of Staff for Civil Affairs), backed up by an American, Brigadier General Julius C. Holmes, a former diplomat and soldier selected by Smith and McSherry, as his deputy. Grassett assumed his new job in mid-April.[3]

With G-5's organizational and command structures now decided, Cain received a summons to report to General McSherry on Saturday, April 15, 1944. (It had probably been McSherry who had pulled the strings necessary to overrule General Crane's attempt to keep Cain in Italy.) Cain reported to him at SHAEF's new headquarters located at Bushy Park, in a southeastern London suburb near Kingston-on-Thames near Hampton

Court Palace. The place was little more than a rapidly growing maze of Quonset huts, tents, and temporary buildings, growing in the ancient royal forest.[4] Directed to Wing 8 in Section E, Cain found McSherry in an office identified as the "European Contact Section." After a first failed attempt, Cain finally got in to see his former commander in the Naples area. In a rush of words, McSherry told Cain that civil affairs was misunderstood and maligned by some of those around Eisenhower. It was time to improve their public relations performance, and for that, they needed "a man of judgment, tact and finesse" to lead the effort. In short, they were looking for someone, preferably a newspaperman, to handle high-level VIPs and the press. They had scoured through the credentials of all of the available officers without success. The job was Cain's for the asking. "I would have an office in London, circulate in high military and political circles, anticipate public opinion in America, and channel all public relations after the continent was reached," he wrote in his journal. Cain told McSherry that while he was highly complimented by the offer, he really wanted to go to the field and get on with fighting the war. He had tentatively been offered a job by General Middleton. McSherry persisted and asked him to think it over for a couple of days. He then played his ace in the hole. As Cain was walking out the door, McSherry said, "Remember, in your considerations, that I *need* you!" Just as with the request from those organizing Tacoma's Golden Jubilee, Cain couldn't refuse. McSherry later told Cain that if he had refused his suggestion, he would have ordered him to take the job anyway.[5]

What Cain didn't know at the time was that he at least partially owed his new job to another Washingtonian, Major Melvin B. Voorhees, a former Seattle newspaper editor who was also serving in civil affairs and waiting for an assignment at Shrivenham. Voorhees had already been interviewed for the job and had turned it down, but not without first telling McSherry's staff about Cain. "There is a guy here who has no newspaper background but is the right man for this job—name's Cain."[6]

Cain was probably selected for other reasons as well. Again, he was at the right place at the right time. McSherry knew him and had appreciated his work in Italy. Ike's chief of staff, Bedell Smith, and McSherry preferred career officers for these high-profile jobs, but, while Cain was a politician, he had been an officer in the Army Reserve and had a record of getting along well with senior officers. He was observant. He was active.

He was articulate and an excellent writer. In short, he was an excellent match for the job.

On Thursday, April 20, Harry Cain was back in McSherry's office to accept his new job. McSherry was delighted but in a hurry. Cain was to be responsible for the Psychological Warfare and Public Relations Division. He would report directly to General Grassett who, as Assistant Chief of Staff (G-5), was the official civil affairs spokesman for the whole European Theater of Operations. Cain was shown the office he was to occupy next door to Grassett's and one door away from another reserved for the use of U.S. Ambassador Anthony "Tony" Biddle when he happened to be at Bushy Park. Cain worked all weekend and, on the following Tuesday, briefed McSherry and Grassett about how he planned to approach his new job.[7]

In an effort that could only be chalked up to wishful thinking, Cain tried to find a room at the Mayfair, Park Lane, or Cumberland Hotels in Central London. Not a chance in the world. He ended up in a closet-sized room on the fourth floor of an annex of the Green Park Hotel on historic but decidedly seedy Half Moon Street, not far from Hyde Park. He commented in his journal, "The stairs are so narrow that I almost have to walk sideways. Had I not seen a lot worse, I would have been very unhappy. The bathroom was on the floor below and toilet even further below that."[8]

On the job less than three weeks, he confided to his journal, "My work is all and more than I anticipated. . . . There is more to be done than time allows but order is on the way. Need a phone and clerk badly and they have been promised before long." He said that he and his six assistants arrived at work before nine in the morning and left twelve hours later. One of his first assignments was to work on a propaganda film with Archibald MacLeish, the American poet, writer, and future librarian of Congress, who was now the Assistant Director of the Office of War Information.[9]

Cain also renewed his acquaintance with Harold Laski, the leftist British politician, economist, and author, whose lectures Cain had attended at the London School of Economics in 1935. Laski maintained a kind of salon at his home for intellectuals, writers, and (mostly socialist) politicians, and Cain attended from time to time. Cain didn't always agree with what he heard but enjoyed the intellectual stimulation. Cain carefully balanced Laski's opinions with the views of England's conservative elite, like Lady Ravensdale, daughter of Lord Curzon, the former Viceroy of India and British Foreign Secretary, whom Cain had met socially. Many members of the British upper class had supported former Prime Minister Neville Chamberlain's policy of appeasement because they felt that Communist Russia posed a far greater future threat to England than Nazi Germany. Cain also enjoyed listening to even more non-conformist views, particularly those expressed by the speakers at Hyde Park Corner, as he had done often during his previous visit to London.

SOMETIME IN APRIL 1944—about a month after he had arrived in England—Cain received a surprise cable from Marj in Tacoma. Her short cable said only that she had been contacted by certain unspecified "Republican leaders," who wanted Harry to run for the U.S. Senate. She explained that they were requesting a statement at once and that the necessary filing papers were apparently in the mail. He was told to expect a series of letters from Tacoma, written on April 7 and 8, which would contain information about the campaign organization that was being formed. The seat was available because the incumbent, Democrat Homer T. Bone, had been appointed to the U.S. Court of Appeals by President Roosevelt earlier in the year. Luck—or at least opportunity—was again knocking on Harry Cain's door.

The cable was the answer to a long-held dream. While still mayor of Tacoma, Cain had often pondered the potential of his political future. How far could he go? Could he advance so far as to become a United States Senator? In those days, the dream had not been framed in a partisan light. He was seen as a future political star by both parties. Many—including most Democrats—saw him as a traditional Southern conservative who was pro-business and moderate on social issues. Washington State, however, had many qualified, upwardly mobile Democrats with potential futures. The Republicans did not. Republicans were looking for popular candidates, and Harry Cain stood out in stark contrast to any of the possible competitors.

Cain had previously discussed the possibility of higher office with his friend and political mentor, Arthur Langlie. On April 8, 1943, a month before he was sworn into the army, Cain had met with Langlie and Major George LaFray in the governor's office to discuss the army's new military government branch but then had met privately with Langlie to discuss the possibility of Cain's becoming a Republican candidate in the upcoming 1944 U.S. Senate race.[10] Cain later claimed that Langlie had again approached him about running when he "was at Tizi-Ouzou in the mountains of Algeria."[11]

In the privacy of his journal, Cain dispassionately evaluated his possible candidacy. The Republicans were courting him while the Democrats were not. An opportunity was at hand—earlier than he had ever dreamed possible. Confiding his inner thoughts to his journal, he wrote, "I have learned not to fool myself very much, so I can do nothing other than admit that the possibility of going to the Senate has aroused every fiber of my thinking. It is what I have dreamed of for a very long time and now that some sort of a chance [presents itself] I am thousands of miles away. What to do? I haven't the semblance of an idea. That I am normally thought of as being a Democrat is another thought-stimulator. It is true that I am a liberal, but likewise I have had no strong party affiliation and I would feel no apology [necessary] to any man for selecting as my own ticket the one which promised the greatest chance of success. Who *are* these Republican leaders? Is Arthur Langlie among them? Does he still feel as he did the day he called me down to Olympia to find out where I stood?"[12]

Cain later remembered this period and reflected on the process of becoming a Republican after the opportunity presented itself. "It was then that I began to think that if I aspire to the Senate of the United States, what am I in terms of politics? It was then I decided, on balance, that the Republican Party was somewhat more cautious in dealing with other people's property and money. That isn't to say they were reactionary, but that I felt that they would move with less speed in economic areas which I felt were important."[13]

Cain consulted the Judge Advocate General's office for advice and was told that while an officer could run for elective office, he could not campaign for that office in any way. He found an article on the same subject and sent it to Marj, with the comment that he doubted whether any man could be elected under such circumstances. A week went by without the arrival of the promised letters from home. He confided to his journal, "There isn't much time left; I think the filings close about the middle of May. Those needed letters better come and come soon, and when they do I will get off an answer in prompt fashion. It will include whether I will or I won't; what is to be done about the job I treasure at home; and my affection for those who have been thinking of a fellow a long way from home."[14]

The anticipated letters, including one from Arthur Langlie arrived on April 20. Langlie was encouraging and thought that Cain should try for the seat. A letter from Marj provided more information about the "Republican leaders" who wanted him to run. They included his former boss, Herb Raleigh, the former mayor and his early mentor, J. J. Kaufman, and a number of other well-known Tacoma business leaders. Reno Odlin, the Tacoma banker who had recruited Cain for the Golden Jubilee celebration and had himself run unsuccessfully for the Senate in 1934, was a dissenting voice, concerned about the logistical problems posed by a candidate who would be both absent from the campaign and silent about his political philosophy.

After returning to London from Bushy Park that afternoon, Cain ran into Floyd Oles, another old Tacoma friend who was then serving on active duty in London. Oles said that he had been looking for Cain for days, even driving out to Shrivenham to find him. He had news from home and was able to add some more detail about Langlie's thinking and about the level of political support back home. The conversation crystallized Cain's thinking, and he now made up his mind, if he hadn't already done so. He sent cables to both Marj and to Langlie saying essentially the same thing: "I can't refuse. My considered answer is a thoughtful, grateful, enthusiastic YES."[15] However, after his conversation with the Judge Advocate General's office, he also disclosed the caveats under which he would agree to run: 1) he would answer no political questions while he remained in the army, 2) if nominated, he would not leave the army to campaign, and 3) if elected, he would not serve until the war was over.[16]

The news of his decision traveled quickly. On the morning of Monday, May 1, Frank McSherry poked his head into Cain's office with a cheery "Good morning, Senator." On May 4, all of the Seattle and Tacoma papers carried short announcements that Cain would file for the Senate. The *Tacoma News Tribune* reported that "his friends said that appeals have come to them from all parts of the state asking that his name be placed in nomination. This demand, they maintain, results from the many analytical discussions of state, national and international affairs he has presented before groups in communities and rural districts throughout the state."[17] On May 24, a statewide campaign organization was announced, to be led by the former mayor, J. J. Kaufman.

The campaign must have suffered some early moments of anxiety. Writing to Marj on June 10, Cain told her—although she probably already knew it—that Kaufman had cabled him asking him for permission to withdraw his name from the race if they felt it necessary. Cain told them to do whatever they thought best but that he would have nothing to do with it. In his journal, he confided, "It's important that people believe what I say; they must be made to understand, too, that until it is time to do something else, I shall continue to be a soldier, first, last, and all the time."[18] Privately, he thought that many of his friends were naïve enthusiasts who imagined that all would be well if only he would come home to campaign. There was no need for concern. By the end of June, "Cain for Senator" clubs had been organized all over the state, and Kaufman was telling the *Tacoma News Tribune*, "All of Washington is now underway for Cain."[19]

BUT THE EVENTS in far-off Washington State were about to seem very far away, indeed. The long-anticipated invasion of Normandy began on June 6, 1944. Because of his public relations responsibilities and high-level contacts, Cain was well aware of its planning and the deep concern that many felt for its success. In a partial entry to his journal, written back on April 18, Cain mentioned the concerns of some high-ranking officers who claimed to have seen the invasion plan. "I found a lot of shuddering over what is to come. . . . They are anything but happy." There were concerns that Rommel knew the details of the Allied invasion plans and was poised to inflict massive casualties on the assault troops unless the Allies landed where he was not expecting them."[20]

Cain's letters to Marj from this period clearly reflect his frustration at having to remain in England while the real battles were being fought in France. His public relations duties seemed much less important now that the fighting was underway in Normandy. He wanted to get back to the field, to where the fighting was. His days were spent "seeking answers to seemingly insoluble problems. Agreements and propaganda and reactions fill each day. A very close friend just came by to say he was going out in the tanks. Maybe that's why I groan a little at being left behind. I didn't care much for Salerno, and that's no understatement, but I would rather be among those who went than to read about it in the papers." Wistfully, he told her that if he had he not been assigned to his current job, "it would have been my good fortune to have gone in from the air [perhaps a reference to connections he already had or was quietly pursuing with the 82nd Airborne Division]. I was looking forward to telling you how it felt to jump for the first time. Just between us, I would have thought, half way down, that it was a hell of a way to make a living. Ha!"[21]

These were difficult days in London. The Germans began to bombard the city with V-1 rocket-propelled bombs on June 13. The impersonal nature of the attacks, occurring suddenly at all hours of the day and night, seemed particularly cruel and monstrous to a war-weary nation. Cain told Marj that they "turned day into night and the other way round." He felt "depressed and dispirited" by the war and its suffering. He sometimes "walked among those living in the underground shelters, to make the more certain that I won't forget. Cute ones like Buzzy and Candy are learning how to sleep on a concrete floor on the edge of the subway. They can accustom themselves to anything; it isn't right, and it simply mustn't happen again. . . . Had Buzzy lived here, he would now know nothing but war with its tragedy and grief."[22] He longed for his loved ones at home. "I wish I wrote more often for it would permit me to restate in a hundred different ways my love and affection for the three at home. That feeling seems to grow the stronger as I remain away, but it's strong enough for a long time, thank you."[23]

Although Cain didn't refer to it in his letters to Marj at the time, his service records indicate that he was promoted from major to lieutenant colonel on July 1. With the promotion, his duties shifted from being responsible for G-5's Public Relations Section to being, as he called it, "the alter ego and gate keeper" for Lieutenant-General Grassett, to whom he already reported.

GOOD FORTUNE SMILED again on Harry Cain as the state primary campaign got underway back home. While Cain was not well known in Eastern Washington, he was clearly the most well known of the ten other Republican candidates—some serious and some just hopeful—whom he faced in the Republican primary on July 11. He chuckled as he recalled that while promoting their own candidacy, the other candidates always went out of their way to promote his, noting that he couldn't be there, because he was over in Europe fighting the Germans. The unintentional combination of Cain being in Europe and not saying a thing and the other candidates crisscrossing the state and, in one way or another, saying positive things about him, could only help. But others were not so sure.

Between July 12 and July 14, the results of the primary election trickled in. Cain couldn't sleep on the night of the 12th. He got up and tried to get more news without success. The situation was still confused the next morning. He tried to do a little work. No use. Then, a wire report from *Stars and Stripes* said that Cain was "practically" assured of the nomination. What did "practically" mean? Finally, on Friday, the 14th, he received a cable from his campaign manager, J. J. Kaufman, saying the newspapers had named him the winner. In the end, Cain beat the second-place finisher, Walla Walla attorney Cameron Sherwood, by more than 15,000 votes out of a total of 364,356 cast for the eleven Republican candidates. Cain noted that his friends and associates were excited and delighted at his victory. They held a party for him and "even three-star generals stopped by to ask questions."[24]

Cain's primary victory set the stage for one of the more curious election campaigns in Washington history, in which four-term Democratic Congressman Warren G. Magnuson, just returned from the navy and campaigning vigorously, contested Republican Harry P. Cain, still only a major in the army when the campaign began, located 7,000 miles away, and vowing not to campaign at all.

In 1944, Magnuson was a young, handsome, and well-liked New Deal Democrat with a reputation as something of a playboy. He had been orphaned at an early age and worked his way through the University of Washington, driving an ice wagon, ultimately earning a law degree, and going into politics. Magnuson was first elected to the state legislature in the Democratic landslide of 1932, next as King County's Prosecuting Attorney in 1934, and then in 1936 to the U.S. House of Representatives, where he became friends with another freshman congressman, Lyndon Baines Johnson of Texas, and occasionally played poker with a young senator from Missouri, Harry S. Truman. Magnuson joined the U.S. Navy after Pearl Harbor and served on an aircraft carrier in the South Pacific. He took advantage of a one-time offer made by President Roosevelt in 1944 that allowed officers to resign and return home to campaign for public office at a time when Roosevelt knew that he would need all of the sure Democratic votes in Congress he could find.

On October 2, Cain's general election campaign was kicked off at a free, two-hour vaudeville show and rally thrown in honor of Tacoma's "fighting mayor" at Tacoma's Temple Theater, attended by hundreds of enthusiastic supporters, including Governor Arthur Langlie, former mayor J. J. Kaufman, and current mayor Val Fawcett. Soon, a number of surrogates, including many of Cain's former primary opponents, were crisscrossing the state, stumping for the absent Cain. He received an endorsement from well-known radio commentator Fulton Lewis, Jr., who called Cain "courageous and extraordinarily able" for his opposition to the Japanese internment camps earlier in the war.[25]

A significant newspaper advertising campaign was rolled out featuring countless one-column, eight-inch ads promoting Cain as "Equipped for Statesmanship," or "A Fighter for Good Government," and possessing "Courage, Sincerity and Leadership." The ads appeared in every daily newspaper in the state, as well as most of the local ethnic and labor papers. A campaign brochure provided "The Average Voter's Size-Up of Harry P. Cain."[26] There was also a successful attempt to familiarize the general public with Cain and his family through extensive, non-paid background articles written by friendly reporters in papers, such as the *Seattle Times*, that editorially supported Cain. Between June 18 and October 22, the *Times* carried three full-page spreads about Cain and his family in its Sunday Magazine section.[27]

Even the popular and politically astute Magnuson found that running against a phantom candidate like Cain was something of a challenge. Like the other Republicans who had run against Cain in the primary, Magnuson couldn't really get at him because he was off fighting the war. By all accounts, Cain had an excellent military record in Europe and an obviously effective public relations effort at home. While Magnuson couldn't effectively attack Cain's record, he could—and did—attack his *lack* of one in terms of statewide experience and issues. Magnuson's ads reminded voters that "This State Has an Investment in Warren G. Magnuson—Keep Him on the Job." His campaign brochure called him "One of the Nation's Ablest Men in Congress." Influential Spokane businessman and former state senator, Joseph Drumheller, sent out flyers reminding the recipients that "Cain is a former president of the Young People's Democratic Club of Pierce County. We are supporting Warren G. Magnuson—a candidate who files on his own ticket—a man who stands proudly on his own record—a man who meets every issue intelligently and courageously."[28] Former U.S. Senator Homer Bone was quoted as telling Magnuson that

"Cain knows as much about the problems of Washington [State] as my poodle dog knows about differential calculus."[29]

A number of statewide political insiders probably agreed. Cain was like an explosive shooting star, streaking across the political horizon to an unknown destination and an uncertain end. He was possessed of impressive rhetoric, a reformer's image as mayor of Tacoma, and a well-publicized war record, but he had never held statewide office, was not known for compromise, and his in-depth political views were almost completely unknown—although organized labor viewed him with deep skepticism. On the other hand, some conservative Republicans felt that Cain was a New Dealer who was only posing as a Republican.

Cain was also viewed as something of a curiosity on Eisenhower's staff, with fellow officers and some of the most famous newspaper reporters in the country following his progress with good-natured interest. He was careful, however, not to make any comments of a political nature to them or mix his day job in any way with the far-off campaign going on in Washington State.

Not surprisingly, Cain was being pressured by his wife and supporters to come home and campaign. Apparently, there were even some rumors that Langlie would appoint him to the vacant Senate seat if he would return and campaign in person. "I guess that if I was appointed and came home, I might get away with it. I would take my seat and then promptly light out for the tag end of the campaign in Washington. I think I could answer all the opposition arguments but I would fail miserably in answering my own. I would simply be another guy looking for a chance to edge up real close to the public trough. . . . If, on our terms, I can win, I shall truly be a representative of a State to the extent unknown by a long line of predecessors. If, on those terms, I lose, my only regret will be for our friends, not for us."[30]

As the campaign heated up, Marj continued to press him to come home and campaign or at least to give them some material, such as statements or highlights of his record and duties that the campaign could use. In late August, she had written to him again, asking a series of questions about his duties at SHAEF, his uniform, and even his medals. In a response fairly dripping with frustration, he explained in general terms how SHAEF was organized, making sure that he emphasized his relatively unimportant position in the larger scheme of things. He explained his role on Grassett's staff, describing himself as "the one to whom others come when they can't get to him. It is for me to know what he would say and do and what he has in mind." He explained that he also served other bosses. "At last count, I had fourteen generals for whom I do what I can. When they have an idea, I try to put it in words, or have others better qualified do it for me."[31]

He scolded her over her questions about his uniform and decorations. "Does it seem reasonable to you [that I would] exploit my uniform [in order to] come home to campaign? [That] seems flatly incomprehensible. I won't permit any mention to be made of my job other than the fact that, for the present, I am a part of SHAEF. Have I made myself clear? And will you remember to refer to me as a soldier and nothing else. The Senate is important, but as compared to what goes on around here it is meaningless."[32] Then, in the middle of his curious campaign for the Senate, Harry Cain's career took another turn. Again, he was in the right place at the right time.

IN LATE AUGUST, the headquarters and some advance units of the conventionally configured U.S. XVIII Corps had arrived in England from the United States. It was almost immediately re-designated the XVIII Corps (Airborne), as a part of the preparations being made for the largest air assault in the history of warfare being planned for September. Because of his position at SHAEF and his contacts with friends in the airborne forces, Cain was fully aware that the new corps would be led by Major General Matthew B. Ridgway, who had commanded the 82nd Airborne Division in North Africa, Sicily, and Italy, and that Ridgway was putting together a new staff. He was keeping only three of the previous corps staff, and one of the new assistant chief of staff positions to be filled would be in civil affairs.

Generals Grassett and McSherry, among others, were well aware of Cain's desire to return to the field and get into the war. He wanted the job and nearly begged them to recommend him to Ridgway. We don't know how it happened, but Cain's name was brought to the attention of Ridgway or his chief of staff, Brigadier General Ralph P. (Doc) Eaton. Ridgway was interested, but he wanted to resolve the issue of Cain's political status. He checked with Eisenhower's staff to see how they felt about the possibility of Cain going home to campaign. They replied was that there was no problem at their end—individuals friendly to the military were needed in Congress and, as the nominee of his party, Cain was free to leave if he wanted. That was not the answer Ridgway was looking for; if he hired Cain, he wanted him around for the duration. He called Cain in for an interview and confronted him on the matter. Cain responded that until he was elected or until the war was won, his place was with the XVIII Airborne Corps. Nothing more was ever said about the matter.

Cain arrived at Ridgway's headquarters at Ogbourne St. George, located only eleven miles south of the civil affairs training camp at Shrivenham, for orientation on or about September 10, because ten days later he wrote from there to tell Marj, "Ten days ago I was a part of the designing of broad, general directives. Today, I sit where we crystallize those directives and turn them in to working plans, and tomorrow I expect to be a workman with a plan in hand. I will learn to ride in a glider and 'hit the stick' [parachuting from a troop transport], but how much safer and satisfying that is than to trust to luck in avoiding the promiscuous savagery of the Doodle Bugs [German V-1 rocket-guided bombs over London]."[33]

The XVIII Airborne Corps consisted of the 82nd and 101st Airborne Divisions—both of which had participated in the Normandy invasion and were rebuilding back in England—along with the newly formed 17th Airborne Division, then in transit from the United States. At the same time as the U.S. XVIII Airborne Corps was created, the British established a similar formation, and both of these, and their troop carrier transport wings, were incorporated into the newly formed First Allied Airborne Army (FAAA), commanded by Lieutenant General Lewis H. Brereton of the U.S. Army Air Corps.

Operation MARKET GARDEN was the code name for British Field Marshal Bernard Montgomery's audacious plan for a multi-division airborne assault upon key bridges spanning three great river barriers—the Maas, the Waal, and the Neder Rijn—all branches of the lower Rhine and obstacles to any Allied advance into northern Germany. The U.S. 82nd and 101st Airborne Divisions, as well as the British 1 Parachute Division, participated in the operation that took place between September 17 and September 25, 1944. While Ridgway and his staff were present with the 82nd Airborne, he was not in overall tactical command of the operation. The operation failed to achieve its objectives, and all three Allied divisions suffered heavy casualties (the operation was made famous in the 1977 film, *A Bridge Too Far*). Cain missed out on MARKET GARDEN because he was still needed in London to ease the transition of his replacement on Grassett's staff. Cain officially reported to Ridgway as Assistant Chief of Staff (G-5) on October 4. He was in for an immediate surprise.

In a radio interview conducted many years later, Cain chuckled when he recounted how Ridgway had asked him what he knew about gliders and parachute-jumping when he reported for duty. "'Not a thing,' I responded. I'd never seen a glider [not *quite* true], and I certainly have not had anything to do with parachutes. Two hours later, I was up in a glider with a young second lieutenant. When we came down, he referred me to a captain who had made more than 50 jumps who assured me that he would show me how to do it."[34] Cain qualified for his Glider Badge that afternoon.

Matthew Bunker Ridgway was one of the great fighting generals in U.S. Army history. As a result of several post-World War I assignments in Nicaragua and the Philippines, Ridgway became an aide to General George Marshall, already slated to be Chief of Staff of the Army, on a special assignment to Brazil. In 1939, Ridgway was another of Marshall's protégés, assigned to the War Plans Division at the War Department, and then promoted to command the 82nd Division when it was activated. He parachuted with it into Sicily and then joined the division after it landed at Salerno. Ridgway jumped again into Normandy, where he led the division with great personal gallantry.

Cain found that working for Ridgway, who was often out among his soldiers and who expected a high level of energy and commitment from his staff, was very different from the shirt-tie-and-uniform-blouse-life that he had led in London. As an aide to Grassett, Cain had dealt with individuals and issues at a very high level. As a staff member to Ridgway, Cain could count on living in whatever conditions the front provided, to be on call at any hour of the day or night, and often to occupy an open Jeep for long hours. With a small staff and no outside help, Cain coordinated the training of the civil affairs staffs of the three divisions under Ridgway's command and the detailed planning of military government activities related to their future military operations. A new assignment required that Cain develop a plan to deal with the large numbers of displaced persons whom the various combat commands would encounter as they moved forward across France and Germany. Under normal circumstances, his duties involved everything from making sure that visiting reporters were properly escorted to tending to the relationships with local officials and planning for the care of civilians and displaced persons in future operations. Under less favorable conditions, such as those the XVIII Corps would soon face in the Ardennes, his duties could include just about anything else.

HARRY CAIN HAD not forgotten about the campaign going on at home, but it must have seemed very far away, indeed. "I have read something of the activities of the opposition and it seems to me that they are pressing a trifle. If it wasn't that the heart of politics was fundamentally worthwhile, its framework would have no appeal for me."[35]

By October, the polling numbers from home were looking good, raising the possibility that Cain might, indeed, pull off an upset against the better-known Magnuson. In a letter to Marj on October 15, he said, "Tonight I will send Tommie [Irving Thomas] some statements. Wonder which he will use?"[36] In a later taped interview, Cain said that he had prepared two statements, one on either side of a sheet of paper, which he sent both to Governor Langlie and to J. J. Kaufman, so that they would be ready, depending on which one was needed.[37]

Finally, the fateful day was at hand. Cain could find no news of the election in Washington by 9:45 a.m. on November 9. Then, the early reports that did come in were fragmentary at best. "Nineteen hours have gone their way since the first report and I managed the interim as best I could. Everybody on the post has been busy with pen and paper trying to work out a result in my favor. That none of us have any true base from which to figure is quite beside the point. Needless to say, I didn't fly back to the big city [London] or make any comments by air. Instead, I went a distance into the country to spend the evening with a war correspondent friend who is resting from his labors. A good enough dinner, a highball or two, a fire in the grate, and two dogs on the hearth . . . I just slept like a child until midnight when they took me home."[38]

By the summer of 1944, a clearly frail and dying Franklin Roosevelt had been President of the United States for twelve years—the entire lifetime of some younger Americans. Many Americans were tired of the war, tired of the New Deal, and tired of the Democrats. The Republicans, frustrated with their inability to defeat Roosevelt in the past and frantic to return to office, sensed victory. But there was still a war going on, and Roosevelt—no longer the progressive New Dealer but a pragmatic wartime leader—was still the nation's President and, to many, its father figure. In addition, Magnuson, who had served four terms in Congress, knew Washington, DC, and had close ties to many Washington State industries, like Boeing, that were vital to the war effort and supported him, along with their unions.

Cain later said that he felt that the tide of the election turned when the Republican presidential nominee, Thomas Dewey of New York, attacked Fala, Roosevelt's Scottie dog, resulting in such an effective rebuttal by the President that he proved that he had not lost his political touch.[39] When the final Washington State returns were tallied, it was not a good night for the Republicans. Roosevelt defeated Dewey by more than 125,000 votes, Magnuson beat Cain by 88,000 votes, and even Arthur Langlie had been defeated for re-election by Monrad (Mon) Wallgren, a former U.S. Senator and close friend of Magnuson's, by 28,000 votes.

Writing to Marj on November 15, Harry said that he had just received a "splendid cable" from J. J. Kaufman and Irving Thomas. It said that they had no regrets. Cain confided that "no possible statement could have pleased me more. My one deep fear has been that some might be too deeply unhappy." They had gotten as far as they could "against a national sentiment which was in opposition. If people aren't downhearted or discouraged or too tired, they haven't lost a thing . . . for their methods will result in certain victory if they will but keep in condition and try again."[40]

Harry Cain had served on the SHAEF staff in London for approximately five months. For most of that time, he was involved at some level with the curious campaign being waged in his name half a world away. Although he dearly would have loved to have done so, he had successfully avoided having to take a stand on the controversial political issues that would have been required had he been actively campaigning. In light of his future Senate term, perhaps he was fortunate to have dodged a bullet. Certainly, he was very disappointed about the outcome of the election—he always hated to lose. But, against the odds, he had taken a chance. He had rolled the dice. He had answered the call. He had come closer to winning than most had expected. He had increased his name familiarity in the state and put the Democrats on notice that he was someone to be reckoned with in the future. At the same time, he had successfully and professionally handled several important and sensitive assignments at SHAEF. He made many excellent contacts in the news media, some of which would last for years. He had helped to define how

Americans and others viewed the war in Europe. It was not the role he wanted to play, but it was the role he was assigned, and he had soldiered on. In the meantime, there was still a vicious war to fight, and by arranging his transfer to Ridgway's staff, Cain had insured that he would be right in the middle of it.

1., 2. Harry's parents, Elizabeth Grace Pulliam and George William Cain, Jr., at the time of their wedding in 1902. Grace was already a published author. Will worked for the publications branch of the Board of Missions of the Methodist-Episcopal Church in Nashville.

3. Harry was named for Grace's favorite older brother, Harry Clay Pulliam; sportswriter, newspaper editor, and president of the National Baseball League. He committed suicide in 1909.

4. Harry and his twin brother, Bill, were born in this family home, known as "Mapledale," in a fashionable area of East Nashville.

5. Grace with Harry (l.) and Bill (r.) in Tacoma, c. 1915. Increasingly suffering from depression, she committed suicide two years later.

6. Cadet Harry Cain, age 14, upon entering Hill Military Academy in 1920. He become class president, Cadet Captain, and a star athlete.

7. Located in Portland's Pearl District, Hill Military Academy consisted of a number of individual houses that served as offices and classrooms and of athletic fields that saw double duty as a drill grounds. Cain was associate editor of *The Adjutant,* the school's yearbook, and editor of *The Hill Cadet,* the student newspaper.

8. Cain entered the University of the South at Sewanee, Tennessee, in 1925. He studied history, literature, and languages, lettered in four sports, and edited the school's newspaper and yearbook.

9. Sewanee's central campus, with its traditional Gothic architecture, quaint traditions, and strict honor code, provided an ideal opportunity for students to become fully immersed in academic and campus social life.

10. This 1934 newspaper clipping shows Cain and Marjorie Dils on their wedding day, following a ten-day whirlwind courtship.

11. Washington National Guard troops use fixed bayonets and tear gas to confront 500 striking lumber workers during the "Battle of the 11th Street Bridge" in downtown Tacoma on July 12, 1935. Cain considered himself a friend of organized labor but was concerned about the influence of radical elements in some unions.

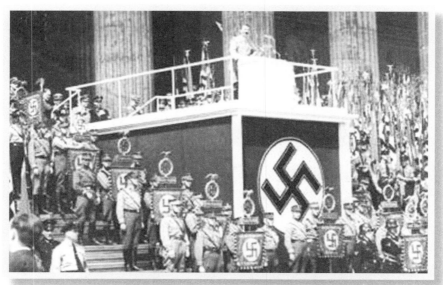

12. Adolf Hitler speaking in Berlin in May 1936. Harry and Marj spent a year in Europe in 1935–1936. After he returned home, Cain made more than 150 speeches, warning state and local audiences of the threat posed by Nazi Germany.

13. In 1939, Cain was picked by Tacoma civic leaders to manage the massive Golden Jubilee Celebration that commemorated fifty years of Washington statehood.

14. Campaigning for mayor in 1940. Cain ran third in the primary but was elected when the leading candidate died four days before the general election. At thirty-four, Cain was the youngest mayor in Tacoma's history.

15. Master of public relations. This newspaper photo shows Cain taking a walk across the unfinished Tacoma Narrows Bridge three days after becoming mayor. He completed it with 2,026 steps in 20 minutes, 29 seconds.

16. Cain was also the first Tacoma mayor to use radio to communicate. He wrote the scripts for his weekly broadcast himself, beginning each with his trademark, "Good evening, Tacoma. This is Harry Cain."

17. Cain attracted national attention to Tacoma in October 1940 by hosting the Warner Bros. premier of *Tugboat Annie Sails Again*. Here he is shown with the film's stars: (in front) Donald Crisp; (l. to r.) Alan Hale, Marjorie Rambeau, Cain and columnist Hedda Hopper; (in back) Ronald Reagan.

18. Tacoma was soon gearing up for World War II. Local shipyards were busy once again, and thousands of soldiers and airmen were training at local military bases. Here a battalion of the 3rd Infantry Division parades in downtown Tacoma in October 1941.

19. Cain faced numerous unanticipated challenges, including the collapse of the Tacoma Narrows Bridge collapsed into Puget Sound, November 7, 1940.

20. Japan attacked Pearl Harbor, Hawaii, on December 7, 1941. Six days later, First Lady Eleanor Roosevelt met with Japanese students in Cain's office. Cain was one of only two elected officials on the West Coast to oppose the internment of the Japanese.

21. Movie star Lana Turner kisses a Tacoma businessman who just purchased $550 in war bonds in June 1942, while Mayor Cain looks on in amusement.

22. Tacoma faced a long-term housing shortage that had existed since the 1920s. The needs of defense workers and the military only made it worse. This is the massive, 1600-unit Salishan development under construction in 1943.

23. Vice and political corruption defied Cain's efforts to clean up Tacoma. His battles with his fellow City Commissioners grew worse by 1943. Here Cain (far right) argues the impeachment charges against Public Safety Commissioner Einar Langseth (far left) for neglect of duty.

24. Increasingly frustrated, Cain joins the Army's new Military Government Branch. Here he shakes hands with Washington Governor Arthur Langlie and Major George LaFray after being sworn in on May 5, 1943.

25. Home for a short leave after completing military training, Harry meets his new daughter. "Can she talk yet?"

26. After graduation from the School of Military Government at the University of Virginia, Cain received his orientation in North Africa and Sicily. He landed on the beachhead at Salerno with the 325th Glider Infantry Regiment of the 82nd Airborne Division on September 15, 1943.

27. Cain later served as "chief gatekeeper" for Lt. Gen. Kenyon A. Joyce, commander of the Allied Control Commission for Italy. They had previously met when Joyce was stationed at Ft. Lewis before the war.

28. Transferred to London in May 1944, Cain served on the Civil Affairs staff at SHAEF. He reported to (l. to r.) British Lieutenant-General Arthur E. Grassett, Brig. Gen. Frank J. McSherry, and Gen. Dwight D. Eisenhower (supreme allied commander).

29. In October 1944, Cain arranged a transfer from SHAEF to serve as Assistant Chief of Staff for the newly-formed XVIII Airborne Corps, commanded by Major General Matthew Ridgway. He joined just in time for the Battle of the Bulge.

A Fighter
for good
Government

HARRY P.
CAIN
(REPUBLICAN NOMINEE
FOR U. S. SENATE)

Now a lieutenant colonel in the American armed forces in Europe, Harry P. Cain has never hesitated to fight for better government. Known as Tacoma's fighting mayor, he has always battled for the right where the fight is hottest. He will return to fight for a lasting peace and a free and better world.

(Paid Adv.)

30. In 1944, Cain was drafted by Washington Governor Arthur Langlie to run for a vacant U.S. Senate seat as a Republican while still on the SHAEF staff in London. The campaign was underway when he became G-5 of the XVIII Airborne Corps. Cain declared that he would not serve until the war was over. Instead, his supporters made extensive use of newspaper advertising utilizing hundreds of ads like this one.

6

"The Fur Is Flying"

HARRY CAIN WROTE to his wife Marjorie from Germany (probably Aachen) on November 24, 1944, during the deadly, grinding battle for the Hürtgen Forest. He told her that he had been "constantly on the move since the last time [I wrote] but it's no time to settle down. Everyone is on the move in spite of rain and snow and mud galore." The casualties were heavy; the weather was terrible, "but our side picks up a little [each] day and that is what counts."[1] It looked like the German defenses might finally be softening, and there were even optimistic estimates that the major fighting might be over by Christmas. Five days later, he wrote, "From now on don't say publicly where you think I may be and if I have mentioned the Divisions with our Corps please don't admit it. Things are on the move and there must be no suggestion of anything. Aside from knowing how to knock you down, Jerry tops the list at being able to ferret out what is brewing."[2]

Cain wrote home again on December 9 from the XVIII Corp's forward headquarters located in the French countryside at Epernay, south of Rheims. He said that he had spent a lot of time "in the mud" since he had last written. "Death and destruction aren't pleasant things to see, but progress demands a heavy price. . . . The longer I am in this business, the more I want to be a simple soldier, with a single track mission of destroying the enemy and all he stands for. It's some of that chance I had a part of and more lies ahead."[3]

It had been nearly a month since Cain's election defeat, and he was expecting a flood of post mortem letters from home. He said he still had no regrets and that he hadn't "even cast a thought about what the future holds politically and won't look that way until [this] prevailing madness is out of the way and done with."[4]

The Ardennes sector of the Allied front, an area of heavy forests and rugged, broken ground cut by deep ravines, narrow valleys, steep hills, and numerous streams about 130 miles northwest of Epernay, served as the dividing line between the U.S. First and Third Armies. Because it was such difficult terrain—a most improbable place to stage an attack in mid-winter—it was lightly defended by U.S. commanders who were facing severe troop shortages, even in their more active sectors.

Into this unlikely area, in the early morning hours of December 16, 1944, stormed the whole of the German Fifth and Sixth Panzer Armies across a sixty-mile front. Overruling the opinions of some of his subordinate commanders, Eisenhower quickly determined that the attack was not a feint but a massive, German counterattack. The Allies were not unaware of a German buildup but had thought that it was related to the defense of Roer River dams and the impending Allied advance into Germany.

Within hours, the U.S. 7th Armored and 30th Infantry Divisions were on the move to try to stop the German flood, but it was a case of too little, too late. The real problem was that there was virtually no pool of reserve manpower left on which to call. Eisenhower's "broad front" advance to the Rhine had consumed men as fast as it had fuel. The only strategic reserve consisted of the still-depleted 82nd and 101st Airborne Divisions of Ridgway's XVIII Corps recovering near Rheims, more than a hundred miles away, in the middle of the worst winter on record.

To make matters worse, Ridgway and much of his staff (including Harry Cain) were in England reviewing the newly arrived 17th Airborne Division that was working up after its arrival in England. About 2:15 on the morning of December 18, Ridgeway received orders detaching his corps from the First Allied Air Army, attaching it to Omar Bradley's Twelfth Army Group, and ordering him to concentrate his forces to meet the attack. Within the hour, Ridgway and his staff were on their way in fifty-five quickly commandeered troop transports to the front. Even before they could arrive in France, new orders were received detaching the 101st Airborne and sending it to the beleaguered VIII Corps in the Bastogne area. Ridgway was to take the 82nd Airborne to Werbomont, Belgium, about forty miles north of Rheims, in support of the 30th and 17th Divisions, which were falling back before the German onslaught.

All of a sudden, Harry Cain was right in the middle of a very hot war. There were no front lines. The 101st Airborne was soon surrounded at Bastogne. The Germans interdicted the route to Werbomont immediately after Ridgway and his staff had passed by. The weather was bitterly cold with blowing snow. No one knew who was a friend or a foe. Ridgway assumed command of the 7th Armored and the 30th Infantry Divisions that were trying, without success, to plug a gap in the Allied lines near St. Vith, through which the Germans were pouring with overwhelming force.[5]

Cain found himself in the middle of the fighting but, amazingly, found time to write home about it in the early morning hours of December 19. "Yesterday in England; tonight a long and contrasting way from there. The papers have told you that Jerry is up to no good and we are here to sort of convince him that there isn't any point in his trying to go in any other direction save backwards. It's too early yet to determine if he is going to listen to our authority now or later on. I moved in today on a Belgian family of seven and their living room is my office, dining room and bed. Some of my men are packed about four deep on the kitchen floor and others are deeper than that in the hay loft. The family, all seven, are listening to the 9 o'clock news. They wonder if the rumor that Jerry will overrun us tonight is based on fact. [I] remember thinking a year ago in Italy that the war would be over by now and yet the pattern today is just about the same. Guesses are about a dime a dozen but I think we are on board for the last lap. To my mind, what happens in the next few days will have a definite bearing on the ultimate result."[6]

By the morning of December 20, Ridgway was able to create a thin defensive line that plugged the gap at St. Vith. Writing home again that night, Cain told Marj that he had said too much when he had written the previous night. "Enough to know in general where I am and that the fur is flying. This business is anything but gay, but I couldn't wish to be anywhere else. That's why I couldn't wait for the election to be over so I could take a seat with the greatest guys on the globe. Living is simple. I don't shave very often, or eat very much, or sleep on a bed, but I am well and vitally interested in living."[7]

The only war story Cain's son, Buzz, remembers his father telling him occurred at this time. Cain said that he had been "pinned down" with many other guys for days near a disabled train. They had no water, but the train was loaded with champagne, which they used for both personal hygiene and liquid refreshment. "Dad was never able to drink champagne after the war, and he said that that experience was the reason why."[8]

The Americans were forced to retreat from St. Vith on December 23 when German forces streamed around their open right flank. Another hastily constructed defensive line finally held against intense and repeated German attacks. With major reinforcements now squeezing the German salient from both the north and the south, Ridgway went on the offensive, regaining the territory his units had just lost. By early January, the crisis had passed and by January 23, St. Vith had been recaptured and the Germans were streaming eastward in defeat.[9]

During the battle, Cain, without the benefit of staff, personally coordinated the activities of the other military government officers caught in the path of the German attack. As the Allies successfully re-grouped and started to push the Germans back, Cain worked with local civil authorities to coordinate assistance to the more than 100,000 terrified civilians who had been caught in the German breakthrough. According to his Legion of Merit citation, Cain "oversaw the evacuation, housing, clothing and feeding of 15,000 civilians without interference with the tactical situation and without dependence upon the military for supplies, transport or personnel."[10]

We have an interesting first-hand account of Harry Cain's actions during the battle for the Ardennes. Jack Bell, then a wire service reporter covering the battle (and later a columnist for the *Miami Herald*), was interviewed for a story about Cain that appeared in *Collier's* magazine in 1949. He said that in the middle of the battle, with the opposing armies surging back and forth and the Belgian refugees left to fend for themselves as they walked along the roads in the freezing weather, American troops had been ordered not to pick them up because every vehicle was needed to transport the troops. On a night when the temperature was five degrees below zero, Bell found himself riding in a Jeep with an American officer when they came upon a barn jammed with people. "Twenty-four children were huddled under a single blanket. All around stood men and women, some of them old and sick, shivering in the icy air. One Belgian Red Cross nurse was on duty. An ambulance took two old men away. Another died on the floor. There could be no fire because the barn was filled with straw."

Bell returned to town horrified, wishing he could do something. He did. He found Lieutenant Colonel Harry Cain. "It took courage to call a colonel out of bed in that freezing cold at one in the morning," he related. "He thanked me. The next morning those 147 Belgians had been removed from the barn and transferred to a theater lobby which was enclosed and heated. They had been fed and given dry clothing. An

6. *"The Fur Is Flying"*

army doctor had delivered a baby and all was well. At noon mess I was telling the officers about Colonel Cain. 'Oh, he's just a politician,' they said. 'He wanted a story.' But I defended Colonel Cain as a guy who did a hell of a good job in a large hurry, no matter what his motives. He was a right good officer."[11]

The tide of battle was finally turning, but danger and frequent tragedy were a part of everyday life. Cain wrote in a year-end letter to Marj, commenting that, in spite of the cold, they didn't put the tops up on their Jeeps because there, "was too much to look at. . . . It's kind of important to watch the brush and one of the crew keeps his eye on the sky. And whenever in doubt you take to the ditch, making certain if you can that no SOB has left a gadget called a mine for a treat. None of us has changed clothes for two weeks and I don't know of a store within miles, Ha Ha! [I] haven't had a bath either and no prospect in sight. But there isn't anybody to dress up for and no plan to go for dinner. Meals are eaten when and where food and time find you." Frustration with his inability to care adequately for the civilian population under his control was evident. There were periodic tragedies. "Last night we drowned the larger part of a truck load of youngsters for, in saving them from a city destroyed, we couldn't save them from a river bank down which they plunged."[12]

The six weeks of battle in the Ardennes forest became known as the Battle of the Bulge. It was the costliest single battle ever fought by the U.S. Army. American forces suffered more than 100,000 casualties, and Harry Cain was very lucky not to be one of them.

FOR MONTHS, EVEN before the battle for the Ardennes, an equally intense battle was being waged among the Allied commanders—particularly Eisenhower, Montgomery, and Bradley—that nearly fractured the alliance. Montgomery wanted Bradley's U.S. Ninth Army assigned to him, more or less permanently for the remainder of the war, in order to capture Antwerp—a vital Allied objective—and launch a massive set-piece attack across the Northern Rhine and into Northern Germany. There was much to recommend the idea. It was the shortest way into Germany, it bypassed the heavily defended Ruhr industrial region, and it would likely liberate the Scandinavian countries. From Montgomery's standpoint, it had several other advantages. It would be a British operation, wildly popular on the home front, and if successful, would cement Montgomery's legacy as the premier British military commander of the war.[13] From the American point of view, the operation would divert valuable troops and supplies, including precious fuel, from the rest of the broad (primarily American) front that was approaching the Rhine. The final decision was important enough to be bumped all the way up to Roosevelt and Churchill.

While grand strategy was being sorted out, it was also important—to the degree the weather would permit—to pursue the Germans retreating east out of the Ardennes salient. Therefore, Omar Bradley, commanding the middle of the Allied front, ordered his troops to continue their advance through the outmoded Siegfried Line and on to the Rhine River fifty miles beyond—his goal being not only to cross the river but to capture the important cities of Cologne and Mainz on the other side. Bradley's advance involved three corps—including Ridgway's XVIII Corps—now expanded to four divisions, including the 82nd, operating as conventional infantry. By mid-February, the advance had bogged down because of the terrible weather and road conditions, and the operation was cancelled. Ridgway's corps reverted to inactive status at their base at Epernay in order to prepare for the airborne operations that would be a part of Montgomery's impending campaign to cross the Rhine.

Cain used this time to carry out a complete reorganization of the XVIII Corps' civil affairs and military government staffs. Cain's recent experience gained during the Battle of the Bulge convinced him that the existing personnel and equipment dedicated to civil affairs activities were completely inadequate to meet the needs of the increasingly large numbers of both occupied and displaced populations. Cain developed recommendations calling for additional resources, presented them personally to officials at SHAEF, and was given the increases he requested. He then had to find and train the additional personnel required for the four divisions now assigned to the corps.

On February 8, 1945, Montgomery launched his massive three-army offensive aimed at crossing the Rhine and sweeping into Northern Germany. It would include a massive airborne operation—Operation VARSITY—to secure the eastern side of the river so as to improve the chances of the armies who would be crossing the river in landing craft and boats. Overlooking his own British airborne commanders, Montgomery asked Eisenhower to assign Ridgway to him in order to plan and command the VARSITY operation. Ridgway tried to resist the assignment as he had recently led conventional ground forces during the advance to the Rhine, and he rather liked the experience. His objections were overruled, and Eisenhower decided that Ridgway and the VXIII Corps would be loaned to Montgomery.

Ridgway determined that VARSITY would be a very different type of operation from MARKET GARDEN. It would be much more like the airborne operations in Normandy than the aggressive forward reach that had characterized the air drops in Holland. There would be other differences as well. Because of the past problems with glider accidents and friendly fire incidents, Ridgway and his staff would cross the Rhine on landing craft rather than in gliders. The airborne troops would also be used differently. Two divisions would land simultaneously in one lift, during daylight, in the largest air assault in history. For some reason, no letters from Cain during this period have survived. He was probably very busy planning how the civilian population and the inevitable refugees would be handled during the advance into Germany. Ridgway recognized and appreciated his efforts, and on March 16, Cain received a battle-field promotion to the rank of Colonel for, as he later put it, "outlasting everyone else" during the Ardennes campaign.[14] A story announcing the promotion appeared in the April 2 issue of the *Tacoma News Tribune*.[15]

Montgomery's massive crossing of the Rhine finally began on the night of March 23. It consisted of 250,000 men (the equivalent of twenty divisions), 1,500 tanks and 31,500 other vehicles, 5,500 artillery pieces, and 256,000 tons of supplies. By 9:30 in the morning, VARSITY was also underway. With Prime Minister Winston Churchill and other top British military leaders watching from the west bank of the Rhine, a single massive stream of 1,545 transport planes and their escorts, along with 1,305 gliders, dropped and landed the first four regiments of the airborne assault force. The troopers from the 17th U.S. and 6th British Airborne Divisions cleared the drop zone and prepared it for the additional 8,000 glider troops who would land just minutes behind them.

Ridgway and his staff, including Colonel Harry P. Cain, crossed the river in a British amphibious tracked vehicle and then boarded Jeeps to make a run through the "no man's land" —much of it still held by German troops—to the drop zone where Ridgway would establish his corps headquarters. Cain found himself once again on—or rather between—the front lines. Rounding the corner of a road, they came face to face with a manned German foxhole. Fortunately, all of the Germans were dead.

A short time later, they came across another roadblock, which included anti-tank guns. Thankfully, it too, was deserted.[16]

As the Allied armies surged to the east, a large number of German troops had been trapped in what became known as the "Ruhr pocket," an area that had been bypassed by the Americans as they moved into Germany. General Omar Bradley assigned three full corps to the task of eliminating the salient, including Ridgway's, which was now withdrawn from Montgomery. Again, Ridgway was unhappy about his new assignment. After VARSITY, he had been led to believe that he would accompany Bradley right on to Berlin. Indeed, he envisioned his 82nd Airborne as being among the first to enter the enemy capital. He was given four divisions for the Ruhr operation, but the 82nd and 101st were not among them; they were going to be held in the Düsseldorf-Cologne area as a strategic reserve. Ridgway was given responsibility for collapsing the southern side of the Ruhr pocket, anchored on the left by Bonn along the Rhine, and extending sixty-seven miles to the east where his sector joined III Corps.

The operation against the pocket began on April 4, with Ridgway's troops joining the attack two days later. The German command was in disarray and, when they saw that further resistance was futile, more than 300,000 German troops surrendered. Cain was responsible for coordinating all of the civil affairs and military government activities of the four divisions reporting to Ridgway, including the care of more than 300,000 refugees in addition to the 300,000 Germans soldiers who had surrendered. According to his Legion of Merit citation, Colonel Harry Cain, "at great personal risk, personally assumed control of the City of Wuppental and . . . 40,000 drunken and disorderly displaced persons who were looting, murdering and raping indiscriminately throughout the city of a half million persons."[17]

Following the elimination of the Ruhr pocket on April 25, Ridgway's XVIII Corps was returned to Montgomery for the final push on toward Berlin. When the war ended on May 7, Cain was at Ridgway's headquarters at the town of Hagenow—about fifty miles east of Hamburg, thirty-five miles south of the Baltic Sea, and twenty-five miles east of the Elbe River. He became the senior military government official, essentially the governor, for Mecklenburg and Western Pomerania, located along the North Sea in what remained of the former Pomerania, much of which now belonged to Poland. Cain's duties again involved the control, housing, and feeding of approximately 500,000 people and the creation and management of fourteen displaced-persons camps. He worked with former civilian civil administrators, as he had in Italy, to get the local governmental and administrative machinery re-established and functioning, more or less efficiently, within five days of the conclusion of hostilities.

Harry Cain's own war ended with a bang—literally. Only twenty-four hours before the end of hostilities on May 7, he was hit by shrapnel (probably grenade fragments) around the elbow area of his left arm during an engagement with German troops. He later told a reporter that "there had been a lot of shooting going on, and there were a lot of soldiers running. I was running, too. The enemy didn't discriminate. I got it in the arm, that's all."[18] He was treated in an evacuation hospital where doctors wanted to fly him either to France or England for further treatment. "That would have meant four or five weeks or more and, Goodness knows, what will happen in that time. I was more than willing to compromise by trading that promised leave for an armful of morphine, codeine, and Novocain."[19]

The next day, regardless of his physical condition, he was asked by Ridgway to perform a duty that would be vividly remembered by the general thirty-four years later. There had been a small concentration camp located near Hagenow. The conditions they found there were shocking. In his memoirs, Ridgway said that no scenes of death on the battlefield could prepare a soldier for such a sight. "Since Harry had been the mayor of a city, I felt it appropriate that he talk to the citizens and officials of the town. We brought them all out to the cemetery, and I went along. By my order, we assembled the authorities in town and all the citizens we could round up, and took them to the place where we had laid out the bodies of some two hundred poor creatures, prepared for decent burial. We paraded them past the graves, so that they could look upon their handiwork."[20]

On Ridgway's orders, Cain prepared a short speech to the living about responsibility, past and future, which he then delivered to the stunned Germans. "Harry drove those Germans to tears. His speech was one of the most effective I have ever heard." (See Appendix 2 for the complete text of Cain's speech.) Ridgway included the incident in his memoirs, and in an interview with Howard Kleinberg of the *Miami News* held after Cain's death, he said, "It was memorable. They [the Germans] said it was hard to believe that what Harry was telling them was so. But it was, and Harry really chastised them."[21] Cain's comments to the Germans were deeply personal. In a letter written that evening to Marj, he told her that his remarks had been "what I feel deep down inside."[22]

Ridgway was impressed with more than Cain's rhetoric. He recommended him for another Bronze Star Medal for his service between December 17, 1944 (the start of the Battle of the Bulge), and February 13, 1945, and for the Legion of Merit for his service between November 12, 1944, and May 12, 1945. Ridgway's recommendation for the latter award was five pages long. In addition, for his services in connection with the liberation of France and Belgium, Cain was also awarded their respective Croix de Guerre Medals with Palm. In the process, Cain had won three more battle stars, bringing his total to five.

Matthew Ridgway never forgot Cain's service with him during World War II. Upon hearing of his death in 1979, Ridgway—then eighty-four—sent a personal note to Cain's widow. "I do want you to know of my great admiration for Harry, and of what splendid service he rendered on the Staff of the XVIII Airborne Corps in Europe in World War II. His rich experience as mayor of Tacoma before the war made him invaluable in his dealings with the authorities of the civilian population in the German territories through which we operated, and I have always been proud to have been privileged to share that service with him."[23]

Hagenow was located east of the Elbe River in what would become the Russian Zone of Occupation. In his letter to Marj of May 8, Cain noted that the "Russians are all over the place, but when they will actually take our place no one seems to know." There were already rumors that Ridgway and his staff would be transferred to the Pacific. "If there is a job in the Pacific and they insist they want me for it, I won't argue or try to evade that issue."[24]

In the meantime, Cain seemed to have plenty to do at Hagenow. During the 1952 U.S. Senate race, a story surfaced about Cain's successful efforts to repatriate 10,000 American prisoners of war who were being held in German camps behind the Russian lines not far away. A widely syndicated columnist, Canadian Bruce Barton—who was there—recalled that "there were about 10,000 American prisoners in one P.O.W. camp who had been on starvation rations, sleeping on straw mattresses in unheated homes—some for three years." Negotiations ensued to repatriate the prisoners, since the camp was located only a few miles from the American lines. "Suddenly came the staggering news that they were not to be allowed to be repatriated across our lines, but through Odessa, a seaport nearly 1,500 miles away. At the hour when things looked darkest, the news spread around that an American colonel had arrived to talk to the Russian authorities, and that he was the kind of spokesman whose words were loud, vigorous and could not be misunderstood. The result of his talk was that enough B-17s arrived immediately at the Barth airport, and before the Russians had time to object further, the prisoners were loaded and well on their way to France and England. Needless to say, that American colonel was Harry Cain."[25]

On May 15, Cain wrote home to say that Ridgway had received an inquiry from SHAEF about his availability for duty with them, probably in Berlin. Ridgway responded that Cain was not available since Ridgway had already told Cain he wanted him to come to the South Pacific with him. On the 20th, Ridgway was notified that they were to move back to their headquarters in France two days later. Cain wrote to Marj, "I can't begin to define properly what this experience has meant up here; but I am thoroughly tired, along with other members of my staff, and we are looking forward to a few days of doing just nothing." He said that he might not have the chance, "because if SHAEF is still curious about my whereabouts, I must be rather rapid on my feet to keep out of their way."[26] In spite of Ridgway's protestations, SHAEF was able to locate Harry, and orders soon arrived telling him to rejoin Frank McSherry and the rest of his former civil affairs associates from London, now relocated to Frankfurt. In his new position, Cain would serve as a military government field inspector, and his new duties reflected the changes in civil affairs and military government that resulted from the changeover from SHAEF to the new American Forces Command, European Theater of Operation (ETO).

Cain's first assignment was a tricky and politically sensitive one—to inspect the military government personnel and procedures being employed in Bavaria. Officially, Cain reported directly to General George S. Patton, the commander of all Allied forces in southern Germany, but in reality, he reported directly to Eisenhower and to General Lucius D. Clay, his deputy governor for all of occupied Germany, both of whom were keeping their eyes on Patton. After the war ended, Patton was placed in command of the occupation forces in Bavaria. He repeatedly clashed with Eisenhower and Clay over his use of former Nazi officials to administer the regional and local governments. He also believed that the German army should be rebuilt as an ally for a potential future war against the Russians, whom

Patton notoriously despised and considered a much greater menace than the Germans. Patton's disagreement with higher authority became public when he openly accused Eisenhower of caring more about a possible political career than his military duties. That was enough for Eisenhower. Patton was relieved of his command and sent home.[27]

Cain's inspection duties in Bavaria were difficult and taxing. "I cover two cities or towns a day and spend those times yowling, praising, groaning, helping, advising, promoting, demoting, chopping some heads and sending others home." On July 1, he wrote to say he might be coming home soon. "Going back to Frankfurt to talk to [the] Generals about the [possibility of leaving Germany on the] 15th."[28] He also mentioned that a future job opportunity had surfaced. Former New York Governor Herbert Lehman was now administering the United Nations Relief and Rehabilitation Agency (UNRRA). He contacted Cain in Frankfurt and asked him to stop by Washington, DC, on his way home to discuss "a post of some importance in the Middle East or Europe." Cain told Marj that he thought it was worth "a conversation at least." The job turned out to be the Director of UNNRA's Division of Displaced Persons in Europe. Cain asked that Lehman's staff send him more information about the job, including those he would be working with, funding, and program priorities.

Cain was able to make the July 15 deadline for leaving Germany, but not without incident. In a letter written on August 29 from London, Cain shared for the first time that he had suffered a serious recent health scare. He told Marj that he had begun feeling ill several months before he left Germany but that "I couldn't very well say anything for there was ever that deadline against which I was working to get home to you." Cain was able to finish his work in Frankfurt and then get away without his friends' suspecting that he was concerned. In Paris for a week of vacation, he went to an army hospital, and "they went over me like a hawk, found poison in the system of a kind hard to define, put me to sleep for most of eight days, and woke me up feeling hazy but fit again." He traveled to London, hoping to get passage on the *Queen Elizabeth* but missed it by a day. He used his remaining time in London to see old friends and to try to catch up on what was happening on the other side of the Atlantic. "Talking to all I can find about everything, politics included. [I had] lunch today with Ed Murrow [the by-then famous CBS radio reporter stationed in London], [and] yesterday with Wilmot Ragsdale, formerly of Tacoma, now, and for many years, with *Time* and *Life*. They are good observers and I am content to listen."

Cain was already thinking about his future political career. "What has Tacoma in mind for me? Will it expect me to talk, when and where, and how often? [I] would prefer a single speech, open to anyone interested; but, above all, I want to refrain from hurting feelings [probably a reference to acting mayor Val Fawcett and the other commissioners, whose management of the city Cain had found wanting in his absence]."[29] He was finally able to board the *Queen Mary* on September 5, 1945, and sail for home.

Tacoma's papers tracked Cain's every move on his journey home. He arrived back in the United States on Monday, September 10. After a quick visit to Washington DC, to talk with officials of UNRRA, he boarded a westbound train two days later. Cain had told Marj from London that he was going to try to avoid stopping in Kentucky to see his relatives on the way home. He did, however, stop in Milwaukee to see his favorite uncle, John Page Pulliam, a wealthy retired electric railway executive whom he hadn't seen in many years. Cain boarded the Milwaukee Road's *Olympian* on Thursday and arrived in Tacoma at 9:35 on Sunday morning, September 16.[30]

Marj, Buzzy, and Candy were all at the Milwaukee's east-side Tacoma terminal to welcome their husband and father home; but so were Irving Thomas, a delegation from the local American Legion post, and reporters and photographers from both Tacoma newspapers. Overcoming his emotion as he looked at the contingent who had come out to welcome him home, he told Marj that "It's been a very long time. . . . Great to be home again."[31] Cain told the reporters that he was "keen to return to his office as mayor." He had little to say about his political future except that his first order of business Monday morning was to go to city hall to "express my gratefulness to Mr. Fawcett for doing a double job while I have been away," something Cain would repeat often in the months ahead. "As long as I'm in the Army, I don't wish to discuss politics," he told the reporters. "I have learned a lot. I have definite plans. What they are I will tell you after my separation from the service."[32]

Cain had not lost his flair for publicity. On the train ride west, he had prepared an extensive statement, which he handed out to local reporters upon his arrival and from which they quoted liberally when they filed their stories that evening. "If I could describe the stark, savage misery of most of those people, you would be horror-stricken. It is not surprising that there is very little moral responsibility in the war-ravaged countries. 'Good' people have turned 'bad' as well as anyone who has been deprived of food, clothing and shelter. . . . They look to us for guidance and a proper definition of 'the democratic way of life.' If America could not effectively provide democracy and find democratic leaders, they "will soon be 'heiling' some other person now that Hitler is no longer at the helm."[33]

Cain was soon out on the speaking circuit, addressing sold-out audiences in Tacoma and around the state. On October 4, Cain left on a weeklong "vacationing trip" to Eastern Washington, speaking to the state convention of the American Legion in Spokane and stopping by the Veterans Administration hospital in Walla Walla to check on the progress of his recovery from the shrapnel wound and his subsequent mysterious poisoning episode.

While he was gone, reports began to arrive in Tacoma from "usually reliable sources" in Washington, DC, that Cain was about to be tapped to return to Germany to direct the entire de-Nazification program in the American zone of occupation. The reports suggested that Cain would be able either to accept or reject the offer. If he accepted, the sources said, he would be promoted to the rank of Brigadier General, which would require congressional approval. The story also speculated on the role that Cain had played in the recent confrontation between Eisenhower and Patton that led to Patton's being recalled. Cain refused to comment on the rumors. Asked about the report after addressing a convention of the American Legion in Spokane, Cain refused to comment, saying, "As an officer, I am not in a position to comment on any plans the army may or may not have for me."[34] He also decided to turn down the job with UNRRA. He had received a thick packet of information about the job from Stanley S. Sommer, Acting Director of the Division on Displaced Persons at UNRRA. At the bottom of one of the pages, Cain wrote, "Wrong people. Insufficient authority. Last priority."[35] Although he didn't say so publicly, Harry Cain's attention was focused on getting to Washington, DC—if he could find a way to get there—and not on returning to Europe.

On November 3, Cain drove to the separation center at Fort Lewis to be officially discharged from active service and then to be sworn back into the Officers Reserve Corps, receiving a World War II Victory Medal in the process.

6. *"The Fur Is Flying"*

The war, as for most veterans of World War II, had been a defining period in Harry Cain's life. In it, he found a sense of drama and meaning that could not be matched, except perhaps by the possibility of service in the United States Senate. Indeed, Cain's wartime experiences often influenced his later political decisions. Cain could not help but feel that he had been challenged and had met the test, making it easier to overcome different but potentially greater challenges in the future. He had first seen combat and unimaginable suffering in Italy. He had successfully tested his administrative and management skills there.

For the next five months at SHAEF, Cain had been exposed to the highest levels of the Allied command and directly involved with how their command decisions were portrayed to the rest of the world. He had made many useful contacts in London, some of which would be of long-standing importance. His work for Generals Grassett and McSherry had been interesting, but not his preference—he had wanted to serve in the field. By coincidence, this period also coincided with his 1944 race for the U.S. Senate. Almost certainly, there were those in London who saw him as simply a politician serving in the army. But his letters and personal journal tell a different story. They clearly show a man who, while vitally interested in the progress of the campaign, never let it get in the way of his day job—severely chastising any, including his wife, who tried to get him to campaign for the office.

His final year on active duty was in the field—where he wanted to be—and often under combat conditions. By all accounts, Cain was an excellent officer: adept at dealing with complex issues, an able communicator who made his commanding officers look good, a brave and vigorous officer. His commander, General Matthew Ridgway, a stern, no-nonsense soldier, certainly thought so and maintained an affection and respect for Cain until the day he died. Although as a senior staff officer, Cain was engaged daily with politics of the lower-case "p" variety, he did not have to engage in partisan politics except for the Senate campaign in which army regulations precluded him from campaigning or even expressing his opinions publicly. The voters back in Washington State supported Cain—or not—based on what they *thought* he represented. He had been, in effect, shielded from politics.

There is also no question that Harry Cain was repeatedly in the right place at the right time during the war. His commander at the Allied Control Commission in Italy, Major General Kenyon Joyce, had known

Cain as mayor of Tacoma, had observed his ability to administer tasks assigned to him near Naples, and asked for him on his staff. His former commanding officer at Naples, Brigadier General Frank McSherry, selected him for a key job at SHAEF. By serving in that capacity, Cain had been in a position to know that Matthew Ridgway was assembling the staff of the XVIII Airborne Corps. Cain had been promoted twice in nine months, the second time for his actions on the Ardennes battlefield. At the end of the war, there had been reports that the army thought so highly of him that they wanted to retain his services and promote him to brigadier general. He had been awarded two Bronze Star Medals, the Legion of Merit, five battle stars, and both French and Belgian Croix de Guerre Medals with Palm.

Cain had also been very lucky: lucky that he survived the Battle of the Bulge; lucky not to be more seriously wounded or worse, killed, the day before the end of hostilities; lucky to be in the right place at the right time when opportunity knocked.

Harry Cain was a young man, only thirty-six, when he entered the army. He was still a young man—not yet thirty-nine—when he came home. But he was older than his years. He had seen many things. He had gained confidence and experience. He returned home with a vision of running again and, this time, winning a seat in the U.S. Senate. Cain's appetite for playing on the national political stage had been whetted, and he believed, as he always had, that he possessed the skill, the drive, the experience—and certainly, the ambition—to make his vision a reality.

7

"I Wouldn't Trade Places with Any Man"

BEFORE HARRY CAIN could do more than consider his political future, he had to deal with very real matters at hand. He returned to his duties as mayor, attending his first meeting of the commission on Monday, December 3, 1945. It was the first time all the seats at the table had been filled in two and a half years. Asked about his plans now that he had returned, he provided a list of city problems requiring action that sounded as if he'd never been gone from office: rising venereal disease rates, disposition of USO facilities and government housing units, traffic congestion and overcrowded parking facilities, and growing strains in community race relations.[1]

Almost immediately, Cain began to meet privately with local supporters of his 1944 Senate bid. Irving Thomas, Ernie Wetherell, and Harold Bird took up their familiar positions as his unofficial advisors, but others stepped forward to help as well. The advice Cain received, not surprisingly, coincided with what he already believed—that he was in the right place at the right time—to run again for the U.S. Senate.

After Washington's junior Senator Monrad C. "Mon" Wallgren left the Senate unexpectedly to run against, and then defeat Arthur Langlie for governor in 1944, Wallgren had quickly appointed Hugh Mitchell, his aide since 1933, to fill the remainder of his term. Mitchell was a liberal, New Deal Democrat who excelled at policy but had never before run for elective office. The scholarly and soft-spoken Mitchell was affable, competent, hardworking, and decidedly uncharismatic. In the opinion of Harry Cain's advisors, he was also something else— vulnerable.

After discussing the matter with his wife and holding more strategy meetings with his advisors, Cain made his decision. On December 10, "in order to satisfy speculation," Cain announced that he would not be a candidate for mayor in the general election to be held the following June. He would leave city hall for a "venture yet to be determined," saying that he "had become a controversial, partisan, political figure" and that this "lessened his future usefulness to Tacoma" unless he saw fit to deny his own future political ambitions. "Tacoma has been exceedingly good to me. . . . I doubt if any man could be more sincere in the appreciation I want to extend to every citizen."[2]

Besides the opportunity, his availability, and Mitchell's perceived weakness, several other factors entered into Cain's decision. He had been a popular mayor—re-elected in 1942 by the largest plurality in the city's history. He had an excellent war record. His experiences during the war had increased his self-confidence and certainly expanded his worldview. His 1944 Senate race had brought him name familiarity. Now, it looked as if 1946 would be a Republican year across the nation and in Washington State. If he ran, Cain believed that he would win. That was the upside. The downside (which was also a positive in terms of making his decision) was that, if he ran for re-election as mayor, he would almost certainly win and (unless Tacoma's form of government were somehow changed) face four more years of constant bickering, or worse, with his fellow commissioners. There had been tension, jealousy, and resentment among them before, and there would only be more of it if he remained. It was time to move on.

As he planned his political future, Cain took some steps to return his personal life to some semblance of normalcy. He bought a new car, and in January, he and Marj purchased an attractive home overlooking American Lake on the grounds of the Tacoma Country and Golf Club. They would later add some adjacent rental properties to help defray the costs of maintaining the residence. His children remembered that any one of the rentals might end up serving as a temporary home during future visits back to the state.[3]

Even without Cain in the race, Tacoma's first post-war municipal elections turned out to be a lively affair, and Harry found the means to become involved in them in a way he hoped would work to his political advantage. Paul Olson, a former aide to Democratic Congressman John M. Coffee, was running against Val Fawcett for mayor. Allegations were made by a local contractor that, back in 1941, during the massive expansion of Fort Lewis, Olson had acted as an intermediary between the contractor and Coffee and that money had changed hands. Although the contractor eventually received the contract, he continued to hold a grudge against Olson and Coffee, providing Cain with photocopies of a $2,500 check and several letters that supported his claim of a shakedown.

Cain released the material to the press in a six-page, typed press release and then flew off to Washington, DC, to testify at a Senate hearing at which his efforts to repress prostitution while mayor of Tacoma were receiving national recognition. While he was there, Cain also provided the material on Olson and Coffee to the Justice Department. Cain determined from a meeting with congressional staffers that if the money delivered to Coffee had been a campaign contribution, it had been unreported. Cain promptly announced this development to the press.

On March 5, 1946, Olson challenged Cain to a debate on the matter. Cain readily accepted—with the proviso that the auditorium be hooked up for a live radio broadcast. Six days later, on the night before the election, the two men squared off for a highly touted "acrimonious" debate before a standing-room only audience of 1,600 people at a local school auditorium. Punctuated by the unanticipated appearances on the stage of J. J. Kaufman, the former mayor, and then by the contractor himself that "kept the overflow audience in an uproar," the two men leveled charges and rebuttals at each other for ninety minutes. Olson apparently lost the debate because on the following day he also lost the election to Fawcett by a margin of 523 votes. Cain received more headlines than either of them.[4]

Cain attended his last city commission meeting on May 31. He used the opportunity to promote some of his favorite causes. He presented the commissioners with a letter urging them to engage an outside consultant to review the structure of the Police Department. Cain also proposed a draft resolution establishing a new city-sponsored Unity Committee, a move designed to help decrease the racial tensions that had begun to build in Tacoma during the war. The resolution was placed in a file along with his letter, and without further comment, the meeting was adjourned to attend the swearing-in of the newly elected officials.[5] Harry Cain had ample reason to believe that he had made the right choice in deciding to leave the mayor's office.

ON TUESDAY, FEBRUARY 12, 1946, a month after he announced that he would not seek re-election, Cain made what he told reporters beforehand would be his "first party political speech" to the annual Lincoln Day Dinner of the Thurston County Republican Central Committee in Olympia. In it, Cain responded to critics who claimed that he had once been a Democrat, saying that he had been "castigated as a renegade by those who stole and mongrelized the party of Thomas Jefferson." He went on to describe the Republican Party as an alternative to "that mess in Washington," noting that he had adopted the Republicans "because the party into which I naturally fell by birth and environment has long since lost any trace of its Jeffersonian principles. . . . There is no Democratic Party anymore. It's a hodgepodge held together by one thing only—the determination to stay in power and enjoy the political spoils and advantages that power gives them." Declaring himself a Republican by "deliberate choice," Cain told his audience, which included many Republican officeholders who were in the state capital for the legislative session, that "should you look in my direction for a helping hand, I shall proudly preach the gospel of a strong and clear program as the creed of my party."[6]

Cain waited two more months until Friday, April 12, to formally announce his candidacy. "This action will not surprise the many who have known, since the day of my defeat two years ago while overseas, of my desire and intention to campaign for the Senate in 1946, but it will publicly advise every other interested citizen that I am a candidate and ready for what promises to be a tremendous and vital contest."[7]

Cain remained in Tacoma until the end of his term as mayor on June 3 but then set off on a whirlwind campaign tour through Eastern Washington, speaking in Yakima on the 12th, in Richland a day later, up in Spokane on the 14th, and Pomeroy, a small town in northeast Washington, on June 15. On June 17, Cain was in Seattle speaking before a capacity crowd of 500 enthusiastic partisans at a dinner meeting of the Young Men's Republican Club. Cain pointed out that, frankly, he was *not* making "a strictly partisan appeal for support. We Republicans should lead, but we should let the bars down and take [in] all who believe in the free standards that have made America great." Cain framed the coming campaign in terms of a "test between two different concepts of government." He decried the tendency, espoused by many in his party, toward isolationism. "It should be our intention to participate in a sympathetic way with all nations. We must prevent wars, but our government should be for America first, last and all the time."[8]

Cain faced the unknown J. Parkhurst Douglass in the July 9 Republican primary. Cain enjoyed far greater name familiarity, was the clear choice of the state's Republican leadership, and overwhelmingly defeated Douglass by more than 13,000 votes in a lack-luster primary campaign. As expected, Hugh Mitchell defeated State Treasurer Russell H. Fluent and Sam C. Herren of Bremerton to win the Democratic primary.

Mitchell had grown up in the newspaper business in Montana and had attended Dartmouth College for three years before family finances forced him to drop out in 1929. He moved to Washington and worked as a reporter for the *Everett Herald* newspaper. He became a fervent supporter of the New Deal and joined the staff of Second District congressman Mon Wallgren in 1933, following him to the Senate in 1940. Wallgren defeated Arthur Langlie for governor in 1944, whereupon Wallgren appointed the loyal Mitchell to replace him in the Senate. Mitchell supported the establishment of a national homeland for the Jewish people in Palestine, children's welfare reform, a national aviation policy, and federal support for state institutions. When Washington's other Democratic Senator, Homer Bone, was appointed by Roosevelt to the Ninth Circuit Court of Appeals, Mitchell became the primary advocate for the Columbia Valley Authority (CVA). The CVA's complicated and competing policy implications—trying to balance the needs of irrigators, hydro-based industries, recreation interests, public power enthusiasts, and salmon advocates—was just the kind of issue that Mitchell enjoyed most. Cain's view of the CVA was much less nuanced. The huge federal program was too expensive, too intrusive on the private sector, and limited states' rights. It wasn't needed. Instead, development should be supported through existing agencies and the private sector.

More than 2,500 Republican delegates and alternates held their state convention at Seattle's Civic Auditorium on Saturday, September 21. Iowa Senator Bourke B. Hickenlooper was in town to deliver the keynote address at the evening rally. Harry Cain was named the permanent chairman of the convention and presided over the adoption of a brief, plain-spoken, nine-point party platform that had been hammered out earlier in the day. In adopting the document, Cain told the delegates that the "scent and flavor of coming victory permeates every corner of this auditorium. . . . It's good to be an American. It's time to get under way. Let's go!"[9]

Cain immediately returned to the campaign trail, driving his 1946 two-door Ford Sportsman convertible from town to town as he traveled around the state, his shapeless, beat-up fedora perched jauntily on the back of his head, with Arthur Burgess, a former Associated Press and

Seattle Times newspaperman, who handled Cain's publicity, along for company. Often speaking four times a day, Cain delighted in reminding his audiences of the battle going on between the moderate/conservative and liberal wings of the national Democratic Party while trying to connect Mitchell to the leftist Seattle congressman Hugh DeLacy, and the Washington Commonwealth Federation who "go down the Communist Party line for appeasement of Russia."[10]

On September 26, in the Mason County timber community of Shelton, with many union members in the audience, Cain spoke to a second campaign theme, the "government dictatorship of labor unions." He reminded his audience that President Truman had recently threatened to use the Army to break the coal and railroad strikes and was threatening to do the same in a West Coast longshoreman's strike. Cain again expressed his belief that many employers were not anti-union; they were glad to have unions in their plants because it "makes for unity of purpose."[11]

The experienced Associated Press political writer Jack Bell—the same reporter who got Cain up in the middle of that frigid night during the Battle of the Bulge—was in Seattle in early October to size up the Cain-Mitchell race. Writing under his byline on October 12 in a story carried in the *Tacoma Ledger*, Bell said that the race shaped up as "one of the country's few clear-cut tests between the major parties' national political policies." Bell said that both candidates might have been lifted bodily from their respective parties' national publications." Cain claimed to be "a conservative liberal" and said that the Republican Party was actually the liberal party "for it seeks to conserve the liberties of the people," while Mitchell was a "radical liberal."[12]

Mitchell, strongly backed by the state's major labor unions, reminded the voters that the Democratic Party was the party of Franklin D. Roosevelt and of his successor, Harry S. Truman. Mitchell supported the continuation of Roosevelt-era wage and price controls, while the nation adjusted to the post-war economy. Cain wanted to end price controls and let wages and prices return to a free market. Both candidates brought in outside surrogates to promote their candidacies. Former presidential candidate and Minnesota Governor Harold Stassen, along with Senators Wayne Morse of Oregon, Kenneth Wherry of Nebraska, and Bourke Hickenlooper of Iowa stumped the state for Cain. Former Vice President and Secretary of Commerce Henry A. Wallace, former New Deal Public Works Administrator Harold Ickes, and Senate Majority Leader Alben

Barkley of Kentucky campaigned for Mitchell. Unfortunately, Mitchell hadn't served in office long enough, nor was his personality strong enough, for the voters to get to know him.

By the middle of October, state Democratic leaders were becoming increasingly concerned about the potential of losing Mitchell's Senate seat. The state's two senior Democrats, Warren Magnuson and Mon Wallgren, came to Mitchell's aid on the campaign trail. In a campaign line simply too good to pass up, Cain tagged the Democratic trio as "Maggie, Mitch and Mon," while reiterating his campaign theme that "the New Deal is living in the past, but the Republicans are looking forward to the future."[13] Cain's campaign was in high gear. His personality was well captured by an adoring backgrounder written by Ashley Holden, the influential political writer for the *Spokane Spokesman-Review*—"Harry Cain, Man of Action."[14]

Finishing strong, Cain traveled 15,000 miles, visiting every corner of the state, effectively using the radio as he had in Tacoma, and making eight formal addresses during the last week of the campaign alone. On October 21, before a crowd of more than 1,000 in Olympia, Cain claimed that "whatever the merits of the New Deal had been, it was a political philosophy whose time had passed." It had descended into "political quackery" and had become "extravagant, careless, greedy for power, and reactionary."[15] The next night in Tacoma, Cain spelled out the fundamental issue of the campaign: "[A]re the people of this country going to continue to accept the theory of the Democratic administration that government is all-wise and powerful, or adopt the principle of the Republican Party of having faith in the dignity, courage and hope of the individual human being?"[16] The scholarly Mitchell was simply outmatched by the dynamic Cain and his campaign rhetoric.

As the campaign reached its climax, Cain finished with an October 26 speech in Wenatchee that emphasized a point he had been making throughout the campaign. He agreed with Senator Robert Taft's assessment that the Democratic Party was "dominated by a policy of appeasing the Russians abroad and of fostering Communism at home," that if Truman "wanted to elect a Republican Congress, he could not be doing a better job."[17] But then, against the advice of his advisors, he went even further. Referring to a report issued by the House Un-American Activities Committee that had not been released to the public, Cain claimed that Seattle congressman Hugh DeLacy was one of the leaders "of the Communist Party's front movement in the United States" and that the

Truman Administration knew it, being aware of the unpublished report, and wasn't doing anything about it. "Is that the kind of government you want? Is that what you go to the polls for? I think not, and I think you will know what to do about it on November 5."[18]

On Election Day, November 5, 1946, Washington's voters, along with voters in much of the rest of the country, voted for change. Harry Cain finally fulfilled his dream of being elected to the United States Senate. Voters turned out in large numbers, and Cain beat Mitchell by more than 60,000 votes (55 percent to 45 percent, receiving 358,847 votes to Mitchell's 298,683 votes). Cain carried all but twelve of Washington's thirty-nine counties, but significantly, because of heavy opposition from organized labor, he failed to carry his own Tacoma and Pierce County. Completing the sweep, Republicans carried five of the state's six congressional districts, defeating Hugh DeLacy in the First District and leaving Henry M. Jackson in the Second District as the only Washington Democrat in the House of Representatives. For the first time since 1930, the Republicans would control Congress with majorities in the House of 245 to 188 and in the Senate of 51 to 45.

Cain listened to the returns all night on the radio—coatless, tie loosened, and drinking black coffee with Marj, Buzzy, and a group of supporters at his side in the Army-Navy Suite at Tacoma's Winthrop Hotel. In the early morning, the family returned to their home on American Lake, where a steady stream of visitors, telegrams, and telephone calls stretched breakfast from mid-morning into mid-afternoon. Cain's son, Buzzy, told a reporter that he'd never be a senator "because you always have to have your picture taken."[19]

In a post-election interview with the Associated Press, Cain reiterated his earlier campaign themes of opposing what he called a "bloated government bureaucracy," supporting a strong and bipartisan foreign policy, and working for "the rights of labor." The news story carried the headline "Cain Hews Liberal Line."[20] Oregon Senator Wayne Morse, the leader of the liberal wing of the Republican Party, had endorsed Cain for election. Following his victory, he told *U.S. News and World Report* that "Harry Cain, of Washington, is expected to be active in the liberal, pro-labor Republican bloc."[21]

Some conservative Republicans, reading the stories, agreed. They questioned whether Harry Cain was a Republican at all. Whatever they thought of him, Harry Cain remembered that "people, of every political point of view, wanted a change—they wanted new faces."[22] While that was true, Cain was also fortunate. He was lucky to have faced the colorless and uninteresting Hugh Mitchell instead of the far better-known, better-organized, and more popular Warren Magnuson.

Harry Cain was certainly *qualified* on the basis of his past experience to be a member of the U.S. Senate, but was he adequately *prepared* to be one? When he was elected as Tacoma's mayor at age thirty-three—only six years earlier—he had been a somewhat brash, but popular, young man who had achieved his position as a consequence of an untimely death and a close vote. Even some of his supporters then questioned his qualifications. Like most businessmen, Cain had opposed Roosevelt's actions during the Second New Deal and still considered himself to be a fiscally conservative, if socially liberal, Democrat. Since the mayor's office was officially non-partisan, Cain's decisions there were driven more by local issues than by political philosophy. Cain's foreign policy views were more well defined, having been framed by his experiences in England and Germany in 1935–36 and further shaped and hardened as a result of his war service. Having played a personal role in defeating Italian Fascists and German Nazis and then interacting with the Russians both in Italy and occupied Germany, Cain had come to respect the toughness and single-minded focus of the Soviets but had also come to the conclusion that international Communism posed a far greater threat to America's future than Fascism or National Socialism ever had.

In 1944, Cain had decided that he was a Republican after being recruited to run for the U.S. Senate, but his political philosophy had not been tested during that campaign. With Cain forced to remain officially silent because of army regulations, only one candidate—Warren Magnuson—was in a position to speak out on the issues. In some ways it had been an unknown blessing. When Cain ran again for the Senate in 1946, his political views became far better defined and more widely known. While he still called himself as a "conservative liberal," his views had become more conservative and partisan, reflecting both the evolution of his own thought process and the influence of his new advisors—mostly conservative, small businessmen from Tacoma. Cain had developed a strong aversion to Franklin Roosevelt's domestic agenda and, after Roosevelt's death, to almost all of the policies of his successor, Harry Truman. The Democrats had been in office for far too long, and it was time for a change.

Only thirty-nine years old at the time of his election to the Senate, Cain's background was devoid of legislative experience or any history of compromise and negotiation. He had spent only three and one-half years as an elected official. Tacoma's form of government hadn't encouraged interaction between officials; the military didn't encourage its officers to engage in politics. Over time, Cain had developed a concept of public service and a belief in limited government, free markets, the sanctity of an individual's civil and property rights, and personal responsibility. With limited experience in partisan politics, Cain believed that he had been elected to lead and elected to act on basis of *his* views (which he assumed to be the views of the majority of those who elected him). Cain believed that the times required action, that he had been given the opportunity to act, and *act* he would! It is not clear that he really understood what lay ahead.

After a series of post-election meetings with state Republican officials, a quick but difficult visit to Portland during which he committed his brother Bill to the Oregon State Hospital, and a brief vacation in Southern California with Marj and the children, Cain set about the business of becoming a member of the U.S. Senate. He named his long-time friend and supporter, Irving Thomas, as his new chief of staff. He named Arthur Burgess, who had handled his publicity during the campaign, as his press secretary. Ernie Wetherell, the former editor of the *South Tacoma Star*, had been his secretary while he served as mayor of Tacoma and would continue on in that position. Burgess was sent ahead to begin to organize an office at the Capitol and to interview other potential staff members.

The new Congress was scheduled to convene on January 3, 1947, at which time, under normal circumstances, the nineteen new Republican and five new Democratic senators would be sworn into office. But seniority is important in the Senate and, therefore, important to a state. Seniority controls a member's committee appointments and even the location of his or her office. When Democrat Warren Magnuson was elected in 1944, Republican Governor Arthur Langlie—certainly no fan of Magnuson's—agreed to appoint him to fill the vacancy that had been created by Homer Bone's appointment to the Court of Appeals, thus permitting Magnuson to resign from the House and begin his Senate term a month early. Now, the shoe was on the other foot. Wallgren had grave reservations about Cain but decided to follow Langlie's precedent and appoint Cain to the vacant Senate seat, if Mitchell would agree to resign early. In an act of great generosity, Mitchell agreed to resign on December 26 (losing some of his Senate pension in the process). Wallgren, already in Washington, DC, on other business, notified the Senate of his decision to appoint Cain on the same day. Cain couldn't be sworn in until the Congress convened, but his tenure would date from the day of his appointment. In a 1949 interview, Cain said that he hadn't asked for the early appointment and didn't know why Wallgren did it.[23]

News of the interim appointment created chaos in the Cain household. Harry decided that he needed to leave for Washington, DC, as soon as possible. Marj had to pack up the family, decide what Christmas toys and other items were going to be taken along for the children, close up their house on American Lake, and get to the train station, all with less than a day's notice. Harry notified his newly named staff to be ready to accompany him. The next evening, Cain and his family, Irving Thomas, Ernie Wetherell with his wife and daughter, and a secretary, Marian Goodwin—a party of nine altogether—were boarding the Milwaukee Road's eastbound *Olympian* on their way to the nation's capital. Saying goodbye to friends and well-wishers who had come to see them off, Cain was typically upbeat. "I wouldn't trade places with any man who walks the face of the earth."[24]

Harry hadn't lost his flair for publicity. Also traveling with the Cain party on the train was Stub Nelson, a political writer for the *Seattle Post-Intelligencer*, who was along to chronicle Cain's first days as a senator. Later that night Nelson filed his first story, datelined "EN ROUTE TO WASHINGTON, D.C., Missoula Mont., Dec. 27.—Harry Cain's first day as a United States Senator was devoted to work in a temporary mobile office on wheels. Busy at a compartment desk as the *Olympian* twisted through the rugged snowbound Montana mountains, Cain dictated letters, dozens of them. While Marian Goodwin typed, Cain pored over data related to the job that officially became his as dawn broke today." Perhaps having filed his story late enough in the evening to have availed himself of the train's bar car, Nelson reported that "getting into [his] senatorial toga was a comparatively simple matter," because Cain had unknowingly left behind the bag containing his pajamas. At Cain's request, Nelson made sure that his story included a message to longtime Cain supporter Harold Bird to forward the errant bag as soon as possible."[25]

In a typed, three-page letter written on January 22, Marj shared with her friends back home just how chaotic the past few weeks had been for the family. She said that the train's compartment provided only two and one-half beds for a family of four. Every possible combination of sleeping arrangements was tried without success. The train was so crowded that they could not find a seat in either the bar car or the dining car. They managed to survive with a bottle of Scotch and food from a picnic hamper provided by friends before they left Tacoma. They had intended to stop in Milwaukee to see Harry's favorite uncle, John Page Pulliam, but through a mix-up in communications, they were not awakened in time, leaving assorted relatives looking for them on the platform in Milwaukee as their train pulled out the station on its way to Chicago. Marj managed to lose her purse during the layover in Chicago. Buzzy lost his glasses. The overnight trip on the Baltimore and Ohio's crack *Capital Limited* from Chicago to Washington was "terrible" and only the "sheer genius of my husband" kept them from a brawl.[26]

Arriving at Washington, DC's cavernous Union Station on the morning of December 30, "exhausted, stressed out, and homeless," Cain told an Associated Press reporter, "I think my best contribution to the State of Washington at first will be to keep my ears and eyes open—and my mouth shut. After all, I'm a freshman here, and freshmen are not supposed to talk until they know what they're talking about."[27] It was an admonition he quickly forgot.

But the Cains now faced a much more immediate problem. Traveling across the Dakota prairies in below-zero degree weather, Cain's train stopped long enough in Aberdeen, South Dakota, to receive a telegram from Art Burgess, already in Washington, DC. His wire said that in two weeks he had been unable to find either an apartment or a home that could be rented for less than $200 a month. The group held a hasty, frantic meeting to decide what to do. As a last resort, they decided that they would try to rent a large house where all of them could live together until other arrangements could be made. Upon their arrival, they checked into the Statler Hotel (now the Capital Hilton) to await events.[28]

The housing shortage in Washington was every bit as serious as Art Burgess had said it was. Marj told her friends by letter that by "employing the help of the Army, Navy, G.O.P., Real Estate Boards both locally and nationally, and publishing plaintive stories," they finally found a one-bedroom, unfurnished apartment on 16th Street, NW, and then had to scramble to "buy, beg and borrow a few pieces of furniture and china" to furnish it with.[29] Marj further told her friends that when Harry first walked into the room—which was smaller than their living room in Tacoma—he said, "Well, Bunny, if you can be happy here, I guess I can." They managed by sending Buzzy to boarding school in Warrenton, Virginia, until they could find larger accommodations.[30] Their housing crisis was finally resolved five months later when they were able to find an apartment in the prestigious eight-story, 525-unit, brick and sandstone Westchester Apartments at 4000 Cathedral Avenue, NW, only three short blocks from the grounds of the National Cathedral. Its residents included two cabinet members, thirty-one congressmen, twelve senators, and fourteen judges.[31]

Marj was immediately swept up in a "whirl of appointments, receptions, teas and formal dinners," laid on for, and by, the Republicans as they returned to power. Senate leaders like Robert Taft and John Bricker of Ohio took Harry under their wing, according him instant recognition, while Marj socialized with the wives of Taft, Arthur Vandenberg (R-Mich.), and Owen Brewster (R-Maine).

HARRY CAIN HAD been elected to the Senate at a transformational period in the history of twentieth-century America. The Great Depression, the New Deal, and conflicting federal policies during the second half of the 1930s had each brought great change, but the war brought even more. As professor Richard Kirkendall has written, the consequences of two of those changes were not yet fully understood. The Depression and the New Deal's intervention in the economy resulted in American capitalism becoming much more organized, centralized, and managed. Because of the war, America had become a global power.[32] The war had accomplished what the New Deal had been unable to do: it moved the American economy from depression to recovery. As the economy boomed, American society changed, higher-income families received a smaller share of the national income, and millions of families emerged from poverty.

At the same time, the Democrats, who had led the nation through the Depression, the New Deal, and then the Second World War, had been in office a very long time. They had became an increasingly fragmented coalition of big-city bosses, intellectuals, socialists (and some communists), and Southern conservatives who vied for power within the party. These various interests competed in many ways, but none more obvious than during the run-up to the national election of 1944. Franklin Roosevelt, increasingly ill, was the only one who could both hold the party together and win the war, but who would be his running mate and successor? Conservative Democrats were determined that it would *not* be the liberal current Vice President Henry A. Wallace. The alternative turned out to be Missouri Senator Harry S. Truman.

Roosevelt died soon after he began his fourth term, and Harry Truman became President of the United States. He inherited a Cabinet loyal to Roosevelt and many skeptics, including Harry Cain, who questioned his qualifications for the job. But Truman surprised many and turned out to be a man of independent mind. His political compass, he told his old Senate pal, Mon Wallgren, in December 1945, was "a little left of center."[33] He crafted an administration that reflected his own priorities: fiscally conservative, internationalist in foreign policy, and generally supportive of the status quo in domestic policy. However, with the end of the war, it seemed that the stopper popped open from a bottle full of difficult social, economic, and political issues that had been fermenting inside for years and even decades. The Democrats' leadership, now much more fragmented than it had been under Roosevelt, faced growing unemployment, increasing inflation, a severe housing shortage, the consequences of the vast internal migration that had occurred during the war, the changing role of women, and growing problems with labor-management and race relations. As if these were not enough, there were growing fears about the threat of Communism—both internal and external.

The 1946 off-year elections were widely seen as a referendum on the Truman presidency and his handling of these difficult issues. His approval rating, as measured by the Gallup Poll, stood at only 32 percent. In many ways, Truman was his own biggest liability. He was not a great communicator, and his obviously limited grasp of the issues made him seem indecisive and not in control.[34] When he *did* forcefully confront an issue, as he did when he addressed a series of massive nationwide strikes, it seemed to work to his disadvantage.

During the war, labor and management had generally honored no-strike pledges, and the labor disputes that did occur were of short duration. But after the war ended and inflation became a greater problem, organized labor began to demand higher wages and other benefits to compensate for inflation and to redress many issues that had been building over time. A series of high-profile strikes began in November 1945 and carried on through the mid-term elections a year later. Truman reacted strongly to the labor unrest. He was no fan of the major union leaders. When the United Mine Workers struck, Truman ordered the federal government to seize the coal mines. When a national railroad strike loomed, he threatened to do the same thing and even asked for authority to draft striking railroad workers into the Army. His actions allowed the Republicans, still struggling to find their own political identity, to use the public's dissatisfaction with Truman and the economy to win control of the Congress for the first time since 1930. Both sides were mad and spoiling for a fight.

IT WAS IN this partisan environment that the newly elected 80th Congress convened on January 3, 1947. The new senators were escorted down the aisle—in Cain's case by Warren G. Magnuson—and took the oath of office in small groups administered by the Acting President of the Senate, Arthur H. Vandenberg, who officiated due to the vice presidential vacancy caused when Harry Truman assumed the presidency. Cain's family watched his swearing in from the Senate Gallery.

"Maggie," as he was uniformly known, was a well-liked politician with a low profile at home and a growing reputation for effectively representing the needs of the people and industries of his state. It was not widely known that he was also one of the capital's most active bachelors or that he belonged to the inner circle of powerful Washington, DC, insiders who regularly played poker with the President of the United States at the White House. Maggie was habitually cooperative with the rest of his state's congressional delegation, as he was now with Cain and the other new Republicans who had just been elected. Thor Tollefson, who had replaced John Coffee in the Sixth Congressional District, quickly received a call from Maggie, wanting to know if there was anything he could do to help. Magnuson was instrumental in getting Tollefson appointed to a seat on the Merchant Marine and Fisheries Committee. "He had great influence with President Truman, but he had influence everywhere. He was a long-term player and a team player. He handled himself in order to be able to work with everyone—a pol's pol."[35]

But Magnuson, who had defeated Cain in 1944, was puzzled by his new Senate colleague. Writing to Seattle real estate tycoon Henry Broderick, he said, "Confidentially, I don't know how it is going to work out with our friend from Tacoma. I have been deliberately more than cordial. Of course, it takes a little time to get adjusted here to the fact that

Democrats and Republicans don't hobnob together on a friendly basis. But the best interests of the state require a great deal of cooperation of all representatives, regardless of party. You may be sure that I'm going out of my way toward that end."[36]

While he snubbed Maggie's overtures, Cain felt that his Senate term started off well-enough. His seniority over the other freshman senators and his early contacts with the Republican leadership led to some good committee assignments. Cain was appointed to the Small Business Committee, the Public Works Committee (where he chaired the Subcommittee on Public Buildings), the Banking and Currency Committee (where he chaired the Subcommittee on Rent Controls), and the District of Columbia Committee (where he chaired the Fiscal Affairs Subcommittee). Seen by the Republican leadership as a potential rising star who was also an accomplished speaker—one who could be counted on to campaign for Republican candidates around the country—he was also named to the National Republican Senatorial Campaign Committee.

His seniority also allowed Cain to select his choice of four available office suites. In his enthusiasm, Cain picked the first one he visited. Room 455 in the Senate Office Building (now the Russell Senate Office Building) was actually a three-room suite overlooking First Street on the fourth floor of the "new" wing of the building, which had been completed in 1933. While the rooms were fairly large, they didn't seem so after a staff of eight, along with their desks, filing cabinets, and a small reception area were crammed into the two offices that remained after Cain occupied his inner office. In 1950, Cain moved to the much more convenient Room 226 in the original wing of the building with its ground-level entry onto Delaware Avenue, a short walk across Constitution Avenue to the Senate Chamber. Unusual for a freshman, Cain was initially assigned a desk in the front row of the Senate Chamber. He began at Desk 1, on the far left of the front row facing the dais, moving toward the center to Desk 3 and later Desk 4, in each of the next successive Congresses.[37]

Cain, who had just turned forty on January 10, was the fourth-youngest member of the Senate. Senator Joseph McCarthy (R-Wis.) was thirty-seven, and two other newly elected Senators, William Knowland (R-Cal.) and William Jenner (R-Ind.) were both thirty-eight. The average age of the new Senate was 56.4 years.[38] One feature writer who interviewed him remembered that Cain "might almost be mistaken for a somewhat weather-beaten college boy turned loose among his elders." Cain had "managed to keep the lean, wiry body of a youth." It was not surprising then, that Cain was turned away on his first attempt to take the "Senator Only" elevator up to his new offices. The young operator looked him over and said, "This elevator is for Senators only." Cain was so surprised that he backed out and walked up the stairs to his office.[39]

The next months were a swirl of activity: listening to the floor debate, acquainting himself with the Senate's arcane procedures, and meeting with constituents and others who wanted to size him up or ask for a favor. Cain had lunch with his former commander-in-chief, Dwight Eisenhower, who was then writing his memoir *Crusade in Europe*. Ike wrote in his diary after the meeting that Cain was "energetic, logical and friendly. He ought to be a fine Senator."[40]

Cain was on the floor of the House chamber to attend his first State of the Union address on January 6, 1947. President Truman began his speech by looking to his left front toward Cain and the rest of the Republicans and quipping, "It looks like a good many of you have moved over to the left since I was here last!" Like other presidents before and since, Truman asked for bipartisanship and cooperation. He called for strenuous efforts to balance the budget but said that considerable funds would be needed for domestic programs, aid for veterans, alleviation of famine and suffering around the world, and to maintain the national defense. He proposed new domestic initiatives aimed at reducing the current labor strife, a new Welfare Department, new housing and efforts to reduce urban blight, and greater protection for civil rights. To help pay for them, he suggested retaining some business taxes that were soon set to expire. In foreign affairs, he called for the speedy ratification of a number of pending peace treaties, additional help for displaced persons, and maintaining adequate military power to protect America's interests. "Our goal is collective security for all mankind."[41]

The new Republican majority was strongly representative of business interests, farming, and small-town America. They were overwhelmingly conservative and many carried a chip of resentment on their shoulder against the Democrats, a chip that had been growing over the fourteen years they had been frozen out of power. They formed a loosely organized, bipartisan coalition with conservative Southern Democrats, who resented the influence of the Northern urban interests, intellectuals, and organized labor in their own party and who opposed anything that might threaten segregation. Together, they opposed almost all of the President's domestic program, and within eighteen months, Truman was calling them "the good-for-nothing, do-nothing, Eightieth Congress."[42]

Looking back, Cain admitted his bias in a 1956 interview in the *New Republic* magazine:

> I know I was considered a cantankerous reactionary in the Senate. I was. The Democratic Party back home had been taken over by New Deal extremists. They completely sold out to organized labor. There was no deviation. They called it liberation. I thought it was the damndest kind of reaction I had ever seen. I had respect for Roosevelt at first. His program was bold and imaginative—just what we needed when the country was sick. But he continued to treat us as sick even when we had become well again. I thought the third term was a terrible thing. All this, plus the war, put quite a chip on my shoulder. I had deep-rooted prejudices. Anything the Trumans were for, I was against.[43]

Within weeks, the Republicans were engaged in proposing new tax cuts and trying to pare $4.5 billion from the administration's proposed budget. Harry Cain, along with Senator Homer Ferguson (R-Mich.) agreed with the proposed budget cuts but felt that they could be cut by even more—by $6 billion—if the army and navy were merged and flight pay for aviators suspended. Not surprisingly, the military howled until Ferguson's fellow Senator from Michigan, Arthur Vandenberg, intervened to stop the grandstanding.[44]

Although Senator Wayne Morse (D-Ore.), who had campaigned for Cain, forecast that Cain would join them in the progressive, pro-labor faction of the Republican Party, Cain quickly gravitated to the predominantly Midwestern conservative bloc of the Republican Party led by Robert A. Taft of Ohio, who now served as the new Senate Majority Leader. Taft was the clear leader of the Senate's Republicans. Cain genuinely admired Taft and agreed with his view that the growth of the government generally resulted in the loss of individual freedoms. Cain also understood that Taft could probably do more than anyone else to advance his Senate career. While he would later disagree with Taft on public housing and urban renewal, Cain was more than willing as a freshman senator to be guided by his party's leadership. Besides, Taft and other conservative Republicans had gone out of their way to befriend Harry and Marj after they arrived in Washington and had been helpful in securing his committee assignments. In addition to Taft, the group included Ohio's other Senator, John Bricker, William Jenner of Indiana, and Owen Brewster of Maine. Together, they shared a basic conservatism, an isolationist view of America, a background in partisan politics, and a hatred of the Democrats. Harry also got to know and become personal friends with another relatively unknown freshman Senator, Joseph McCarthy of Wisconsin. At the time, Cain was said to have "followed Taft around like a shadow, supporting him on every important issue."[45] Many years later, Cain remembered that "Robert Taft was a remarkably able and astute man but very few people came to hear him speak. They would *read* what he had to say, but he did not have the ability to stimulate people."[46]

While the standoffish and intellectually arrogant Taft was the undisputed leader of the Senate Republicans, particularly on domestic issues, the elderly, but highly respected Arthur H. Vandenberg of Michigan had become the leader of the internationalist faction of the Republicans in the Senate. Cain developed a real friendship with Vandenberg, who was twenty-six years his senior. The two shared both an interest in the newspaper business, as Vandenberg had once been a newspaper editor, and similar views about foreign policy. Until the start of World War II, Vandenberg had been one of the Senate's greatest isolationists, but he gradually changed his mind during the war. One historian of the period said that "Vandenberg became a Senator on March 31, 1921, and a statesman on January 10, 1945, when he delivered a speech on the Senate floor renouncing isolationism in favor of internationalism."[47] Cain later attributed his ability to change his mind on complex issues to the influence of Vandenberg. "He was one of the few people from my time in the Senate, when the Senate would, almost by some instinctive process, show up [when he] was going to give a speech. Even people who disagreed with him would come to listen to his eloquence."[48] The two powerful Republicans, Taft and Vandenberg, shared an often strained relationship as Taft led his party in general opposition to the Truman Administration on domestic policy, and Vandenberg led a group of internationalist Republicans who allowed Truman to achieve some important victories in foreign affairs.

An early defining issue was President Truman's nomination of David Lilienthal to head the Atomic Energy Commission. Widely esteemed by New Deal liberals for his management of the Tennessee Valley Authority

(TVA) but criticized by conservatives for what they believed was his pro-Communist viewpoint, Lilienthal's nomination split the Republicans. Vandenberg and his moderates supported the nomination while Taft led the opposition, backed by a group of hard-line conservatives (including Harry Cain), who were usually even less flexible than Taft was.

Three things quickly became apparent about Senator Harry Pulliam Cain. The first was that he was going to oppose any domestic policy initiative that had a liberal or progressive tinge to it. The second was that he was going to represent his own views and not necessarily those of his constituents in Washington State. At the time, he said that he believed "in representing the entire nation." After hearing that, one visitor to Cain's office commented after he returned home, "Every state in the Union has two senators except the State of Washington. We have only one and one-forty-eighth, because Cain belongs to the nation."[49] The third was that Cain was unpredictable. After only two weeks in office, he received 108 nearly identical telegrams as a result of a campaign organized by a New York banker asking him to support a reduction in rent controls—an issue he agreed with. He sent a favorable response to the banker, along with the stack of telegrams, asking the banker to copy his response and send it along at his own expense to the others. His unpredictability surfaced again several months later when Cain and Senator John J. Williams (R-Del.), both members of the Public Works Committee, decided to drop in unannounced at the White House while President Truman was welcoming Mexican President Miguel Aleman to Washington. They were on a fact-finding trip to determine the number of officers needed on the White House police force. They inspected the premises thoroughly, including a turkey that was being cooked in the White House kitchen for the state dinner.

As a senator, Cain continued his previous practice of using the radio to communicate with his constituents, writing the scripts himself for a weekly, fifteen-minute commentary that was broadcast over a statewide network of twenty-one local radio stations. Cain returned frequently to the state. By November, he was able to claim that he had made five transcontinental air trips to his home state and back, made one car tour through fifteen states, and visited both Alaska and the Russian Zone of Occupation in Germany.

Cain was surprised to be asked to chair the Rents and Housing Subcommittee of the Senate Banking and Currency Committee. It seemed like a great honor for one so new and inexperienced. The Committee's chairman, Charles Tobey of New Hampshire, quickly set him straight. "This assignment may be the roughest of all appointments and if you don't accept it there will be no committee, for everyone else until you, has turned it down." Cain accepted.[50] Cain joined the arcane debate about housing and rents with a surety that was missing from some of his other assignments. Wilson Wyatt, President Truman's National Housing Administrator, had known Cain when both were mayors. Wyatt had been delighted when he heard of Cain's election, remarking to a friend that here was one Republican, at least, who would understand something about the nation's housing problems.[51] Wyatt would soon be disappointed.

The post-war fight over public housing and rent control became the on-going signature battle of Cain's senate career. Other controversial issues came and went away, but housing remained until Korea and foreign affairs pushed all else from the public's attention after 1950. Some saw the issue as a simple battle between the supporters of free enterprise and government involvement, but it was much more complicated than that. It was a battle over how the nation's massive post-war housing demand would be met, and the stakes were high. It matched a business coalition consisting of the National Association of Real Estate Boards, the Mortgage Bankers Association of America, and the National Association of Homebuilders and their local members against a coalition of community development and community activists who felt that the government's housing programs should serve a larger purpose than the simple enrichment of the real estate and mortgage banking interests. Certainly, the bankers and the home construction industry would profit from an expansion of the nation's housing supply, but they were strongly opposed to what they saw as an unwarranted intervention by the government in an important sector of the economy. The community groups were willing to go along with new programs supported by the President, so long as they accommodated low- and moderate-income homebuyers and delayed the bankers' attempts to privatize public housing and lift rent controls until the pent-up pressure for new housing had been met. The community activists believed, along with President Truman, that the Republicans who opposed controls were helping to fuel the nation's persistent problems with inflation.

While he normally followed Taft's lead on domestic policy issues, Cain disagreed with him on housing. Taft believed that public housing was not a radical idea at all but a practical means of achieving a conservative ideal—a decent living environment for families. Taft's change of heart had occurred after Stanley Rowe, his neighbor and chair of the Cincinnati Housing Authority, had persuaded him to tour the city's slums.[52] As early as 1945, Taft—then in the minority—had joined with Democratic Senators Robert Wagner of New York and Allen Ellender of Louisiana to stimulate post-war residential construction and improve the housing of all income groups through combination of private enterprise and public entities. The so-called W-E-T bill, which received its initials from the last names of its three main supporters, provided grants and loans to local governments, expanded federal financial aid to the private housing industry, liberalized terms on federally insured mortgages, and authorized the building of 500,000 units of public housing over four years—the first such authorization since 1938.[53] Republican opposition to the public housing provisions of W-E-T stymied the passage of a comprehensive housing bill for another four years.

In his State of the Union message, Truman had again called for passage of a comprehensive housing bill. Taft continued to support the legislation, and the bill's informal title was changed to T-E-W, reflecting Taft's new status as Senate Majority Leader. T-E-W had only lukewarm support in the Senate, with conservative Republicans and Southern Democrats opposed for different reasons. There was even less support for it in the House.

Cain, influenced by friends and supporters in the real estate, mortgage banking, and homebuilding industries back home, believed that government should get out of the housing business as quickly as possible. Through their auspices, he became closely tied to the national trade associations that represented these groups. His office was soon believed to be the principal conduit for providing internal government information to the industry. Columnist Drew Pearson was soon calling him "America's No. 1 Real Estate Lobbyist."

Within three months of being sworn in, Cain was fully engaged in trying to modify the provisions of T-E-W. Cain proposed a 15 percent rent increase for tenants of federal housing and introduced new legislation, along with Senator Richard Russell (D-Ga.) that would dispose of the agency that administered all of the war-era public housing altogether, making the units available instead to veterans. Cain believed that "rent control" was a misnomer. "It wasn't rent control, but a freeze. Rents were controlled as to income while the costs of maintenance and operation were unregulated. Once this undeniable fact became clear, my simple mind said either balance the two sides or get rid of it."[54] In July 1947, Cain chaired a hearing on the subject in Seattle. About eighty low-income residents of Seattle's public housing projects demanded his recall and picketed the hearing, fearing that they would be dispossessed by his proposal. Cain invited the pickets into the hearing room and defended his position vigorously during a three-hour meeting. Later, angry picketers surrounded him as he attempted to get to his car.[55] T-E-W narrowly passed the Senate but died in committee in the House of Representatives.

In 1948, a pared-down, noncontroversial version of T-E-W was introduced. Taft felt that they had to pass something they could point to in the coming election. The new bill included the more popular provisions of the former bill—liberalized mortgage terms and guaranteed profits for private investors of large-scale rental housing—but little else. Cain and Wisconsin Senator Joseph McCarthy (then more interested in housing than in Communists) opposed even this pared-down measure because of the rental housing provision. Again, the proposal passed the Senate, but Cain tried at the last moment to sabotage it in a ploy that angered even his supporters. On April 30, 1948—the day before the Kentucky Derby, a day on which by longstanding common agreement no substantive business was conducted so that the senators could leave for the Derby—there was a previously scheduled routine motion to extend the funding for the Federal National Mortgage Association (FNMA) for three months, until the House could pass a similar measure. With the contrivance of the Republican floor leader, Kenneth Wherry of Nebraska, and without warning, Cain introduced a motion to extend funding for FNMA for a full year. He and those in on the plan realized that if funding for FNMA could be secured, the real estate interests would have time to attack T-E-W in the House where they had more support. The ploy was caught just in time, and voting on Cain's proposal was delayed until the following week when it was overwhelmingly defeated. His breech of senatorial courtesy was not appreciated by his colleagues.[56] When it finally passed, Truman belittled the Housing Act of 1948 as a paltry gesture and went on to make the housing issue a centerpiece of his presidential campaign against the "do-nothing Eightieth Congress."

The Rent and Housing Subcommittee was not Harry Cain's only thankless committee assignment. He served on the District of Columbia Committee. The Committee had long been the purview of Southern conservatives who chose to serve on it in order to make sure that the city's majority African American population could not vote in national elections. Other members generally saw it as a useless, backwater assignment. Cain was appalled that his colleagues should be debating just how much to *tax* the voteless residents of the District of Columbia. He weighed in on the subject during a caustic nationally broadcast Sunday night radio interview program, calling the citizens of the nation's capital "political serfs." The next day, his remarks were the subject of the lead editorial in the *Washington Evening Star* that noted, "It could be wished that more members of Congress would approach consideration of Washington's problems from Senator Cain's point of view. But, until Americans in Washington are given the right of bona-fide representation in the Government which taxes them and sends them to war, the 'serfdom' to which Senator Cain refers will continue."[57]

On March 12, President Truman spoke for the second time in three months before a Joint Session of Congress to propose what became known as "The Truman Doctrine." It was the beginning of the administration's policy of "containment" of the Soviet Union. The policy was built on the premise that the United States, then in sole possession of the atomic bomb, could control the expansion of the Soviet Union and other Communist states with a relatively small military establishment and a moderate amount of foreign aid to help other nations protect themselves. Because budgets were tight, aid would largely go to Europe, the primary target of Soviet expansion, rather than to Asia. In his speech, Truman requested $400 million dollars in military and economic aid for Greece and Turkey as well as authorization to send American economic and military advisers to the two countries as well. The legislation passed, due in no small part to the supportive role played by Arthur Vandenberg. Cain reluctantly supported the legislation, "not because it even approximates an answer to the problem, but because it was presented in such a way that I can't resist it."[58]

On the other hand, Cain was a strong proponent of Universal Military Training (UMT), which was also being proposed by the Truman Administration as an alternative to reinstituting an unpopular military draft. In a time of growing threats and reduced budgets, Cain thought UMT provided a trained pool of manpower without spending the funds needed for large standing forces. In the April 26 issue of the *Saturday Evening Post*, Truman's Secretary of War, Robert P. Patterson, wrote an article advocating UMT. Cain agreed. "We learned two things from World War II: one is that modern wars come suddenly; the other is that nations which are poorly prepared pay the highest price."[59] UMT failed to pass the Congress, so Truman regretfully adopted the other alternative in July and instituted only the second peacetime military draft in American history. Truman also supported the reunification of Germany under a federal form of government and the withdrawal of Allied occupation forces, replacing them with an Allied police force—actions which the Russians would certainly have opposed given their distrust of Germany and their growing distrust of the Allies. Responding to a question about the subject on the March 6 radio program, *America's Town Meeting of the Air,* Cain said, "To my mind, the safest guarantee for the future peace of the world is the peaceful, democratic Germany."[60]

Because of his experience in dealing with displaced persons in Europe, Cain was asked to join a group of powerful Judiciary and Appropriations Committee members on a European tour to look into the plight of millions of displaced persons. The group visited England, Germany, Austria, Switzerland, and Italy, where they met with Pope Pius XII at Castel Gandolfo on October 31. Writing to Marj, who was back at their home in Tacoma, Cain described the Pope as being "a gracious, intelligent, and very alert personality. Some thirty minutes spent in musing over the state of a troubled world. My next wish is to meet Mr. Churchill. That would be enough for one hectic trip."[61]

The most controversial and contentious issue that Harry Cain had to deal with during his first two years in the Senate had nothing to do with foreign policy. It was the effort by the new Republican majority to redress the balance between labor and management and to reform what they considered the inequities of the 1935 National Labor Relations Act— the Wagner Act—that protected workers' rights to unionize and created the National Labor Relations Board (NLRB) to enforce the Act. At the time, the Roosevelt Administration and the overwhelmingly Democratic Congress were responding to the argument that, since America already had large-scale business organizations, it needed large-scale labor organizations in order to offset them. Indeed, there was a strong belief that it was the business community that had largely created the Great Depression in the first place.

Now, with the Republican majority in Congress, there was finally the political will and the opportunity to redress the balance between labor and management. Cain believed that labor and management should operate on a level playing field with workers deciding on what was best for them in their individual circumstances. He had always nursed a lingering hope that his views might somehow appeal to both business and labor. Those hopes were certainly fading after the 1946 election, but Cain would often express his view that "hope springs eternal," one of his favorite expressions. Years later, Cain told an interviewer, "The only way I could have maintained my friendly relations with labor at home was to vote no to everything [to modify the Wagner Act] when I felt strongly that yes votes would benefit the nation, including labor."[62] It was an issue that would come back to haunt him for the rest of his life.

The vehicle chosen by the Republicans to amend the Wagner Act was the Labor-Management Relations Act of 1947, or the "Taft-Hartley Act," as it came to be known. It was first introduced in 1946 and was one of more than 250 anti-labor bills pending in Congress when Harry Cain joined the Senate. The bill was a direct response to the postwar labor unrest caused by the wage controls imposed during the war but was, in addition, a longer-term reaction against the political power that organized labor had developed since the passage of the Wagner Act more than ten years before. It was seen as a means of demobilizing the labor movement by imposing limits on labor's ability to strike and by prohibiting Communists and other radical elements from their leadership.

Not surprisingly, organized labor—particularly the industrial CIO unions—fought the proposed legislation with everything at their disposal, referring to it as a "slave labor bill." However, Taft-Hartley's outcome in the Republican 80th Congress was never in doubt. In fact, more conservative and moderate Democrats joined the Republicans in voting for the legislation than voted against it. Bowing to the power of organized labor in his own party, President Truman vetoed the legislation. On June 23, 1947, the President's veto was overridden by a vote of 68 to 25—including twenty Democrats who voted with the majority. However, Taft-Hartley as an issue had "legs." It played an important role in Truman's upset 1948 election victory. "Labor did it," he proclaimed after he won.[63] Notwithstanding his veto, Truman went on to use the provisions of Taft-Hartley twelve times during his presidency.

Shortly before the vote to override the President's veto, Cain was visited in his office by Dave Beck, originally from Seattle, who was then the executive vice president of the powerful Teamsters Union. Beck told

Cain in no uncertain terms that the Teamsters had helped to elect him and that he should change his vote on Taft-Hartley. Cain later remembered, "There were some rather harsh words. [I told him,] Mr. Beck, I've gone through all of this turmoil—soul searching, if that's what you want to call it—and if other Republicans in the State of Washington voted against Taft-Hartley, I have voted for it because I thought the Wagner Act had gone too far and that Taft-Hartley would help to restore the balance. You are merely talking to the wrong guy!" According to Cain, Beck told him "that he would get me politically if it was the last thing he ever did." He proved true to his word. "I didn't like some of the provisions in the Taft-Hartley Bill but I felt that the bulk was good and it would get rid of the Wagner Act's lopsidedness and inequities. I voted yes." [64]

After a year in the Senate, Harry Cain could look back on his record and take pleasure in the fact that his votes had been generally consistent with his campaign pledges. He had voted for measures to reduce the size and cost of government, to redress the balance between labor and management, and, when it became necessary, to support the administration's efforts to contain the spread of Communism, although he had reservations about their cost and effectiveness. Some of his votes were viewed as uncaring or detrimental to the best interests of the state, such as those opposing a proposal to build a score of new federal post offices (which had been strongly pursued by Senator Magnuson) or access roads into Forest Service lands to facilitate the harvesting of timber or opposition to the creation of a Columbia Valley Administration. His vote on Taft-Hartley, of course, eliminated—once and for all—any hope of future support from organized labor, if, indeed, that had ever been a realistic possibility.

It is questionable whether Cain recognized them at the time, but these and other controversial positions represented danger signals that would become even more obvious in the future. The first was how he was viewed by his peers and how he viewed himself in the Senate. When Harry Cain arrived in the Senate, the new Republican leadership identified him as someone with real potential. Because of his early appointment, Cain held seniority over the other freshman senators. His obvious skill as one of the most articulate and partisan Republican spokesmen meant that Cain would be equally useful campaigning for Republican candidates or during debate on the Senate floor. Because of this, Cain was encouraged by his mentors, as if he really needed encouragement, to speak out on issues that often had more to do with the national partisan debate than they did with the needs of his constituents at home. In the process, Cain may have come to see himself more as a national political figure and less as a champion of his state's interests.

Often encouraged by others in the Senate, Cain was often more likely simply to oppose an issue rather than try to seek a compromise that could eventually lead to his support. Whether on the floor of the Senate, meeting with constituents in his Senate office, or back in his home state, Cain was more often talking than listening. Cain increasingly followed his own instincts rather than the advice of his staff or political advisors. There would be a number of controversial issues in the months and years ahead, and the decisions Cain made would largely establish his legacy as a member of the U.S. Senate.

8

Controversial Decisions

HARRY CAIN BEGAN his second year in the United States Senate feeling that, after a generally successful beginning, he finally *belonged* in what he liked to refer to as the "most important legislative body" in the world. Cain had become one of the most outspoken conservative members of the Republican caucus and had established a strong reputation on such issues as reducing the federal deficit, fighting to free controls on housing and rents, and for redressing the balance between labor and management by supporting Taft-Hartley.

Cain worked easily with most of the members in his own party and developed a deep respect for some of the more conservative members of the Democratic caucus, like Richard Russell of Georgia and Harry Byrd of Virginia. On the other hand, Cain's relationship with Washington's senior Senator, Warren Magnuson, was officially correct but strained. With most other senators, Cain's relationships were cordial and professional, often involving a game of golf or a friendly drink, but were not really close.

Cain was self-assured and comfortable in his role as a member of the U.S. Senate. He enjoyed relaxing in the Senate cloakroom during debate, often engaging in animated conversation with Arthur Vandenberg or Russell Long of Louisiana. Cain could also be found in the Senate gym, either swimming in the pool or sparring in the ring with Kenneth Wherry of Nebraska. Cain enjoyed attending local sporting events, like the Washington Senators' baseball games, often attending with his close friend Joe McCarthy, but on most weekends, Cain could be found on the golf course at Burning Tree or Congressional with constituents, lobbyists, or other fellow legislators. In addition to these pleasures, there was always the constant press of constituent meetings at the office, at lunch in the Senate Dining Room, over drinks at the Statler or the Mayflower Hotel, or dinner at the Occidental Restaurant, next door to the Willard Hotel, or at the venerable Old Ebbitt Grill, then located on F Street.

Even a casual observer could see that Harry Cain loved his job. An otherwise derogatory article about him in 1952 revealed an obvious truth. Cain was a player on what he considered the greatest stage in the world. "Unlike his colleagues who play their roles with monotonous pomposity, Cain knows that for each scene there must be an appropriate, and different, mood. Even a dull colloquy of a committee hearing can be tremendously enlivened, if only someone, e.g. Harry Cain, can work in enough striding to and fro and burying of face in hands before thrusting the telling question at an unsuspecting witness. His committee audiences have been known to burst into spontaneous applause." One government administrator who had faced Cain in such situations was quoted as saying, "You know, I can't help but feel when I am facing that man that he is not completely serious. No matter how he carries on, he seems to me to have his tongue in cheek, to be perfectly aware that he is playing a part."[1]

In actual fact, Cain took his role in the Senate very seriously. He still retained his somewhat idealistic concept of senatorial responsibility—voting one's conscience, even when it proved to be unpopular, and putting what he believed to be the national interest ahead of more parochial state interests. Cain candidly discussed his philosophy in a 1949 interview. "I had decided to listen only to my conscience and my instinct and do what seemed right at the time. Why not? A man in public office might as well play it the way he thinks he should. There is no sure way to stay in public office. Anyone may get licked, no matter what he does, so why not do what he wants to?"[2]

His pragmatism was combined with a healthy dose of self-confidence, bordering on an egotism that was often supported by enablers around him. This led to a continuation of the series of controversial votes and unpredictable actions that characterized the remaining years of his Senate term. Taken together, they would destroy his national political career.

CAIN ATTENDED THE opening of the Second Session of the 80th Congress on January 6, 1948, after spending the Christmas recess with his family at their home on American Lake in Tacoma. In his third State of the Union address, delivered the following day, President Truman again called for bipartisanship in dealing with America's challenges, civil rights for all citizens, and the extension of unemployment compensation, old age benefits, and survivors' benefits for the millions who remained unprotected. Truman told the Congress that they had a special responsibility to help rebuild the European economies destroyed by the war and to help care for the millions of displaced persons still living in refugee camps. While he didn't specifically mention the Soviet Union in his speech, Truman said that a growing "Cold War" had been waged for the past year.

The highlight of the speech was a call to authorize the expenditure of $6.8 billion over the next fifteen months for European recovery. "We are fighting poverty, hunger, and suffering. This leads to peace, not war," Truman said.[3] The so-called "Marshall Plan" was designed to rebuild the shattered economies of Europe's democracies as a means of protecting them from the possibility of a Communist takeover, particularly in Italy and France. The aid program was originally offered to the Russians, as well as to Western Europe. When they obligingly refused to participate and convinced the Eastern European countries they occupied to do the same, they actually helped Truman. Soviet acceptance of American aid would have made passage of the Marshall Plan almost impossible in the Republican-controlled Congress.

The Marshall Plan, with the support of Republicans like Arthur Vandenberg, was passed by Congress in April. Robert Taft resisted the idea of bipartisanship in foreign policy and rejected the concept that America could materially improve the domestic condition of foreign countries, writing to a friend saying that "the sooner we get free from the idea that we are bound to cooperate on everything, the better off we will be."[4] Cain voted with the majority, but with deep reservations about the proposed cost and the propriety of trying to prop up foreign nations that should be expected to manage themselves. In a note written to Marj when he had returned from the Senate-sponsored trip to Europe, Cain worried that "whatever we do for Europe is certain to be both right and wrong. Instead of coming home with a simple black and white picture I have a frame in which hangs a series of bewildering contradictions."[5]

Cain told his constituents essentially the same thing. Noting that he had lived in Europe for a year before the war and then traveled extensively throughout the continent during the war, Cain had assumed that he would understand what he found on his trip. "No assumption could have been farther from the truth. I returned a week ago . . . without a solitary, single conviction. The task which confronts the world . . . is too monumental and contradictory, too confusing and uncertain for any given individual to understand."[6] While the cost of the Marshall Plan was of great concern to many, including Truman, the potential future cost of *not* saving the European democracies seemed even greater. The Russians again helped the passage of the Marshall Plan by staging a coup in February to remove the elected government in Czechoslovakia and by actively supporting Communist Party movements in several Western European countries. The Marshall Plan recognized two major truths that were well understood within the Truman Administration but not adequately explained to the majority of the American people. The first was the administration's clear emphasis on assisting Europe at the expense of Asia; the second was the administration's desire to spend America's limited resources on economic reconstruction rather than on national defense. Both would result in unintended consequences.[7]

Cain's vote on the Marshall Plan was not considered controversial, except to the most dedicated isolationists, but that was not the case with his position on an issue that came to a vote in May. During the waning months of World War II, the military leaders of the then-U.S. Army Air Force (USAAF) began to worry about the impact that the almost certain post-war demobilization would have on its future strength and mission. Now the youngest of the armed services, the newly independent U.S. Air Force felt that they needed to protect their share of the defense budget, particularly against the navy, which always seemed to out-compete them for available funding. The air force promoted a 400,000-man establishment, including twenty-five groups of new strategic bombers, as their best chance to improve their share of the defense budget.

Truman's first Secretary of Defense, James V. Forrestal, a man greatly admired by Harry Cain, supported a strategic bombing role for the navy and promoted the construction of the first super-carrier. Truman believed that the cost of Forrestal's "balanced forces" approach was not sustainable in the Congress. Forrestal's increasing on-the-job stress and a clandestine 1948 meeting with Republican presidential candidate Thomas Dewey led to Truman's loss of confidence in him and a request that he resign in 1949. His successor, Louis Johnson, recommended cancellation of the aircraft carrier and, instead, supported the development of new strategic bombers. The matter was now before Congress. The recommendation brought forward by the Senate Armed Services Committee fell short of committing the Congress to carry out the air force's full four-year, 70-group program, but it did allow them to begin their modernization program. The recommendation also injected fresh life into America's aircraft industry, keeping it healthy in case of future need. Not surprisingly, the bill was strongly supported by the Boeing Company, Washington's largest employer and the likely manufacturer of most of the new bombers.

Cain was one of only two Senators to vote against the measure when it was overwhelmingly approved by the full Senate on May 6. Many friends urged him not to vote on the issue at all, and indeed, he didn't vote on the first roll call. However, after more personal consideration, he decided to vote against the measure on the final vote. Cain said that his "no" vote was essentially a vote of confidence in Forrestal, whom he greatly respected. Cain later said that he was also put off by "the political hocus pocus" that accompanied the vote. He knew that the "people who were supporting the authorization were the same people who were in the process of cutting down the appropriations and I wanted to know why we should fool the country," but that didn't convince voters at home, many of whom worked either for Boeing or its suppliers and who belonged to its unions.[8]

About this time, Cain received a visit from his old friend, Melvin Voorhees, a former newspaper editor from Seattle, who had known Harry when they served together in Europe and who later recorded his impressions of Cain at this time. "I had heard that he was 'in bad' with many of his constituents. His youthful zest, I heard, had been swallowed up by conservatism. Was it so? I've never been sure. But Harry Cain had changed. He talked at me, not to me. He seemed oddly dogmatic."[9]

The remainder of the year was taken up with the 1948 presidential election. Truman was assailed by Southern Democrats for his support of civil rights through his executive orders on July 26 ending segregation in the armed forces and guaranteeing fair employment in the civil service, and by liberal Democrats for his unceremonious dumping of former Vice President Wallace. Truman was now also attacked by the resurgent Republicans, who had been doing all they could since 1946 to scuttle his "Fair Deal" domestic proposals. Harry Truman was in trouble. On the home front he was faced with labor unrest, unemployment, inflation, and a growing hysteria about internal security while overseas he faced the massive job of rebuilding Europe, the repatriation of millions of displaced persons, the fallout from his support of Israel, a possible

Communist victory in China, and an increasingly uncooperative and aggressive Soviet Union.

The Republicans smelled victory. Their 1948 National Convention began in Philadelphia on June 21. They again nominated New York Governor Thomas E. Dewey over the vigorous objections of Senators Robert A. Taft and Arthur Vandenberg, both of whom sought the nomination. Cain had been careful not to take sides, but by April 1948, he had moved closer to Vandenberg and perhaps had come to the conclusion shared by a majority of the delegates who believed that the intellectually arrogant Taft "Can't Win." In the months leading up to the convention, Cain and Vandenberg had often been seen in deep conversation on the Senate floor. Vandenberg, serving as Acting President of the Senate, allowed Cain—no longer a freshman, but still a very junior member—to preside over the body for three consecutive days. The Washington, DC, rumor mill had suggested that if the Michigan Senator were nominated for president, a young westerner—a man like Harry P. Cain—might have made an attractive vice presidential choice.[10]

Vandenberg's drive for the nomination failed, but on June 23, Harry Cain made the last regularly scheduled speech at the convention. He warned the delegates that they could win in November but still lose in 1952 if the party "failed in the next several years to live up to [its] platform and fall far short of [its] announced goals."[11]

The Democratic National Convention was held in Philadelphia only two weeks later. It was marked by the emergence of Hubert Humphrey, the dynamic young mayor of Minneapolis, and a walkout by members of the Alabama and Mississippi delegations when the convention narrowly approved a civil rights plank in the party's platform. The contentious convention was soon followed by a full-scale revolt by states' rights "Dixiecrats," who supported South Carolina Senator Strom Thurmond for President. The Democrats were already facing a revolt by a coalition of New Dealers and old-time Progressives who supported Henry A. Wallace, who was now running on the Progressive Party ticket.

What followed was one of the more interesting presidential campaigns in American history. Faced with opposition from both extremes of his own party, Truman campaigned as much against the Republican Congress as he did against Dewey. The Republicans declared their support for American participation in some form of international organization and then spent the campaign attacking the domestic policies of the Roosevelt and Truman Administrations. An overconfident Dewey played it safe, tried not to make any mistakes, and acted as if he were already President of the United States.. The underdog Truman undertook a remarkable 21,928-mile presidential campaign, crisscrossing the nation and making brief speeches to huge crowds from the rear platform of his train in the nation's first "whistle-stop" campaign. The changing momentum of the election went largely unnoticed in the campaign's final days because of the overwhelming conventional wisdom that Dewey would win. With Strom Thurmond and Henry Wallace in the race, Truman received just under 50 percent of the popular vote but still defeated Dewey by more than two million votes. The Democrats also regained control of Congress, gaining nine seats in the Senate and seventy-five in the House.

Cain wrote a somewhat curious letter to Truman on November 9, saying, "Perhaps no single Senator enjoyed working harder for your opponent" than he had but went on to wish him "happiness, health and success," noting that "I shall look for ways in which to support those portions of your coming programs with which I can logically agree. On the occasions when I oppose your recommendations I shall try my very best to do so on the basis of facts rather than on political prejudice."[12] Truman responded with a perfunctory, two-sentence acknowledgement, expressing the hope that the new Congress and the President will be able to "accomplish a constructive program."[13]

Two weeks after the election, Cain watchers received an even greater surprise than Harry Truman's victory when, without warning, Cain's Capitol Hill office issued a press release saying that the Senator and his wife intended to separate and that she would be filing for divorce. The terse announcement said that Mrs. Cain's filing would cite incompatibility and that the couple had arrived at an amicable property settlement. Mrs. Cain would retain custody of their two children and would remain with Candy in Washington, DC, while Buzzy would travel to Florida for several weeks with his father.[14]

Stranger yet, after his office had issued the announcement, Cain left his Bethesda Naval Medical Center hospital bed, where he had gone for observation, to call his own press conference. "If it were not that Mrs. Cain and I are in public life," he said, "there would be no reason for this conference." He said that the suit would be filed in Tacoma, "as soon as the mechanics can be worked out. The situation between Mrs. Cain and myself is something we have been discussing for a number of years—long before I ever came to Washington."[15] While they may have previously discussed separation or divorce, was there something—some event or series of events—that had caused this unexpected and precipitous announcement? Perhaps. In their 1972 biography of Henry M. Jackson, William Prochnau and Richard Larsen tell the story of an unexpected encounter between Marj Cain and another woman when they both visited Cain's hospital room at the same time.[16]

The Cains' marriage combined two very strong personalities. They had many common interests—theater, golf, and being in public life among them. Harry loved his family, but as he became increasingly self-absorbed in his Senate duties, he left Marj with the responsibility of caring for their two small children. During the week, his Senate duties and the hosting of constituents often meant that he didn't return home until late at night. There were rumors of an affair with a congressional staffer, an event not at all uncommon in Washington, DC. The divorce was filed in Tacoma several months later by Marj's attorney, citing a "burdensome home life" and an "indifferent attitude."[17] In the end, the couple decided to reconcile. His son later said, "My impression/assumption (though I can't back it up) is that Dad both outgrew his attraction to whoever the secretary was, and realized that his political career would be damaged if the divorce went through. Also, he always felt love and respect for Mom—but was good at showing it only in his letters, not in person."[18]

IT WOULD BE hard to overstate the desperation and agitation suffered by the Republicans after their losses in the 1948 election—the failure to recapture the federal bureaucracy with all its rewards and the loss of the Congress after only two years in control. Harry Cain was now a member of the minority party, although he had advanced nearly twenty places on the Senate seniority list. He was able to keep his committee assignments on the Banking and Currency and Public Works Committees and gained a non-voting seat on the powerful Appropriations Committee.

The new Congress began on January 3, 1949, with President Truman delivering his State of the Union Address two days later. It was his shortest State of the Union speech to date and showed his clear frustration with the prior Congress. "We have rejected the discredited theory that the fortunes of the Nation should be in the hands of a privileged few. We have abandoned the trickle-down concept of national prosperity." He was still requesting that Congress deal with the same catalogue of domestic issues he had been pushing before—civil rights, education, help for farmers and the rural poor, health care, housing, and Social Security. "The recent election shows that the people of the United States are in favor of this kind of society and want to go on improving it." He also called for the repeal of Taft-Hartley, a return to the provisions of the Wagner Act, and the continuation of rent controls.[19]

In February 1949, the Democrats—now again in the majority—once more took up the T-E-W housing bill. The scope of their proposed Housing Act of 1949 was grand: "the realization as soon as feasible of the goal of a decent home and a suitable living environment for every American family." Cain opposed both the urban renewal and the public housing portions of the proposed legislation. The urban renewal provisions were designed primarily to help provide inner-city housing rather than new commercial development. Cain and Ohio's other Republican Senator, John Bricker, sought to kill the bill. In the Banking Committee, and later on the Senate floor, they introduced a whole series of unsuccessful amendments, including one that would allow for local communities to provide public housing if approved by a vote of the people with a potential match to be provided by the state.

Cain and Bricker also understood that the housing legislation was supported by two diverse groups—Northern liberals and Southern conservatives—who both, but for different reasons, wanted the federal government to finance public housing in their cities. Cain and Bricker hit upon a unique ploy to separate the two groups—they introduced an amendment that flatly prohibited racial segregation in public housing.[20] The liberal Illinois Senator Paul Douglas, who had better civil rights credentials than most, was outraged by what he described as the cynicism of the Bricker-Cain amendment and urged Northern liberals to vote against it. "I am ready to appeal to history and time that it is in the best interests of the Negro race that we carry through the housing program as planned, rather than put in the bill an amendment which will inevitably defeat it, and defeat all hopes for re-housing 4,000,000 persons."[21] Douglas noted with pointed sarcasm that Bricker had already announced that should his amendment fail, he would still vote against T-E-W.[22] The Bricker-Cain amendment was defeated in the Banking Committee. Cain later said that he had opposed the legislation for two major reasons. "I thought that the least that public housing ought to do was to be competitive with private building and construction." The second reason was that much of the proposed new housing would be segregated. "I felt that no federal money conceivably could be spent for one segment of our population to the exclusion of any other, equally in need."[23] In the end, Harry Truman's come-from-behind victory in the presidential election provided the momentum to pass the Housing Act of 1949. It was his only major domestic legislative victory that year.

One of the most controversial episodes in Cain's Senate career also occurred that February. President Truman decided to nominate his good friend, former U.S. Senator and Washington's recently defeated governor, Mon Wallgren, to be Chairman of the National Security Resources Board (NSRB). The two had served together on the Senate Committee to Investigate the National Defense Program, not surprisingly, referred to simply as the "Truman Committee." The NSRB was one of the agencies created by the sweeping National Security Act of 1947. That legislation combined the Army and the Navy and the recently independent Air Force into the newly created National Military Establishment, later renamed the Department of Defense, established the National Security Council within the executive branch, and created the Central Intelligence Agency. The NSRB's goal was well-intentioned—it was responsible for long-range planning to prepare for mobilization in the case of a national emergency—but in practice, the NSRB was a flawed entity. Under the legislation, the NSRB's eight members shared responsibility for their actions. Truman sought to change that by vesting all of the Board's power in its chairman, who would serve *ex officio* as one of only seven permanent members of the National Security Council. Giving Mon Wallgren that level of responsibility was too much for Harry Cain.

Wallgren's nomination required the advice and consent of the Senate. Since he had also previously served in the Senate and was a well-liked member of the "club," Wallgren's approval was expected to be routine. Against what appeared to be overwhelming odds, Cain decided that he must oppose the nomination. Other senators and friends advised him not to do it. One senior Republican senator estimated his chances of derailing the appointment at "2,000 to one."[24]

Cain was undeterred. His opposition to Wallgren was based on both personal and professional considerations. Although as governor, Wallgren had made Cain's Senate seniority possible by his early appointment, Cain had never liked or respected the man, considering him little more than a congenial backslapper and a political hack. Much of Cain's antipathy had probably been shaped by Arthur Langlie, whom Wallgren had defeated for governor in 1944. At the time, many had questioned why Wallgren would give up a seat in the United States Senate to run for governor of Washington. His argument had been, "I'm running for governor because the people of this state will overwhelmingly vote to reelect Franklin Roosevelt." While that was true, it also quickly became evident that Wallgren intended to look after himself and his friends in Olympia. The state purchased a ninety-foot yacht, on which Wallgren entertained President Harry Truman, and bought two new Cadillac limousines. Wallgren was quite open about his spending. During the 1944 campaign he had famously quipped, "If the voters don't want to go first class, they better get another Governor."[25] Cain could acquiesce to the appointment of such a man to some lesser job in the administration, but he had grave concerns about Wallgren's leadership and executive abilities as chairman of the NSRB.

The Senate Armed Services Committee had jurisdiction over Wallgren's nomination. Cain invoked senatorial privilege in order to testify before them. In a lengthy statement to the Committee on February 17, he contended that Wallgren "conspicuously lacked both the background and capability for the job." Wallgren had been in the optical and jewelry business in Everett until 1932 but had since served as a member of the House of Representatives, in the U.S. Senate, and as governor of Washington. Calling the appointment "the most capricious and potentially dangerous and injurious nomination of the twentieth century," Cain claimed that Wallgren was "a man who had prospered in and through politics." Based on research, which he had conducted himself, and on information he had heard from others, he characterized Wallgren as someone who had been expelled from high school, had owned a pool hall, and had worked in his family's jewelry business when it had financial difficulties. "I know of scores of persons who think well of him as a companion at the pool table, in the banquet room and when the fish run high."[26] In an even longer statement before the committee on February 28, requiring fourteen pages of fine print in the *Congressional Record*, Cain narrowed his criticism down to two points: Wallgren was "incompetent to fill the office of Chairman of the National Security Resources Board"; and "his appointment would represent a distinct danger to the security of the United States" because of his "continued association with persons whose loyalty is subject to doubt and his complete inability to recognize the manifestations of communism."[27] Wallgren, who was present during Cain's testimony, responded to questions from other senators, but because of committee rules could not rebut Cain's remarks directly during the proceedings. He attempted to do so in subsequent written statements that he provided to the committee. In them, he accused Cain of conducting a "personal vendetta" against him and tried to address the issues that Cain had raised.[28] He also appealed to his close friend, the President of the United States. When Senator Millard Tydings of Maryland, the Chairman of the Armed Services Committee, wrote to President Truman after Cain's testimony to say that Wallgren's nomination could be in trouble, Truman responded by writing a letter he never sent. In it, he told Tydings that "there will be no retreat on my part and I had expected none on yours. Were our positions reversed, Mon's confirmation would go through. I know that you can put it through and I am requesting you, as a personal favor, to put it through. The Senate will have come to a pretty pass when it lets a minority political scalawag run the majority. As far as I am concerned the fight goes to the bitter end."[29]

Cain was no less adamant. Having previously sent a copy of his upcoming statement to Dr. John Steelman, an assistant to the President, on February 25, Cain wrote to the President on the same day he delivered his additional testimony, providing the President with a copy of his remarks to the Armed Services Committee. His cover letter said, "My opposition to Mr. Wallgren is both firm and honest. In the problem before us I respectfully suggest that the nominee, while perhaps possessing virtues required by some assignments, is singularly lacking in what you require from advisers and assistants whose sole objective is that of keeping our nation free at home and secure against aggression from abroad." Asked about the letter in his press conference of March 3, Truman said that he had not yet received the letter but denied that "he was in controversy with Senator Cain."[30]

Cain decided to take his fight to the Senate floor and to filibuster the nomination. Southern senators were already in the middle of a filibuster opposing the President's Civil Rights legislation, so Cain's effort constituted a filibuster within a filibuster. The Senate's rules on cloture having been set aside for his speech, Cain took the floor of the Senate at 2:15 p.m. on Tuesday, March 8, 1949, wearing a pair of carpet slippers and telling the senators, "This will take some time, quite a good deal of time."

It did. He spoke until nine that night—six hours and forty-five minutes. While Cain was a gifted extemporaneous speaker, he had carefully practiced what he planned to say about Wallgren. Not content to read the DC telephone book or use similar ploys often resorted to in previous Senate filibusters, he was armed with a blue notebook containing 78,300 words on 261 pages that contained a few of his reasons for opposing Wallgren's nomination and a series of large charts showing the organization of the NSRB and its relationship to other federal agencies. His secretary, Ernie Wetherell, hovered nearby, providing him with coffee and tea, and helping him change, several times, in and out of two pairs of "warm" shoes that he had brought for the occasion.

Cain's wife, Marjorie, who had filed for divorce several months earlier, watched sympathetically from the gallery, but only seven senators heard Cain's entire presentation. Cain contended that Wallgren lacked the capacity to function as the NSRB chairman because of his "incompetence, lack of executive ability, inability to analyze, or to understand important issues of the day." He added that however adept Wallgren might be as an ex-champion billiard player, hole-in-one golfer, fly fisher, or duck shooter, he could not master the NSRB job and "will, in terms of swimming, go down three times and come up only twice, and the country will be the loser."[31] In a comment that would come back to haunt him later, he described Wallgren as neither a "Communist or a fellow traveler," but added that he was "painfully naïve . . . unusually uninformed . . . and had been soft and unintelligent in his treatment of Communists and fellow travelers in Washington State." Summing up, dead tired, and losing his voice, he argued that, "government by [Truman's] cronies must end."[32] Ten years later, in 1959, he remembered the occasion in response to a question from his son, Buzz, who was writing a graduate school paper about his father. "I do not recall much of what I said in opposing Wallgren before the Armed Services Committee or in my long Senate speech. What I recall most vividly about the speech is that Arthur Vandenberg came to me after I had been speaking six or seven hours and quietly suggested that I had won and that further argument was unnecessary. I didn't hesitate. I stopped without bothering to finish the paragraph." Vandenberg later wrote a congratulatory note to Cain. In it, he said, "I have been in the Senate for a long time. You are the only member I have ever known who can run a shoestring into a shoe store."[33]

Wallgren responded to Cain's attack in his own way. On March 10, 1949, the Seattle-based Acme Detective Agency began an extensive investigation into the rumors of mental illness in Cain's family. The investigation, which extended over a period of several months and involved extensive travel by several investigators to multiple states and the nation's capital, was apparently funded by Wallgren, since some of the reports generated by the investigators were addressed to him at his residence at the Wardman Park Hotel in Washington, DC. The investigation primarily focused on Cain's brother, Bill, who had been admitted to Oregon State Hospital in Salem in December 1946. The report somehow made its way to Henry Jackson before or during his 1952 senate race against Cain, but there is no indication that Jackson ever used it in his campaign.[34]

The Armed Services Committee ultimately exonerated Wallgren of the charges Cain had made about his integrity, but the questions about his competence remained unanswered, and no one seemed to be able to overcome that problem. After Senator Harry F. Byrd (D-Va.) independently came to the same conclusion as Cain, the Armed Services Committee narrowly voted 7 to 6 to table the nomination. Some felt that Byrd and other Southern senators like Richard Russell (D-Ga.) were also using the Wallgren nomination to get back at Truman for his support of civil rights. Truman bowed to the inevitable and, on May 17, 1949, wrote to his close friend:

My dear Mon:

It is with the deepest regret that I yield to your request to withdraw my nomination of you to be Chairman of the National Security Resources Board.

Like you, I am convinced that had your name been permitted to go before the whole Senate, the nomination would have been confirmed.

I want you to know that my faith in you is undiminished. From experience, I know the qualities of integrity, industry and high intelligence that you would have brought to the position for which I selected you. It is unfortunate in the public interest that the Committee charged with considering your nomination saw fit to lay it aside. For the reasons you so compellingly state, I have no choice now but to withdraw the nomination.

With deep appreciation of the fine spirit which prompted your request, I am, as always, with affectionate regards,

Very sincerely yours,

HARRY S TRUMAN[35]

Cain's action to block the Wallgren nomination was followed in June by his opposition to another Truman appointee. He joined with Senators Bricker of Ohio, Homer Capehart of Indiana, and an unlikely ally, Lyndon B. Johnson of Texas, to block Truman's re-appointment of the liberal regulator, Leland Olds, to another term as chairman of the Federal Power Commission. The conservative Republicans opposed Olds because of his politics. Johnson opposed him because Olds had opposed an oil and gas pipeline that Johnson favored. Again, Truman had to back down from a favored appointment.[36] The President, however, ultimately got the last word by appointing Wallgren to replace Olds as chairman of the Federal Power Commission. Cain opposed this nomination, too, but without his former vehemence. Still, he managed to couple his opposition with a criticism of Truman for not yet filling the NSRB opening.

The vehemence of Cain's attack was remembered by his critics for the rest of their lives. Letters to Magnuson's office likened Cain's actions in office to those of former Washington congressman Marion Zioncheck, whose escapades included dancing in a DC fountain and driving on the White House lawn. One writer asked Magnuson if Cain had "gone crazy or [was] just plain nuts?"[37] But Cain had no regrets. He later said, "I simply did not think him big enough."[38]

Cain's opposition to Wallgren showed another side of Harry Cain that is not generally known. His opposition to an individual or an issue was often very personal—more than political grandstanding. Cain often conducted extensive private research, spending considerable amounts of his own time and money (the latter always in short supply). Perhaps it was the former newspaperman in him. In 1940, Cain had uncovered unfavorable financial information about Melvin Tennent during the 1940 Tacoma mayor's race, but never used it publicly. Later, during his term on the Subversive Activities Control Board, Cain would use his own funds, even traveling around the country, to check out the stories of individuals who claimed that they were being unfairly targeted by the federal government's internal security program.

In September 1949, Cain announced that he was considering a scheme that was bizarre even for him. With more than two years remaining on his own Senate term, he began to actively consider a campaign against the state's senior Senator, Warren Magnuson, who was up for re-election in 1950. Cain would not have to resign his own seat in order to run, and if he lost, he could return to the Senate. If he won, Cain was confident that Arthur Langlie—once again the state's governor—would appoint another Republican to replace him. No senator in history had ever run against another sitting senator from his own state. Because of that and the obvious political benefit, Cain liked the idea.[39] Cain believed that Washington's voters should have the opportunity to choose between a conservative like himself—a "*true* liberal"—and a "Fair Dealer" like Magnuson.[40] Cain also felt that there was much to run against in Magnuson's record and personal life—all the more so if the important Sand Point Naval Air Station was closed as a budget-cutting measure or Boeing decided to move to Wichita in order to cut costs. "Friendship and common sense necessarily dictate that I give the proposal my earnest consideration. In the meantime, the Washington state Republican party may develop one or more candidates against Senator Magnuson that would make it unnecessary for me to follow the suggestions of my friends."[41]

However, while many business leaders supported Cain's conservative views, they valued Magnuson's influence in Washington, DC, even more. After all, hadn't "Maggie" saved Boeing? One Cain supporter expressed his loyalty in a letter to Cain's secretary but said that the idea that Cain might challenge Magnuson "was as punk an idea as could be dreamed up. Maggie gets a lot of Leftist votes, but there are also a lot of Republicans who are Magnuson advocates. Cain against Magnuson is a screwball idea." He predicted that "if Harry Cain goes against Magnuson, Harry would lose."[42]

Another problem was Cain's changing relationship with his early mentor, Arthur Langlie. The latter belonged to the "big tent" faction of the Republican Party, which believed that they needed to court organized labor and appeal to a wide spectrum of viewpoints in order to win statewide elections in Washington State. The moderates believed that Cain and the conservatives practiced what they called "Kamikaze politics" and held no-compromise views that only polarized the electorate. Cain and other conservatives believed that the moderate's "wishy-washy" approach was a violation of core Republican values and that the party should oppose the Democrats rather than try to mimic them. [43] In the end, after a careful consideration of the political realities, Cain decided not to run against Magnuson, and that honor fell to the moderate W. Walter Williams, a Seattle mortgage banker, who beat the red-baiting Albert Canwell in the Republican primary but lost by a large margin to the popular Warren Magnuson.[44]

His consideration of a race against Magnuson only added to the dismay and growing concern by some of his advisors, supporters, and constituents at home. They were increasingly concerned about the effectiveness of Cain's staff and his willingness to listen to them. Marian Goodwin and Ernie Wetherell had returned home at the end of 1948. Art Burgess was then promoted to replace Wetherall as Executive Secretary in November 1948. Perhaps there was no one left on his staff who had the ability to rein in his potentially self-destructive instincts. They decided that Emily Walker, a close friend of Cain's for many years, who had worked for him during the Golden Jubilee Celebration and supported him while mayor, should join his staff to try to calm things down. A no-nonsense newspaper reporter and columnist, six years his senior, Walker seemed like the perfect choice. She moved to Washington, DC, and tried to exert a restraining influence on him. She recalled that "things were beginning to deteriorate after he'd served in office for two years. That was when I joined his staff at the behest of his supporters here (in Tacoma), who thought I might be able to steer him back onto what they thought was the right path. They were mistaken. He was off and running in the direction he followed until his defeat, often with powerful support [from some of those] in the Senate [who urged him forward] on some of the issues he fought for or against."[45] Unfortunately, those senators didn't vote in Washington State.

The Cains were more or less able to repair their marriage, and the family returned to their hectic routines. Marj took care of the children's needs and socialized with friends, taking advantage whenever possible of Washington's meager theatrical scene. It was a difficult time for the children. They would spend all or most of the year attending public school in Washington, DC, and their summers in Tacoma, having to live in one or another of the rental units the family had acquired. It is not surprising that the children's fondest memories were of those summers, spent among old friends in Tacoma.[46]

It was also at about this time that Cain began to have his first serious difficulties with the press. Previously, his personal and professional relationships with the media had generally been excellent. As a former newspaperman, he understood reporters and their needs—having the occasional drink, providing them with good copy and frequent photo opportunities, and making them feel important. In the past, his friendship with them was real, and they responded in kind. However, the national press corps was different from their counterparts in Tacoma and Washington State—then, as now, they were more aloof, more cynical, more conscious of their exalted positions and reputations, and far less likely to overlook faults and weaknesses. He had recently provided the national press corps with lots of copy, and much of it hadn't been positive. In a friendly 1949 story about Cain in *Collier's*, feature writer James C. Derieux described him as "an energetic, gesticulating speaker who uses an extravagant number of words." He noted that "while some of the national press rated Cain as one of the ablest of extemporaneous wordsmiths in the nation, others substituted the adjective 'extraneous' for extemporaneous."[47]

In its October 24, 1949, issue, *TIME* magazine's influential Capitol Hill reporter Frank McNaughton referred to Cain as a "garrulous lightweight"[48] and then went after him again in the March 20, 1950, issue penning a derogatory story called, "The Senate's Most Expendable." McNaughton's story began:

> In the Senate Restaurant, and along the tiled Senate corridors, Senators are known not only by the headlines they make but also by the company they keep; by their native ability and practical effectiveness as legislators; by the work they do, or avoid. A favorite pastime is picking the worst of the lot. It involves standards of comparison.

> It is easy to sigh for the days of Senators with tongues of silver and minds of steel, to forget that some of today's Senators rank high in character and vision, and that few of the present Senators are as bad as some specimens of recent history—the Bilbos, Huey Longs, "Pappy" O'Daniels and "Cotton Ed"

Smiths. Some are merely time servers and seat warmers who are as incapable of harm as of greatness. There are others whose antics are sometimes cheap and whose motivations are sometimes sordid. But their faults in one area of lawmaking or politicking are offset by their usefulness in others. After allowances are made for such human frailty, these eight would turn up on most lists of the Senate's most expendable men:

Kenneth D. McKellar, Democrat from Tennessee, 81, relentless in his prejudices, vicious in his vendettas.

Patrick A. (Pat) McCarran, Democrat from Nevada, 73, pompous, vindictive and power-grabbing—a sort of McKellar with shoes on.

William E. Jenner, Republican from Indiana, who is devoid of influence among his colleagues and partisan-minded to the last brain cell.

Glen H. Taylor, 45, Democrat from Idaho, the banjo-twanging playboy of the Senate.

William Langer, Republican from North Dakota, who was almost barred from his Senate seat in 1941 on grounds of "moral turpitude" growing out of some old charges of corruption while he was governor of North Dakota.

George W. Malone, isolationist Republican from Nevada, a onetime prizefighter who fights a loud, long fight for narrow sectional interests.

Elmer Thomas, Democrat from Oklahoma, 73, who votes pro-labor often enough to win labor's support at elections, but owes much of his backing to oil and private utilities.

and,

Harry Pulliam Cain, Republican from Washington, 44, tall, lean, friendly—and a lightweight.

McNaughton's article included a short paragraph about each senator that justified his presence on the list. About Cain, he said:

As early as 1947, he urged withdrawal of occupation forces from Germany, and an end to the denazification program. On occasion, he subjects the Senate to hammy theatrics and wild filibusters. Some of his Senate colleagues would be inclined to rate him as no more than a noisy nonentity if he were not something more bothersome—the real-estate lobby's warmest friend.[49]

Cain was outraged by the story. Rather than let it go, he responded with a two-hour long diatribe against *TIME* and McNaughton delivered from the Senate floor. He began reasonably enough by recounting a series of tongue-in-cheek correspondences he had conducted with the magazine's editors over the past two days in which he attempted to determine who had written the article. (Cain knew exactly who had written the article and that he was sitting at that moment in the Senate press gallery.) Cain noted that *TIME* had recently taken advantage of certain tax breaks provided earlier by the government.

If he had ended it all there, it might have all been considered good fun, even though it took up the Senate's time. But he didn't end it there. Cain then unleashed a long and personal attack on McNaughton, who had previously written two sympathetic books about Harry Truman, saying that he had dropped out of the University of Missouri and had never registered to vote, and branding him, "4-F in peace and war." (The 4-F was a Selective Service deferment for men who were physically unfit for the draft.) Cain described McNaughton as "smug, arrogant, self-centered, vain, and frustrated." When he finished, the Senate was hushed. In the press gallery, Frank McNaughton sat imperturbably, as he had throughout Cain's diatribe.[50] Cain should have known better as a result of his previous long experience with the press. Other senators, reporters, and the staff of the Senate were not amused. They considered it beneath a senator's dignity verbally to assault a relatively unknown member of the press from the Senate floor. One wrote that Cain should "pick on a Pygmy your own size." Cain's outburst was, of course, duly reported in wire service reports and in the columns of political pundits in papers across the nation—including those back in Washington State.

9

"The Guy in the Sky"

PRESIDENT TRUMAN DELIVERED his fifth State of the Union Address on January 4, 1950, the day following the start of the Second Session of the 81st Congress. His words were prophetic: "The first half of this century will be known as the most turbulent and eventful period in recorded history. The swift pace of events promises to make the next 50 years decisive in the history of man on this planet." Noting that the "false promises of Communism" presented more than a military challenge, Truman called for continuing support for the United Nations, the European recovery program, and the passage of legislation then pending before the Congress to increase technical assistance and capital investment for underdeveloped regions.[1]

In domestic policy, the President called for curbing big business monopolies, aid for small business, and creating new independent business enterprises. Truman again urged the repeal of the Taft-Hartley Act, calling it "punitive in purpose and one-sided in operation," and told the lawmakers that the nation still required more new housing, particularly "housing for the lower and middle-income groups, especially in large metropolitan areas,"[2] and called for the extension of rent controls for another year. An abrupt end to controls would "precipitate a wave of exorbitant rent increases."[3] Truman twice asked for the passage of legislation that would create a new Columbia Valley Administration—a key goal of Pacific Northwest public power enthusiasts—and called for the enactment of the civil rights proposals he had first proposed in February 1948. To pay for these initiatives, Truman asked that federal expenditures "be held to the lowest levels consistent with our international requirements and the essential needs of economic growth, and the well-being of our people." Looking to his left at the Republicans, he told them not to forget that last phrase. Continuing his thought, he warned the Congress that it must "guard against the folly of attempting budget slashes which would impair our prospects for peace or cripple the programs essential to our national strength."[4] Truman spoke to Congress from a decidedly weakened position. Allegations of corruption among some of his staff members, foreign policy reverses, spy scandals, and charges of Communist influence in the State Department during the previous year had all taken their toll.

For Harry Cain, the new term began as a continuation of the previous one, with another fight over the President's proposed extension of federal rent controls, set to expire on June 30. With the extension looking as if it would pass the Senate, Cain announced in June that he would filibuster the measure. Fortified by pickles and coffee, potato chips and milk, and dressed in a tan gabardine suit with a special device strapped to his leg so he could relieve himself, he made the longest single speech of his Senate career, "rasping on," according to *TIME,* for twelve hours and eight minutes. "My fight is for fair play and freedom," he began.[5] Cain claimed, among other things, that rent controls were an illegal invasion of private property that led landlords into "involuntary servitude."[6] It was the fourth-longest filibuster on record, but it was all for naught. Cain, mouth drooping from exhaustion, agreed to end his filibuster if a vote to return the bill to committee was called. This motion failed by a vote of 44 to 25, and the bill passed the Senate by a vote of 36 to 28. The *Washington Post* seemed to sum up the views of many in a June 12 editorial that said, "Apart from the fact that the Cain filibuster has been a senseless waste of time and an exhausting ordeal for busy senators, it has distracted attention from the merits of the controversy over rent control."[7] An unintended result of Cain's filibuster was a series of nationally syndicated photographs showing him walking out of the Senate chamber, looking disheveled, exhausted, and decidedly un-senatorial. It was not good publicity.

At the same time, the Congress was also considering a bill to extend coverage to about ten million more persons under Social Security's old-age and survivors insurance program and to expand benefits substantially to the rest of those covered under the law. The President had included the proposal in his January budget message, and its provisions were essentially the same as those he had proposed unsuccessfully in 1948 and 1949. While conservative senators were unenthusiastic about the proposal, most felt that a vote against expanding Social Security would be political suicide. That didn't deter Cain from voting "no." The measure passed the Senate overwhelmingly with only two senators in opposition—Harry P. Cain of Washington and Hugh Butler of Nebraska. Cain later said that he wanted Social Security left as it was, pending a thorough and independent review of needed changes and new legislation to be offered in the next session of Congress. He later said that he didn't vote against Social Security itself but planned to strengthen the program by offering amendments to the program after he was re-elected in 1952. "I would say that probably half the Senate shared my view in whole or in part about the need for amendments, but I found myself in a position of voting "no" out of stubbornness."[8] Cain sent 500 letters to leaders throughout the country to try to explain his vote, but his reasoning failed to convince.

Truman's State of the Union Address also called specifically for the passage of the Columbia Valley Authority, another issue where Cain was at odds with a great many of his constituents. Actually, the issue had been around since long before Cain came to the Senate, but Truman's specific support for it in his 1950 State of the Union message placed the controversial issue on the front burner of debate over domestic policy.

The passage in 1933 of legislation creating the Tennessee Valley Authority (TVA) had been acclaimed as one of the greatest triumphs of the early New Deal. The legislation combined the powers of some twenty federal agencies into one coordinated regional planning and public works program covering parts of seven states. The states were among the poorest in the nation, but they were represented by some of the nation's most powerful federal legislators. Soon after the creation of the TVA, Washington Senator Homer T. Bone proposed a similar Columbia Valley Authority (CVA) to manage the Bonneville and Grand Coulee dams. Bone was joined by proponents of public power who felt that they had suffered at the hands of the private utilities for many years. They were joined by advocates of new industries dependent on cheap electricity, by farmers and orchardists who sought irrigation for their crops, by flood-control enthusiasts and assorted civic boosters who believed that an injection of federal funds into the area—even if it didn't match the level of the TVA—would be good for business.

By 1944, planning for the CVA had progressed far beyond the dams, but it was not yet a reality. Bone then left the Senate, and Hugh Mitchell, appointed to replace him by his former boss, vigorously took up the cause before he was defeated by Cain. When Cain had arrived in Washington, DC, he had hoped to finesse the issues. Using talking points that had been handed to him by Spokane Chamber of Commerce officials during a stop there on his train trip east, he called for a well-rounded, harmonious program that would expedite the "steady and intelligent" development of the Columbia Basin. "All persons concerned either directly or indirectly with public and private power and reclamation, must assume responsibility for a program that will be positive, logical, and understandable. . . . It should not be the program of one party or one group."[9]

To Cain, the proposed creation of the CVA represented everything he hated about big government and the Democrats: public sector competition with private enterprise, out-of-control federal spending, a new, bloated federal bureaucracy that increased its power at the expense of state and local government, the potential for transferring electricity generated in the Northwest to California, and a system of top-down management so extreme "that [it] borders on Communism."[10] Most important, Cain didn't want to create a massive, popular program for which the Democrats could take credit. However, by the time the Congress could take up the CVA again, foreign policy considerations, and then the Korean War, had intervened.

Although foreign policy was an area about which Cain felt he possessed considerable expertise, his votes on a series of foreign policy issues during his final two years in the Senate were as controversial as his votes on other issues. He had voted reluctantly to approve the Marshall Plan but then voted against the 1949 Military Assistance Act that provided arms for Western Europe and Korea. He then voted against the Point Four Program, a measure that provided technological skills and equipment to various poor countries, and later voted for a Republican-backed effort to end the Marshall Plan prematurely, contending that the cost of the Marshall Plan was no longer justified because of Europe's recovery efforts.[11] Cain later told his son, "Some colleagues thought my NATO votes contradictory. Horseradish!" Cain's view was that the NATO allies should first take an inventory of what they actually needed and that the U.S. should verify those needs. He did not agree that "we needed to 'crash ahead' because of the threat of war."[12]

When asked, Cain would often defend his Senate votes by saying that the only person he listened to when he had a tough decision to make was the "Guy in the Sky." He once told an interviewer that he listened to only three persons in making his toughest and most controversial decisions. "I am one, a dead man is the second, and a 'Guy in the Sky' is first."[13] The reference to the dead man was to Dr. G. B. Kerstetter, the front-running candidate who had died at Cain's feet only four days before the 1940 Tacoma mayoral election, paving the way for his election to public office. "When I am in a political jam, not certain what to do, that man stands before me. Maybe I'm under some kind of special obligation because of the way I won my first public office. I don't know. But I certainly feel that I must not let him down."[14] In 1960, he told a Miami reporter that the experience of watching Kerstetter die before him had become his "greatest strength and my greatest weakness. It gave me courage to act as I wanted to act—regardless. But it sometimes weakened the votes."[15]

By this time, his voting record and some of his personal decisions had become so controversial that some state Republican Party leaders questioned whether they should even use him to campaign statewide for local candidates in 1950. Langlie and the moderates controlled the state party apparatus, and together, they effectively kept Cain out of the state during the campaign. His only appearance was for Payson Peterson, who was running a hopeless race against Henry Jackson in the Second District.[16] Cain had very much wanted to campaign in the state as a means of promoting either his candidacy against Magnuson or his reelection bid in 1952 and never forgot the slight. State Democrats only added to the Republicans' discomfort when Art Garton, the state's Democratic Party chairman, sent a telegram to his Republican counterpart, J. M. (Bud) Dawley, on the eve of the Republican state convention challenging them publicly either to endorse or repudiate Cain's actions.

THE KOREAN PENINSULA had been partitioned mid-way between North and South since the end of World War II. The Soviet Union had declared war on Japan two days after the first atomic bomb was dropped on Hiroshima and, by August 15, 1945, had advanced to the 38th Parallel dividing the country. Following the war, the Soviets formed a Communist government to administer the North, and when their puppet government refused to participate in a United Nations-supervised national election in 1948, separate governments were created in each of the occupation zones. Both claimed sovereignty over the entire peninsula and sought to re-unite it under their respective forms of government. While the two governments engaged in occasional talks, they more often engaged in cross-border skirmishes and raids. These escalated into open warfare in the early morning hours of June 25, 1950, when North Korea invaded South Korea. There has been much speculation about the causes of the war—perhaps North Korea's Russian and Chinese benefactors misread America's foreign policy intentions in Asia following its disengagement from China or simply saw the situation as an easy way to unify the peninsula under Communist rule—but the North's attack clearly caught the United States and her allies off guard and unprepared. In accordance with the demobilization at the end of the war, the few U.S. infantry divisions remaining in the Pacific had been reduced to only 62 percent of their authorized firepower, and none of them was stationed in South Korea.[17]

Two days later, President Truman ordered U.S. forces to come to South Korea's defense, following a United Nations Security Council Resolution that had been passed while the Russians were boycotting the organization. Three days later, on June 30, Harry Cain was on the Senate floor, speaking in favor of an appropriations bill to fund the 1951 Military Assistance Program that he now knew would be painfully inadequate. Suddenly, a piece of ticker tape was handed to him. Pausing, he read it to the expectant senators. "The following is the text of the White House announcement authorizing the use of ground troops in Korea." He stopped. "Why should I read any further, Mr. President?"[18]

The Korean War was by far the most serious international crisis of Truman's presidency. It immediately changed his priorities, essentially ending his efforts to enact his Fair Deal domestic agenda and, at least temporarily, suspending the administration's "Europe First" strategy. Truman's decision to intervene in Korea was not dictated by the belief that the remote peninsula held any great significance for the United States; it was based on the premise that North Korea was acting on behalf of the Soviet Union, which was seeking to expand its influence into North Asia.

General Douglas MacArthur, a man with a storied military career, an outstanding record as the military governor of Japan, and a long-held, deep distrust of politicians and his own military superiors, was named commander of all U.N. troops in Korea. By the end of July, the situation was dire: his under-trained, under-equipped, peacetime soldiers were pushed back to a very tenuous perimeter around Pusan at the southernmost tip of the country. The only things that saved them were the Allies' control of the air and sea and the fertile, strategic mind of their commander.

9. "The Guy in the Sky"

On September 15, MacArthur countered North Korea's invasion with a brilliant amphibious invasion of his own at the South Korean port of Inchon, halfway up the western side of the Korean peninsula and within easy striking distance of Seoul, effectively cutting off the invaders. The U.N. troops broke out of their Pusan perimeter and began to move northward in the hope of cutting off and surrounding the retreating North Koreans. But re-establishing the original status quo was not enough for MacArthur—he now advocated a full invasion of the north while the North Koreans were in full retreat.

While they respected MacArthur's tactical victory at Inchon, Truman's military and political advisors believed that his proposal to invade the north all the way to the Yalu River was costly, unnecessary, and dangerous. If MacArthur's plan failed, the U.S. and its allies could face the possibility of an all-out war with both China and Russia. As Truman explained, "We are trying to prevent a world war—not to start one."[19] In the final analysis, Truman was not willing to expand a limited war to preserve the remaining Nationalist-held territory in South China or to start a general war in Asia to defeat the Chinese Communists and return the Nationalists to power. The long-term focus of the Truman administration was on Europe.

On September 11, with mixed advice coming from his advisors and with various warnings of a possible Chinese intervention being ignored, Truman allowed MacArthur to invade the north after a short meeting with him at Wake Island in the Pacific. MacArthur assured the President that there was very little possibility that the Chinese Communists would win the war and told reporters that the troops "would be home by Christmas." On October 2, Chairman Mao Tse-Tung met with members of the Chinese Politburo to discuss military intervention. Warned that America possessed overwhelming firepower, Mao reportedly told India's Premier Jawaharlal Nehru, "China has millions of people. They cannot be bombed out of existence. The death of ten to twenty million people is nothing to be afraid of."[20]

On October 19, the Chinese, who had secretly massed more than 450,000 men along the North Korean border, attacked south with overwhelming force, sending the U.N. troops reeling back to the 38th Parallel with heavy losses in the dead of winter. The situation was finally stabilized by MacArthur's new ground forces commander, Lieutenant General Matthew Ridgway, who restored the front lines to roughly where they had been along the 38th Parallel. In the meantime, MacArthur, seemingly unraveled by China's intervention, lobbied both the Truman Administration and Republicans in Congress to expand the war by re-arming the Chinese Nationalists and using atomic bombs to seal off the Korean peninsula and obliterate China's major cities. After suffering several days of anguish, in which MacArthur defied a direct order to cease his back-channel communications with the Republicans, Truman finally had enough and relieved MacArthur of his command on April 11, 1951. "I fired him because he wouldn't respect the authority of the president," Truman said. "I didn't fire him because he was a dumb son of a bitch, although he was, but that's not against the law for generals." [21]

Four days later, Cain and Democratic Senator William Benton of Connecticut squared off in a nationally broadcast Sunday night debate on CBS Radio's *People's Platform.* Cain called for a declaration of war "against all of the enemies of the United Nations either fighting in Korea or using contiguous and adjacent territory from which to launch attacks," and said that he would soon introduce legislation to that effect.

Cain followed up on his threat by introducing two totally conflict-ing resolutions simultaneously on April 17, 1951. The first was entitled "Declaration of State of a War between the North Korean Regime, the Chinese Communist Regime, and the Government of the United States," effectively a declaration of war against China. The second called for with-drawing from Asia altogether. It was entitled "Proposal for the Orderly Withdrawal of the Armed Forces of the United States from Korea." In his remarks supporting the resolutions—in between calling for the atomic bombing of China—Cain said that freedom "must either fight and sacri-fice; struggle and die to survive, or . . . withdraw in the hope that another opportunity to be successful will be afforded." The Senate was not ready to choose between those grim choices, and neither resolution ever saw the light of day. [22] Those choices *did*, however, provide an effective campaign issue for Cain's opponent in 1952.

MacArthur's dismissal by the already unpopular Truman set off an uproar in the Congress and across the nation. Wisconsin Senator Joseph McCarthy's immediate reaction was, "The son of a bitch should be impeached." [23] A Joint Committee of the Armed Services and Foreign Relations Committees was formed to investigate and hold hearings on MacArthur's dismissal, and Harry Cain was appointed to it. On June 25, Senator Richard Russell of Georgia, the Committee's powerful chairman, said that he hoped that the hearings would pave the way for re-creating a "genuine nonpartisan foreign policy." Cain issued his own statement, saying that he felt that the Chinese bases in Manchuria should be bombed "with everything we've got" until there is a peace agreement "satisfactory to us."[24] The hearings generated great public attention and bitter partisan infighting. The Democrats safely controlled the Committee and produced a final report that supported Truman's decision to fire MacArthur. Cain led a group of Republicans who drafted a minority report that proclaimed, "General Douglas MacArthur has set forth the only positive program for winning the Korean War."[25] The draft also accused the Truman Administration of failing to support the Chinese Nationalists and the Roosevelt Administration of losing the Chinese mainland as a result of decisions made at the Yalta Conference.[26]

MacArthur had been fired, not so much for believing that the United States should undertake a broader war but for actively conspiring with the Republicans to pressure the administration to undertake that general war. In the first instance, he was only guilty of gross insubordination. In the second, Truman and his advisors believed he was guilty of political treachery. At first, it appeared that MacArthur's position might prevail. The popular general undertook a triumphant tour of American cities after he returned home, defending his position and bitterly attacking the administration. MacArthur and the congressional Republicans had a strong ally in William Randolph Hearst, the now-conservative, rabidly anti-Communist czar of the nation's largest mass communications empire. In April 1951, Hearst warned his son Bill "not to let up on front-page publicity for General MacArthur."[27]

On November 14, 1951, MacArthur visited Tacoma, and Harry Cain was there to introduce him to a capacity audience at the College of Puget Sound's Memorial Fieldhouse. He called MacArthur "the greatest citizen your junior Senator has known." MacArthur replied with equal praise. "I don't think you people in this part of the world understand what a great record he [Cain] is making in the other part of the world. His fearlessness, his courage, and his Americanism are hard to realize unless you are in the halls of the U.S. Senate itself."[28]

The concerns about the war and dissatisfaction with the Truman Administration led to Republican victories in the midterm elections of 1950. The Republicans picked up five seats in the Senate and twenty-eight in the House, not unusual by normal standards, but a blow all the same for Truman, who had refrained from campaigning because of the war.

President Truman's sixth State of the Union address—his first as a war president—was delivered on January 8, 1951. It focused almost entirely on foreign policy. For the first time, he directly warned against "the threat of world conquest by Soviet Russia," and said that Korea represented "an attempt of the Russian Communist dictatorship to take over the world." Gone were the past references to his Fair Deal programs and the need to protect the nation from internal security risks.[29]

Cain's primary committee assignment also changed with the opening of the 82nd Congress from the Banking and Currency Committee to the Armed Services Committee, a change that Cain had actively sought. From that point forward, however, Cain was almost totally silent on housing and rent control issues. A man who had worked closely with him on the Banking Committee told an interviewer that Cain had said, "Being the nation's No. 1 real estate lobbyist is no way to become a second-term Senator from Washington or any other state."[30]

THE WAR IN Korea and MacArthur's firing only highlighted the rising tide of fear about the threat from Communism—both internal and external—that had been slowly building in the country since the end of the Second World War. Indeed, what eventually became known as the Cold War with the Soviet Union began almost immediately after the cessation of hostilities and lasted for more than twenty years. Particularly in the early years of this high-stakes confrontation, a nearly continuous series of events seemed to suggest that America was under assault by Communism both from within and without. First, there had been the well-publicized conviction of several American Communist Party leaders under the 1940 Sedition Act. That had been followed by allegations that some State Department officials had supported the Chinese Communists in their 1946–1949 civil war against Chiang Kai-shek, followed by the charges from the China Lobby that the Truman Administration had "lost China" because of the Communists' 1949 victory. Then came the surprise announcement in August 1949 that Russia had developed its own atomic bomb, followed by allegations of spying by a senior State Department official named Alger Hiss in 1948, his conviction for perjury

9. *"The Guy in the Sky"*

in 1950, and, finally, by the war in Korea, which started in June 1950. Truman's Gallup Poll approval rating dropped to only 22 percent.

The public's fears and passions were inflamed by the conservative media and by politicians like Harry Cain, Joseph McCarthy, and Richard Nixon, who were honestly concerned about the Communist threat but who were not above using the subject to their own political advantage. Allegations of Communist Party membership or even questionable associations had become an issue in a growing number of election campaigns between 1946 and 1950 and would become an even greater issue in the future. Harry Cain had used the issue against Seattle Congressman Hugh DeLacy and the leftist Washington Commonwealth Federation in 1946, indirectly helping to cause DeLacy's defeat. But no one characterized the indiscriminate use of Communism for personal gain more than Harry Cain's close friend, Wisconsin Senator Joseph McCarthy. Cain and McCarthy became more than close friends. Their lives would be intertwined for nearly a decade until their political views—but not their friendship—separated.

Two years younger than Cain and elected with him to the Senate in 1946, McCarthy came from a hard-working, devout Catholic farm family and grew up in decidedly austere conditions during the Depression. Through hard work and personal effort, McCarthy went on to earn a law degree at Marquette University and was elected as a state circuit court judge in 1939. During the war, he joined the Marine Corps and served as an intelligence officer in a dive-bomber squadron in the Pacific.

Like Cain, McCarthy started his political life as a Democrat. Like Cain, he had run, and lost, an election for the U.S. Senate in 1944. As with Cain, his war service was instrumental in his winning his Senate seat. Once in the Senate, the two gravitated toward each other. Both disdained Washington's social life and had decidedly unpretentious tastes. Both shared a love of sports and perhaps more than an occasional drink. They were both shameless self-promoters who thirsted for public recognition. Both held decidedly anti-East Coast establishment political viewpoints, and some believe that this bias had a great deal to do with the fervor of McCarthy's attack on the Dean Acheson-led State Department in 1951.[31] Cain and McCarthy were also alike in that neither one of them could be controlled in the conventional sense. However, unlike Cain, who had become a highly recognizable member of the Senate in a relatively short period of time, McCarthy spent his early Senate career as a relatively undistinguished back-bencher. Taft and the Republican leadership paid little attention to him. When committee assignments were announced in January 1949, McCarthy complained bitterly, saying that his second-rate assignments would be "extremely embarrassing to me in my State."[32] By flouting Senate customs, ignoring established courtesies, and failing to defer properly to seniority, McCarthy never became a member of the Senate "club," and this, ultimately, had much to do with his eventual undoing.

On February 9, 1950, McCarthy made a speech at a Lincoln Day Dinner to the Ohio County Women's Republican Club at the McLure Hotel in the unlikely location of Wheeling, West Virginia. Few in the audience of local Republican women had ever heard of McCarthy. He didn't even have a prepared speech. Speaking from a pile of loose notes, McCarty claimed that four years earlier, former Secretary of State James F. Byrnes had responded to an inquiry from a congressman about the progress of a program that was then being used to screen State Department employees to determine their loyalty. Byrnes had reported back that his department had found 284 individuals unfit to serve because of former Communist Party activities but that, to date, only seventy-nine had been dismissed. This presumably left 205 "known Communists" working in the State Department. Only the right-wing *Chicago Tribune* reported McCarthy's remarks in a few paragraphs on its inside pages. The next day, however, the story was picked up by the national wire services, and Joseph McCarthy, the junior senator from Wisconsin, become an instant celebrity.[33] Overnight, McCarthy had finally found an issue that would lift him from the anonymity of his back-bench Senate career.

Joseph McCarthy gave the anti-Communist movement a name and, in return, they gave him his agenda and much of his ammunition. McCarthy brought to the cause his enormous energy, a genius for publicity, and a complete unwillingness to play by the rules. He had always been an outsider—a renegade. In a 1960s interview, Cain said that McCarthy had talked with him about his Wheeling speech prior to making it. "All of us questioned the number of Communists or fellow travelers in the State Department he included. He admitted the lack of factual knowledge and said he would leave this number out. In giving the speech, the number was about twice what he had tried out on us."[34] Republican leaders privately advised McCarthy to get some help in verifying his numbers. Publicly, they refrained from criticizing their colleague, but privately they were concerned. Robert Taft, an ardent anti-Communist like his father, told a friend that McCarthy had "overstated a good case . . . he made allegations which are impossible to prove which may be embarrassing before we get through."[35]

But the timing of McCarthy's speech couldn't have been better. A few weeks before the Wheeling speech, Alger Hiss, a former senior U.S. diplomat, United Nations official, and president of the Carnegie Foundation for International Peace, had been convicted of lying about his past connections to Russian intelligence courier Whittaker Chambers. The publicity resulting from the conviction, and then the guilty verdict itself, convinced large numbers of Americans who had not previously taken the charges of Communist espionage very seriously that there was, indeed, a growing threat to America's internal security.[36]

In the days and weeks that followed, McCarthy had trouble proving his allegations or even keeping his numbers straight. The Senate's Democratic leadership, forced to react because of the growing sensationalism surrounding McCarthy's charges, created a subcommittee of the Foreign Relations Committee, chaired by veteran Senator Millard Tydings of Maryland, to look into his charges but, in reality, to try to discredit McCarthy. The resulting hearings, which began in March 1950, were marked by partisan infighting, with the Committee's report calling McCarthy's charges "a fraud and a hoax" and Republicans calling the report a "brazen whitewash of [a] treasonable conspiracy." Ultimately, the full Senate had to vote three times to accept the Tydings Committee report, with the Democrats winning each time on a straight party-line vote.

In July, a month after the outbreak of the Korean War, columnist Drew Pearson, in a further effort to discredit McCarthy, charged that he had falsified part of his Marine Corps combat record. At McCarthy's request, Cain personally examined McCarthy's complete military service file and then answered McCarthy's critics with a long and thoroughly documented rebuttal on the Senate floor.

McCarthy came to be a feared, potent force in American life. Many believed that he played an important role in helping to defeat Millard Tydings for re-election in Maryland in 1950 and in electing a young John F. Kennedy in Massachusetts by pointedly *not* campaigning for the Republican incumbent, Henry Cabot Lodge, following a personal request by Kennedy's father. It was rumored that the aristocratic Lodge would not appear on the same platform as McCarthy.[37] Whether McCarthy had any real impact on Tydings's defeat or on Kennedy's election was immaterial. Others *thought* he had, and that was enough to create panic and fear throughout official Washington, DC.

Following President Truman's firing of General MacArthur, McCarthy's attacks on the Truman Administration became, if possible, even more intense. Alonzo Hamby, one of Truman's best biographers, writes that within two months in 1951, McCarthy accused the President of being a drunk and his two top national security officials, Secretary of State Dean Acheson and Secretary of Defense George Marshall, of being traitors.[38] Most Republicans still refused to denounce him publicly. Robert Taft came close. "Marshall," he said, had followed "the most stupid possible policy [as Secretary of State in 1947 and 1948] . . . and subsequent events in Formosa and Korea stemmed directly from it." But "I do not agree with Senator McCarthy's accusations of conspiracy or treason."[39] Harry Cain kept silent. He agreed with the spirit, if not necessarily the substance, of McCarthy's allegations.

Although Cain was often accused of being a "follower" of Joseph McCarthy, such was not the case. While they were close personal friends, he was never a *follower* of McCarthy. As we have seen, Cain became concerned about Communist influence within the Washington Commonwealth Federation as early as the late 1930s and attacked one of its founders, Washington congressman Hugh DeLacy, during the 1946 election by claiming that DeLacy was both a Communist and the subject of an unreleased report by the House Un-American Activities Committee.

All of this happened well before McCarthy's 1950 Wheeling, West Virginia, speech. From that point on, Harry Cain generally supported McCarthy but became increasingly concerned about his methods and some of his later choices of targets. Cain waited longer than most—until he was out of the Senate and serving on the Subversive Activities Control Board—finally to break ranks with McCarthy, although they remained personal friends and Cain never criticized him by name in public. As Cain later remembered, "It was a strange, perplexing and interesting relationship I had with McCarthy. For several years before his death we were the best of friends but unrelenting enemies. He never attacked me personally as he did many others, and I never referred to him in any speech. We just felt differently and acted accordingly. Joe used to grin, express regret that I had grown soft, and then in confidence confess that if my views picked up much more public support he would be forced to find another issue. He was, indeed, an amazing fellow."[40]

9. *"The Guy in the Sky"*

About the same time that McCarthy began televising his investigation of Communists in government, Senator Estes Kefauver (D-Tenn.) was beginning to investigate the involvement of organized crime in the nation's cities and in interstate commerce. In May 1950, the Senate created a five-member Special Committee to Investigate Organized Crime in Interstate Commerce, and Kefauver, a former Tennessee congressman, who had been elected to the Senate only two years earlier, arranged to be appointed its chairman. Tall and sanctimonious, Kefauver had a reputation in the Senate as a maverick and had few friends or even admirers. One Democratic insider referred to him as the most hated man in Congress.

As "reality television" (a term that would not become known until decades later), the Kefauver Committee hearings far surpassed McCarthy's televised grilling of little-known witnesses about the arcane details of American foreign policy. Instead, Kefauver's hearings featured well-known Mafia crime bosses and their often colorful and humorous associates and provided a fascinating picture of organized crime in America. Beginning in May 1950, they lasted for fifteen months, were held in fourteen cities, and questioned at least 600 witnesses—often disclosing ties with state and local Democratic officials.

On March 26, 1951, as the hearings were winding down in Washington, DC, two members of the Cleveland crime syndicate, Morris Kleinman and Louis Rothkopf, were called to testify. Kleinman refused, saying that "I am not an actor and have had no public speaking training. From newspapers I can demand a retraction or sue for libel. I cannot check on what is happening to me on the television or radio. If the television industry wants me to boost their sales, I am entitled to be consulted. This is a violation of my constitutional rights. I will not perform to help TV. I will not proceed further until this apparatus is shut off and removed." Kefauver decided to charge them with contempt of Congress and to have them held in lieu of $10,000 bail.[41]

Cain became increasingly dubious both about the methods used and the results obtained by Kefauver's committee. "The longer I watched these hearings, the less I could understand what some of the harassment and some of the circus antics had to do with the development of information. It mattered not to me that their reputations were unsavory or that they might be using the lights and TV cameras as an excuse not to testify. In my judgment, their contentions were reasonable and valid."[42] When the contempt resolution against Kleinman and Rothkopf was brought before the Senate for a vote, Cain defended them. He believed that their constitutional rights had been violated. In an eleven-page speech delivered on August 9, Cain denounced the hearings as "television extravaganza tactics" and a "vaudeville show."[43] When it came time to vote on the contempt resolution, Cain was one of only thirteen senators to vote "no." The charges were later overturned in court. Cain later remembered that "more than one came to me and said quietly, 'Gee, you couldn't be more right, and your logic is undeniable, but we had to vote against you because we can't take time to go home and explain why we were defending those crooks.'"[44] Perhaps Cain should have listened to them. As his own re-election campaign approached, it was hard for Cain to explain to Washington's voters why he had apparently been defending major Mafia crime bosses while Estes Kefauver campaigned for his opponent.

Two other Cain actions in late 1950 were noteworthy in appearing to highlight his well-developed unpredictability. The first was his personal defense of Anna M. Rosenberg, a Hungarian immigrant who had served with distinction in various positions during the war and had been honored with the Medal of Freedom and nominated by the President to be Assistant Secretary of Defense. Her liberal politics and wide range of associates led McCarthy and others to launch an all-out campaign to oppose her nomination on the grounds that she was a Communist or, at least, a Communist sympathizer. Rosenberg was hauled in before the House Un-American Activities Committee, where most of McCarthy's objections were proved to be groundless. When her nomination reached the Senate Armed Services Committee, of which Cain was a member, he saw nothing inconsistent in defending her against McCarthy's unsubstantiated allegations. "I was shocked by the allegations offered by witnesses without supporting evidence and became convinced that perjury was being committed."[45] When her nomination was approved later that month, Cain was generally given the credit.

The other action involved Cain's support of military aid to Spain and its dictator, Francisco Franco. With the United States fighting the Communists in Korea, Spain's economy in shambles, and the conservative Franco increasingly opposing the Soviet Union, Cain's view was that the U.S. should support any nation that was friendly to us. Repeating Robert Taft's oft-used remark to Ashley Holden of the *Spokane Spokesman-Review*, Cain said that "Never again, am I going to vote for a bipartisan foreign policy just because it is bipartisan."[46] Truman was disgusted by Franco but acquiesced to Acheson and Marshall, who were looking for possible U.S. bases in Europe. Formal diplomatic relations with Spain were finally restored during the Eisenhower Administration.[47]

BY THE START of 1952, it was clear that the popular, six-term Democratic congressman from Washington's Second District, Henry M. "Scoop" Jackson, would be Harry Cain's opponent in the upcoming U.S. Senate race. A son of hardworking Norwegian immigrant parents, Jackson grew up in a socially conservative family in Everett, Washington, a radical, blue-collar mill town known as "The City of Smokestacks."

Jackson's father once worked at the Anaconda copper smelter in Montana and had been a police officer, a concrete worker, and later, an independent contractor in Everett. He was a union man—the Plasterers and Cement Masons Local 190 elected him as their treasurer for twenty-six years—but he was not a radical. Jackson's daily life was largely influenced by his mother and his older sister, Gertrude, who would both play a prominent role in Jackson's future political life. Jackson was a hardworking and thrifty young man. He earned his nickname "Scoop" when he was fifteen, earning a national award for delivering 74,880 *Everett Herald* newspapers without a complaint.[48]

Jackson entered the University of Washington in 1930, living at home, working his way through school, and commuting thirty miles each way with a friend who owned a car. A serious but not an exceptional student, he graduated from the University of Washington Law School with an interest in politics. In 1932, Jackson and his longtime friend and associate John Salter formed the Roosevelt First Voter's League. Initially, they were the group's only members. Jackson and Salter saw the pain that hard times inflicted on everyday citizens at the relief office where they both worked.

With the help of his sister Gertrude, Salter, his Delta Chi fraternity brothers, and other friends, Jackson ran for and was elected as Snohomish County's youngest-ever Prosecuting Attorney at age twenty-six. In 1940, with the incumbent Democratic congressman Mon Wallgren eyeing a run for the U.S. Senate, Jackson decided to run for the seat and defeated six other Democrats to be elected to the House of Representatives. At twenty-eight, he was the youngest member of Congress. He was a quiet, hard-working congressman who shied away from the limelight, worked hard for his constituents, and gravitated toward mentors like Speaker of the House Sam Rayburn, Washington's senior Senator, Warren Magnuson, and Estes Kefauver. Like other prominent Washington State Democrats, Jackson was a strong supporter of public power and the proposed Columbia Valley Authority. Significantly, Jackson was the only Democrat in Washington's congressional delegation to survive the Republican landslide of 1946. Learning his job from Warren Magnuson, Jackson became adroit at the "bring home the bacon" style of Washington politics. Like Magnuson, Jackson joined the military in 1942 and completed army basic training, but he took advantage of the same one-time offer by President Roosevelt that allowed Magnuson and other members of Congress to return to their legislative duties before the 1944 elections.

Jackson and Cain also shared some similarities. They both grew up in working-class towns during the Great Depression. Both supported the election of Franklin Roosevelt as young men and founded political organizations to support him. Both had experience in cleaning up vice in their communities. Jackson had even once voted to extend the life of the House Un-American Activities Committee but then voted not to fund it.[49] The two men generally agreed when it came to the threat posed by the Soviet Union. Under other circumstances, the two men might earlier have developed the friendship and respect that they established later in life. But by 1952, Cain was vulnerable, and Jackson was ambitious.

Jackson had long considered running against Cain and had turned down an offer from President Truman in 1950 to be appointed Under Secretary of the Interior in order to be ready to run for the Senate when the opportunity came. John Salter and Magnuson thought the time was right but didn't want a costly primary race between Jackson and the other likely Democratic contender, Hugh Mitchell. Magnuson talked Mitchell into running for governor in 1952 while Jackson's staff, with the help of the CIOs and other union research departments, prepared a meticulous account of Cain's controversial voting record.[50]

Flanked by his mother and sister at their family home in Everett, Jackson announced his candidacy on his fortieth birthday on May 31, 1952. Not directly referring to Cain, Jackson noted that "senators who have repeatedly tried to scuttle our foreign aid programs, military and economic, are penny-wise and pound foolish. . . . The future cannot be won with faint-hearted, confused policies. It calls for aggressive, intelligent, stable leadership in the Senate. It calls for men in the Senate who understand our state's potentialities. It calls for two senators who will work together."[51]

Cain later remembered his 1952 Senate campaign as a "no-holds-barred, rough and tumble contest in which little was spared by either side."[52] Cain was busy with his duties in the Senate but tried to fly home to campaign as often as possible. On June 8, Cain made a late-night speech on the Senate floor chiding his colleagues for failing to follow through with an investigation of the "China Lobby." With only one other senator present and sitting in the presiding officer's chair, Cain spoke for an hour and inserted seventy-three pages of material into *The Congressional Record*.[53]

Congress adjourned on July 7 to allow its members to go home and campaign. The Republican National Convention began in Chicago later the same day. It was the first political convention ever to be nationally televised. Cain, who had supported Eisenhower for the Republican nomination—much to Taft's disappointment—delivered the final speech of the convention on July 11 in the normal Cain fashion, shirt collar open and tie loosened. Entitled "Young Americans, The Future Belongs to You," his speech encouraged the youth of America to support the Republican Party.

Cain entered into the campaign against Scoop Jackson supremely confident that the power of incumbency, plus an electorate tired of Harry Truman, would carry him and the national Republican ticket to victory in November. However, it soon became clear that Cain's candidacy was in trouble. His support of Taft-Hartley had insured the dedicated opposition of organized labor and their supporters. Other controversial votes, his penchant for filibusters and publicity stunts, the rumors of his affair and other recent unflattering publicity, along with his support for Joe McCarthy, led many moderate Republicans and independents to conclude that Cain was out of touch with both them and his state. He had become a polarizing figure. Voters were either for or against him, and there was little room for middle ground.

An added problem was that in early June Cain discovered that he needed a throat operation that required a brief hospitalization and a month's rest, effectively keeping him off the campaign trail at a critical time. He spoke publicly only eight times between his operation and August 15.[54] Within the family and his campaign organization, the forced absence from the campaign trail was considered to be a major problem.[55]

An even bigger problem was the fact that his opponent ran an innovative and thoroughly modern campaign. Jackson's advertising campaign stressed the congressman's integrity and record of accomplishments, while plastering the state with large billboards featuring a full-color picture of Jackson and the slogan "Jackson will make a *great* U.S. Senator." Salter, always the political insider, made sure that the socially inhibited Jackson stayed connected with Democratic politicians throughout the state.

While he had a liberal voting record on domestic issues, Jackson was one of the Congress's leading experts on atomic energy and national defense. Cain tried to attack his liberal voting record and paint him as being insufficiently anti-Communist. It was difficult, but Jackson successfully resisted the temptation to respond to Cain's "soft on Communism" charges until the very end of the campaign, effectively keeping the innuendoes from becoming a campaign issue. The Jackson camp also turned down any and all attempts by Cain to hold face-to-face debates, recognizing Cain's penchant for oratory and his record as a political body-puncher. Even so, Cain's continuing charges, and the fact that Joe McCarthy had announced that he was coming to Washington to campaign for Cain, caused Jackson some sleepless nights.

Cain campaigned under the banner "Retain Cain." On August 14, he was the keynote speaker at the American Legion's statewide convention in Tacoma. In a voice still strained and raspy from his throat operation in June, he sharply attacked America's foreign policy, telling the Legionnaires that America could not "buy security." The result of trying to do so in Europe, Greece, and Turkey had "dangerously weakened the integrity of the American dollar." Cain said that the war in Korea "has taught us what the major weaknesses of the United Nations are. For so long a time as the power of the veto is permitted and exercised [in the United Nations], so long will [it] remain as a debating society."[56] Cain later remembered that when he arrived at the auditorium, the Jackson forces had already distributed a flyer, the substance of which was that "this fellow Cain had never voted yes for anything in his life. That he was against everything except that nefarious slave-labor Taft-Hartley law. It was a very persuasive piece of information."[57]

Cain also continued his efforts to generate support from organized labor, but with little success. Labor was solidly behind Jackson. Cain claimed that labor leaders had "stacked the deck" against him, organizing political seminars in which Jackson supporters were allowed to speak but Cain supporters were not. Cain claimed that the State A.F. of L. had Jackson in its pocket and tried to practice "mind control over the workers of Washington."[58] Ed Weston, the president of the Washington State Federation of Labor, which had supported him in 1946, promised to "slit . . . Cain's political throat from ear to ear," because of his past votes on labor issues.[59] It was not just state labor leaders who were after Cain. In his news conference of August 14, 1952, the President was asked about his reaction to the latest issue of the *CIO News*, which had listed Cain as one of labor's eight "worst enemies." The reporter wanted to know whether the President included Cain on his list of "those you would most like to see replaced this fall." Truman responded with more equanimity than might be expected. "I want to see Democrats elected everywhere. I have no special pick on anybody."[60]

Cain also faced problems from within his own party. The 1952 Republican campaign to select their presidential nominee was one of the most contentious of the century. The conservative Robert A. Taft of Ohio and his supporters battled the more moderate Dwight Eisenhower and his followers as the party divided along bitter and uncompromising lines. In Washington State politics, Langlie epitomized the moderate Eisenhower wing of the Republican Party, while Cain typified its conservative-isolationist congressional faction led by Taft. While Langlie enthusiastically supported Eisenhower, Cain at first leaned toward Taft but ultimately supported Eisenhower when it became clear that 1952 was going to be a Republican year. Langlie soon began to distance himself from Cain over his votes on Taft-Hartley and other issues, but by 1950, their differences had grown even deeper, although both denied their disputes and complained of deliberate attempts by the press and others to exploit their differences. However, by 1952, their policy differences were so great that Langlie actually considered running against Cain in the Republican primary before deciding to seek a third term as governor.[61] The *Seattle Times* reported that state Republican leaders were trying to negotiate a cease-fire but felt that it had about the same chance of success as the on-and-off peace negotiations in Korea.[62] In the end, Langlie effectively disassociated himself from Cain's reelection campaign in 1952. While he appeared with Cain and candidate Dwight Eisenhower during the latter's campaign tour of Washington State, his presence was meant to support Eisenhower, not Cain.[63]

For his part, Jackson in the early months of the campaign generally stuck to broad issues, such as keeping the nation strong and promoting the peaceful uses of atomic energy. Behind the scenes, however, his workers and surrogates tirelessly attacked Cain's "sorry" voting record on Taft-Hartley, the 70-group air force, Social Security, and Columbia River development projects. They reminded voters of his recent marital problems and the time that he had once introduced two completely contradictory resolutions in the Senate on the same day. Reprints of negative national publicity, such as *TIME*'s "Senate's Most Expendable" story, a Joseph Alsop column in the *New York Herald Tribune* that claimed that Cain was "endowed with a matchless ignorance of foreign affairs," or the *Fortune* magazine article that had called him "not only remarkably negative but occasionally screwball" were widely distributed.

The state's primary election was held on September 9. Cain faced opposition from perennial Republican candidate Carl Viking Holman and Ed F. Oldfield, while Jackson ran unopposed in the Democratic primary. The result was one that could be interpreted either way. Jackson received approximately 65,000 more votes than Cain, but the combined Republican vote was larger than expected. Holman then asked his 50,000 supporters to switch and vote for Jackson. It was not good news for an incumbent Republican senator in an election that was otherwise shaping up to be a landslide year for the Republicans.

As the campaign began to heat up in September and October, both candidates hit each other hard—but not face to face—frustrating Cain to no end. Jackson continued to attack Cain's voting record. "Cain can talk from now until doomsday," Jackson said, "but he cannot escape the fact that he and the Left-wing Senator from Idaho, Glen Taylor, were the only two senators who voted against a 70-Group Air Force." Or, on another occasion, "Imagine, with our state facing a brownout in its defense plant operations . . . with thousands of acres of land thirsting for irrigation, Harry Cain turned his back on his constituents and voted against his state, national security and the prosperity of the region" by voting against an appropriation for Grand Coulee Dam.[64] After all was said and done, Jackson's strongest campaign point was that Harry Cain "cannot escape the fact that his six-year voting record, on both domestic and foreign policy, is a source of continuing embarrassment, even to his own party."[65]

The race was watched closely across the country. Sensing a potential Jackson victory, Cain was targeted by the national Democratic Party and organized labor. The Democratic Senatorial Campaign Committee flooded the state with materials that mirrored the points about Cain's voting record that Jackson was making. Cain attempted to refute the charges by releasing a detailed, seven-page press release that addressed each of the twelve charges with a detailed rebuttal that would be read only by his most avid partisans. A similar item-by-item defense of his voting record was sent out from his campaign headquarters in the form of a newsletter to supporters.[66] He also stepped up his campaign rhetoric against the AFL-CIO and the Washington State Labor Council for their "blind support" of his opponent. His fierce attacks only encouraged their belief that Cain's campaign lacked focus. To make matters worse, Cain also seemed to be targeted by the national press that began to use with their stories the highly unflattering pictures that had been taken of him following his twelve-hour housing filibuster—looking exhausted and disheveled, his facial muscles drooping from the effects of his childhood bout with Bell's palsy.

President Truman, Democratic presidential nominee Adlai Stevenson, and Senator Estes Kefauver, whose crime hearings Cain had attacked, all campaigned in the state for Jackson. In October, Republican presidential nominee Dwight D. Eisenhower visited Washington State. Cain and Governor Langlie joined him in Spokane for a cross-state "whistle stop" journey by train. At each stop, Ike urged voters to return Harry Cain to the Senate. Some of Cain's strongest supporters in the Senate, including Robert Taft, Styles Bridges, Everett Dirksen, William Knowland, and Joseph McCarthy, campaigned for Cain.

Seattle Times political writers William Prochnau and William Larson, in their biography of Jackson, penned a wonderful description of Cain's speaking style during the campaign. "Cain's voice was like thunder filtered through gravel. His personal appearance was electric. His speeches, delivered in a loosened-necktie, let's-get-down-to-business style, were almost hypnotic. His mobile face could change from an expression of joy to dark outrage in an instant. Always his hair was tousled. Just as he had jumped from airplanes into the action in Europe, he delighted in jumping into the midst of the political action, wherever it was."[67]

On October 3, Cain addressed a statewide radio audience to respond to remarks that the President had made while campaigning for Jackson throughout the state during the previous two days. With his voice fairly dripping with emotion, full of feigned anger, astonishment, and sarcasm, Cain appealed to his radio audience. "Tonight, I shall not say that our President abused your hospitality by telling you one lie after another, but I shall prove that our President insulted your collective intelligence and took for granted that you are among the most uninformed citizens to be found anywhere."

He then went on to refute, point by point, the President's characterizations of Republican opposition to a number of Pacific Northwest issues, including public power, land reclamation, and regional development. More than halfway through his fourteen-minute speech, he finally got around to his opponent, claiming that Jackson "thinks and acts in the image of Mr. Truman, but he has none of Mr. Truman's courage. Mr. Jackson, like Mr. Truman, has said many things about my own record in the Senate that are not true. I think I could make this Mr. Jackson eat his words if he would only dare to say in my presence what he says so willingly behind my back. Jackson of Everett is a coward who doesn't tell the truth!"[68]

It was clear that there was no love lost between Cain and the President. Cain was one of the most vocal members of what Truman called "the good-for-nothing, do-nothing, Eightieth Congress," and, never one to mince words, the President reprised the line at every stop on his campaign swing through Washington State. He went out of his way to make sure he spoke against Cain in Tacoma. The *Tacoma News Tribune* speculated, not without reason, that Truman did so in order to pay Cain back for blocking the nomination of Truman's old friend, Mon Wallgren.[69] Cain returned the President's feelings in kind. In a later interview taped not long before his death in 1979, Cain remembered that "I was a real opponent and antagonist of Harry S. Truman. I thought that when he was talking like that it was pure downright nonsense and I went around the country saying so. Subsequently, I have learned not to revere, but to admire and respect the memory of Mr. Truman." The President never forgot Harry Cain either. In later years, the two would occasionally meet each other at some event or other, and Cain recalled, "We were not close friends at *any* time, but he knew me and he would come up to me with a smile on his face and say, 'Hello,' and ask me, 'What kind of battle are you in now?'"[70]

Senator Joseph McCarthy flew into the state during the last days of the campaign, with the Cain camp hoping that his appearance would help to pull out a last-minute victory. McCarthy arrived tired and surly. He had recently undergone an operation for a hernia, and the incision was still painful. Scheduled to speak in Jackson's home town of Everett, McCarthy was set to remind the locals of Jackson's votes against the

House Un-American Activities Committee and his support for George C. Marshall and Alger Hiss. Unfortunately, McCarthy's plane was diverted to Portland by bad weather, and he missed the Everett rally.

The next day, he was scheduled to appear at what was billed as a press-club dinner and, later, a live television appearance before a large in-house and viewing audience. The press dinner turned out to be a raucous "roast" affair sponsored by the local press association in which McCarthy was to be pitted against Victor A. Meyers, Washington's longtime secretary of state, lieutenant governor, and its reigning political comedian. By the time McCarthy arrived late, still not feeling well and worried about getting to the TV interview on time, the audience had spent far too much time at the bar, with McCarthy's supporters and opponents already shouting at each other and even engaging in fist-fights. Someone threw a dinner roll at McCarthy while he was waiting impatiently to speak. He got angrier and angrier, according to Jackson's publicity director, Gerry Houck, who was there. "Finally, he pounded the lectern and said, 'God dammit, I did not come three thousand miles to be funny.' Vic Meyers walked up to the podium and said, 'I did not walk six blocks to be serious.'"[71] McCarthy was due at the television station and left the banquet hall, now in complete chaos, just before the police were called.[72]

McCarthy never let Cain forget that night. "He was rudely and roughly greeted in Washington State and he never recovered or forgot the treatment given him [at the] Press Club gathering in Seattle. Years later he implored me to determine the names of several who heckled him, for even then, he wanted to get even. He was indeed an amazing fellow."[73]

The TV appearance at Seattle's influential KING-TV turned out to be another fiasco. The station's attorney objected to certain passages in McCarthy's prepared remarks and told the Senator that he could not make them on the air. Angered by the decision, McCarthy decided to give no speech at all—not for Harry Cain and not about the allegations of Communist sympathy for Scoop Jackson—and stormed out of the studio.[74]

In the end, Cain decided to fall back on his greatest asset, the power of his own words. In a statewide radio address delivered in prime time on Friday, October 31, and framed as a letter to his son, Buzzy, then in his first year at Vermont Academy, Cain called Jackson a "moral coward" who "runs away from any and every opportunity to test the quality of his competence, capacity and knowledge against your dad." He thanked those fellow senators who had campaigned for him and mentioned letters of support he had received from Generals Matthew Ridgway, Mark Clark, and Douglas MacArthur. He contrasted his military service to Jackson's, who had only completed basic military training during the war. On the other hand, he decried the use of "malicious criticisms" published in national publications like *TIME*, *Red Book*, and *Pageant*, which his opponents had "reprinted and practically mailed from door to door."

Reminding his listening audience that in 1946 he had campaigned against the left-leaning wing of Washington's Democratic Party, he noted that since that time most of them had been defeated and discredited, but not all. Referring to Jackson and to Hugh Mitchell (who was then running for governor), he said, "Jackson and Mitchell are neither Communists nor fellow-travelers. They are merely the front men behind which the others remained unmolested in recent years gone by. I have no personal grievance against either man. I am against them because they are weak and spineless men." He ended his speech repeating the same ten points he had been using throughout the campaign and a verse from an inscription on a World War I memorial located in Edinburgh, Scotland, from which Matthew Ridgway was fond of quoting:

> If it be life that waits, then I shall live forever—unconquered, If it be death, then I shall die at last—strong in my pride and free.[75]

Cain's son Buzz has no memory of ever reading the letter that formed the basis of his father's final campaign speech. "Maybe I did get a copy back then, my first fall at Vermont Academy, but I doubt I would have paid much attention to it. Clearly I was not the primary audience that Dad had in mind. The tone of it suggests to me that he knew he had lost, and was very angry and frustrated as a result."[76]

Both major Seattle newspapers and the *Tacoma News Tribune* endorsed Cain, but in spite of their support, the polls showed that Harry was trailing badly. A little over a week before the election, columnist Drew Pearson alleged on his weekly radio program that the national Republican Party had given up on Cain and cut off all further financial support for his campaign. The story was quickly denied by the Cain campaign, but the damage was done. A last-minute advertising campaign tried to attach Harry to the coat-tails of the popular Eisenhower by emphasizing that Cain was a part of the larger Republican ticket.

9. *"The Guy in the Sky"*

That night, Richard Nixon, the Republican vice-presidential nominee, was in Tacoma to make his final address of the campaign. Cain was
tasked with making the introduction but spent much of his time defending
Nixon's candidacy. It was hoped that this final appearance with a member
of the popular Republican national ticket would allow Cain to squeeze
out a victory on Election Day the following Tuesday. But it was not to be.
Jackson overcame a Republican landslide in Washington State and across
the nation to win an anticipated but, nevertheless, impressive victory
over Cain—56 percent of the vote for Jackson (595,288) to 44 percent
for Cain (460,884). Otherwise, the scale of the Republican victory was
so great that the *Seattle Times* story about the election results in the next
morning's paper didn't even mention Jackson's victory until the ninth
paragraph.[77] Cain put the best face he could on the election results. He
told the *Tacoma News Tribune* that his joy in the Republican landslide
left him with no "tears or room for personal regret."[78] Privately, however,
Cain could not understand why the voters could not see the logic of his
past decisions.

In later years, Cain's decisions and his controversial voting record
in the Senate would be the subject of much conjecture and speculation
among his friends, former associates, and even his detractors—just as it
had been during his Senate campaign. In light of his later well-deserved
reputation as a civil libertarian, they wondered how a former progressive
mayor could have been transformed into a dogmatic, ultra-conservative,
reactionary U.S. Senator and then switch back to being a liberal again.

Cain never publicly answered that question adequately to most
people's satisfaction. It must have been difficult for him to talk about,
although he had always referred to himself as a liberal. Cain did, however, offer a few hints. He once told the author that he had believed that
"men were elected to the Senate to lead and not to be led" and that their
decisions "should be made, not by the force of public opinion but on the
basis of knowledge which a Senator has reason to doubt is available to
his constituents at home."[79]

In a 1961 interview with the author, Cain said, "You know, freshman members of the United States Senate are, historically, encouraged
to be seen and not heard, and that makes a lot of sense because one goes
to the Senate for a six-year term, so what is the rush? A large number
of Senators are re-elected again, and the object is to make a career of it;
therefore, why not be seen and not heard? *It was not possible for me to*

observe what made all kinds of sense [emphasis added]. How long had the Senate been controlled by the Democrats? The Republicans had been out of power for decades, almost. The very same people who advised me to be seen and not heard necessarily were the very same leaders who said you *must* be heard. And I just say it as a flat fact that Harry Cain . . . talked too much, too quick, and that was just not the right thing to do."[80]

Harry Cain, of course, was right. By any objective measurement, his term in the Senate was a personal and political disaster. Cain nearly lost his marriage. His unpredictable behavior led his enemies, and more than a few friends, to worry about his mental health. He had always been successful in dealing with problems and issues, less so in dealing with politics. In the highly partisan environment of Capitol Hill in the late 1940s, politics were often more important than issues. His controversial and often contradictory votes confused Cain's friends and confirmed the worst fears of his enemies. His strange inability as an accomplished communicator to adequately explain and defend his conservative-libertarian positions only added to Cain's problems. Undermined by less-than-flattering portrayals of him in the national press, Cain came to be seen as a caricature of the Republican right wing. Even when Cain dealt in detail with issues about which he was well informed, like the real estate industry, he came across—and not without reason—as the tool of vested interests.

In a typed, multi-page, 1971 letter to a Seattle film critic who had referred to Cain in a film review as "one of the most reactionary United States Senators in the history of the body," Cain responded to the charge with an amazingly introspective look back at his Senate career. "As a reactionary I reacted strongly against measures [I] believed to be adverse to the public interest. It seldom bothered me that a number of my positions were supported only by a small minority. Had I been concerned with self rather than country I would have acted much differently. My outstanding weakness was in mostly failing to adequately explain my actions to constituents and the general public."

Cain then cited as examples his long filibuster against rent controls, his opposition to most public housing proposals, his support of integrated public housing, his 1950 vote against extending Social Security, and his vote in favor of Taft-Hartley. To those he could have added his votes against the 70-group air force, and his filibuster against Mon Wallgren. "An idealist is one who represents things as they might be rather than as they are. Certainly I went to the Senate with stars in my eyes. Compromise came hard for me. . . . I was often angry and too impatient for my own good. After having served recently abroad in the military for several years I saw no need for compromise or delay."[81] Cain's perceptive self-awareness with the benefit of hindsight was impressive, but it must have made the fact that he was no longer a member of the U.S. Senate even more painful.

Many years later, his son Buzz was even more candid in summing up the reasons for his father's defeat. "Subsequent history suggests that he became a senator from Washington due to a very unusual and fortuitous set of events, and that his chances of remaining a senator from there were slim to none. His personal philosophy ran against the grain of the majority views in Washington, and he was never enough of a politician to try to disguise his own views. Some of his actions as senator, like making a symbolic vote against something Boeing really wanted, or purposefully antagonizing Dave Beck, show either unusual naiveté, a dangerous disdain for politics, or a really unbounded confidence in his ability to explain himself to the public, or maybe all three."[82]

10

"Can Freedom and Security Live Together?"

AFTER HIS SENATE defeat, Harry Cain may well have thought that his public career was ended. Following the election, he wasted no time leaving Tacoma for Washington, DC, taking the train on an indirect route by way of New Orleans on his return to the capital. Rampant speculation about his next career move began within a week. There were rumors about a TV network "news commentating" job or a position in the newly elected Eisenhower Administration. "I've been mulling over a lot of things in the last two months and now I have to make up my mind," he told the Washington correspondent for the *Tacoma News Tribune*.[1] Senator Joseph McCarthy lobbied the new Secretary of Defense, Charles E. Wilson, to consider Cain as a candidate for Secretary of the Air Force or Assistant Secretary of the Army. These reports were offset by a conflicting rumor that former Massachusetts Senator Henry Cabot Lodge, a close Eisenhower advisor who was helping the president-elect select high-level appointees, was not among Cain's fans.[2] Lodge reportedly carried with him a short, typewritten "hit list" of right-wing Republicans—some of whom had contributed to his recent defeat in Massachusetts—who would *not* find top jobs in the new administration if he had anything to do with it.[3] Although Cain had publicly supported Eisenhower for the Republican nomination, his Senate record may have been enough to sour Lodge on his suitability for high appointive office.

For whatever reason, the desired appointment as either Secretary of the Air Force or Assistant Secretary of the Army failed to materialize. Former Senate colleagues, like Robert Taft and New Hampshire Senator Styles Bridges, along with other friends of Cain, intensified their efforts to lobby the new administration on his behalf. On April 7, ten weeks after Eisenhower assumed office, Charles Willis, an assistant to White House

Chief of Staff Sherman Adams, confirmed to the press that Cain would have his choice of three jobs: a seat on the Subversive Activities Control Board (SACB), a seat on the Civil Service Commission, or a top job in the Veterans Administration. "I understand that Cain has expressed interest in any of those positions and has been endorsed for them."[4]

These reports energized scores of Cain's enemies in Washington State who then flooded Magnuson's and Jackson's offices with angry letters and telegrams, asking them to block Cain's nomination to *any* job. Not surprisingly, many were from local Democratic clubs or labor organizations, but some were from citizens who noted that Cain had been repudiated by 135,000 votes in the recent election and objected to his further service in any governmental capacity. Both Magnuson and Jackson responded with nearly identical form letters that noted that the Republicans were in now in control of the appointment process but that they had made the appropriate congressional committees "aware of all pertinent matters."[5] Magnuson responded to a letter from prominent Democrat and Seattle attorney Solie M. Ringold with much the same answer he had given to the others but with more candor, adding to the standard reply, "There was another factor which influenced us—namely, the appointment runs only to August 3. It is true that if Cain seeks reappointment, the President could give him an interim assignment on an interim basis. Word has leaked to us, however, that he—Cain—intends to go into the TV business."[6]

It is not clear how much detailed scrutiny Cain received in the vetting process beyond what was already known about his successful terms as mayor, his enviable war record, and his controversial term in the Senate. Had those responsible explored his background in more detail, they would have discovered a pattern of defending controversial groups and individuals he felt had been unfairly accused. Those had included the Japanese-Americans in the hours and months following Pearl Harbor, the liberal Anna Rosenberg when McCarthy and others tried to discredit her nomination as Assistant Secretary of Defense, and then McCarthy himself when columnist Drew Pearson attacked his war record, and even two Cleveland mobsters Morris Kleinman and Louis Rothkopf, after Cain came to believe that their civil rights had been violated by the Kefauver Committee.

Having filled most major appointments with moderates, Eisenhower was interested in placating Taft and other conservatives (with whom he would have to work in the Republican-controlled Congress) by appointing some of their own, including Harry Cain, to important, but lesser, positions. The President's older brother, Edgar, a prominent Tacoma attorney and Cain's neighbor at the Tacoma Country and Golf Club, later indicated that he had also played a role in obtaining a position for Cain in the administration.[7]

Cain decided to accept the SACB job, even though he had no prior background in national security matters beyond his casual involvement with them as a member of the Senate Armed Services Committee. Cain later said that Senator Taft advised him to accept the appointment "so the President would have at least one conservative near him."[8] In a 1958 letter to Edgar Eisenhower, written after the two had fallen out over Cain's disagreements with the administration, Cain explained his reasons for accepting the SACB position. "The assignments I wanted in the Defense or State Departments were not offered, and I was less than enthusiastic about a tendered assignment on the SACB. . . . I chose the [interim appointment on the SACB] . . . [because] it would make me familiar with the work and [allow me to] determine whether the White House wanted me as a member of its 'team' or whether it [the appointment] had [been] intended to placate Mr. Taft by assigning me to political 'Siberia.'"[9]

On the afternoon of April 10, following a meeting with the President, attended by Cain, former Ohio Governor Thomas J. Herbert (another new appointee to the SACB), and White House Chief of Staff Sherman Adams, Cain was officially nominated to fill a vacant, four-month term on the five-member SACB at the then-handsome annual salary of $15,000. He was assured that he would be re-appointed to a full three-year term in June.

Cain later described the marching orders he thought he received from the new President in his letter to the President's brother, Edgar. Cain said that Eisenhower had "indicated that he had little knowledge about the status of internal security," and that he knew almost nothing about the SACB. The President was concerned about the potential for Communist infiltration, Cain felt, but thought that the existing "constitutional guarantees" were adequate to defeat both the spread of domestic communism and to "undo the damage generated by the spread of so-called McCarthyism." Eisenhower asked Cain to brief him on all these matters "after a period of study" if Cain thought it necessary.[10]

The Senate Judiciary Committee promptly held confirmation hearings for Cain and Herbert. During his hearing, Cain's opposition to Mon

Wallgren's nomination came back to haunt him. In "sharp" questioning, Democratic Senator Thomas C. Hennings of Missouri asked Cain whether the "yardstick of defeat in your own state should be applied for determining your qualifications," an argument that Cain had used against Wallgren. Cain insisted that his primary objection to Wallgren's nomination had been his belief that Wallgren was simply not competent to hold the National Security Resources Board position. Cain further pointed out that he had raised no serious objection when Wallgren was later nominated to serve on the Federal Power Commission. Cain was questioned sharply by Hennings and the Committee's chairman, Republican William Langer of North Dakota, about the depth of the political opposition to him in his own state and about the theory of "guilt by association" as proof of Communist membership or association.[11] Cain promised that he would not consider the latter in his deliberations at the SACB. When asked by reporters, both of Washington's Democratic Senators, Warren Magnuson and Henry M. Jackson, said that they would not oppose Cain's appointment.[12] The Judiciary Committee approved the nomination on April 27, and the full Senate voted without objection to approve it the next day. Cain's conservative reputation in the Senate and his excellent war record led both his friends and his potential enemies to believe that he would be a hardliner member of the SACB.

AN ACTIVE THREAD of radicalism had been present in American life since the beginning of the Republic. In the nineteenth century, it was adopted in various forms by anti-immigrant and anti-Catholic nativists, abolitionists, socialists, labor union organizers, and agrarian reformers. Each of these groups, in one way or another, faced repression by the majority led by powerful business and political leaders, often supported by vigilantes, private security forces, mainstream newspapers, and state and local law enforcement.

The fear of communism in America first emerged as a potential threat after the Paris Commune of 1870–71, but America's working class, though it unionized enthusiastically, never embraced widespread socialism, let alone communism's appeal to revolution. The 1917 Russian Revolution and the end of the First World War energized the fledgling communist movement as never before. Seeing the success of communism in Europe, it seemed to a fearful, anti-labor business community and their allies in government that America might be the next to fall under communism's sway. In 1918, Congress passed legislation that allowed it to target individuals for deportation simply because they were thought to belong to a suspect organization. More than 4,000 were arrested, and 591 aliens were eventually deported in what became known as the "Red Scare of 1919–1920."[13] In 1921, the American Communist Party (CPUSA) was formed from two groups that had split off from the Socialist Party in 1919, but it held little appeal for American workers during the increasingly prosperous 1920s.[14]

The economic collapse of 1929 and the Great Depression that followed changed all that. With the nation's economic future in question, the CPUSA, while never large, was able to convince thousands of new members that it held the answers to the nation's distress. Many remained in the party only briefly, and most were drawn to communism more by the promise of reforming America's economy or opposing German and Italian Fascists than by any primary loyalty to the Soviet Union. On the right, a small and disparate assortment of fascist organizations, like the German-American Bund, also thought it saw the answer to America's problems in National Socialism.

Communists became active in the union movement and in government and, indeed, served in the New Deal agencies of the Roosevelt Administration. After 1936, their presence began to attract the same powerful (and some new) enemies that had confronted earlier radical groups—the anti-labor business community, the Roman Catholic Church, the conservative media led by William Randolph Hearst and his communications empire, and law enforcement—but now they were joined by the more traditional labor unions of the AFL, the American Legion, and even some socialists.[15] As before, these forces appealed to a sympathetic Congress for help. Their timing was excellent because, after the midterm elections of 1938, Congress was largely controlled by a coalition of conservative and Southern Democrats, who were increasingly at odds with the Roosevelt Administration.

Congress quickly passed a series of new laws that laid the basic groundwork for the post-World War II Red Scare. The 1938 Foreign Agents Registration Act required anyone issuing political propaganda on behalf of a foreign nation to register with the State Department. The 1939 Hatch Act denied federal employment to anyone with "membership in any political party or organization which advocates the overthrow of our constitutional form of government."[16] The 1940 Alien Registration Act, more commonly known as the Smith Act, resurrected most of the provisions of the 1917 Espionage Act and applied its provisions during peacetime for the first time. The Smith Act also required all resident aliens to register with the government and be fingerprinted. Other regulations authorized the Armed Services to summarily dismiss any civilian worker whose continued employment was deemed contrary to national security.[17]

In 1938, the House of Representatives had also created the House Un-American Activities Committee (HUAC). It was chaired by Congressman Martin Dies, a staunchly conservative, anti-Roosevelt Southern Democrat from Texas. In the beginning, with war in Europe threatening, Congress's intent had been to focus the HUAC primarily on the German-American Bund and other fascist organizations, but under Dies's leadership, it directed most of its attention to the threat of communism. Historian Geoffrey Stone has written that the "Dies Committee's proceedings were often wildly irresponsible and, as a result, were given spectacular coverage in the media. The first volume of the committee's hearings named 640 organizations, 483 newspapers, and 280 labor organizations as 'Communistic,' including the Boy Scouts of America, the American Civil Liberties Union, the Catholic Association for International Peace, and the Camp Fire Girls."[18] Dies, through his unauthorized leaks of internal government information and his irresponsible claims of the numbers of Communists in the government, would provide the model for Senator Joseph McCarthy a decade later.

Once America entered World War II, the Roosevelt Justice Department found itself having to deal not only with the disposition of alien residents (see Chapter 3) but also with the public hysteria emanating from the Dies Committee and other anti-Communist conservatives. But, while the Hatch Act was helpful, as far as it went, there was no effective means of determining the loyalty of federal employees who might belong to a Communist organization but did not advocate the overthrow of the government. Therefore, in 1942, in concert with the Congress and the FBI, Attorney General Francis Biddle developed a list of forty-seven "subversive" organizations, the largest of which were the CPUSA and the German-American Bund. Until its existence was revealed at the end of the War, the Biddle list remained largely unknown to the press or the general public and was used quietly to provide cover for the FBI's loyalty investigations of federal employees.[19]

10. "Can Freedom and Security Live Together?"

With the end of World War II, the United States was, as noted earlier, almost immediately drawn into the Cold War with the Soviet Union. The Soviet occupation of Eastern Europe, the Berlin blockade, the fall of China, and then the Korean War all had different causes, but they were seen by many as part of one broad conspiracy to control the world. Many Americans saw not only an international Communist conspiracy but an internal one as well. Republicans successfully waged the 1946 midterm elections, at least partially, on the basis of claims that the Roosevelt Administration—and, more recently, the Truman Administration—had been "soft on Communism."

On November 25, 1946, two weeks after the election, President Truman, at the urging of Attorney General Tom Clark and FBI Director J. Edgar Hoover, suddenly decided to appoint a Temporary Commission on Employee Loyalty (TCEL) on the publicly stated premise that past government efforts had been ineffective in barring "any disloyal or subversive person" from government employment." Truman's timing of the announcement and his call for a report within two months were widely interpreted as trying to forestall any action on the loyalty program by the new Republican-controlled Congress.[20] The TCEL never defined the term "disloyal" but recommended six types of activities that could be considered in determining whether a federal employee was disloyal. These included "sabotage, espionage, and related activities; treason or sedition; advocacy of the illegal overthrow of the government; intentional or unauthorized disclosure of confidential material; serving a foreign government in preference to the United States; or membership, affiliation or sympathetic association with an . . . organization . . . designated by the Attorney General as totalitarian, fascist, Communist or subversive." The latter category was clearly modeled on the Attorney General's list used during the Roosevelt Administration which, itself, was partly modeled on the Hatch Act criteria.[21] We now know that Truman Administration's concerns were well founded. Thousands of recently released Soviet intelligence and other classified telegrams sent between 1940 and 1948 show that more than two hundred Americans were working as Soviet agents during and after the Second World War and that the CPUSA was working in close concert with the Soviet intelligence agencies.[22]

On March 21, 1947, Truman signed Executive Order 9835, based on the TCEL recommendations, which created a new loyalty program for all federal civilian employees.[23] The EO declared that the "presence within the Government service of any disloyal or subversive person constitutes a threat to our democratic processes," and required that all prospective federal employees, whether a scientist at the Atomic Energy Commission or a janitor at the Department of Agriculture, be screened for loyalty. Previously, only those employees who were alleged to be disloyal were screened. At the heart of the program was a new listing of proscribed organizations developed by Tom Clark, Truman's Attorney General, which incorporated the previous Biddle list but also added the six criteria of disloyalty recommended by the TCEL. It created a new Loyalty Review Board (LRB) that would provide guidance to all federal agencies in making their employee loyalty determinations. The Justice Department provided the LRB with a list of all organizations that met the six TCEL criteria. The LRB then disseminated the list to all federal agencies where, to one degree or another, it was used in determining the loyalty of their employees. Over the next five years, the program produced no public evidence of espionage and found fewer than three hundred people believed worthy of dismissal from the federal government.

In actual practice, EO 9835 was remarkably difficult to implement. To begin with, the media's reporting about the new loyalty program was confused as a result of the imprecise language used by both the administration and the media to describe the negative impacts resulting from an organization's being listed, or by the members of such groups once they were identified. The program also failed to provide any significant information about the groups on the list, such as when they had been, or became, "subversive." Moreover, since the list was established by Executive Order rather than by congressional action, its implementation was purely an administrative matter—it contained no clear standards for placing an organization on the list beyond the TCEL recommendations, no criminal penalties, and no hearing or appeals process for those charged. Finally, unlike the Biddle list, the Clark list was made public, thereby inviting intense public scrutiny of the organizations on the list—which was, of course, the whole idea. The FBI made sure of it by leaking information about the targeted groups to friendly media outlets and to Congress. Years later, civil liberties historian, Robert Justin Goldstein, the author of *American Blacklist,* the definitive history of the Attorney General's List of Subversive Organizations, coined a comprehensive acronym for such cataloguing—AGLOSO, "a list of groups in which membership was officially designated as grounds for possible exclusion from federal employment," that was used to refer to the Truman list as well as those that preceded or followed it.[24]

Until President Nixon was forced to discontinue the AGLOSO in 1974, two months before his resignation, the list remained clouded in confusion, controversy, and partisan politics. Ultimately, approximately 300 organizations appeared on the list, most of them extremely obscure and very small. Many of the organizations folded quickly after they appeared on the list or were already defunct. More important, the use of the list extended out far beyond its originally intended purposes to become a virtual "blacklist" used by thousands of state and local governments, school boards, and even private corporations in making employment decisions.[25]

The Korean War, which began in June 1950, only served to further the anti-Communist hysteria that had been building for years. First, there had been the well-publicized conviction of several Communist Party leaders under the Smith Act in 1949, followed by the Alger Hiss trials in 1949 and 1950. Then, in February 1950, it was discovered that Klaus Fuchs, a member of the British mission working on the Manhattan Project, had provided atomic secrets to the Russians, and he was arrested. That revelation was quickly followed by the arrest that summer of Julius and Ethel Rosenberg, accused of spying for the Russians. Finally, came the dramatic allegations that senior State Department officials had supported the Chinese Communists in their civil war against Chiang Kai-shek. To make matters worse, Senator Joseph McCarthy, now well beyond naming suspected Communists in government, was essentially charging that Secretary of State Dean Acheson and Secretary of Defense George Marshall were traitors.

In September 1950, in response to these events and the resulting public alarm, Congress hastily, but overwhelmingly, passed the McCarran Internal Security Act (ISA). The McCarran Act, named for the rabidly anti-Communist Senator Pat McCarran of Nevada, required all "Communist-action" and "Communist-front" organizations to register with the Attorney General. A Communist-action organization was defined as one "substantially directed, dominated, or controlled by the foreign government or foreign organization controlling the world Communist movement," while a Communist-front organization was defined in broader terms as one that is "substantially directed, dominated, or controlled by a Communist-action organization" and is "primarily operated for the purpose of giving aid and support to a Communist-action organization, Communist foreign government, or the world Communist movement."[26]

At the heart of the McCarran Act was a provision that created the Subversive Activities Control Board (SACB). Correcting a deficiency in the purely administrative AGLOSO process, the McCarran Act gave the SACB the authority to hold quasi-judicial hearings to determine whether an organization, based on the recommendation of the Justice Department, essentially an indictment, would have to register with the Attorney General and have its activities restricted in other ways. This provision of the Act also provided a formal appeal process that could be utilized when the SACB agreed with the Attorney General's charges. No organization was ever cleared by the SACB after the Attorney General petitioned it for a finding that the group was a "Communist-action" or a "Communist-front" organization, but several groups had their SACB finding overturned on appeals.[27]

Another provision of the ISA mandated the detention of likely spies and saboteurs during an internal security emergency declared by the President.[28] President Truman was a committed anti-Communist but was concerned about some of the more draconian provisions of the Act. He vetoed the legislation, claiming that it "punished opinions rather than actions." Reflecting the tenor of the times, Congress overrode his veto by a vote of 248 to 48, and the Act became law. As a senator, Cain voted both for the original legislation and to override the President's veto.

There has been a great deal of confusion between the AGLOSO and the SACB. Both contain the word "subversive" in their titles. Both involved the Department of Justice. But, as we have seen, the AGLOSO was a purely administrative process used to provide guidance, after EO 9835, to the Loyalty Review Board and, through them, to other federal agencies. It had no basis in law and could exact no legal penalties or provide a legal process for organizations that found themselves on the list. The primary benefit of the AGLOSO was in the publicity it attracted and the public onus it placed on listed organizations and their members—which, of course, was the main idea—but another "benefit," depending on how one looked at it, was the broad, if often unauthorized, use of the list for other, unrelated purposes.

The SACB, on the other hand, was an independent, quasi-judicial entity created by Congress to determine—based on formal testimony presented before the board by the Justice Department and the accused organization—whether the organization in question should be forced to register as a Communist-action or Communist-front organization. Rulings of the SACB could be appealed all the way up to the U.S. Supreme Court.[29]

THE PUBLIC'S FEAR of communism provided the Republicans with a potent campaign issue in the 1952 national election. The Republican Party Platform charged the Democrats with "shielding traitors" and "undermining the very foundations of our Republic." Realizing that he was going to have to face the issue of McCarthy and communism in the coming campaign, Eisenhower fought hard to have Richard M. Nixon chosen as his running mate. Eisenhower wanted a vice-presidential nominee who had a strong record of anti-communism. Nixon was eminently qualified in this regard due to both his role as a member of the House Un-American Activities Committee during the Alger Hiss trial and his 1950 Senate campaign against Helen Gahagan Douglas in California.

Once in power, however, the Republicans, like the Democrats before them, found that the internal security issue was more complicated than they had ever anticipated. Eisenhower's Attorney General, Herbert Brownell, wrote in his memoirs, "The challenge we faced was to draw an appropriate line between the needs of national security . . . and the rights of the individual as set forth in the Bill of Rights. The bounds of both concepts . . . are imprecise when one attempts to think about them in the abstract. They are even more difficult to define in practical application, especially since they have been given differing interpretations in war-time and in peacetime over the years. We faced an added complication: Where should the line be in time of cold war?"[30] Brownell remembered that internal security had been a particular concern of Eisenhower's during the campaign, and remained so after the election, when he asked that new procedures be put in place to better define what constituted a "security risk."[31]

Brownell's answer was contained in a new Executive Order 10450, prepared by the Justice Department and signed by the President on April 27, 1953, only two months following his inauguration—the same day that Harry Cain's nomination to the SACB was approved by the Senate Judiciary Committee. The new Executive Order reflected both the President's and the Attorney General's view that the Truman Administration's loyalty-security program was not working and that a new approach was required.[32] There was considerable ambivalence within the Justice Department about the "loyalty" emphasis of the Truman list. Therefore, the most significant change made by EO 10450 was in broadening the criteria used for investigating new and existing federal employees. By adding "security" to "loyalty," the new criteria greatly expanded an employee's grounds for dismissal.

Rooting out Communists from federal employment remained the stated purpose of the list, but the definition of security was expanded to include not only subversion but also drunkenness, drug addiction, unusual sexual practices, conviction of a felony, membership in a nudist colony or anything deemed "inconsistent with the national security."[33] Suspicion of disloyalty could result in suspension and dismissal, prior even to a hearing on the matter.[34] What would prove to be the final additions to the list were announced by the Justice Department on December 30, 1954. While it expanded the criteria for dismissal from federal employment, EO 10450 did not change the responsibilities or procedures of the SACB, which proceeded slowly and methodically to concur with the Attorney General's recommendations regarding the reputed subversive organizations brought before it.

Like the Truman program, Eisenhower's loyalty-security program was meant to quell criticism. Instead, it only encouraged it. Four months after the signing of the EO, 1,456 federal employees had been dismissed—all but five of them hired before the Eisenhower Administration took office. By the end of 1953, the administration had shown that it was just as willing as McCarthy and the other Red-hunters to capitalize on the internal security issue in order to keep the various factions of the Republican Party together and to prepare for the 1954 mid-term elections.[35] Between 1947 and 1956, the various loyalty-security programs resulted in the firing of 2.700 federal employees and the resignation under pressure of another 12,000.[36] Most of the firings and resignations may have been justified, but many were not.

HARRY CAIN REPORTED to work at the SACB's offices, located on Vermont Avenue NW, across Lafayette Park from the White House, and immediately immersed himself in learning his new job. According to another member of the SACB, Dr. Kathryn McHale, Cain "did little talking and a lot of listening. He read voraciously . . . everything he could find that bore on his new job and responsibilities. He worked hard, very hard, at home, in the office and everywhere, to think this thing through."[37] For eighteen months, as Cain sat and listened to the tedious arguments of the lawyers arguing their cases in front of the Board—restricted from actively participating in the debate—Cain became increasingly frustrated by his new job. He later claimed that the period of time he spent listening and learning had occasioned a "spiritual awakening" and permitted him to reflect upon "fundamentals."[38]

Cain also used the time to establish or re-establish relationships with important contacts in the four-month-old Eisenhower Administration. It seems reasonable to assume that Cain was aware of the political and administrative challenges of the new administration and the criticism it was receiving from Senator McCarthy and others on the right, as well as being at least generally aware of the internal workings of the Eisenhower White House itself. After all, Cain had served on the President's staff in London during the war.

The Eisenhower Administration was a major departure from its predecessor in many ways. Unlike Truman, Dwight Eisenhower never considered himself to be a politician, even though he had successfully navigated the upper echelons of multi-national politics at the highest level. Before he had agreed to run for the Republican presidential nomination, he had twice turned down similar offers from President Truman to run as a Democrat. Eisenhower once told his chief of staff, Sherman Adams, that "when I declared myself a Republican in 1952, I did so upon the representations of some of my friends in whom I had the greatest confidence. I believe the more enlightened principles of the Republicans were closer to my own beliefs than those of the other party. But I could have been a conservative Democrat."[39] Eisenhower accepted the Republicans' call, he said, because he assumed that they wanted someone with his wartime and NATO experience and believed that he stood the best chance of containing communism and bringing peace to the world as a Republican president.

It came as an unpleasant shock to him to learn that many Republican political leaders were simply using his prestige and popularity as their best shot at breaking the Democrats' twenty-year grip on the presidency. To make matters worse, many of the influential conservative Republicans in Congress had not supported Eisenhower for the nomination, nor did they accept the premise that his election had largely saved their party from irrelevance. Eisenhower's distaste for partisan politics reflected itself in his unwillingness to take firm control of his party, preferring to leave the operation of the political machinery to others.

Another factor in the Eisenhower presidency was the way in which he governed. As a career military man, Eisenhower was committed to, and expected, a well-tuned staff system. Fortunately, unlike Truman's staff, which improved over time but was always small, Eisenhower's White House staff became a smoothly functioning machine administered by Sherman Adams, one of the most powerful presidential chiefs of staff in the history of the office. H. R. Halderman, Richard Nixon's chief of staff, referred to Adams as "an alternate President. If you put [John] Ehrlichman, [Henry] Kissinger, and me all together, then you might have Sherman Adams."[40]

While Cain didn't know Governor Adams (he met Adams for the first time during his preliminary interview with Eisenhower), he did know, and counted as a friend, Maxwell Rabb, a lawyer, former staffer to Senator Henry Cabot Lodge, and an Eisenhower campaign worker who now held the dual positions of Cabinet operations officer and associate counsel to the President. Rabb was generally considered to be the Administration's point man on minority affairs and reported to Sherman Adams. Rabb was the closest contact Cain had to anyone in the White House, and the two would carry on an anguished exchange over the next three years.

Eisenhower ran his administration through Adams and a group of generally competent Cabinet secretaries, who were given considerable freedom. As an example of his confidence in them, Eisenhower told his Cabinet members that they were free to speak their minds publicly on the issues of the day and that he would back them up "when he could." Eisenhower wanted no repeat of Henry Wallace's outspoken opposition to Truman's Cold War policies. Eisenhower's solution was simple. Speeches that contained no direct reference to the President or the White House did not need to be approved in advance, thus allowing the President the freedom to respond or not, depending on the occasion.[41] Over the years, Eisenhower had also developed a means of dealing with individuals who irritated him. "With a guy like that," he once told Sherman Adams, "I simply write his name on a piece of paper, put it in the lower desk drawer and shut the drawer."[42]

10. "Can Freedom and Security Live Together?"

HARRY CAIN WAS still learning his new job in late 1953 when he received a telephone call from a "Mrs. Smiley," a former Seattleite whose husband, a research biologist at the National Cancer Institute, had been suspended as a security risk from his job. She claimed that she had sought help from the members of Washington's congressional delegation without success and was calling Cain as a last resort. "Can I come and see you?" Cain met with the woman and after doing some independent research agreed to look into her situation. It turned out that the couple had belonged to the left-wing Washington Pension Union in the mid-1930s and that "unknown accusers" were claiming that the scientist had been a Communist Party organizer.

After looking into Smiley's case for six weeks at his own expense, Cain became convinced that Smiley had not been a Communist because he had never pled the Fifth Amendment and was willing to take a lie-detector test. Smiley was doing important scientific research, and his fellow workers were willing to be character witnesses for him. Cain later told an interviewer, "But aside from that, here is what disturbed me. None of the charges had anything to do with his conduct for the past ten years." Convinced of the man's (at least recent) innocence, Cain decided to make his argument to the departmental loyalty board that was currently handling Smiley's case. The board disagreed with Cain's argument, and the man was subsequently fired. Cain then helped him find a new job in the private sector.[43]

When the word of Cain's quiet assistance to Smiley became known to other government employees who had similar problems, they also began to call on him for help. Some found out from unlikely sources about Cain's willingness to help. A former government attorney in search of another federal job was having trouble and came to Cain for help. Cain asked the man who had referred him. He replied, "Why, _____ of the Justice Department. He said if anyone could help me it was you." The man he named was the chief assistant to William F. Tomkins, the Assistant Attorney General in charge of the government's internal security program.[44]

While these cases, technically, had nothing to do with Cain's duties at the SACB (most of those who contacted him were facing difficulties at their federal agencies resulting from their past or present membership—or some other connection—with an organization listed on the AGLOSO), his duties at the SACB were not onerous, and he had more than enough time available to look into some selected cases as a private individual. As he did so, Cain began to see what he believed was a consistent pattern: one in which the administration's fixation with employee loyalty was interfering with their civil liberties. "When first they started to come to me to discuss their difficulties, I thought perhaps they were over-emphasizing the problem. But the more I looked into their cases, the more I began to understand that the very system we had developed to protect freedom was a system which, if we didn't manage it more intelligently, was destined to destroy freedom."[45]

The cases set off multiple alarms in Harry Cain's mind. In some cases, he believed that the employee's basic constitutional guarantees were being ignored. The manner in which many of the cases were being handled smacked of intrusive big government at its worst and of poorly trained, ill-informed bureaucrats trying to implement a none-too-clear AGLOSO. To make matters even worse, the lives of the employees and their families were being adversely impacted—sometimes severely so—by unproven allegations and smear tactics, making it hard for them to get another job, if they had to, or even to live in their own communities. If something wasn't done, this could become a public embarrassment to the President. Once again, as he had in the Senate, Harry Cain decided to listen to his conscience and do what seemed right to him at the time.

Cain later recalled, "After I went to the SACB, and through the first year of that experience, I became amazed by what I had not known and astounded by what I had forgotten about the lessons offered by history concerning man's struggle to become and remain free. . . . In the Senate I was dealing mostly with theory. . . . I was not on any committee investigating domestic Communists. . . . My great error was in assuming that congressional committees and the government would treat fairly with every suspected or accused person, and that every organization on the Attorney General's List of Subversive Organizations had been listed for cause."[46]

Cain began to express his concerns privately with Maxwell Rabb and to others. He didn't want to weaken the security setup. He only wanted the existing one to be "fair as well as firm. . . . If [an agency] security officer has charges that can stand up, then I'm on his side. . . . I am still as anti-Communist as I have always been—only now I know a little bit more about it."[47]

Years later, he remembered that many of those he talked to shared his concerns but that no one in the administration was willing to risk his or her career to do anything about it. "By that time, they had built an octopus, and psychologically this even covered the President. Their greatest fear was that any move to correct unfairness might be construed by the general public as being 'soft' on Communism. I said at that time that the worst thing that has happened to my country in my lifetime is that the historic custom of assuming that an American citizen is innocent until proven guilty has been replaced by the requirement of a citizen to prove that he is innocent."[48]

Privately, Cain was told by Rabb and others that the administration was not likely to change its policies on the basis of his concerns. Change would require more pressure being brought to bear on the administration by Congress and less pressure being brought to bear by the right wing of Republican Party. Cain assumed (perhaps because he wanted to) that he was being told indirectly that he might quietly help to speed that process along. Could he take his concerns public so long as he did not try to speak for the President? Could he help his own chances of advancement within the administration by trying to protect the President from near-certain criticism? Could he even perhaps advance his own chances of returning to the U.S. Senate? Cain decided to speak out.

Cain's first speech on the subject was given to the Goodwyn Institute in Memphis, Tennessee, on November 16, 1954, and was entitled "Communism and the Counterattack." In it, Cain evenly described the roles of both the Justice Department and the SACB under the current law. He hinted at his growing civil liberties concerns without expressly discussing them. "If the Communists seek to import that tyranny (tyranny over the minds of men), and they do, the more reason why we should not let them provoke us into adopting the weapons of tyranny which, though intended to be used only against Communists, might later be turned against ourselves also."[49] The speech was not widely reported and elicited no response from the White House or the Justice Department.

Cain's speech to the Goodwyn Institute came at a time when the administration's internal security program was coming under increasing scrutiny. The Korean War was over, and the nation, while still mindful of the threat of Communism, was increasingly focused on fighting it externally, rather than internally. The Army-McCarthy hearings had concluded in June, greatly damaging McCarthy's reputation and exposing his political vulnerability. In December, the Senate would vote to censure him. More important, the Democrats had won decisive victories in the 1954 mid-term elections and would take control of the Congress in January 1955 after only two years of Republican leadership.

McCarthy's career may have been in decline, but McCarthyism was still alive and well. In December 1954, a national firestorm erupted when it was reported that Wolf Ladejinsky, a well-known and respected agricultural economist and a refugee from the Russian Revolution, had been fired by Agriculture Secretary Ezra Taft Benson as a security risk. Ladejinsky was a well-connected Washington, DC, insider. He was a protégé of Rexford Tugwell, a member of Franklin Roosevelt's original brain trust, and had served as a former State Department advisor to Chiang Kai-shek in China and General Douglas MacArthur in Japan on land reform. The reason given for Ladejinsky's firing was that he would have "required a clearance from the Communist Party" to act as an interpreter for Amtorg, the Soviet Union's national trading company, back in the 1930s. Ladejinsky also had three sisters who still lived in Russia. The Agriculture Department claimed he was a security risk while the State Department defended him. The furor had found its way all the way up to President Eisenhower, who had declined to become involved.

Cain was incredulous. It was clear to him that Ladejinsky's case had been mishandled and that the coordination between the two departments involved had been abysmal. On December 29, 1954, he wrote to his friend Max Rabb at the White House. "The unfolding of the Wolf Ladejinsky case is almost unbelievable, isn't it? My guess, in three parts, is: (a) the Secretary [of Agriculture] has never seen the file on Ladejinsky, (b) the Secretary has considered only those negative excerpts from that file in the State Department written by a security officer, and (c) the security officer in the State Department has but recently assumed his duties which demand the highest character and balanced judgment."[50] Cain decided to speak out.

The opportunity presented itself when Cain received an invitation to speak to the conservative Fifth District Republican Club in Spokane on January 15, 1955. Cain decided to use the Ladejinsky example to showcase his broader concerns with the administration's internal security program. When his wife, Marj, heard what he was planning to say, she tried to talk him out of it, telling him that it was the wrong speech, at the wrong time, and in the wrong place. "I thought it would ruin him politically." Marj knew, however, that once his mind was made up, no one was going to change it. As Cain boarded the plane for Spokane, all she could do was wish him luck.[51]

Cain's speech—entitled "Can Freedom and Security Live Together?"— was the opening round in what subsequently became known as the "Cain Mutiny." In the speech, Cain summarized his past two years as a member of the SACB, comparing it with his term in the Senate. "For the better part of two years I have been sitting, listening and thinking" while admitting that, in the Senate, he had "lost sight of some fundamentals which have returned to focus during the past two years." Cain told his audience that "I am here as a proud Republican, but I am speaking as one who feels that his basic allegiance is to his Nation rather than to the political Party of his deliberate and considered choice."[52]

Cain then noted that the nation needed to be prepared to meet the Communist threat, but in doing so, it needed to keep three things in balance—"Justice, Security and Freedom." It was his "generally considered view" that the nation's security system had "worked well and fairly on the average," but that there were "conspicuous and inexcusable examples" to the contrary that were far too common. Cain then proceeded to cite the Wolf Ladejinsky case as one of those examples. The Ladejinsky case "points up practically every weakness which we can find or trace in our prevailing security system. It includes evidences of the shortsightedness, ruthlessness, smugness and brutality of bureaucracy at their worst." He said that Ladejinsky had been saved only "because he had friends in high places, but men and women of smaller reputations might only consider themselves caught in a trap without knowing where to turn for help."[53]

Cain then offered several suggestions for making the existing internal security program more effective while decreasing its current negative impacts on innocent citizens and noted that changes in both attitudes and procedures were needed to avoid making "cowards and mental robots of free men and women." Cain's suggestions, which he had already discussed with Rabb and others, included referring contested decisions to a higher authority for final determination, more care in the selection of security officers at government agencies, considering the use of professional hearing examiners, allowing agencies to tailor "security to the job" (where an individual who was unsuited for one job might be able to fill another, less sensitive one), and more specificity in the use of the term "security risk." "A loyal person can be a security risk and a security risk can be truly loyal."[54]

With his libertarian instincts firmly on display, Cain told his audience that an individual's "opportunity to be different" must not be lost in the nation's search for security. Cain asked his audience, "What is loyalty? Is it orthodoxy? Is it conformity? Though government workers must be loyal, there is no reason why they must be rigidly orthodox in their thinking. In order to be loyal must you agree with courses of action laid down by your government which you believe to be totally wrong?" Concluding his remarks, Cain told his audience that "a whole clique of spies could hardly do as much damage to us as could our failure as a government to have confidence in our own people."[55]

Cain wanted to make sure that his comments were heard by a larger audience than the Republicans in Spokane, so before flying west, he provided copies of the speech to reporters from the *Washington Star* and the *Washington Post*. As Cain knew they would, both ran front-page stories in their Sunday editions that included extensive excerpts from his speech. Their stories were immediately picked up by the wire services. The liberal *New Republic* also reported extensively on his speech, and its reporting was then reprinted in the *Congressional Record*.[56]

The reaction to Cain's speech was immediate—particularly given his strong Republican credentials and his current position as a member of the SACB. *The Washington Post* editorialized that Cain's speech was "remarkable on two counts. It presented a reasoned, compelling indictment of the excesses in the Federal employee security program in terms that invoked the highest values of the American past. And it also presented to the Republican Party a persuasive argument on practical political grounds for a drastic reform of security procedures."[57]

Three different Supreme Court Justices, either personally or in writing, praised Cain for his comments. A number of liberal members of Congress called to congratulate him. Liberal columnists like Marquis Childs, who had been no friend of Cain's during his years in the Senate, now complimented him on his clarity of vision and purpose. Playing on Cain's words from the Spokane speech, Childs wrote that "two years of sitting, listening and thinking" would "do a great deal for those who administer the security program." It certainly had "worked an extraordinary transformation" on Cain.[58] Responding to the support he was receiving, Cain told the *Washington Post*, "We can be safe and free at one and the same time but it is possible to become so safe that nobody can be free."[59]

10. "Can Freedom and Security Live Together?"

Congressional Republicans remained largely silent but were nonetheless incredulous. Ultra-conservative Indiana Senator William Jenner said that "Cain's comments had been the subject of a lot of cloakroom conversation. . . . No one knows the answer. We just keep asking one another the question." Even Cain's close personal friend, Joseph McCarthy, was baffled. "I can't understand him. You know how unpredictable he is."[60] Conservative commentators were more vocal in their indignation. Fulton Lewis, Jr., the nationally syndicated columnist for the Hearst Corporation, lamented in a special two-part column called "Left Wing Darling" that Cain had "completely gone over to the other side."[61] Others, like Willard Edwards, writing in *American Mercury*, suggested that Cain had been bitter and frustrated after his Senate loss, had not been too mollified by his appointment to the SACB, and now enjoyed all of the publicity and notoriety he was receiving after his comparative obscurity over the last eighteen months.[62]

Cain later claimed that he had not become a "liberal" as some had suggested. He said that his change of mind was confined only to the one issue of internal security. Cain told Edgar Prina in an in-depth interview in *Collier's* that, were he back in the Senate, he would be voting as a conservative on most foreign and domestic issues. Cain also claimed that he was "totally unprepared and amazed" by the national reaction to his comments, but that is hardly credible given Cain's background in media relations. Cain certainly understood that his speech would be both newsworthy and controversial. Otherwise, why leak it to the Washington, DC, press corps in advance of his speech?

The White House and the Justice Department, blindsided by Cain's unexpected comments, were understandably furious with him for forcing them to read his comments on the front pages of the Washington, DC, papers. To Sherman Adams, Cain's actions represented both a breach of courtesy within the chain of command and a lack of willingness to be a "member of the team."

In his January 19 news conference, the first ever to be filmed for television, a question from a reporter for the *Providence Evening Bulletin* asked the President about Cain's criticism of the administration's employee security programs over the weekend. The President responded, "Well, Mr. Cain, like everybody else, has his right to criticize." He then went on to say, "The system that he criticizes, I believe, is fairly well conceived. Certainly it is the best that we have been able to devise in view of the conflicting considerations that apply. And they are also sensitive considerations, sensitive on the side of the Government and sensitive on the side of the individual. In their application always there is human failure; I admit that, and I don't claim any kind of perfection. Now, so far as I know, Mr. Cain has not submitted to any responsible official in the executive department a summary of his objections or on what he bases his criticism. I did read part of his speech, and that is all I know about it."[63]

Cain later said that he had failed to provide an advance copy of the speech to the White House because they didn't "ask for one." The truth is almost certainly closer to the answer he gave to L. Edgar Prina in their interview—that he had *wanted* to make the speech. The consequences of his decision were predictable. According to Prina's article in *Collier's* magazine, there had been two telephone messages waiting for Cain when he returned home from Spokane. One was from Maxwell Rabb, which he returned immediately. Rabb asked, "Harry, why didn't you let us screen that speech?" Cain replied candidly, "Max, because I wanted to give it."[64]

The other call was from Sherman Adams. He asked Cain to stop by his office as soon as he could arrange an appointment. Cain met with Adams in his White House office on January 20, the day following the presidential news conference. The diminutive Adams was sitting behind a large desk with a replica of the Great Seal of the United States carved into the front panel as if to remind his guests of the source of his power. In what Cain termed "a terse discussion," Adams proceeded to give him "unshirted hell." Cain said that he tried explaining his criticisms without success. Adams wasn't interested in hearing explanations. Cain later quoted Adams as saying, "To hell with the merits of what you have to say! That's what you're paid for—to know more about this than anyone else—and I assume that everything you say is right. But that's beside the point. You're rocking the boat and, by God, it's going to stop right now."[65]

On January 22, a day after their meeting, Cain wrote to Adams. "You may be certain, sir, that I shall not soon, if ever, forget the hours we spent together yesterday during which you officially reprimanded me for having spoken out in Spokane last Saturday. . . . My only distress comes from being advised that I may have unintentionally embarrassed the President. If I did so embarrass him, I apologize most feelingly. My intention was that of really helping him and the political party to which we all belong." Cain went on to urge that "those concerned carefully analyze the contentions and suggestions" he had offered in the speech and reminded Adams that, "almost nothing was said about the merits of my views in their meeting. In the long run, I must be judged on the substance of what I said rather than on the basis of why I spoke out. The latter can be considered to have been an indiscretion, but the former may yet be considered as a sturdy contribution to the common good."[66] Cain apparently also promised Adams that he would not speak again on the subject for a month or so while the Attorney General looked at making some improvements to the program.

If possible, the Attorney General's reaction to Cain's Spokane speech had been even more intense than that of Sherman Adams. Herbert Brownell was one of the President's closest political advisors. He also administered the government's employee loyalty program. Brownell was furious that Cain was out on the stump talking about matters that were completely outside of his formal responsibilities at the SACB and, worse, that he was playing into the hands of McCarthy and others who were criticizing the administration for not being tough enough on communism. Even though McCarthy had recently been censured by the Senate, the last thing the administration needed was another critic of their security program—particularly one of their own.

One high-ranking Justice Department official, speaking off the record, wondered, "[Has] Cain got any friends left in the Administration? He never discussed his criticisms with anyone in the department before he teed off on us. He should have fought this battle within the Administration. If he lost, and still felt deeply about it, he should have resigned. Then he would have been perfectly free to belt us to his heart's content." The official then made a second point. Cain was also speaking outside of his field of responsibility. "For him to be talking about the employee security program is like a guy who has been delivering babies all his life suddenly performing a delicate brain operation."[67] Brownell, a former head of the Republican National Committee, was even more specific when speaking on the record to a group of reporters in Seattle. Asked about Cain's recent criticism, Brownell responded, "I wouldn't know what's in Cain's mind. You'd have to ask him. The people out here must know about him—they elected him to the Senate."[68] During the same trip, he reportedly told a group of state GOP leaders privately that Cain didn't have the foggiest notion of what the security program was all about and that he was one of the most disruptive influences in the administration.[69] These comments, of course, immediately made their way back to Cain.

In March, word leaked out that Cain was working on another speech. He must have been unhappy with the pace of the "improvements" that Brownell had said he was working on and with the behind-the-scenes criticism of him by Justice Department officials. News of the new speech prompted another call from Sherman Adams. According to a story later reported in the *Washington Evening Star*, the conversation went something like this:

Adams: It has come to my attention that you are going to make a speech Friday. What kind of an organization is it?

Cain: Well, Governor, it's the same organization Herb Brownell addressed last year.

Adams: You haven't forgotten our little talk after you got back from Spokane, have you?

Cain: Why, Governor, it might just as well have been yesterday. I remember every word of it.

Adams: What are you going to talk about?

Cain: I am only going to talk about the Bill of Rights and man's dignity. The same things Herb Brownell talked about. Of course, I might give them a different twist.[70]

Adams ordered Cain to provide him with copies of this and any future speeches. Almost certainly, Adams also began to have his staff explore how they could get rid of what was becoming a bothersome distraction. They soon learned, however, that they had a problem in this regard. Most administration officials serve at the pleasure of the President and can be dismissed without cause. SACB members were different. The SACB was a creation of the Congress and the McCarran Internal Security Act of 1950 and was independent and quasi-judicial. The President appointed its members with the advice and consent of the Senate. Board members could be removed for only two reasons: malfeasance in office or neglect of duty.

As ordered, Cain duly sent copies of his upcoming March 18, 1955, speech to the National Civil Liberties Clearing House in Washington, DC, entitled, "Strong in Their Pride and Free," to Adams, Brownell, and Max Rabb but not in enough time for them to do anything about it. In a note to each accompanying the speech, he said, "I have never tried so hard to be objective and constructive in committing these views to paper. I applaud what the administration has done to improve our security systems but I am venturing some suggestions which may anticipate future requirements."[71]

Cain's speech began by citing various public statements by the Attorney General that stressed the importance of civil rights to Americans. He then went on to trace the development of civil rights in America and to note that in the past both Democratic and Republican administrations had mixed partisan politics with internal security. Cain found the government's recently announced improvements in the program to be "indecisive" and called for the creation of a bipartisan commission to review the current program. He again pressed for modifications to the program. These included better training for government employees involved in internal security issues, ending the practice of suspending employees until their hearings had been held, providing legal counsel to the accused (similar to the military practice in court martial proceedings), and clearing any employee who had belonged to an alleged Communist organization—other than the CPUSA—but who had resigned prior to 1947 and had not subsequently engaged in any suspect activities. "A person may have been a dupe in joining a listed organization which is thought now to have been subversive, but it does not follow that he necessarily was disloyal."[72] An accused employee should have the right to know the source and nature of the derogatory information being used against him. "The Attorney General's list ought, in my judgment, to be liquidated through procedures which our country supports."[73]

But the biggest news to come out of the March 18 speech was that Cain finally parted company politically with his longtime friend, Joseph McCarthy. Although he refrained from mentioning McCarthy by name, Cain defended the use of the Fifth Amendment against self-incrimination and chastised *those who referred to witnesses before their committee as* "Fifth Amendment Communists" *because they* chose to invoke their Constitutional privilege against incriminating themselves. "Those who use the Fifth Amendment as an adjective of disapprobation modifying the noun 'Communist' are as guilty of disrespect for the Constitution as any Communist could be." It was a favorite phrase of McCarthy's and a clear reference to the Wisconsin senator.[74]

Interviewed by newspaper columnist and former staffer Emily Walker only two days after the speech, Cain dropped yet another bombshell.

He admitted that he had acted improperly in accusing Mon Wallgren during the NSRB hearings of being soft on communism. He said that he had not known then, and still didn't know, whether all the charges he made against Wallgren were true. He made them based on information he received in telephone calls from Wallgren's enemies without asking them on what "precise information" their allegations were founded. "I am willing to agree that I didn't know what I was talking about. I didn't have justification to say that about Mr. Wallgren. I didn't like him, and I was willing to treat him differently than someone I liked."[75]

Ten days following his March 18 speech, Cain appeared on the NBC television program *Youth Wants To Know*. He again called for the establishment of a system under which the organizations on the Attorney General's list could contest the fact that they had been listed and get a fair hearing. "Some organizations have been on that list since 1947 without ever having a chance to clear themselves against the charges" made against them. Cain again called for differentiating those employees who were "unreliable," such as those with a drinking problem, from those who were "disloyal." Most of the firings that had taken place were of people who were unreliable. It is "persecution rather than prosecution" to classify a drunk as disloyal, Cain said, "for such a label makes it almost impossible for him to get another job."[76]

Cain's latest speech generated another round of glowing comments from the liberal media but set off another round of speculation regarding his motives. On March 23, Emily Walker filed another story for the *Tacoma News Tribune* from her perch in Washington, DC. She asked the questions that everyone else had been thinking about. "What happened to Cain? Why did he do it?" Walker offered three possibilities. The first was that his speech had really been motivated by an honest concern about the need to reform the nation's internal security program. The second was that he was bored at the SACB and was hoping the publicity arising from the speech would lead to another, more important position within the government. The third was that he was hoping that the publicity would help pave the way for a return to politics in the state of Washington.[77] Cynics seemed to focus on the third possibility. Cain addressed that possibility directly in a March 18 interview with a reporter for the *Washington Evening Star*. He was asked directly whether he was trying to generate publicity in preparation for another run for the U.S. Senate in Washington. He responded that "there is no truth to reports that I am going to run for the Senate again."[78] While that statement was technically correct, it is also clear that a return to the Senate was never far from Cain's mind. He often remembered his time in the Senate with fondness and nostalgia in later interviews and, in October 1955, hinted to the *American Mercury* that he was at least thinking of a possible 1956 race against Warren Magnuson for his Senate seat.[79]

Cain later told his son that it "generally puzzled me that many writers were puzzled because my conduct was seemingly different as between the Senate and the SACB. Maybe many in public life who take a position never change it. Writers or reporters tend to be skeptical and suspicious. Many thought for quite a time that I was up to some political trickery, trying to curry favor, get revenge or preparing to run again for the Senate or some other political office."[80]

But even if Cain's explanations to Sherman Adams and the press regarding his motives are taken at face value, they still don't explain his actions. His concerns with AGLOSO were already known to the White House and the Justice Department. Cain had discussed them privately with Max Rabb and others, if not with Adams and Brownell personally. In addition, one has to assume that Cain could have expressed his concerns directly to the President, at least prior to making his Spokane speech, had he wanted to. Cain already had the President's permission to report back to him, dating from their meeting on April 10, 1953, which Adams attended. Since Cain didn't request a meeting, the only conclusion to be drawn is that he didn't want one. Cain wanted, as he told Max Rabb, to make the speech. Cain wanted to bring his concerns to the public's attention in his own way—a way that would certainly attract attention to himself.

In deciding to go public with his concerns, Cain set into motion a series of events that would unfold over the next eighteen months, alienating him from the President who had given him his job, leading supporters and detractors to question his judgment and motivations, and, ultimately, costing him his job. In the beginning, as Cain told several interviewers, he felt that the logic of his arguments would bring changes to the security program by discussing the need for them within the administration. When it became obvious that, for its own reasons, the administration was not open to Cain's suggestions, he decided to take his concerns to the public. When officials at the Justice Department impugned Cain's motives and tried to discredit him, the battle was on. Brownell and others felt that the only honorable course for Cain to follow was to resign and continue his fight from outside the administration as a private citizen. Cain believed this argument to be "nonsense." "Had I resigned, my effectiveness would have been nil. Everybody knew this, but the critics had to say something. My views prevailed in the end and nothing else mattered."[81]

11

The Cain Mutiny

WHAT BEGAN AS a difference of opinion about the merits and application of the administration's internal security program and then expanded to questions of judgment and motivations continued to escalate into something just short of all-out war. The rift between Cain, the White House, and the Justice Department was well known within the administration and by some Washington insiders but was not generally known to the public. Cain believed, and with some reason, that the administration—and most particularly, the Justice Department—was trying to discredit him professionally and to muzzle his criticisms. In 1961, Cain told the author that his differences with Brownell eventually became "irreconcilable." His opposition, Cain said, couldn't be avoided in good conscience. "I've never found a counterpart of the Attorney General's list in any dictator country on the face of the globe. This has been the most extraordinary departure from tradition that the United States has ever known."[1]

To the administration, of course, Cain was a "loose cannon" who was involving himself in matters outside of his area of responsibility and, in so doing, was not only being disloyal to the President who appointed him but was also causing a considerable public distraction away from the administration's quiet efforts to distance itself from its anti-Communist critics. An indication of the administration's displeasure with Cain can be gathered from an exchange of notes between Deputy Attorney General William P. Rogers, who would later serve as Attorney General and Secretary of State, and FBI Director J. Edgar Hoover. Rogers sent a copy of Cain's earlier letter to Sherman Adams on to Hoover, asking him to return it to him "after you have had the agonizing experience of reading it." Hoover sent it back the next day with a note, referring to the letter as a "diatribe written by 'Wordy' Cain" and commenting that no one in Washington had ever exceeded Cain's use "of the personal pronoun, I." A further indication of the displeasure of senior Justice Department officials with Cain can be found in an April 15, 1955, memo from Oran Waterman, head of the Justice Department unit responsible for designating AGLOSO organizations, to his supervisor, David Irons, chief of the Subversion Organization Section. In it, Waterman wrote that Cain's attacks on the list had "caused serious disservice" and were "inimical to the interests of the internal security program."[2]

Cain was aware of the administration's displeasure with him but felt that it might yet be possible to push for some changes to the program from within. Following his dressing down by Sherman Adams, Cain spent weeks unsuccessfully trying to arrange a meeting with Brownell, still believing that the logic of his arguments would ultimately begin to bring the Attorney General around to his point of view. A meeting between the two men was finally arranged for Friday, April 1—perhaps an inauspicious date. Assistant Attorney General William F. Tompkins and SACB chairman Thomas Herbert sat in on the three-hour meeting. Cain again laid out his concerns about the administration's loyalty program and particularly about the AGLOSO. These were essentially the same points that he had made in his Spokane speech and in subsequent conversations. In response, Brownell focused on the fact that he had been embarrassed and disturbed by Cain's speeches, which dealt publicly with matters outside of the jurisdiction of the SACB. In frustration, Brownell asked to know what Cain planned to do or say about the security program in the future. Cain said that he would think about it and get back to him.[3]

Following the meeting, Cain wrote to both Brownell and Tompkins. He asked Brownell to "give additional consideration to the cut-off date for your list of un-American organizations [the suggested 1947 date prior to which alleged questionable activity would not be considered] and to explore ways in which the potential of the [SACB] can be more fully developed." In his letter to Tompkins, he said, "As I see it, your first concern has been with security while mine has been with the individual. I want to believe that we are each anxious to contribute constructively to the end result."[4] On April 7, Tompkins responded, almost certainly with Brownell's permission, thanking Cain for his earlier letter and proposing that they get together for a series of meetings in late April and early May to discuss Cain's suggestions. When asked, the SACB's chairman, former Ohio governor Thomas Herbert, walked a fine line about Cain's feud with the administration, saying, "Harry Cain is doing a fine job on the Board. As to the other matters to which he has been addressing himself, he is speaking as an individual and not for the Board. I think he has made that abundantly clear."[5]

However, before Cain received Tompkins's reply, he decided to fire off another letter to Brownell on April 5. In a single-spaced, ten-page letter, he acknowledged Brownell's concern that he had been speaking out on subjects that were outside of the purview of the SACB. Echoing Governor Herbert's comments, he wrote, "I made it clear that I have been speaking on my own responsibility as a citizen and as a member of the Board, but not for the Board." In a not very veiled warning, he told Brownell that he did not intend to speak again about these matters until the latter part of May but that he would "then speak about things as they are."[6]

Cain then proceeded to unload on the Attorney General in language very few cabinet officers ever receive in writing from another member of their administration. Again raising a point that had upset the Attorney General during their meeting, Cain said that he was "not convinced you appreciate the vast difference between your public pronouncements and the lack of achievement [in combating communism]" by the Justice Department and criticized Brownell for his "failure to prosecute your cases before the SACB 'more energetically.'" Cain continued by quoting passages from some recent speeches made by the Attorney General to the effect that subversives posed a real threat to the nation and that the Justice Department was actively prosecuting them. "It [has] become distressingly apparent that something was organically wrong with your department. The threat of Communist subversion and infiltration is either real, as you constantly say it is publicly, or it is more fanciful than real, as this board's workload might indicate."[7] He ended the letter with a challenge. "You like plain talk and so do I. . . . I think it self-evident that most of us should put up or shut up."[8]

Brownell's reaction to reading Cain's second letter can only be imagined, but again, he did not respond. The meetings between Cain and Tomkins, however, went ahead as planned. The two met for more than ten hours in two meetings—with more scheduled to follow. Cain felt confident that he had won Tompkins over on at least two issues: allowing an employee to remain at work until a hearing could be held regarding the charges made against him and providing employees with legal representation in the same way as the military provides for their personnel in court-martial proceedings. A final meeting on the matter was supposed to be held on May 16, but it never occurred. Tompkins contacted Cain to say that he needed more time.[9]

Because of all the publicity being generated from his Spokane speech, Cain was now invited to speak to a succession of civil rights and civil liberties groups—organizations very different from those who had supported him while he was in the Senate—and to testify at a series of congressional hearings on the internal security program now being organized by the new Democratic majority. These included the Senate Government Operations Subcommittee, led by Senator Hubert Humphrey of Minnesota, the Senate Post Office and Civil Service Subcommittee, chaired by Senator Olin Johnston of South Carolina, and the Senate Judiciary Committee, chaired by Senator Thomas Hennings of Missouri.

Not surprisingly, the Eisenhower Justice Department took a different view. In an interview published in the *New York Times Magazine* in August, a senior administration official was quoted as saying that the internal security had improved because "the security program has re-established public confidence in the civil service. . . . The program has accomplished its purpose of restoring respectability to Federal employment as well as protecting the national security. The Government is starting out again with a clean slate, so to speak, and everybody is feeling better about it."[10] "Everybody," clearly, did not include Harry Cain.

As promised, Cain refrained from making any new speeches until the fourth week of May, but then, on the 23rd of that month, he delivered a speech entitled "Truth or Consequences" to B'nai B'rith, the Jewish humanitarian and civil rights organization, at its annual convention in upstate New York. "I tell you that the Attorney General's list is vastly misleading because it indicates that the United States is confronted by a far larger assault against our security by organized groups of Communists or fellow travelers than is the fact. . . . Of the 275 listed organizations [on the AGLOSO], approximately 150 of them have long since gone out of business. . . . This list is the warped and wormy measuring rod which, for eight years, has served as the main index to the loyalty and trustiness of employees in the federal and defense industry establishments."[11]

On June 2, Cain testified before the Senate Post Office and Civil Service Subcommittee. Cain called the security program "totalitarian in practice and result." It deprived Americans of the "dignity and self-respect to which every human being is entitled." He claimed that the practice of using past organizational membership to determine an individual's current security risk could even be used to cast suspicion on current members of Congress who may have belonged to an organization before it was "taken over by the Communists."[12]

On June 5, the same day on which his son was graduating from Vermont Academy without him, Cain was on the CBS television program *Face the Nation* in Washington, DC. Two exchanges were noteworthy.

> Edward M. Hines (Sunday editor of the *Washington Evening Star*): "So then, are you saying that really there is no need for an Attorney General's subversive list—period! Is that correct?"
>
> Cain: "I am saying that the time has come when we ought to consider whether or not the Attorney General's list . . . isn't doing infinitely more harm to the republic than it is doing good. In addition, to which, sir, the Constitution of the United States . . . speaks out boldly in opposition to *ex post facto* laws . . . and though the Attorney General's list is not a law in itself, it has inherent within it the spirit of opposing the Constitution."

The other came when one of the panelists asked Cain if he would run again for public office again. Cain replied, "To be very practical, blunt, and pointed about it, I don't think I could be reelected."[13]

Cain's views were finally gaining some traction in Congress where some of his proposed reforms enjoyed broad bipartisan support. But the most unexpected congressional attack on AGLOSO came on June 28, when the Senate Internal Security Subcommittee, chaired by Senator James Eastland of Mississippi and widely known for its anti-Communist views, issued a report that specifically criticized the Attorney General's list and included many of Cain's recommendations. The report declared that AGLOSO had been "greatly and quite generally misconceived" as well as "widely misunderstood and misapplied." It urged the Attorney General "as promptly as possible" to publish a handbook containing the kind of information about the listed organizations that Cain had been requesting.[14] Indeed, the committee report was so consistent with Cain's recommendations that many felt he had helped to craft its language.

The abrupt interruption of the meetings with Tompkins only increased Cain's sense of frustration. He decided to unburden himself in a seven-page, single-spaced letter to Sherman Adams on June 30. "In five months and more there has hardly been a single word of encouragement, approval, understanding, or enthusiasm [from the White House]. Where I have endeavored to convince them [referring to the Justice Department] that the best politics flow from doing the right and logical thing, they have impressed upon me, through direct conversation or in remarks which naturally get back to me, that I have been a disturbing member of the team." He continued, "It seems distressingly clear that much of the internal security advice which others have given to the President has been negative, restricted, and unimaginative. My every effort has constituted a responsible citizen's advice to the President which I have not been encouraged or allowed to discuss with him personally during the more than two years I have served in my important capacity."[15] Adams did not directly respond to Cain's letter, but it quickly made the rounds of his critics.

By mid-1955, evidence began to accumulate that Cain's efforts were finally paying off. In July, Agriculture Secretary Benson withdrew his charges against Wolf Ladejinsky. The press gave Cain some of the credit for the decision, but others were more appreciative. From Saigon, Cain received a telegram: "Profoundly grateful for your support and magnificent statement. [signed] Ladejinsky."[16] Across the country, other factors were at play. McCarthy's voice had been marginalized, if not silenced. Congressional hearings and proposed legislation seemed to support Cain's concerns, and media coverage had been generally positive. A series of stories in the *Christian Science Monitor* gave Cain much of the credit. In a June 11, 1955, article, reporter William Stringer declared that a "significant change in attitudes on the whole controversial question of security-loyalty procedures is evident in Washington." He listed five recent events as causes, in which Cain's "sharp testimony" against the current program was listed first.[17] In another article in the *Monitor* three days later, Josephine Ripley credited Cain with having waged a "one-man crusade" that was largely responsible for a "sudden reassessment of federal security regulations." On June 29, she wrote that it was Cain who had first lashed out at the AGLOSO in its present form in a "series of sizzling speeches."[18] On August 14, the *New York Times Magazine* carried a long article entitled "The Security Issue: A Changing Atmosphere," written by John M. Oakes, a member of the paper's editorial board, that noted the shift in the public's attitude and prominently quoted Cain.[19]

11. The Cain Mutiny

In its October 1955, issue, *American Mercury* magazine ran an in-depth article on Cain's transformation, saying, "there is some reason to believe that 'the Cain mutiny,' as punsters have dubbed it, may mark a significant shift in the political trends of the times."[20]

As public opinion appeared to shift and interest in the internal security issue waned, Cain's speeches began to receive far less attention than they had previously—perhaps because the novelty of his comments had begun to wear off. A speech to the American Civil Liberties Union (ACLU) in Los Angeles failed to generate even a local story in the *Los Angeles Times*. An August 15 speech to the national convention of federal postal employees generated attention only because Cain drew attention in it to the fact that the President had in the prior week announced the creation of a federal Commission on Government Security—an idea Cain had championed.

That all changed when Edgar Prina's detailed, in-depth interview with Cain in *Collier's*—entitled "The Harry Cain Mutiny"—hit the news-stands on August 18. Cain's revelations about the depth of his rift with the administration immediately became front-page news. The details of his conversations with Adams and Brownell, in particular, provided a rare look into the inner workings of the Administration. Cain provided a "No Comment" when asked about the story by a *New York Times* reporter but didn't deny any of the details. Cain tried to downplay his frustration with the White House, saying that "I am not presently in disagreement with Mr. Adams about anything. I hold Mr. Adams in high regard."[21] Cain's motivations for conducting the candid interview with Prina can only be imagined. It followed the termination of the meetings with Tompkins and the lack of response to his letters to Adams and Brownell. It certainly served to re-stir the pot, but perhaps that was the whole idea. Relations between Cain and the Justice Department continued to seethe after the publication of the *Collier's* story, and it was not long before there was another confrontation.

Cain decided to make another speech. Keynoting the 10th National Conference of Citizenship on September 19, Cain continued his attack on AGLOSO in a speech entitled "The Blessings of Liberty: Unto the Least of These, Thy Brethren." Noting that America's totalitarian enemies would never be able to prevail unless or until "America is so divided by fear and suspicion, and so torn by internal dissention and distrust, as to be unable to resist domestic pressures." In this connection, Cain voiced concern that "in the vital area of human relationships, and more particularly the relationship between the American citizen and his government, we have . . . gone backwards. . . . We are not nearly so free in 1955 as we were in 1945."[22]

Cain compared the process employed by the SACB, where the Attorney General "must establish his allegations to be true," and where the board's decisions "were subject to judicial review" to the use of the AGLOSO, a public document "available to and employed extensively by states, municipalities, and private agents or agencies from coast to coast." The list provided "the foundation for present-day guilt by association. Because of the list, we are much less free to speak, to think, to join, to learn and to travel than we were ten years ago. . . . Unless we define more clearly what it represents and until we flatly refuse to assume that guilt flows from mere membership, past or present, the Attorney General's list will continue to operate as a blunderbuss of insecurity." As an example of what he was talking about, Cain described the plight of a federal employee who was separated as a security risk from the federal service the previous April because his parents had once been active in a lodge of the International Workers Order. There was no allegation of any wrong-doing on the part of the federal employee, but when the employee requested a hearing, he was told that the "provisions of Executive Order 10450 preclude appointment of an individual where the facts establish a close and continued association [in this case, with his parents]."[23] At the time of Cain's speech, the case had continued to drag on for months without being resolved.

While Cain had not mentioned either the name of the individual or the agency involved, the Treasury Department announced on the day following Cain's speech that it had decided to review the case of William Taylor—a man whose case exactly fit the circumstances of the case Cain had described in his speech. Cain hadn't mentioned it, but he had recently and privately asked the Treasury Department to re-open the case. Taylor was reinstated several months later.[24] Taylor's case was just one of at least "a score" of cases, by his own estimate, in which Cain played a role in helping to reverse the government's decision in federal employee security cases. Most of these efforts remained unnoticed and uncommented upon.

On September 28, nearly ten days after his speech, Cain sent Max Rabb a note from Seattle, where he was presiding over the Washington

Pension Fund hearing (see below), enclosing a copy of a recent column written by Roscoe Drummond, the highly respected editor and columnist for the *New York Herald Tribune,* which was complimentary of Cain's speech. Mindful of the criticism against him by some in the administration, Cain penned a handwritten note on his letter to Rabb. "Have been here [Seattle] for several weeks on the government's case against the Washington Pension Union. Haven't said boo—but am being treated as though I am no longer dead. I consider this reaction to be as unexpected as it is pleasing."[25] Cain didn't send Rabb an article from that day's *Seattle Post-Intelligencer* in which its political writer, Stub Nelson, said that he had recently checked with state GOP leaders about rumors that Cain might like to try for a political comeback, perhaps against Representative-at-Large Don Magnuson. Their collective answer was, "We are not interested in Cain's candidacy for any office." As if to emphasize the point, they said that they would not even be interested in Cain as a "second choice," saying, "If we have to, we would rather go with a new face."[26]

CAIN SPENT MOST of October 1955 in Seattle, presiding over the SACB hearing on the Washington Pension Union (WPU). Cain knew the WPU well from his years spent in his home state. Probably because of this background, Harry Cain was appointed as the hearing examiner in the case. The WPU was an outgrowth of the Washington Commonwealth Federation (WCF), the same organization that had spawned the political careers of Hugh De Lacy, Howard Costigan, and other liberal, Seattle-area Democrats in Washington politics. The WCF disbanded in 1945, but the WPU soldiered on, advocating social policy issues and seeking to raise public awareness about public assistance grants and the state's aid-to-dependent children program. WPU leaders openly admitted their earlier affiliations with the Communist Party as well as the fact that they had become active in the liberal wing of the Democratic Party during the 1930s and that they were proud of their more recent political activities on behalf of the poor. But back in 1949, Cain had told the Senate Armed Services Committee that "the Washington Pension Union is one of the most notorious Communist-front organizations in our state and its entire high command has been identified as belonging to the Communist Party."[27]

Once hugely important in Washington politics, the WPU by 1952 was under siege by the government. At that time, the Justice Department arrested seven members of the Communist Party in Washington, including William Pennock, the president of the WPU. Pennock and the other six members of the "Seattle Seven" were then prosecuted and convicted under the Smith Act. During the course of the trial, Pennock committed suicide. Their convictions were overturned on appeal in 1958.

When the WPU case first came before the SACB, its lawyers—fully cognizant of Cain's former views about the organization—asked that he be disqualified as the hearing officer in the case. The SACB had denied their request, and since then, both sides had been gearing up for the hearings. At that point, strangely, the Justice Department stepped in to take up the WPU's "bias and prejudice" case against Cain, citing comments he had made in an article he had written for the November 1955 issue of *Coronet* magazine. In it, Cain retold the story of the Smileys (the scientist who had worked for the National Cancer Institute and his wife) who, Cain said in the article, had "joined an outfit called the Washington Pension Union because it worked for free milk and pensions. Occasional WPU meetings were held at the Smileys' home. There was excited talk of 'saving the workers from starvation.' Some years after the Smileys had left the WPU, it was placed on the Attorney General's list of subversive organizations."[28] In the article, Cain said that the list "has helped create an atmosphere of intolerance and suspicion" and noted that "no organization should be placed on it without a judicial hearing." A *Seattle Times* editorial on October 24 applauded Cain's comments in the *Coronet* article and his handling of the WPU hearing. "Cain's fair and judicious conduct of the Pension Union hearing has made an excellent impression in Seattle—one that lends weight to his views on questions of federal security procedures."[29]

By their action, the Justice Department lawyers were essentially giving the WPU another chance to disqualify Cain. However, the lawyers for the WPU now came to Cain's defense, saying that during the earlier hearings Cain had been free of bias and now accused the government of using "incredible tactics" against Cain because he had "refused to knuckle under to their demands."[30] Cain was intensely relieved when the board rejected the government's challenge to his impartiality. In the *Coronet* article, Cain wrote, "The question of my prejudice had to be submitted to the SACB. So easily they could have said that I was prejudiced. That wouldn't [cause me to] lose my job on the SACB, but it would have discredited me with everyone and I would be over and done with."[31] Ultimately, Cain rejected all sixteen motions by the WPU for dismissal of all or parts of the Justice Department's case and voted with the majority to order the WPU to register as a Communist-front organization with the Attorney General. The organization finally disbanded in 1963.

THE WASHINGTON PENSION Union case created more publicity for Cain in his home state than at any time since his defeat by Henry M. Jackson three years earlier. Cain clearly enjoyed it and used it to prompt new speculation about his political future—a train of thought that was never very far from his mind. On October 27, Cain wrote a letter to Max Rabb that confided, "One might think from the press coverage that I was an active participant in Washington State politics. Such is not the case, but the assumption causes me no displeasure." Cain further attempted to dispel administration criticism of his attacks on the AGLOSO. "The fact is that during my month at home, I have refused to say anything publicly about any question unrelated to my assignment. The irony of political life being what it is, this conduct has made me much more of a force than had I employed the hearings, as one could do so easily, to serve any political ambition I might have in mind."[32]

Cain then went on to discuss his own political future within the administration. "It seems a fact that our national climate, in terms of moderation in security matters, is vastly more refreshing and healthy than it was twelve months ago. We agree that my conduct during this period has annoyed some of those in authority but perhaps we agree as well that I am in some substantial respect responsible for the improved national climate. It is undeniable that I am made very welcome in quarters where most Republicans are opposed or misunderstood. It ought to follow that I can speak for the Republican cause where other Republicans are refused admission.[33] Making an argument to use his services during the 1956 election campaign, he reasoned, "Had I not been advocating reforms for our existing internal security systems, the advocates for reform would be monopolized by the opposition. It seems self evident that most of what I have advocated must be adopted in due time. Your colleagues ought, I think, to recognize that no one yet has been remotely successful in attacking or destroying the validity of my recommendations. You will note, moreover, that I have always contended that I was speaking in support of what I believe the President believes to be true. I want to think that my [views] will someday be acknowledged publicly by you and others who represent the Administration."[34]

It was an attempt to find out where he stood. Cain was using Rabb as a conduit to those who refused to meet or speak with him. "I urge you to talk with the Governor [Sherman Adams] about the substance of this letter. I shall not be interested in any so-called special favors but it would be unreasonable and truly unfair if I did not seek to determine my relationship with the Administration months before the expiration of my term."[35]

Cain wrote to Rabb twice more before the end of the year—on November 3 and on December 20. In November, he wrote to inform Rabb of the successful outcome of a case in which a civilian employee of the army, Walter Novak, had been restored to his former job after Cain intervened in the case and arranged for Novak to be represented by legal counsel. "In the absence of an automatic appeals process, [Novak] had been told by nearly everyone that nothing should be attempted, for nothing could be accomplished. During 1955 I have had some small part to play in saving a score or more of Novaks who were otherwise condemned to a life of futility and despair."[36] Rabb must have responded positively to Cain's request for a meeting in a note dated December 15 because Cain replied to Rabb five days later, expressing the hope that "the year to come will have us meeting on many occasions and I hope that it does. I shall relish any chance to talk with you about anything or practically everything."[37]

While Cain was waiting to discuss his future with the White House, the Justice Department on November 15 announced that it would recommend amendments to the law governing the Federal Employee Security Program to Congress so that the heads of departments and agencies would be forced to suspend an alleged security risk without a prior hearing. A week later, the President said that he was making a sweeping study of the federal security program with the aim of correcting any faults that existed in it. He said that hardly a week passed without some phase of the program being brought to his attention and made the subject of a very earnest and "prayerful" conference.[38]

Cain and Rabb finally met on December 28. The news was not good. Rabb expressed his candid opinion that Cain's future "was in dispute and doubt around the White House" but that the differences might still be reconciled.[39] In the meantime, Cain was advised that he should not expect to be representing the administration on the campaign trail and that he should refrain from making any more speeches attacking the administration's internal security program. Looking back at the situation many years after his resignation, Cain finally understood that he had been naïve.

Cain's public differences with the administration were clearly taking a social as well as a political toll on him and his family. Cain told one reporter that "some of our friends who contend that subversion prospers under every bush have declared a state of siege and are not to be seen in my company." His wife, Marj, relayed to another that a Tacoma friend had been told in no uncertain terms that anyone who "kept the company of Marj and Harry was completely off the list—if you were known as a friend of Harry Cain you had gone soft on subversion."[40]

Most of President Eisenhower's January 5, 1956, State of the Union Address dealt with America's international responsibilities and national defense, but there was one reference about internal security. "Of great importance to our nation's security is a continuing alertness to internal subversive activity within or without our government. This administration will not relax its efforts to deal forthrightly and vigorously in protection of this government and its citizens against subversion, at the same time fully protecting the constitutional rights of all citizens."[41]

Because of the signals received during his meeting with Max Rabb on December 28 or, perhaps, in spite of them, Cain decided to speak out again on January 30, 1956. The occasion was the Twelfth Annual Celebration of Independence Day, sponsored by the Chicago affiliate of the Americans for Democratic Action (ADA). Cain opened his remarks by saying that it had been the "planning, skill, and patience employed by you and your counterparts in a far western state" that had "insured my availability to be your guest tonight." He came before them not only as a "proud member of the Republican Party" but as "one of the few individuals whom you have seen in recent years who admitted publicly to being a conservative by deliberate choice." Cain noted that recent "competition to be more anti-Communist than the next fellow" had already led to excesses and extremes that are "self-defeating and may be undermining freedom's foundation stones called the law and fair play."[42] He traced the history of the development of the Bill of Rights by the Founders and the history of abuses of it, normally imposed in times of perceived danger, that dated back to the imposition of the Alien and Sedition Acts of 1798. He then outlined the development and use of the Attorney General's list since it was established during the war, noting how each new version had made it more restrictive. The language in EO 10450 was the most restrictive of all, "permitting the resolution of doubts in favor of Authority rather than in favor of the individual, even before those doubts had been established. Liberals and conservatives alike should be concerned. . . . Personal liberty belongs to every other citizen in the same way it belongs to me. The safest and only durable way for each of us to protect our personal liberty is to make certain that the other fellow is fully protected in his."[43]

On the day following the Chicago speech, Cain sent a copy of the speech to Adams with a note: "Perhaps the President will feel refreshed should he read portions of it." The next day, February 1, he sent Rabb a copy of his speech, along with a copy of his note to Adams. He apparently held out hope of getting Vice President Richard Nixon to support publicly his position. "I have talked with Dick's right-hand man about my willingness [to discuss the matter] and wish to confer with the former."[44] He also hoped to meet with Brownell, sending him a copy of the speech and asking for a meeting, followed by yet another note to Adams, requesting a meeting with the President or Brownell and telling Adams that he had heard informally that Brownell was willing to see him "not at all." No replies were forthcoming.[45]

Continuing to receive the cold shoulder from the Administration, Cain maintained his speaking schedule in February with another of what he now privately referred to as his "open letters to the President." On February 22, he delivered a speech to the annual luncheon of the New York Civil Liberties Union entitled "What Price Security?" The event celebrated the birthday of George Washington. In discussing the views of the Founders as they struggled with the Bill of Rights, which amended the Constitution, Cain noted that Washington, while in office, had opposed every attempt to amend the Constitution, believing that "those thereafter in positions of authority would be just in their dealings with the people," and for most of America's history, that had, indeed, been the case. However, fear and confusion following World War II had resulted in Americans' adopting "procedures and approved policies that are as foreign in origin as they were repugnant in our past."

Cain then went on to describe the history of the government's loyalty-security program. "The first Truman Loyalty Standard of Disqualification was 'reasonable grounds for belief that the person involved is disloyal.' The second Truman Loyalty Order of 1950 revised the Standard . . . to require only that 'reasonable doubt' of an individual's loyalty be determined. In 1953, the Standard of the Eisenhower Federal Security Program was 'that persons were to be employed or retained by the federal service, if their employment or retention was 'clearly consistent with the national security.'" Cain then went on to make his point. The more restrictive language adopted by the Eisenhower Administration permits "resolving doubts in favor of Authority before these doubts have been established to really exist." Under the [existing] regulations, "the individual must assume the burden of proving his loyalty, his security reliability. . . . To my mind, the results are equally unfair to the government and the individual."[46]

Widely interpreted as referring to the President, Cain went on to say that "many a modern-day leader is likewise too remote from Main Street, where appear the victims of injustice or lack of fair play. . . . Leaders will seldom tolerate abuses which they know to exist. But abuses do exist which are not seen or felt by persons highly placed, and it remains for the average citizen to cry out in indignation or alarm when he sees them."[47]

Cain sent copies of the New York speech to Rabb, Adams, and Brownell and added Fred Seaton, Deputy Assistant to the President, to the list of recipients. In his letter, Cain noted that one of the security risks he mentioned in his speech had been restored to his federal job less than forty-eight hours after the speech, although the sixteen months between his dismissal and reinstatement spent trying to defend himself had cost the individual $125,000.[48] Again, he received no responses.

On March 9, Cain wrote yet again to Rabb, inquiring about his future. Cain was winding up the Washington Pension Union case and expected that, following it, "I shall be available for re-assignment, reappointment or some other endeavor. When last we got together around Christmas, my future was in dispute and doubt around the White House. You thought that these differences might be cleared away or reconciled. It did not then seem advantageous to talk with the Governor about the future." Now, he again asked for a meeting with Adams. "Though I remain anxious to assist the Administration during the election period and after that, I am naturally as anxious to fend for myself if re-appointment is not to be offered. It seems reasonable to suggest that I am more widely informed and better equipped to do a more constructive job somewhere than I have ever been. If these tools aren't to be employed by our side, I shall be keenly disappointed."[49]

The changing public attitudes about internal security, driven largely by Cain's speeches and their resulting publicity, did not go unnoticed at the Justice Department. On March 2, Deputy Attorney General Tompkins sent a memo to Brownell recommending that AGLOSO be abandoned entirely. He argued that approximately 230 of the 279 groups then listed were defunct and that other government agencies were no longer relying on it. The list was so misused and misunderstood that it would be difficult to add new groups to the list.[50] In a contentious March 12 conference that included Tompkins, Deputy Attorney General Rogers, and FBI Director Hoover, the FBI declared its opposition to Tompkins's proposal. The FBI's opposition resulted in a convoluted decision by the Justice Department to recommend that AGLOSO be abolished (without informing the FBI in advance) while, at the same time, preparing to add scores of new organizations.[51]

On April 12, Cain again wrote to Adams and Brownell, asking for appointments to see them. Again, neither man responded. On April 30, Cain saw Rabb at a special dinner honoring the tenth anniversary of *Meet the Press.* Some months earlier, he had begun to record his thoughts in a journal, just as he had during the early part of his term as mayor and, then again, during the war. "Rabb was in a very uncomfortable position. There was simply nothing that he could do. It was not profitable to 'rock the boat.' Without bitterness or any feeling I told Max to forget it. I have seldom felt sorrier for anybody. Max Rabb is an important person, the Secretary to the Cabinet, who does not dare to correspond with a presidential appointee who has been Rabb's friend for a long time. . . . It serves no purpose to criticize or condemn. Every man has the right to make his bed and live in his own way."[52]

Cain finally decided that he wasn't making any progress going through the regular chain of command at the White House. He decided, as he called it, to "go for broke." On May 5, Cain spoke at a luncheon of the Jewish Labor Committee of the National Trade Union Conference on Civil Rights held at the Belmont Hotel in New York City. The title of the speech, "The Individual is of Supreme Importance," was based on a recent quote by the President. Cain wasted no time in getting his audience's attention. "For the President of the United States I have a considered admiration and respect. Good fortune has enabled me to serve him in war and peace. I shall strive to serve him well on this occasion. If I speak of and to him bluntly, I do so only because of the faith I have in the quality of leadership which belongs to him in such abundance. The nation suffers needlessly, in my view, because that leadership is neither understood nor being felt in some quarters." Then Cain went on to repeat many of his previous criticisms. "What I must try to accomplish now is to convince the President that the principle which he puts first—the individual is of supreme importance—is being so little understood or dishonored in practice that the internal security of our beloved nation is in danger of being undermined." Trying to deflect any direct criticism of the President, Cain suggested that Eisenhower was unaware of the abuses inherent in his loyalty-security program and that he "has no real knowledge about how the individual is being treated." Cain claimed that the President's advisors "who let it be known that they represent, speak for, and protect him, have never brought him face to face with what I am talking to you about today." He asked his audience, "Have we made more security risks than we have found?"[53]

To emphasize his point, Cain related the story of a young air force civilian accountant who had been suspended as a security risk fourteen months before and had come to him for assistance. Cain didn't mention him by name, but the man was quickly revealed by the *Washington Evening Star* to be Sidney Hatkin. Out of work following his suspension and with a family to feed, Hatkin placed an ad in the local paper looking for work. He was soon contacted by a Mr. Machoff who met with Hatkin and asked him to assist him in doing research into some vital aspects of the aircraft industry. A fee was negotiated and paid on the spot. Hatkin immediately contacted the authorities. Machoff turned out to be a man named Methiov who worked at the Soviet Embassy. Cain asked, "I wonder how many have been approached; how many have closed their eyes to doubts and agreed to work for the other side because they had to eat?" Hatkin's patriotism didn't help him keep his job. Even after he filed an affidavit about the Machoff incident, the Air Force proceeded to fire him, saying that they had concluded that he was not reliable or trustworthy from a security point of view.[54]

Days later, Cain told Emily Walker, "I knew that when I gave this speech I was going for broke. I have tried in every way I know to reach the President in order to apprise him of what I am certain no one else has, namely the tragic things that are happening to individuals whom the government are not treating as individuals at all. . . . I hope that by this means, now that the story has reached the print, the President will become aware of what is going on."[55]

On the Monday following his speech to the Jewish Labor Committee, Cain decided to write directly to the President. He attached a copy of the speech to a note that requested "some expression of your future wishes with regard to myself." Cain told Eisenhower of his unsuccessful efforts to see him and ended with the hope that "it will be proper for me to come directly to you." Two days later, Cain wrote three more letters—one each to the President's brothers, Dr. Milton Eisenhower and Edgar Eisenhower, and one to Vice President Nixon—attaching a copy of his speech and his note to the President to each.[56]

At the same time, Cain sent yet another note to Sherman Adams, enclosing another copy of the speech, and telling him that he was still eager to see him but that "I shall make no further request. Should [the President] wish to see me, I shall gladly join with you at any time or any place which suits your convenience." In a draft of a 1959 graduate school paper, on which the senior Cain collaborated closely with his son, Buzz wrote that his father "was not fully confident" that the President would see either his note or his speech. His father apparently agreed. In a handwritten marginal note, the senior Cain wrote, "Understatement."

Adams later denied that he ever stood in the way of Cain meeting with the President. "Any allegations that I or any other member of the White House staff used presumptuous or arbitrary tactics to keep high-ranking executives or legislators from seeing Eisenhower are completely false."[57] Three days later, Cain wrote a final letter to Attorney General Brownell that began, "It seems unfortunate that you have not responded to any of the letters I have written to you since July 26, 1954. I had wanted to talk with you quietly about the Sidney Hatkin affair."[58]

On May 17, with his term on the SACB scheduled to end in August, Cain delivered what he, by now, considered his swansong to the Colorado Branch of the American Civil Liberties Union. He noted that he was speaking to the group "in my present capacity perhaps for the last time." In his speech, he attacked what he called the administration's "numbers game" (a Republican Party publication had recently used the number of 9,700 as an indication of the Administration's success in dealing with loyalty-security cases among government employees). Cain told the ACLU that "these numbers should be marked POISON and employed with great care. . . . In the eyes of a vast majority of our people [the President] is the champ and this is as it should be . . . but any champion can be made to look like a chump if he leaves himself open to a sucker punch. The figure 9,700, employed without explanation, is such a sucker punch."[59]

Cain's direct references to the President in his last two speeches immediately became front-page news. The *Christian Science Monitor* ran a lead story only three days after Cain's Colorado ACLU speech, noting that "five different Congressional groups, plus the State Department, plus the Air Force, are now looking into the Hatkin story. Mr. Cain may not have saved his own job but he has set off a blast likely to reach the President's ear." William H. Stringer, the Washington Bureau chief of the *Christian Science Monitor*, writing on May 18, said, "Mr. Cain expects that when his term expires in August the Eisenhower Administration will be glad to appoint someone else. Perhaps the President and his advisors should think this over carefully. Sometimes it's useful to have someone who speaks the unpleasant fact."[60]

Writing in *Newsweek*, Ernest K. Lindley said, "No one has ever refuted Cain's specific criticisms. So far as I am aware, no one of consequence has even attempted to do so." Lindley went on to note, using information that must have been provided by Cain, that "sixteen months have elapsed since Cain uttered his first public criticism of the operation of the loyalty-security system. Not once has he been invited to the White House to see the President. In recent months, he has repeatedly written to the Attorney General and not even been given the courtesy of a reply. Cain deserves better treatment than that, if only because he is a man of conscience and intellectual integrity. He has no private means, and by keeping silent he could have looked forward to reappointment to his present job when his term ends in August."[61]

The *Tacoma News Tribune* editorialized, "It is ironic but true that Harry Cain seems about to fade from the national scene at the very height of his usefulness. . . . His failure to live up to his potential during his term in the Senate would be a serious bar to any re-entry into Washington State politics. Further, many of those who supported him in 1946 would be dubious over supporting a man whose political complexion had changed from ultra-conservative to quite liberal and that same change probably wouldn't switch enough labor votes into the Cain camp to make up the deficit. . . . Cain has many friends and admirers who believe that in recent months he has found himself, after a prolonged period of political groping.

They are sincere in their hope that his abilities and his service will not be lost to the public good, in one manner or another."[62]

While he may have held out some remote hope that he could remain, Cain privately agreed with his hometown paper's assessment and understood what lay ahead. On May 22, Marj confirmed to a reporter for the *Washington Evening Star* in a story that was picked up by the *Tacoma News Tribune* that she had rented out their treasured three-story home in the exclusive Foxhall Road district of Washington, DC. Marj had gone to work as a designer in a home decorating shop and had obtained a real estate license. With Buzz off at Stanford, Harry, Marj, and Candy again moved into a one-bedroom apartment.[63] Marj said the SACB job had been a "bone" that had been tossed to her husband that had "become a bomb . . . too hot to handle." She complained that other Republicans had failed to "show appreciation" for her husband's efforts and about the "New England freeze" around the President for whom her husband still had "faith" and "devotion." "When a ship is going into a storm you don't leave all the hatches open. You just fasten down the hatches and ride out the storm together. We are prepared to make any sacrifices necessary for what we believe in so strongly."[64]

Many years later, in a personal interview, Cain said, "You might think me very naïve. I know I have been naïve on occasion, and perhaps I was this time, but I thought—really I thought—I thought that I belonged to a political party that constantly, consistently, was talking about the dignity of the individual. All I needed to do was to be conclusive in my evidence that individuals . . . were being unfairly charged, badly dealt with, stripped for life of their sense of dignity . . . [and] that all I had to do was make these matters absolutely plain and then the President would put everything right. . . . I thought they would do it for *political* reasons. I thought that they would do it for reasons of logic and just for reasons of reason, but again I came back to that old point; when you build an octopus, how terribly difficult to admit that it has any weaknesses . . . and to set those weaknesses right."[65]

Cain's recent speeches and his letters to the President and Adams finally brought the matter to a head. Referring to a question about Cain's May 17 speech to the Colorado ACLU, White House Press Secretary James Haggerty replied that "I never have any comment on Mr. Cain," and gave the same answer to a follow-on question about whether or not Cain had asked for an appointment with the President.[66] Then, during

11. The Cain Mutiny

President Eisenhower's May 23, 1956, news conference, Garnett Horner, a reporter from the *Washington Evening Star* who was friendly to Cain, asked the President whether Cain, who had recently indicated that he expected not to be re-appointed to the SACB, could see the President if he asked for an appointment. Eisenhower, obviously miffed at the question, answered with a terse "Yes."[67] Three days later, columnist Roscoe Drummond, wrote that "every correspondent in the room knew that it was not an enthusiastic or even a very cordial yes."[68]

Upon reading about the President's comment, Cain immediately called Eisenhower's secretary, Bernard Shanley, requesting an appointment. He asked how much time he might be able to expect so that he could prepare for the meeting. "You appear to be well prepared every time you talk," Shanley responded.[69] Cain was told to prepare to meet with the President at 8:30 a.m. on Thursday, June 7. He arrived on time at the White House only to learn that his time slot had been preempted by the Attorney General to discuss "security" issues.

Despite the frustration of the delay, Cain realized that "everything" rode on this meeting. Indeed, he had high hopes for it. He didn't know how much of his year-long campaign against the administration's loyalty-security program had come to Eisenhower's attention, but he had developed his presentation over a series of public speeches and was now prepared to summarize it in what he hoped would be a powerful presentation to the President. He kept detailed mental notes and then committed them to paper as soon as he returned to his office, sharing them with freelance writer Daniel M. Berman, who then used them as well as a personal interview to provide a detailed description of the meeting in the June 25, 1956 edition of the *New Republic* magazine.[70] Cain provided additional detail in later interviews with his son and with the author for term papers they were writing.

It took Cain six minutes and twenty seconds to walk across Lafayette Park from his offices in the Lafayette Building, pass through security, and arrive in the anteroom of the Oval Office for his 3:30 meeting that afternoon. According to Berman's account, President Eisenhower greeted Cain, coolly but civilly, all business, without shaking his hand. Cain sat in a chair alongside the President's desk; Gerald D. Morgan, Special Assistant to the President, sat in another in front of the desk. Leading off the discussion, Eisenhower said that he had had full confidence in Cain when he had appointed him but had "been astounded" when his staff told him that Cain had given them no advance warning of his criticism before he decided to denounce the Administration publicly rather than criticize it in private. "I thought that I could trust you when I appointed you to that job, and now some of my people tell me I can't." Defensively, Cain responded that there was "not a damn word of truth" in what his staff members had told him and what was more, if the President would call them all in—Cain seems to have suspected them of lurking just outside the door to the Oval Office—he would "prove it to him right then and there."[71]

Cain had anticipated and was prepared for the accusation. He recalled that a month before his Spokane speech he had been asked by the "Executive Office" to investigate the case of a female government worker who was suspected of being a security risk. He had and established to his satisfaction that she was guilty of nothing. In spite of this, he said, the woman still remained under suspicion. "I have always tried to tell your people, Mr. President, that we're having too much of this security business."[72] Eisenhower wanted to know what he meant. Cain was again prepared. He reminded the President of three statements he had made in recent presidential speeches: "The individual is of supreme importance" in a democratic society; government must have a heart as well as a head; and federal workers should be treated as people, not as social numbers. "I have always believed these things, Mr. President, and you are the one who can breathe meaning into those words." [73] Cain said that, as important as these principles are in a court of law, they are equally crucial in an administrative proceeding on which people's livelihoods and reputations depend; it is cruel and unfair to expect a man to answer vague and ambiguous charges. Eisenhower concurred: it was not good for charges to be nebulous.

To make his point, Cain then proceeded to describe the cases of Sidney L. Hatkin, the air force statistician, and William H. Taylor, the former Treasury official and a Republican, who had not been given any real opportunity to clear themselves by their respective agencies. Eisenhower noted that he did not like the fact that accused employees were not always given a full statement of the reasons for their dismissal. Cain responded that the current Executive Order 10450 *did* allow for this right, but the section in question had been revoked in the name of administrative convenience. The present system, Cain said, allowed vindictive administrators to dismiss persons for personal reasons and pretend that security was involved. "Those dismissed for disloyalty and those fired for reasons that do not at all reflect on their patriotism are both branded as security risks." As an example, he described the case of Abraham Chasanow, an employee of the Navy Department who, after a public furor, had been reinstated with an apology. The whole problem was that *security* and *loyalty* had become hopelessly confused. "Those dismissed for disloyalty and those fired for reasons that do not at all reflect on their patriotism are both branded 'security risks.' The loyalty criterion should apply only to departments dealing with military secrets. For the others, *suitability* should be the standard by which an employee is measured."[74] Eisenhower expressed surprise at this and questioned Morgan who, participating for the first time, gave a detailed and legalistic explanation as to why this was not being done.

At that point, the meeting had gone six minutes beyond the half hour allotted to it. Eisenhower anxiously looked at his watch, and Cain, noticing, asked if he could have another minute. "No, there is someone waiting for me." "But Sir," persisted Cain, "this case concerns a soldier." The President dropped back in his chair, and Cain related the story of Irving I. August, a Korean War veteran who had been refused the necessary army clearance for an overseas assignment with the Red Cross. He had written to the President, sending back his Combat Infantry Badge, but his letter had been unanswered and, instead, forwarded to the very people in the army bureaucracy who were refusing his clearance. As Cain later remembered it, the President said, "That can't be," and called in his secretary, asking her to track down the veteran's letter. Eisenhower then made a specific suggestion. The Attorney General was responsible for security matters, but Cain should put his thoughts down on paper and then arrange a meeting with Morgan for further discussion. "Do I understand that I have your encouragement and directive to confer with Morgan on this matter?" Eisenhower assured him that he did and rose, for the first time shaking his hand, and ushered him out the door. Cain later remembered, "I knew that I had gotten through to him and disturbed him when, instead of granting my request, he asked me to continue, and in the end authorized me to deal directly with his staff rather than through the Attorney General. He wasn't uninformed in knowing what civil liberties were; he was uninformed in his assumption that they were being respected."[75]

That night, shortly after midnight, President Eisenhower was stricken with a bowel obstruction that was so serious he could have died. As it was, it required immediate surgery at Walter Reed Hospital, essentially reducing his workload and his availability for the next month. That left Sherman Adams running the White House. Cain's meetings with Morgan never took place. Cain later told the author that "Jerry Morgan is a nice follow; an intelligent person, but like others in the Palace Guard, he wanted to insure the President's peace of mind. To hell with the facts if they might upset the 'old man.'"[76]

When he came out of the White House following his meeting with the President, an obviously nervous Cain told reporters, "I don't know what to say or how to say it. . . . The President could not have been more generous with his time. His questions were penetrating and searching, and it was obvious it is his ambition to equate the needs of internal security with the rights of free citizens. . . . From my own point of view, I was satisfied and felt more hopeful about the future in the field of internal security than before."[77]

In his own notes of the meeting, he was more candid. "I would say that had it been possible, he would have gladly chucked me out of his office in the first 30 seconds. There's no doubt about that. What struck me most was the President's certainty that the advisors he relied upon couldn't possibly be wrong, and his total lack of interest in listening to the counter view. Perhaps I changed his position a trifle, but only because I sort of overwhelmed him. I took away the reaction that I had been talking to a man who, in having been told by an intimate what he ought to think, was prepared not to do any thinking for himself. This shocked me for he was the President and I found him to be the most uninformed person [about internal security] I had ever met, and, much worse, a man who was obviously content to remain content by what he had been told."[78]

Cain understood that the meeting had been a climactic moment in his career. He later remembered, "I knew, totally because of the President's illness . . . that I wasn't to be re-appointed. I didn't want that job. I didn't want to spend the next five years of my life in the internal security field. I was sad. It wasn't because I was losing my job, but because I was losing my place in the government. . . . Had the President remained well, he would have been conscious of what I was doing . . . [and] it might have happened that the President would have offered me some other appointment. I was sad because I had been in the City Hall of Tacoma; I had spent several very rich years in one of the great spasms involving my country.... I had spent better than six years in the Senate of the United States where I had made some progress and a lot of mistakes; and I'd done what I thought was a real job of work at the SACB. I would have been quite content to remain a public servant in perpetuity."[79]

On June 12, Cain testified before the Constitutional Rights Subcommittee of the Senate Judiciary Committee. He had been scheduled to begin his testimony on Monday, June 4, but with his meeting with President Eisenhower scheduled for the seventh, he knew that his testimony would further inflame relations with the White House. By quiet arrangement with the subcommittee's chairman, Thomas C. Hennings of Missouri, his appearance was postponed a week. His testimony over two days filled eighty pages of small type in the printed transcript. He began by telling the panel that he believed that President Eisenhower had shown "deep concern and interest" in his proposals for revamping the security-loyalty program but that in the past the "rights of free men and women have been disregarded and mangled" in the operation of the administration's program. In the quote from his testimony that made the news headlines, he said that he hoped that America's efforts to battle communism didn't lead to a pro-fascist revival. "Our nation has less to worry about from the clear and present danger of Communism than it has to worry about the secret and more pernicious danger of fascism."[80]

Continuing his testimony the next day, he told the senators that, of the thousands of government workers listed as security risks over the years, it would be hard to find a dozen of them who actually were found to be disloyal. Cain also repeated his criticism of the AGLOSO list. To list organizations as bad "without those in authority bothering to define why the organizations are bad, is to employ a weapon from the arsenal of the tyrant." Cain said that he had "serious doubts the list is needed in a free society."[81] His testimony generated another round of front-page publicity, but Cain knew that he had already crossed the line in terms of his future.

Cain wrote to President Eisenhower again on June 17, following his Senate testimony. Noting that his term of office was set to expire on August 9, he offered his resignation "should you wish my assignment then to expire." The President responded five weeks later on July 27, accepting his resignation but "hoping that you will continue on until your successor has qualified and taken office." Eisenhower thanked him for his service and wished him "the best of health and happiness in the years ahead." Cain responded to the President two days later, saying that he would gladly continue to serve until his successor had been appointed but asking that he be given some indication of the length of time in question. An answer came promptly from Sherman Adams. "I think it will not be necessary for us to ask you to continue on beyond the first of September."[82]

Harry called Marj, who by then was spending the summer at their house on American Lake with the children, to say that the President had accepted his resignation. When a reporter called for her reaction, she said, "We love the Northwest, and I hope it will be possible for us to come back for good." Harry was undecided. Reached at his SACB office on July 25, he told a reporter for the *Washington Evening Star* that he was "so busy winding up my work here, I've had no time to make other plans."[83] In another interview, with Emily Walker the same day, he expressed his uncertainty about the future. "For the first time in 18 years, or from the day I entered the City Hall as Tacoma's mayor, I am beginning to give real consideration to this matter of making a living. Each thing I have done in the past has been progressively more challenging than that which came before—mayor, soldier, senator, authority on subversion—each has been broadening . . . and each has had something more worthwhile than the one before. At my age [50], one assumes there will be many years ahead, and with my background, I am concerned not only with making a living, but a living with the richness of the past. I am free and will be anxious to start a new career. Where or when, I do not know."[84]

While Cain was still out in Seattle, handing down the final ruling in the WPU case, the White House announced that Dorothy Lee, a member of the Justice Department's Parole Board, would be nominated to the SACB as Cain's replacement. In an August 2 letter to Sherman Adams, Cain expressed his bitterness at the way his resignation had been handled, saying that the process had violated "common decency" and reflected "arrogance and callousness. . . . Your methods astound me." He also complained again about the Justice Department's attempt to discredit him in the WPU case.[85]

On the day following the expiration of Cain's term at the SACB, the *Washington Sunday Star* published an article written by Daniel M. Berman, a political scientist and freelance writer friendly to Cain, in which he—now freed from any constraints by being a member of the SACB—unloaded once again on the government's internal security program. Cain went beyond his previous criticism of the AGLOSO and confided that during the period of the WPU case he had undergone an "agonizing reappraisal" of the McCarran Act itself, coming to believe that it represented a major threat to the constitutional right of free speech in America because it: 1) made people hesitate to join an organization for fear that the government might someday label that organization subversive; 2) made members of such organizations "second-class citizens" and deprived them of the rights to Government employment, travel abroad, and jobs in defense industries; 3) deprived individuals of their Fifth Amendment rights because it forced members of designated groups to brand themselves with a label which negatively impacted on their reputation and, perhaps, their freedom; and 4) because it was almost impossible for an organization, once identified by the government, to obtain an "acquittal" from the SACB. Cain noted that he had "voted enthusiastically" for the McCarran Act, believing that it would strengthen America against its internal enemies. Now, he said, he was certain that the Act had "actually weakened us and wouldn't be worth the price, even if it had really made us stronger. . . . The price we have paid is the abandonment of serious political dissent. America without dissenters might be secure, but it would not be America."[86]

A combination of Cain's public criticism, increased congressional oversight, internal dissention within the administration, growing media skepticism, and decreasing public interest ultimately sealed AGLOSO's fate. Harry Cain's immediate future may have been determined, but both the AGLOSO and the SACB continued on in limbo. By November 1956, the administration had decided to put a stop to any further designation proceedings, and no new organizations were listed for the next thirteen years. The list remained, moribund and unused, until President Nixon tried unsuccessfully to revive it as a tool against his political enemies in 1971.

CAIN STILL HAD a wife and family in Tacoma who were waiting for him to come home. Marj told a reporter, "My husband has great hope, and it is my and the children's hope too, that something will develop here that will make it possible for us to stay here as a family—and I emphasize as a family. What the future holds we do not know but I'm glad he is to have an opportunity to make a choice of what we will do with our lives." Marj noted that her husband's efforts had not been in vain, referring to the fact that Attorney General Brownell had announced earlier that week that 3,000 cases of dismissed civil service employees would be reopened, and that this decision was directly attributable to the "fundamental disagree-ment" between the two men.[87]

Harry returned to Tacoma on September 10, but not before writing to Adlai Stevenson and Estes Kefauver, who led the Democratic ticket then running against Eisenhower and Richard Nixon, offering to help them in their campaign. "Though we have never met, my political effort is freely given. . . . Should it happen that any of my expressed or written views on the subject of internal security are thought to possess value, may I suggest that you employ them as you see fit."[88] A close friend of Cain's in Washington, DC, told the *Seattle Times* that Cain was marking time before seeking a job in the private sector in order to see if Stevenson's presidential campaign would be successful. If it was, Cain was hopeful that a Democratic victory might lead to an appointment where he could continue his work for human rights.[89] It is unknown whether Cain ever received a response from either candidate, but it can be imagined that Cain's known unpredictability and his previous attacks on Kefauver's Crime Committee hearings might have been considered when his letters were received.

As the Cains struggled to plan for their future, Harry's past efforts on behalf of the many individuals he had helped were formally recognized. The Very Reverend Francis Sayre, Jr., dean of Washington's National Cathedral and the grandson of former President Woodrow Wilson, organized a large testimonial dinner for Cain at the National Press Club on October 23, 1956. It was attended by more than 350 civil libertarians, labor leaders, and political admirers. Also attending the dinner were many of the individuals whom Cain had helped. One by one, they read congratulatory messages which had been received from an impressive cross-section of prominent union officials, educators, politicians, and liberal activists, including Eleanor Roosevelt; Ernest Angell, chairman of the ACLU; labor leaders Walter Reuther and George Meany; Harvard historian Arthur Schlesinger, Jr.; the deans of the law schools at Yale, Fordham, Notre Dame, Tulane, and the Universities of Pennsylvania, Illinois, and Minnesota; and seven United States Senators from both parties, including Hubert Humphrey.

The evening's major address was given by Morris Ernst, a New York attorney who had served in three Democratic administrations and was a co-founder of the American Civil Liberties Union. Ernst said that "he had never met Cain, but came to honor him as a man [who] had the courage to change his mind." At the end of the evening, Cain received a plaque from Sidney Hatkin, now re-employed by the air force, which read:

IN TRIBUTE TO HARRY P. CAIN

CHAMPION OF HUMAN DIGNITY, DEFENDER OF CONSTITUTIONAL RIGHTS IN THE SEARCH FOR NATIONAL SECURITY

FROM THOSE WHOSE LOYALTY TO COUNTRY HE VINDICATED AND THOSE WHOSE FAITH IN FREE-DOM HE STRENGTHENED

PRESENTED AT TESTIMONIAL DINNER NATIONAL PRESS CLUB, WASHINGTON, DC 23 OCTOBER 1956[90]

Cain was deeply moved by the evening's tributes and forever cherished the sentiments expressed on the plaque he had been presented. Most of those in the room thought that Cain had completed a remarkable political odyssey—a personal journey from reactionary conservatism to civil libertarian—and celebrated him for his accomplishment. Few realized that Cain's basic political philosophy had not really changed—he was fundamentally still the same Harry Cain. His libertarian belief in the rights of the individual was the same as it had always been, but it had been tested. Cain had come to believe that legislation, no matter how well intentioned, that was designed to counter a basically political concept was inherently dangerous. The place to challenge political ideology was in the "marketplace of ideas," not in the courtroom. In an in-depth interview published in the *Washington Sunday Star* on the day immediately following the end of his SACB term, Cain told Daniel Berman, the writer who had previously written the detailed description of Cain's climactic Oval Office confrontation with the President, that "the reason I fought so hard for people I've never seen or known is that if I don't fight to protect the other fellow's freedom, my own freedom hangs by a very thin thread indeed. I believe with all my heart that freedom is indivisible, and that unless we have it for all, we shall soon have it for only those [who have] nothing to say. I believe in democracy enough to want to supply a platform to its critics as well as its defenders."[91]

Harry left the next day to travel to New York City, where he had an appointment with an employment agency.

TWO ECHOES FROM his SACB years would interrupt Cain's future life. In May 1957, he was called to testify as an "expert witness on Communism" in the contempt of Congress trial of the famous playwright Arthur Miller. The charges against Miller were being brought by the House Un-American Activities Committee (HUAC) in connection with a year-long investigation into a Communist conspiracy to misuse American passports. Cain believed that Miller's constitutional freedoms were being abused by the HUAC in their attempt to win a high-profile victory. In 1957, Miller was one of America's most celebrated dramatists and a Pulitzer Prize winner, having written *Death of a Salesman* and *The Crucible*. While Miller had been cooperative with the Committee in all other respects, he refused to provide them with the names of other alleged Communist writers with whom he had attended meetings in New York in 1947. With his wife, Marilyn Monroe, sitting in the courtroom at great risk to her own film career, Miller fielded the committee's questions for a week. When the prosecution called the staff director of the HUAC as an expert witness, Miller's attorney, Joseph L. Rauh, Jr., sought to have the man's testimony stricken from the record on the grounds that he was not an impartial witness. When the judge declined, Rauh called Harry Cain to the witness stand.

Cain testified that he had read Miller's plays and did not believe that he had been "under the discipline of the Communist Party."[92] Cain said that the way to determine whether a person is under Communist discipline is to observe "how the individual lives, acts, writes and speaks rather than by associations. To base a judgment on associations," Cain said, "is to fail utterly to distinguish between different kinds of individuals who make up our society." In the case of professional writers like Miller, "their writings are the important thing, not their associations."[93] In his autobiography, *Timebends: A Life*, Miller wrote, "Sitting and talking with him [Cain] in the Rauh living room, I saw a man with a special kind of tired, thin laugh that comes to those who have been spewed out by power and know they are not ever coming back."[94]

Then, in the fall of 1962, John Goldmark, a Harvard Law School-educated Okanogan County, Washington, cattle rancher, three-term state legislator, and nephew of U.S. Supreme Court Justice Louis Brandeis, sued his local newspaper, the *Tonasket Tribune*, and four prominent northeastern Washington members of the John Birch Society for libel. Goldmark's wife, Sally, had been a member of the Communist Party while a federal employee in Washington, DC, from 1934 until the time of their marriage in 1943. She later agreed to be interviewed by the FBI, although her past Communist Party connections were not revealed to the public. During Goldmark's 1962 campaign for re-election to the Washington Legislature, Sally's past became known. Ashley Holden, once the political writer for the *Spokane Spokesman-Review* and a staunch Cain supporter during his days in the Senate, was now publisher of the *Tonasket Tribune* (circ. 1,013). Holden ran a news story pointing out Goldmark's membership in the American Civil Liberties Union, which Holden claimed was "closely affiliated with the Communist movement in the United States." Holden had written an editorial in his small, but locally influential newspaper in which he called Goldmark "a tool of a monstrous conspiracy to remake America into a totalitarian state." As a result of Holden's coverage in the *Tribune* and printed materials widely distributed by another defendant, Albert Canwell, a former state representative who was now a freelance anti-Communist "investigator," Goldmark finished fourth in a field of five Democrats vying for his seat in the legislature in his heavily conservative district.[95]

The libel trial began on November 4, 1963, and lasted for two and one-half months, interrupted by the Kennedy assassination on November 22 and a nine-day break for the Christmas holiday. The trial attracted intense statewide and national attention because of the issues involved and because of the appearance of many notable personalities as witnesses who testified for both sides. These notables included Herbert Philbrick, a former FBI counterspy and author of *I Led Three Lives*, for the defense; former U.S. Attorney General Francis Biddle; actor Sterling Hayden; and former senator and SACB member Harry P. Cain, testifying for the Goldmarks.[96]

Cain's surprise appearance in the packed Okanogan, Washington, courtroom on Wednesday, January 8, 1964, caused a sensation that had been unanticipated by the defense. Cain loved the drama and the irony of it. First of all, he had been little in the news, particularly in Eastern Washington, since his 1957 move to Florida. Second, during his Senate term, Cain had been supported by most of the very men that Goldmark was suing.

One of the main issues in the trial was whether the ACLU was a Communist front organization. Cain testified that the ACLU had never been a Communist front, concluding that "the sole function of the American Civil Liberties Union, as I understand it, is to maintain throughout the United States and its possessions those guarantees within the Constitution which deal with liberty for the individual and to advocate those rights in every legitimate way."[97] On January 22, 1964, a jury of Goldmark's Okanagan County peers found in favor of Goldmark and awarded him a total of $40,000, the second-largest award ever made in a libel trial in Washington State up to that time. The verdict included a specific finding that the ACLU was not a Communist front organization, a finding that would affect other future lawsuits across the country.

31. Cain won the Republican primary but lost to Congressman Warren G. Magnuson in the general election. Magnuson went on to hold the seat for the next thirty-seven years.

32. Col. Cain receives a decoration from an unidentified general officer toward the end of the war. He was wounded in action one day before the end of hostilities on May 7, 1945, and ended his service as a military government inspector, reporting to Gen. Lucius Clay and to Eisenhower.

33. Cain returned home to Tacoma on September 16, 1945. He was already thinking about his political future.

34. First-term Democratic incumbent Hugh Mitchell was affable, competent, hardworking, but decidedly uncharismatic.

35. 1946 campaign poster. Cain simply overwhelmed Mitchell in the Republican landslide that regained control of Congress after fourteen years, but Cain didn't carry Tacoma and Pierce County.

36. A happy Harry Cain speaking to a radio audience on November 5, 1946, after it had become clear that he would be Washington's next U.S. Senator.

37. Homeless, the Cain's spend New Year's Eve 1946 crammed into a small room at Washington, D.C.'s Statler Hotel. They finally fit into a one-bedroom apartment by sending Buzzy to boarding school.

38. Cain's official U.S. Senate photo. This one is addressed to "Commodore" Sam Perkins, Tacoma newspaperman and civic leader.

39., 40. Cain's most important mentors in the Senate were (left) Senate Foreign Relations Committee Chairman Arthur Vandenberg (R-MI), and (right) Senate Majority Leader Robert A. Taft (R-OH).

41. Long-time friend, former co-worker, and newspaper columnist Emily Walker was convinced to join Cain's Washington, D.C., staff in 1948 in an effort to moderate his controversial voting record and unpredictable behavior. It didn't work. She later said, "He was off and running in the direction he followed until his defeat."

42. Democratic targets of Harry Cain's wrath. (l. to r.) Washington Governor Monrad C. (Mon) Wallgren, Lieutenant Governor Victor Meyers, U. S. Senator Warren G. Magnuson, and President Harry S Truman (sitting) in the Governor's Office in, Olympia, c. 1948.

43. One of Cain's first big controversial votes was in favor of the Taft-Hartley Act. His relations with organized labor never recovered.

44. Cain quickly became known as a leading opponent of rent controls and retaining public housing. Here he is confronted by pickets during a hearing on the matter in Seattle in July 1947.

45. Cain practices with his props for what would be a six-hour, forty-five-minute filibuster against President Truman's nomination of former Washington Governor Mon C. Wallgren to be Director of the National Security Resources Board.

46. An exhausted Harry Cain recovers with a cup of coffee after a losing twelve-hour, eight-minute filibuster against the extension of rent controls that lasted until 4 a.m. on June 10, 1950.

47. Cain was the final speaker at the 1952 Republican National Convention in Chicago but soon discovered that he needed throat surgery which limited his ability to campaign until August. By then it was clear that his campaign was in trouble.

48. A soggy group of "Youth for Cain" supporters, including daughter Candy (front center) and her older brother, Buzz (2nd from left, back row), rally for Cain in Tacoma.

Jackson

Will make a *Great* **U.S. Senator**

Here is the warm, personal story of one of
the most promising young men in American
public life today. Able, energetic
Henry M. Jackson is a veteran of 12 years
in Congress. Elected in 1940 at the age
of 29, he has built a remarkable record
of service to his state and country.
Those who have seen Jackson in action

49., 50. President Harry S. Truman campaigns for the Democratic ticket at the Tacoma Armory on October 2, 1952. Congressman Henry M. Jackson waged a thoroughly modern campaign to defeat Cain in what was otherwise a Republican landslide election year.

51. While there were legitimate concerns about the nation's internal security, much of the nation's fear was stoked by Senator Joseph McCarthy, Cain's longtime friend, who attached the loyalty of Democratic and Republican administrations alike.

52. The post-war Red Scare prompted a decade of growing concerns about the threat of Communist subversion. Here school district employees take a loyalty oath at a California high school, c. 1953.

53. 54. Key players in the Eisenhower Administration's loyalty-security program. Both FBI Director J. Edgar Hoover (left), and Attorney General Herbert Brownell (right) felt Cain's criticisms were outside of his authority as a member of the SACB.

57. Cain criticized the Eisenhower Administration's loyalty-security program in a series of increasingly critical speeches and interviews during 1955–56. He is shown here speaking to the Colorado Branch of the ACLU on May 17, 1956.

55., 56. Cain was considered disloyal and "rocking the boat" by powerful White House Chief of Staff Sherman Adams (left). Cain tried to explain his concerns to Maxwell Rabb (right), a longtime friend who served as Secretary of the Cabinet.

58. The President successfully avoided Cain's criticisms until he was finally asked if he would agree to meet with Cain during a televised press conference on June 23, 1956. He answered with a terse "Yes."

(60.) This newspaper photo of LaVonne Kneisley ran with the announcement of their marriage in 1957. They had known each other since the mid-1930s.

(59.) After Cain's resignation, more than 300 elected officials, jurists, civil liberties advocates, including many of those whose jobs he had saved, joined to honor him at the National Press Club on October 23, 1956. Here he accepts a plaque from Sidney Hatkin, one of those whose jobs he saved.

(61.) A 1958 newspaper ad for First Federal Presents, Cain's public affairs program on Miami TV.

(62.) Miami was changing rapidly by the time Harry Cain arrived. Both recently-arrived Cubans and historically underserved African Americans were demanding to be heard. Here, protestors march in front of the 1968 Republican National Convention in Miami Beach. Cain quickly became an influential voice for change in both the board room and the banquet hall.

63. Politics were never far from Harry's thoughts. He managed a congressional campaign in 1962 and seriously considered running for the U.S. Senate in both 1964 and 1968, but his views were increasingly at variance with the state's conservative Republican Party. He chaired Florida's Citizens for Johnson-Humphrey campaign in 1964.

64. Cain was appointed to the Miami-Dade County Commission in 1972 and reelected later that year. He championed indoor smoking bans, bilingualism in the county government, and equal rights for homosexuals.

65. During his final visit to Tacoma, in December 1977, Cain was honored by the local Japanese-American community for the support he had provided them thirty-five years earlier during WWII. They presented him with a beautiful, large bronze horse, representing the coming "Year of the Horse" and signifying that, to them, he was their "Man of the Year."

66., 67. Harry Cain is remembered in both Tacoma and Miami, the two cities he called home. In 2009 the Tacoma City Council voted to rename a portion of the Broadway Plaza between the city's new convention center and Hotel Murano (left) the Harry P. Cain Promenade. It was once the center of the Japanese-American business community. In an ironic coincidence, given his opposition to public housing during his Senate career, the Miami-Dade Public Housing Agency in 1989 named a new 14-story, 152-unit senior living facility (right) for Cain in recognition of his many contributions to the Miami community.

12

An Uncommon Man

BACK WITH MARJ and the children in Tacoma since mid-September 1956, Cain tried to regain his bearings. He was unemployed and without serious prospects. The angst of having lost two jobs in a row and the uncertainty of what lay ahead must have been palpable. Cain made some local speeches to test the waters. He spoke with friends and supporters about the potential for a political comeback and, short of that, about job opportunities in the Tacoma or Seattle area. The results of his inquiries were not encouraging. "In a word, I could not go where I wanted to go," he later said.[1] At that low point, word had come of the testimonial dinner to be held in his honor at the National Press Club in Washington, DC. While Cain's spirits were lifted by the outpouring of good will he received at the banquet, his prospects were not—he still had no job and almost no money. He remained in Washington, DC, after the dinner, looking for work.

In November, Emily Walker reported that Cain would be joining a large real estate development company owned by Leon Ackerman of Washington, DC. Ackerman was a successful mega-developer with big plans. Indian Lakes Estates was to be a 7,000-acre planned community in Polk County, Florida, and Cain would "direct its activities" from an office in Dayton, Ohio. He returned to Tacoma for the Christmas holiday. It was a false start. For whatever reason, Cain didn't return to Dayton after the holidays. In April, Cain denied that he had withdrawn from the organization. "I have given the company my suggestions on major policy changes I feel should be made. They are still being considered and will be decided shortly."[2] Whatever those policy changes were, they apparently didn't include Cain.

In the meantime, a temporary opportunity to make some money surfaced in January 1957. It was announced that Cain would become a Chubb Fellowship lecturer at Timothy Dwight College at Yale University for a week, beginning on February 11. Cain later said that he had a "stimulating time" talking about his time on the SACB, the broad field of constitutional rights, and his work as a former U.S. Senator, but it was no answer to his long-term problem.[3]

And unemployment was just one of Cain's problems. He narrowly missed being named as one of ten correspondents in a messy California divorce trial.[4] Marj was again considering filing for divorce. Finally, the matter of his loyalty to President Eisenhower kept surfacing, sometimes at very close quarters. In early February 1958, Marj told Harry of a conversation she had had with Edgar Eisenhower, the President's older brother and a respected Tacoma attorney, shortly before she also moved back to Washington, DC.

Edgar Eisenhower apparently told her that he felt that Harry had not only let him down but had also betrayed his brother's confidence after he appointed Cain to the SACB. Cain couldn't let that go unanswered. In a long, single spaced letter to the President's brother(only the first four pages remain), Cain restated his admiration for the President, noting that in an early meeting between himself and the President, Eisenhower had personally asked him to look into what was going on at the SACB and to report back to him. Cain then went on to retell the story of how he became alarmed that Eisenhower's advisors were operating in a manner harmful to the President's best interests and ultimately his belief that they had done a "hatchet job" on him.[5] If Edgar Eisenhower responded to Cain's letter, it has also been lost.

Cain remained in Washington, DC, after the testimonial dinner, traveling to New York City, where he met with an executive recruitment agency that some friends had recommended. He sought to "re-enter the financial industry in some manner." The discussions went well, and "it looked like I might get a pretty good job with a commercial bank in New York."[6] While he was in New York, Cain received a surprise telephone call from Robert V. Walker, chairman of the board of the First Federal Savings & Loan Association of Miami, an old friend with whom Cain had played golf and fished during previous vacations in Florida. Walker and his three brothers, two of whom also worked for First Federal, were influential in Miami's business community and were conservative Republicans who had come to know Cain during his Senate years because of his involvement with housing legislation. The Walkers hadn't seen Cain in several years but had tracked him down at his New York hotel room. Walker had a favor to ask. Would Cain be available to come down to Miami for a week or ten days as their guest?

During what Cain described as a "glorious holiday," he determined that the Walkers needed a little help with a regulatory matter currently pending in Washington, DC. Cain was only too happy to oblige, spending a day or so in the capital, assisting the Walkers with their problem, and then traveling back to New York to find out how his job prospects were progressing. Back in Florida again to report on his progress, the Walkers asked him a question that must have been music to his ears: "How would you like to stay with us on [a] permanent basis?"[7]

Cain asked for a day or two to think about it, and then contacted the New York employment agency. The prospects for the job in New York looked good but were not yet certain. Cain told them about the opportunity that had surfaced in Florida. "How much are they going to pay you?" they asked. "About a third of what I could make in New York," he answered. "Don't you think you should have your head examined?" Remembering the conversation years later, he responded, "I'm not certain, but considering all things, there may be something more to life than making a great big salary when half of it goes back to the government."[8]

Telling the Walkers that "I am free as I never have been before," Cain accepted their offer on April 1, 1957. Almost immediately, he knew he had made the right decision. It was the beginning of what, in many ways, would be one of the happiest periods of his life. The self-imposed pressure to succeed and the desire to return to the Senate were still there, but they were now tempered with a painful, but somehow peaceful, reality.

POWER IS RELATIVE and comes in many forms. Harry Cain's new job in Florida empowered him to help his community while redeeming his reputation. After the disappointments of the Senate and the SACB, Cain was being given another chance to succeed at a job and in an environment that matched his personal strengths. Assuming that his new employers agreed, Cain could spend his time working on issues about which he cared deeply while, at the same time, promoting both his employers and himself.

The First Federal Savings & Loan Association was a storied financial institution in the Miami area. Dr. William H. Walker founded it in 1933 when, after waiting for three weeks in Washington, DC, for the newly created Federal Home Loan Bank Board to open its doors, he helped its staff to write the charter that allowed First Federal to become the first federal savings and loan association in the United States. When, in 1957, illness required the elder Walker to retire, his son, Robert V. Walker, took over as chairman of the board. Like his father, the younger Walker was active in community affairs, serving on the boards of several institutions of higher learning, the United Way, and the Dade County Community Relations Board.

What the Walkers had in mind for Cain was a good fit for his multiple talents. Long interested in radio and then television, Cain would host *First Federal Presents*, a thirty-minute public affairs television program, which aired every other Monday night on WCKT-TV, then the local NBC affiliate. Cain's Washington, DC, connections ensured a stream of nationally known guests. By February 1958, Cain had attracted to the program Eleanor Roosevelt; Treasury Secretary Robert Anderson; Director of the Budget Maurice Stans; thirteen sitting U.S. Senators; congressmen from twelve states; and his old friend from the Eisenhower White House, Maxwell Rabb. Jack Anderson, the local television critic for the *Miami Herald*, soon nominated Cain for his "unmitigated gall" award, saying that the program's format was "as heretically audacious as a testimonial for atheism in the middle of a church service." First, it was live television, a format that had largely disappeared from the Miami market. Second, it was informative and educational—"no give-aways, no quiz panels, no cheese-cake, and no toothpaste or cigarettes—just a few low-key commercials from Cain's bank."[9]

The program became so successful that the Walkers began to see other useful activities for Cain. In November 1957, they named him vice president for community affairs, the first non-family member to serve as an officer of the institution. The Walkers saw the benefits from community involvement, not only as public service but also as a means of advertising and increasing the size of their institution. Indeed, the Walkers saw Harry Cain as the perfect tool to help them accomplish both goals.

Cain had an even broader view of his job. During his first decade with First Federal, Cain's community relations activities consumed only a third or half of his time. That meant that in his early years in Miami, Cain had free time for community activities as well as golf, swimming, and scuba diving. Often at the suggestion of the Walkers, Cain became more involved in the Miami community, trying to understand the dynamics of its diverse population and assessing the quality of its local leadership. By February 1958, the community was beginning to notice Cain's presence beyond the success of his television program. John B. McDermott, the political writer for the *Miami Herald,* wrote about Cain in a column—a story that Cain may have forwarded to his former staffer Emily Walker in Washington, DC, knowing that she would include it in the column she wrote for the *Tacoma News Tribune.* "A new face has blossomed forth on the political banquet-dinner circuit in Miami. Former U.S. Senator Harry Cain of Washington, now a Miamian, is proving to be one of the most entertaining and capable toastmasters seen in a long time. Furthermore, he may provide the spark which the Republican Party in Florida has been lacking. He is able, witty, has a vast political background and is a top notch speaker. Democrats would do well to keep their eye on him."[10]

After ten years of managing First Federal's public relations activities and troubleshooting various deeply challenged community organizations such as the United Fund, Cain convinced the Walkers that his work at the bank should be expanded and re-focused on improving the firm's relationships with Miami's rapidly changing and diverse population. "When I joined the firm . . . Community Relations was an orthodox, strictly limited endeavor. It could be defined as being Public Relations and often was. The basic emphasis was on advancing a favorable image of the firm within segments of the community from which business came and might be expected to come. Every effort was [directed toward making] the public more aware of our reputation and status in the Greater Miami area. Duties included being often seen and occasionally heard before the accepted and acceptable organized groups in Dade County."[11]

Harry Cain's new life in Miami did not include his wife and family. Harry and Marj had a complicated relationship—two strong, talented individuals who loved and respected each other but had trouble living together in a relationship that increasingly revolved around only one of them. The complications extended to their children. Buzzy and Candy had largely been raised by their mother. Harry was often away—first off to the war and then after he returned, serving in the Senate and then on the SACB. Both children attended boarding schools from an early age. Even when Candy was living at home, she frequently changed schools as her parents moved back and forth between Washington, DC, and Tacoma. Candy remembered of her father that "family never seemed to be his greatest priority, other than being sure we were provided for adequately."[12] When Harry was defeated for re-election, Marjorie had expressed the hope that her husband would be able to find a job in Tacoma. Perhaps without the strain of the constant attention and travel, they could re-build their relationship, but Harry wanted to remain in government. After Cain was appointed to the SACB, he had continued to travel extensively. Marj and Candy, now a teenager, continued to live in their small apartment in Washington, DC, where Candy attended three different schools in three years.

Buzz was completing high school at Vermont Academy. He was a good student and an excellent athlete who had a serious speech impediment. Overcoming this difficulty, Buzz was named valedictorian of his graduating class in 1955. Buzz later remembered, "I was to be honored for various athletic and academic achievements, and I was looking forward to 'showing off' for my parents, especially my father. One of the honors, valedictorian, required that I give a speech at the commencement (which given my stuttering impediment, was a bit of a trauma for me). I turned to Dad for help in writing the speech, which he helped with, by letter, focusing on the Soviet menace facing the country. Then I memorized the speech and was ready to go. The day before commencement only Mom showed up, explaining that Dad had a chance to go on *Face the Nation* at the last minute because the scheduled guest had cancelled, and that was more important than his son's graduation. I accepted that, because it was so consistent with my whole relationship with my father, but somehow I never forgot the disappointment."[13]

In January 1958, Marjorie again filed for a divorce that became final in May. Both the divorce and the settlement were uncontested. In April 1958, she landed a position managing the tour guides at the U.S. Pavilion at the Brussels World's Fair. Marj also found a summer job for Buzz, selling souvenir programs in the American Theatre. Candy finished the ninth grade classes in Tacoma and joined them in Brussels in August.

On July 18, 1958, Harry married LaVonne Strachan Kneisley in a private ceremony in Chevy Chase, Maryland. Harry had known "Bonnie" Kneisley for many years. In 1933, she married Leland "Lee" Hein, a Tacoma accountant. The Heins and the Cains were friends, and Lee (and perhaps Bonnie) were at Tacoma's Union Station when Harry and Marj boarded the *North Coast Limited* at the start of their great European adventure in 1935.[14] The Heins had one son, David, who was twenty-two in 1958 and living in Los Angeles. The couple divorced in 1937. Bonnie moved to Seattle and married Richard Kneisley, an attorney. They divorced in 1945.

While she was in Seattle, Bonnie found work as a stenographer for Ward A. Smith, a mortgage officer for the Seattle Trust and Savings Bank. When, in 1943, Smith and a partner opened their own real estate, mortgage lending, and homebuilding firm in Tacoma, Bonnie, now separated from Kneisley, joined them as the firm's chief escrow officer. By 1949, Smith had become the principal owner of the company, and Bonnie became his administrative assistant and personal secretary. Ward Smith and Harry Cain were close personal friends, and Smith was one of those upon whom Cain relied to provide him with first-hand knowledge and advice about the real estate and homebuilding industry. Bonnie would certainly have encountered Cain again when he and Smith met and socialized during his periodic visits back to the state on vacation or Senate business.

In 1955, Bonnie moved to Washington, DC, to work for Carey Winston, a former Seattleite, who had become a prominent mortgage banker in Washington, DC. Bonnie and Harry reconnected there. Cain's daughter, Candy, remembered that she first learned of her father's second marriage from an article in the *Tacoma News Tribune* just before she left for Europe.[15] She was fifteen.

When Bonnie joined Harry in Florida, the couple first lived in a condominium on Bay Harbor Island not far from the Indian Creek Country Club. They soon moved to 7369 Big Cypress Court in Miami Lakes, a planned community of modest, closely packed, zero-lot-line homes built around a series of artificial lakes and a golf course, nineteen miles north of downtown Miami. Bonnie doted on her new husband—a quality that he enjoyed immensely. With his penchant for nicknames, she forever became "Wiggie," a term of endearment that resulted from one of Bonnie's trips to the hairdresser. The couple became active in Miami society and worked together on many of the community activities in which Harry was involved on behalf of First Federal Savings. Candy visited Harry and Bonnie at Miami Lakes a year later when she was sixteen. Candy came to appreciate Bonnie and the couple's obvious happiness, but it was a difficult adjustment at first. Two years later Candy married Robert Tingstad in Tacoma with both of her parents present.

Buzz graduated from Stanford in 1959, returned to Tacoma to be near his mother, and received an M.A. in political science from the University of Washington in 1961. After completing his military service, Buzz joined Marj in Washington, DC, where, with the help of his father and Senator Frank Church of Idaho, he got a job on the Capitol Hill police force. Buzz later joined the staff of the National Institute of Mental Health and earned a Ph.D. from Brandeis in 1971.

THE FLAT LANDS and marshes that surround Biscayne Bay had been inhabited by the Tequesta Indians for, as far as anyone knew, forever, but the antecedents of the city that would eventually be built there were much more recent. The area was one of the only places in Florida to survive the Great Freeze of 1894. Local citrus growers, with a sudden lock on the northern citrus market, persuaded the Florida East Coast Railroad to extend rail service there in 1896. At the time, Miami boasted a population of approximately three hundred souls. The community prospered along with other waterfront communities in the Florida real estate boom of the 1920s, but fell victim to a major hurricane in 1926 and to the collapse of the economy during the Great Depression. Biscayne Bay was ideally situated to be a training center for the navy's anti-submarine patrol activities during World War II, and many servicemen returned to the area after the war, boosting the population to nearly half a million by 1950.

Harry Cain's arrival in 1957 coincided with the major social and demographic changes that were occurring in the Miami-Dade County area. In 1959, Fidel Castro came to power in Cuba. The overthrow of the corrupt, but business-friendly, Batista regime resulted in a mass emigration of Cuban talent and capital from the island to Southern Florida, something that continued throughout the early 1960s. In 1960, nearly 233,000 or 18.5 percent of Dade County's 935,000 citizens were Cuban. Another 214,000 (17 percent of the population) were African American. At the time, neither played much of a role in the area's social, business, or political life. In 1960, the mainstream of the Greater Miami community was white, segregated, and solidly Democratic.

One of the first activities to occupy Cain's time was the Dade County United Fund, which had transitioned from being the Community Chest to the United Fund in 1959 and now found itself on the verge of collapse. Dr. Walker made it possible for Cain to become the president of the United Fund, essentially giving him a leave of absence to devote his full time to reorganizing and updating its procedures, policies, and operations. The organization badly needed his help. Cain soon issued a candid public statement, pointing out that the organization had been kidding itself and the community by claiming to reach its goals when, in reality, it had been borrowing against its next year's collections. In fact, the United Fund was on the point of disintegrating. Cain's statement had the dual effect of straightening out the organization while, overnight, giving him considerable stature as a Miami community leader.[16]

Cain later confided to a *Miami Herald* reporter that "being President of the United Fund is the last job in the world I'd ever want or seek. But here I am—brimming with the excitement and challenges of it! This is a thing that's important and vital to the community—a job that has to be done."[17] The job was not done by the end of Cain's first term, so Walker arranged with the board to have him serve a second year as the Fund's president. Bonnie helped out—one of 15,000 housewives who served as block workers, going door to door, soliciting contributions.[18]

Cain later said that much of the effort to reconstruct and save the United Fund was agonizing. "It provided a unique opportunity to evaluate the performance of the many health, welfare and educational activities throughout Dade County. In addition, it enabled a newcomer to the local scene to mingle with and take a reading on the capabilities and reliability of scores and scores of leaders in our community. In this realm I probably learned more in two years than an active person would have, under normal circumstances, in ten years or more."[19] Cain completed his two-year leave of absence and, after a month-long visit to Washington State to see his children and friends, he returned to his job at First Federal Savings in February 1961.

Through his involvement in the United Fund and other social service agencies, Cain was exposed, for the first time since he served on the District of Columbia Committee, to the needs and aspirations of the urban underclass and multiple ethnic minorities who were fighting for self-sufficiency and civil rights. Notwithstanding his long-held belief in limited government, it became clear to Cain that only the federal government had the capacity to provide the necessary social and community development programs and to ensure and protect the civil rights of all its citizens—if it only had the will to do so. Cain believed that the private sector also had an important role to play. Whereas the United Fund had been saved by the timely intervention of Miami's business leaders, Cain felt that those same leaders should now focus their efforts on strengthening the entire community. "This can only happen if businesses and other leaders from everywhere contribute intelligence and energy to the unmet needs which confront and trouble our urban society."[20]

Cain foresaw that the growing Cuban community would become U.S. citizens and would vote as a bloc for generations. Because of their strong entrepreneurial focus and virulent anti-communism, Cain was sure that they would become Republicans. Economically, because of their education and resources, the Cubans over time would take care of themselves. Cain's major concerns were with the growing and increasingly restless African-American community and the urban poor of all races.

Harry Cain had long pressed the Walkers to take a greater role in addressing long-repressed social issues that were beginning to become front-page news, both in Miami and the rest of the nation. He argued that the firm's traditional public relations activities, with which he had been intimately involved, were now completely ineffective in "maintaining and advancing the community's tranquility and stability."[21] With the passage of the Civil Rights Act of 1964, First Federal hired its first African American employee in other than a traditional service job. Many more followed. Commenting on the rapid pace of social change and the need for the institution to remain associated with it, Cain wrote, "Social revolutions seldom start at the bottom of any cycle of oppression and neglect. Revolutions have been triggered throughout history when conditions for those oppressed or neglected seem to be improving. When this happens, those who revolt invariably strive to attain in a hurry what has long been denied to them."[22]

Cain's success in straightening out the United Fund and his growing recognition as a leader in the Miami community were satisfying, but he still longed to get back to the big stage. He was aware of an upcoming vacancy on the Federal Home Loan Bank Board and wrote to his friend, Senator Hubert Humphrey, now the Senate Majority Whip, asking him to intercede with the Kennedy White House. On January 3, 1962, Humphrey wrote to Ralph A. Dungen, President Kennedy's special assistant, on Cain's behalf. The desired appointment never materialized. In the meantime, Cain made sure that he became the subject of considerable speculation about his possible political future in Florida.

12. An Uncommon Man

Democrats in Dade County enjoyed a seven-to-one registration advantage over Republicans. The county had a healthy reputation not only for voting Democratic but also for being "ultra liberal." The county's Republican leadership had a reputation for being old guard, conservative, tired, and not very aggressive. Republican candidates tended to be young and attractive, under-funded, almost completely unknown, and totally unsuccessful.[23]

Six weeks before the 1962 general election, Cain responded to a frantic appeal from the campaign of a personable young attorney, Robert A. Peterson, who was fighting an uphill battle against Claude Pepper, a former U.S. Senator from Florida, for the right to represent a newly formed Miami congressional district. Before he would agree to take over the campaign, Cain sent Peterson and his supporters a letter in which he imposed a set of unusual stipulations for financing and waging the campaign. After the election, in a highly unusual move (but not surprising for Cain), he released the contents of the Peterson letter to both the *Miami News* and *Miami Herald,* creating great interest and surprise among local political observers and instantly establishing Cain as an unusual, if formidable, political strategist.

Written on September 29, 1962—already late in the campaign—it contained four "terms and conditions." Cain's decisions would be accepted "without argument or debate." Cain would have sole discretion over campaign expenditures (the campaign had just $360 in its operating account). Cain would further have authority to dismiss anyone from the campaign who violated one of his decisions, "or I will feel free to separate myself from your campaign without notice to you or anyone else." Finally, Cain would not be known as Peterson's campaign manager. "I will be known as your friend who willingly undertakes to accomplish what you ask."[24]

Cain bluntly told Peterson that his campaign had "neither purpose, direction, workers, nor money." Perhaps remembering his own career, he wrote that "the most difficult lesson to learn in politics, and it is generally learned the hard way, is that [y]our friends will often cause you much more trouble than your enemies." You can at least anticipate your enemies. As an example of how friends, regardless of how well motivated, can go wrong, Cain pointed out that "Jewish, Negro, and labor representation was conspicuously absent" from Peterson's campaign executive committee, a situation that would immediately have to change. The campaign would have only two themes: the first would be the differences between Peterson and his opponent, and the other would be "moderation versus extremism."

Peterson's opponent, the sixty two-year old Pepper, who had served in the U.S. Senate with Cain, had once been labeled "Red" Pepper by the state's current Democratic Senator, George Smathers, for his outspokenly liberal views. Cain wrote, "Our intention will be to make your position of moderation appealing to both Democrats and Republicans." Finally, Cain told his candidate, "At no time during the campaign will I discuss with you the chances of your being elected. I commit to you, not because I think you can win, for at this time I do not, but because I think it possible for you to make a good showing and this will be of real benefit to what I believe the needs of our time require."[25]

As expected, Pepper won the race, beating Peterson by sixteen thousand votes, but by Republican standards of the day, the margin almost constituted a Republican victory. Peterson agreed to let Cain release the contents of the letter. It catapulted Cain into the forefront of the Republicans in Dade County and throughout the state. From that point on, his was a voice to be reckoned with in local Republican politics. During the campaign, Cain worked with other Republican candidates to sign a four-point "manifesto" that would become the key to the Republicans' statewide campaign strategy over the coming years. The "manifesto" demanded that Florida's election laws be rewritten so that someone switching parties could run under his new party label immediately. It also included a demand for a constitutional convention to replace Florida's outdated 1885 constitution for state reapportionment and a call for "equal opportunity in all areas of human activity." The outlook for Republicans in Florida was still dire, but Cain was optimistic. He believed that an articulate Republican, adequately financed, could become a good long-shot bet to win statewide office. By that, he meant either governor or U.S. Senator and, presumably, himself. [26]

On May 10, 1963, without Cain's knowledge, Richard Bryce, an influential local Republican leader with forty years in the political trenches, wrote to A. B. Herman, director of Political Organization for the Republican National Committee, suggesting that Cain run for the U.S. Senate from Florida. "Without question, he is the most brilliantly effective speaker in either party. A significant part of his talent is in the fact that his obvious fairness makes him palatable to most partisans."

12. An Uncommon Man

Responding, Herman raised an important point: "Whether the Cain of today is the Cain of 'yesterday' is the question. No one was held in higher esteem than the Cain of yesterday. If you can find *that* Cain, it is my judgment that he could be the first Republican United States Senator from Florida. However, the decision can only be made by one man. Does he have the belly for it?"[27] Cain still had the "fire in the belly" for politics, but he was *not* the same man who had served in the Senate before.

Sandwiched in between the countless community meetings on behalf of First Federal Savings, Cain continued to dispense political advice, and the recipients were not limited to the Republicans alone. On June 3, 1963, in the immediate aftermath of the dramatic civil rights marches that had been met with police dogs and fire hoses in Birmingham, Alabama, Cain wrote again to his good friend Senator Humphrey. The subject of his letter was an issue that has since become a frequent matter of speculation among historians of the Kennedy years—the young President's apparent reluctance to push a strong civil rights agenda.

Cain wanted Humphrey to prod President Kennedy into taking action. "I have no desire to second-guess the President but I think the people, of all races and backgrounds, would benefit were the President to talk to the nation about the racial problem or dilemma which embroils our nation today. In my judgment, the nation is ready to listen—now. He could talk about the whole of the situation and give it the perspective it requires. In a postscript, Cain added, "The door to *an equal opportunity for all* can be opened with far greater speed. The President can't do this by himself, but he stands the best chance to persuade the nation that it can and why it should—not a century from now, but with the passing of each day."[28] And, in a handwritten note to the author on the back of the copy of the letter he had sent to Humphrey, Cain acknowledged that his own personal dream lived on. "I am off on Tuesday for 10 days or two weeks in Washington. There will be conversations about many things, including politics. It is possible, but far from likely, that I might become a candidate. . . . It is a fabulous if perilous period in which to live. Freedom can become much stronger than it's ever been."[29]

Back in Florida, speculation that Cain might run against Democratic incumbent U.S. Senator Spessard Holland continued to heat up through the remainder of 1963, fueled by a series of in-depth interviews Cain granted to local magazines and newspapers. "Sure, I'd like to go back to the Senate," Cain told Joe McGowan, Jr., of the Associated Press.

"It's the best job in the world and I know now that my own term was just long enough to be an apprenticeship. . . . I had some ideas when I went to the Senate, and I'd like to return—with what I know now—to try to put them into effect." Unfortunately, many of Cain's ideas were in stark variance with the views of the mainstream Republicans in Florida or around the country who were, by then, supporting the conservative Senator Barry Goldwater as the Republican nominee for president in 1964. Cain resigned from the Dade County Republican Central Committee in October. Committee members made it plain that Cain would get no support from them unless he was able to win the Republican primary.[30]

Cain ultimately decided that he had neither the political backing of the Republican Party establishment nor the ability to raise enough money from other sources to run a competitive Senate race in 1964. Rather, he turned his attention to the national presidential race. While Cain still considered himself a Republican, his recent battles with the Florida Republican Party, his close friendship with Hubert Humphrey, and his aversion to Arizona Senator Barry Goldwater's candidacy, resulted in a typical Harry Cain reaction—he became the chairman of the Florida Citizens for Johnson and Humphrey Committee, campaigning tirelessly, and in every one of Florida's sixty-seven counties, for the national Democratic ticket. Cain's 1964 campaigning on behalf of the national Democratic ticket was reminiscent of his earlier exploration of supporting the Democratic Party ticket in 1956 after he failed to be reappointed to the SACB.

Not surprisingly, Cain's support of the Johnson-Humphrey ticket infuriated Florida Republicans. In a series of letters and meetings in Washington with Ray Bliss, the chairman of the Republican National Committee, Cain noted that the Florida state committee had not met in 988 days. "It was understood everywhere that I was simply taking a leave of absence from my Party [during the Johnson-Humphrey campaign]. Depending on developments, this may happen again and last longer."[31] While Cain may have still considered himself a Republican, the local party leaders were not so sure. Marcus Kyle, the Chairman of the Republican Executive Committee of Dade County, said that he "would very much like to see this man [Cain] get on the ballot in a Republican primary . . . where only registered Republicans are voting and we will find out once and for all just how much of a following he has in this county."[32] In a letter to the author dated August 31, 1965, Cain mused, "The only way to have any fun as a Republican in these parts is to engage in hassles with other Republicans."

Cain then began to consider running for George Smathers' Senate seat, which would become available with the 1968 election. William Dwyer, John Goldmark's attorney and future U.S. District Court judge in Seattle, had recently written to Cain, encouraging him to get back into politics. "I just might accept his encouragement to return to public life. This isn't likely, but I shall rather enjoy keeping him in suspense."[33]

Cain also raised the possibility of a Senate run when he wrote to Vice President Humphrey on November 19, 1966, to say that his pique at not being chosen for the Federal Home Loan Bank job was not permanent. "I simply thought that some of your associates in the big house weren't very bright. But my indignation at their tedious months of evasive indecision was a thing of the moment and nothing more." Cain went on to say, "While waiting for an opportunity that escaped me, I began to think of a broader one which might be possible. And now, to my astonishment, I am actually not far from declaring my intention to become a candidate in pursuit of George Smathers' Senate seat which will, unfortunately, soon be vacated. Were I to be nominated, a difficult accomplishment, it might follow that I would be a solid and even persuasive competitor in the general election." Florida had never sent a Republican to the United States Senate, let alone one whose primary issue was the need to improve race relations. Cain felt that a moderate Republican could build a strong base among young new voters in Florida's growing metro areas and attract African Americans by standing for improved race relations.[34]

To hedge his bets, Cain continued to seek appointment to a high-level federal job. Cain wrote to his friend, George Smathers on March 8, 1967, to say that he would be "very pleased" if Smathers and Washington Senator Henry Jackson were able to speak with President Johnson about a position for Cain (perhaps an appointment to the SACB).[35] Cain also sent a copy of his letter to Jackson, who wrote back to Cain two days later, saying that he had been in contact with Smathers and that he had "agreed to join me along the lines that you and I suggested."[36] Their efforts were unsuccessful. On July 25, Cain wrote to Jackson saying that "the speed and ease with which LBJ recently appointed an unknown to the SACB made me a trifle sad and finished any lingering expectation that I might be invited to return to the Government. This was the jolt I needed to forget the possibility."[37] Jackson quickly responded to say that he hadn't given up trying.

While Cain was disappointed by being passed over by the Johnson Administration, there was much to occupy his time in Miami. Indeed, Cain continued to bury himself in the complexities of community affairs. By then, Cain was already serving as the chairman of the Dade County Human Relations Board, another organization that was foundering when he assumed control. At one time or another, Cain also served as the chairman of the Governor's Advisory Committee on the Aged, president of the Miami Chapter of Planned Parenthood, assistant to the president of the Florida Chamber of Commerce, vice president of its Governmental Research Council, and as a board member of the Dade County Urban League, the Dade County Chapter of the National Conference of Christians and Jews, Goodwill Industries, Senior Citizen's Day Centers, and the Miami-Dade Tourist and Convention Council.

Cain was publicly honored by the Florida Region of the Anti-Defamation League of B'nai B'rith, the National Jewish Hospital and Research Center, and by the National Conference of Christians and Jews. He worked to establish the Greater Miami Urban Coalition in the wake of five days of rioting in the Liberty City neighborhood in 1968 and used the Human Relations Board as a sounding board for discontents and social reformers.

Cain worked hardest perhaps in helping re-locate the ninety-year old Florida Memorial College, a Black Baptist college, from St. Augustine to Miami. Cain accomplished the move with very little help from the rest of Miami's "liberal" community, whose members were concerned about having a segregated college in their community. Cain felt that the school's low tuition rates would provide local students with a better chance to go to college. Cain permitted himself to be honored by the college at a testimonial dinner on December 11, 1967, allowing the dinner to go forward because all of the proceeds would go to the school. His efforts on behalf of the school were duly noted in the editorial pages of several Miami newspapers. More than a thousand attended the dinner, including the governors of Arizona, New Mexico, Washington, and Wyoming. Governor Spiro Agnew of Maryland was the dinner speaker.[38] The school honored Cain by naming a hall in their new library building for him.

While Harry Cain continued his efforts to improve community and race relations, his mind never wandered very far from the field of politics.

12. An Uncommon Man

He was still thinking about the 1968 Senate race—keeping himself and everyone else in suspense. As the April 2, 1968, filing date approached, Cain unburdened himself to Morris McLamore, the political writer for the *Miami News*. "I don't know if I'm strong enough to reach high noon on April 2 without signing up. I'll not deny the question. Within moments of hearing that George Smathers would not offer again for his seat . . . it occurred to me. That was two years ago. Since then, I have strained the positive elements and the liabilities accumulated in my eleven years in Florida. I am on the verge of making a final, flat decision not to run. Yet, how can I when the challenge has so much appeal"?

Cain understood his major problems: raising enough funding for a competitive campaign and facing continuing opposition from the local Republican Party. "If it were possible for me to gain the Republican nomination, I would consider myself a very likely winner in November." But, by his own admission, Cain had no direct route to Florida's governor, Claude Kirk, or to the state Republican Party organization. In fact, many local Republican leaders were adamantly opposed to Cain's candidacy because of his support of Lyndon Johnson and Hubert Humphrey in 1964.[39] Cain told the campaign manager for former Governor LeRoy Collins, who tried to recruit him to serve on the Executive Committee of Collins's campaign, that because there was still a "remote" chance that he might file for the Republican nomination, he would have to decline. "I don't think I will, but in knowing myself rather well I won't feel comfortable about the situation until one second after high noon on Tuesday, the 2nd of April."[40]

On March 15, at George Smathers's suggestion, he wrote to Marvin Watson, Special Assistant to the President, enclosing a personal message to President Johnson, asking to be considered "for any Federal assignment where such capacity and talents as I may possess seem tailor made for the job."[41] Watson apparently spoke to the President about Cain's request and wrote back to say that an appointment to the Interstate Commerce Commission would have "found favor with the President had it been available." Watson also expressed the view that President Johnson was sincere in his "friendly expressions" toward Cain.[42] In the end, Cain bowed to the reality of the situation and ended up supporting Democrat Collins for Smathers's open Senate seat, which was ultimately won by Republican Congressman Edward Gurney.

The 1968 presidential campaign was an even more difficult choice. Cain had lost confidence in the Johnson Administration over the issue of the Viet Nam War. Accordingly, on August 23, he wrote to Senator Henry Jackson to say that "it seems to me that Southeast Asia is a basic key to what the future holds at home for all citizens. Until we have disengaged ourselves militarily, I do not comprehend how we can take corrective steps domestically which are so imperatively required." Disentanglement from expensive, long-term foreign involvements was consistent with his general position about such matters in the Senate. Another consistent theme was civil rights. Cain told Jackson that "in the meantime, the best we can hope for is to avoid a widening separation between the races. The name matters not, but we need something comparable to the Marshall Plan if we are to save the cities and reconcile differences which prevail among the ethnic and minority groups."[43]

Unenthusiastic about Richard Nixon, Cain supported Governor Nelson Rockefeller throughout the Republican primary campaign. After Nixon won the nomination, Cain reluctantly decided to support him over his old friend Hubert Humphrey. "In the elections of 1964, I stumped the whole of Florida and did all I could to make Hubert Humphrey widely and favorably known. The passage of time has not diminished my affection and admiration for him. But the team of Humphrey and Muskie are associated with and speak for those who have been in command during the past eight years. Hubert Humphrey stands today somewhere between his understandable loyalty to the administration and being his own man. If a change is to be desired, as I believe to be a paramount need, an extension of [Democratic control of] the White House is not the answer."[44]

Cain, whose health had started to deteriorate as a result of his two-pack-a-day cigarette habit, wrote to Joseph Walker at First Federal Savings on Thanksgiving Day 1969. Predicting his death ten years later, he provided detailed directions about what to do in that event and sent copies of the letter and instructions to be signed and returned to him by Bonnie, Marj, Buzz, and Candy. In it, he expressed his fondness and admiration for the Walker family, saying that he had often "pondered why you didn't fire me or I didn't quit. I suppose these thoughts occur in every marriage. Ours has withstood some troublesome times. . . . But you won't think it boastful of me to suggest that in some important and enduring ways we have helped each other. I have gloried in the firm's growth and success. A sly caper on my part was to broaden your horizons where people, here and elsewhere, were concerned. Even now, the difference between attitudes as they were when I joined you in 1957 and [the present time] are startlingly good. Recently it took you about two minutes to agree that I might assume the Urban League's presidency. Had I offered the proposal ten years ago, you would have called the Board into emergency session and summarily fired me on the spot. All of us have learned a lot in our years together."[45]

On November 1, 1970, as Cain approached retirement (he thought), he wrote the Walker brothers a thirty-two page summary of his past and present activities on behalf of the firm, including a detailed description of the strengths and weaknesses of almost forty community organizations. It was an amazing and candid document—the kind that more communities should employ as they look honestly at their strengths and weaknesses. Cain concluded the document with a plea to the Walkers to remain involved in their community after he was gone.[46]

As the 1972 presidential campaign approached, Harry Cain was looking for a candidate. The revelations about the June Watergate break-in caused him to look at President Nixon "with a total sense of disbelief." Accordingly, Cain decided to support Henry M. Jackson, the man who had defeated him for the Senate in 1952. "Senator Jackson is an unlikely close personal friend. Twenty years ago there was reason to dislike him intensely. After months of warfare, both conventional and guerilla, he won and I lost."[47] Cain didn't officially sign on to Jackson's Florida campaign, as he had with Johnson and Humphrey but enthusiastically introduced the Washington senator at a series of appearances and fund-raisers in the Miami area. "I believe he [Jackson] has all the credentials to be an excellent President." After George McGovern ended Jackson's candidacy in the Democratic primaries, Cain remained publicly silent on the upcoming choice for president. He had another local campaign to deal with.[48]

On the same day as the presidential primary, Dade County voters recalled four of their county commissioners for failing to build a hospital that had twice been authorized in countywide referenda. The five remaining members of the Commission had to select four new replacements. Harry Cain agreed to be one of them after rejecting the idea at first. He did so with the understanding that he would not seek re-election.[49] "None pushed me to be a candidate for the Commission. The decision was mine. It came mostly from feeling that the individual should do his best for as long as he is able."[50]

Cain had been interested in Dade County's metropolitan government for years. Often he had come into contact with it through his various community activities. In 1967, as vice president of the Government Research Council of the Miami-Dade County Chamber of Commerce, Cain had fought against an effort to elect the county's nine commissioners by district. While Cain felt that representation by district would improve the chances of minorities to serve on the Commission, he also felt it would polarize decision-making at a time when the commission was facing many other problems and should be accountable to all of its constituents.

Not surprisingly, Cain's debut on the Miami-Dade County Commission was immediately involved in controversy. He had hardly been sworn in before he refused to sign the county's loyalty oath. Red-faced Metro officials found out the next day that the outdated version they had asked him to sign had been found unconstitutional nine months earlier.[51] In May, Cain convinced the rest of his fellow commissioners, many of them chain-smokers, to pass a smoking ban within the Commission's chambers. "I had been a heavy smoker for 35 or 40 years when I did battle with a bout of pneumonia . . . about two months before I was appointed a commissioner. I can still remember my first meeting. [It] went from nine to five and, of course, everyone was smoking all day. . . . I knew I had to do something. So I went to the mayor and told him what I wanted. . . . That was on a Friday. On Monday we voted in the ban." Cain famously quipped, "If I had my way, the only place where consenting adults could smoke would be in the shower."[52] The ban on smoking was soon followed by further bans on smoking in elevators, nursing homes, hospitals, and other health facilities. On a visit back to Tacoma, Cain told a reporter for the *Tacoma News Tribune*, "At one time in my life I thought my work in helping to establish the Seattle-Tacoma Airport was the biggest thing I'd ever done, but not anymore."[53]

Cain found that he really liked serving on the Commission. It afforded him the opportunity for public service unencumbered by partisan politics. He had intended to serve only a three-month appointment and then return to his job at First Federal Savings. However, Cain enjoyed himself so much that he finally decided, instead, to implement the separation from First Federal he had discussed with the Walkers three years before. He told his daughter, "I am working to leave the firm. After 15 years, this isn't easy. The final separation takes place in about two weeks. After that I will become a consultant."[54]

Cain became one of the Commission's outspoken and articulate members on social issues, once questioning whether they should spend $105,000 on police, fire, and other services to help host the Republican National Convention in 1972. He thought the funds might better be spent on social problems closer to home.

His secretary, Lois Gallagher, told a reporter, "He runs us all ragged. He's got more energy than any two other men." Because Harry spent more time in his office than the others, he was the one who usually got to talk with the citizens who came to the commissioners with their problems, including one man who claimed that the false teeth he received free as a welfare recipient didn't fit right. "I'm afraid I haven't been able to do anything for that guy with the false teeth yet," Cain said in a later interview. "The dentists say they've given him three sets so far and he doesn't like any of them."[55]

Howard Ferguson, a columnist for the *Tacoma News Tribune*, wrote about Cain in a March 13, 1977, column on the occasion of Cain's next-to-last visit to Tacoma. Cain talked about an issue that was waiting for him when he returned home to Florida—equal rights for homosexuals. "That's right. About three years ago, I drafted a resolution that provided equal rights in jobs, housing and public accommodation no matter what your religion, color, sex or age. Well, just recently, a woman member of the commission came up with an amendment to that law. It was to give the same rights to homosexuals. I thought about that for a while. Then I called her and offered my help. If you start cutting back on who gets the equal rights, then you don't have any equal rights."[56]

Cain filed for re-election with a minute and forty-seven seconds left before the filing deadline on July 25, 1972. He spent about $1,500 and received enough votes to escape a run-off.[57] In addition to his continuing efforts to limit smoking in public places, Cain introduced successful resolutions that mandated bilingualism in county government, consolidated rural taxicab services, and set staggered terms for commissioners. "Certainly this is the most interesting, provocative, provoking, demanding job I've ever had. The last four years have been extremely stimulating, exciting and worthwhile for me."[58]

In 1976, Cain sought re-election, but he didn't actively campaign. His failing health was making it more difficult to keep up with his busy schedule, to campaign effectively, or even to play golf. Cain sent out a statement saying that "should I be re-elected, I will continue to do the best I can."[59] He was defeated in the primary by a young and energetic union official, William Oliver, who actually campaigned for the job and defeated Cain by a margin of nearly 18,500 votes in a three-man race. The major causes of his defeat were his obvious declining health and a proposal he had supported to increase the commissioners' salaries—a proposal that was also defeated in the same election. Cain expressed surprise at his defeat. "I never thought it would happen. I'll be puzzled over this for a long, long time. I've been an honest, dedicated public servant, and that's hard to beat." *Miami Herald* columnist Charles Whited described Cain as "tired, pouchy-eyed, speaking in that vocal rumble that sounds like a diesel with a loose valve." Cain remembered all those labor groups he had gone to, asking for their vote. "I hardly know Mr. Oliver," he said, "but he had the votes. You've got to give credit where credit is due."[60]

In December 1977, on his final trip back to Tacoma, Cain was honored at a dinner sponsored and attended by the local Japanese-American community to thank him for the support he had given them thirty-five years earlier during the dark, early days following the nation's declaration of war against Japan as a result of the Japanese attack on Pearl Harbor, which catapulted the U.S. into World War II. They presented Cain with a beautiful, large bronze horse, representing the coming "Year of the Horse," and signifying that, to them, Harry Cain was their "Man of the Year." Speaking for the group, Tacoma business leader Joseph Kosai said that local Japanese families "have never forgotten Mayor Cain's support for us in 1942. You will always have a place in our hearts." For once, even Harry Cain was at a loss for words. Through tears, he rasped, "I not only have never had a night like this, I don't know of anyone else that ever had one. All I can say is, 'Thank You.'"[61]

Without the daily challenge of feeling that he was directly "involved," Cain's health continued to deteriorate. He was still involved in many boards and committees, but he was tired much of the time, his energy sapped. On Monday, February 26, 1979, Cain made his last public appearance before the Miami-Dade County Commission, delivering in his unmistakable voice an impassioned and fiery plea for a civilian review board to investigate charges of police brutality. His wife, Bonnie, said that speech—preparing for it and giving it—had taken a lot out of him. "He had been sleeping a lot, day and night. I asked him what was wrong and he said, 'I don't know. I just don't feel well.' On Friday, he stayed home, read the papers and went back to bed." That evening he arose to watch the *Johnny Carson Show* and chat for a while with Bonnie. Harry bid her good night, went back to bed, fell asleep, and didn't wake up. The official cause of death was listed as complications from emphysema, but he suffered from numerous other ailments, including heart and kidney problems.

As soon as they heard the news, editorial writers across the country remembered Harry Cain. The *Miami Herald*, which had followed him closely for twenty years, editorialized "Harry P. Cain is gone. The community that benefited so much from being chosen as his second home is poorer for his passing. . . . Harry Cain spoke his mind, often with humor and rarely with equivocation, and never mind the political consequences. . . . That quality and the man who embodies it so well will be missed."[62] The *New York Times* and the *Washington Post* both emphasized his support of Joseph McCarthy and his criticism of the Eisenhower-era internal security program in their stories of his passing.

The *Tacoma News Tribune* said, "His was a lifetime that spanned some major turning points in the history of his country, his home state of Washington and his city of Tacoma. And Harry Cain made his mark, because he served. [For] 36 years Harry Cain offered leadership, contributed time and participated in public debate. Often he created the debate in which he took part. Of all of Tacoma's mayors, Harry Cain was the most famous. His death . . . signaled an end to a chapter in Tacoma's history. He will be missed."[63] Emily Walker wrote a touching tribute to Harry, remembering her association with him during the Centennial Jubilee Celebration, four years on his Senate staff, and as a reporter in Washington, DC, who often covered his activities on the Subversive Activities Control Board. Walker also remembered the night that Pierce County's Japanese-American community honored him.

Private services for Harry Cain were held on March 6, 1979, following the script he had provided Joseph Walker on Thanksgiving Day 1969, but the Miami community was not about to let Cain go that quietly. On March 12, a memorial service was held for Harry Cain at the Bayfront Park Auditorium, attended by hundreds of friends, business associates, and representatives of the many community organizations he had served. Friends remembered him as a "man of contradictions: cantankerous and courtly, abrasive and compassionate, as an iron marshmallow."[64] Bonnie received letters from Cain's former Senate colleague, Margaret Chase

Smith, and from General Matthew Ridgway, who fondly remembered Harry's service on his staff during World War II. Senator Henry M. Jackson wrote to say that after the hard-hitting 1952 campaign they had become good friends, calling him a "warm and decent human being."[65]

At the memorial service, Henry King Stanford, the president of the University of Miami, who obviously knew Harry Cain well, offered a prayer. In it, Stanford referred to the fact that Cain's intellectual mentor had been the eighteenth century philosopher and statesman Edmund Burke, who had himself been no stranger to championing unpopular causes. Quoting Burke, he said, "'Public life is a situation of power and energy; he who trespasses against his duty sleeps upon his watch.' No one could ever accuse Harry Cain of sleeping on his watch in the public life he led. . . . He was ever alert to opportunities for constructive service." He also repeated one of Burke's famous quotes that Cain was fond of repeating himself: "The thing necessary for the triumph of evil is for good men to do nothing."[66]

In accordance with his wishes, his body was cremated and his ashes scattered along the rough on both sides of the fourth fairway at Burning Tree Country Club in Bethesda, Maryland. The fourth hole at Burning Tree was, and is, one of the most difficult on the course, and as Harry had told his son, Buzz, whose task it was to spread the ashes, he wanted to be able to spook his friends in the middle of their backswings!"[67]

Epilogue

HARRY CAIN FADED from the public's memory following his death and is now largely forgotten. Largely forgotten, but not quite. Cain's hometown newspaper, the *Tacoma News Tribune*, still publishes pictures of him from the extensive photo collection at the Tacoma Public Library, and the paper's columnists still occasionally write about the events of his life. In late 2009, the Tacoma Public Landmarks Commission and the Tacoma City Council approved a proposal to rename the pedestrian portion of the Broadway Plaza between the refurbished four-star Murano Hotel and Tacoma's new convention center as the Harry P. Cain Promenade. The location is a particularly fitting one for a memorial to Cain because, in 1941, the area was the center of the city's Japanese-American business district.

Harry Cain liked to carry with him a list of capital projects he supported when he campaigned for mayor in the early months of 1940. Most of these projects were ultimately included in the comprehensive planning study he initiated in 1942, and many of them were eventually—some *very* eventually—completed. The new Tacoma Public Library building was completed in 1952. The new County-City Administrative Building opened in 1959; the Schuster Parkway, Cain's planned waterfront drive connecting Ruston and Old Tacoma, was finished in 1976; the Tacoma Dome sports stadium opened in 1983; and the Tacoma Convention and Trade Center was completed in 2004. Most have forgotten Cain's vision in planning these projects. About the only physical vestige that remains from Harry Cain's two terms as mayor are his signature and his footprints and handprints in a concrete slab at what is now the Tacoma Soccer Center. On February 19, 1941, Cain dedicated the building as the Tacoma Exhibition Hall after it had been under construction for ten years.

The city was also slow to adopt Harry Cain's recommendations on changing the Tacoma City Charter. The council-manager form of government was finally adopted in 1952 after another very public episode of vice and corruption.

Miami-Dade County, Florida, where Cain spent the last twenty-three years of his life, was much quicker to recognize his many contributions to their community. There is a hall named in his honor at the library at Florida Memorial University, the largely African American Baptist college that Cain had been instrumental in relocating to Miami. In 1984, the Metropolitan Dade County Department of Housing and Urban Development dedicated a $6-million, 152-unit, fourteen-story low-income public housing complex for the elderly in Cain's memory. It is located in downtown Miami, next to Miami-Dade Community College's New World Center campus. The dedication program noted Cain's "sincere and vigorous interest in public housing." It failed to mention that his "interest" had included his fierce opposition to continuing public housing and rent controls proposed by the Truman Administration during his term in the U.S. Senate. However, the Harry Cain Tower was really meant to honor the later contributions of a man whose "life work was guided by a compassionate and constant commitment to social justice, civil rights, and civil liberty for all persons."[1]

Some of Cain's greatest accomplishments as a Miami-Dade commissioner were the cutting-edge causes he championed. Many of them remain potent social issues today. The indoor smoking ban he championed was one of the first in the nation and has now been widely adopted throughout the rest of the country. In 1977, during his final year on the Commission, Cain drafted and sponsored a resolution that provided for equal rights for homosexuals in jobs, housing, and public accommodation—an issue that is still being debated more than thirty years later.

MOST OF HARRY Cain's immediate family outlived him. Tragically, his twin brother, Bill, did not. An excellent student, Bill Cain graduated with honors from what became Oregon State University, where he obtained a post-graduate degree in electrical engineering. Bill was hired by General Electric and was involved in steam turbine research at the company's facilities in Schenectady, New York, and then as a sales engineer at their Fort Wayne, Indiana plant. He married Alicia Mary Ackart in Schenectady in 1931. They had two children; a daughter, Delores, born in 1933, and a son, George William Cain IV, born in 1939. Bill Cain suffered increasingly from depression, leaving his position with GE and moving back to Oregon with his family in 1941. There, Bill found work as an engineer for the Bonneville Power Administration until 1944. He then worked for short periods of time at other jobs until Harry was forced to commit him to the Oregon State Hospital on December 19, 1946. Bill was released in 1947 but recommitted soon thereafter and remained there until his death on January 19, 1966.

Marjorie Cain, following her summer job with the U.S. exhibit at the 1958 Brussels World Fair, worked for the State Department, sold real estate, and ran for mayor of Palm Desert, California. After her defeat, Marjorie said, "Well, I met some very interesting people along the way."[2] In 1978, Marjorie married Dr. Leland Powers, who had once served as Harry Cain's embattled Director of Public Health in Tacoma. It was Powers who had helped Cain to understand the social and economic costs associated with large-scale prostitution and who deserved much of the credit for cleaning it up while Cain served as mayor. He went on to become Washington's State Health Director and, later, the United Nations Relief and Rehabilitation Administration's Chief Medical Officer in China after World War II.[3] Marjorie Cain passed away in 1994 at the age of eighty-five.

A year after Harry Cain's death, Bonnie Cain moved back to Tacoma from Florida. Their many friends and associations in Miami had been Harry's, not hers. Back in Tacoma, Bonnie played cards, loved her cats, and enjoyed time spent with her friends and family. She passed away at age seventy-five in 1985.

Harry P. Cain II (Buzz) met and married Maury Bethea of Memphis while he was working as a Capitol Hill policeman in 1963. Maury was working for Senator Estes Kefauver, with whom the senior Cain had crossed swords during the Kefauver Crime Committee hearings. After completing his master's degree from the University of Washington, Buzz joined the staff of the National Institute of Mental Health, earned a Ph.D. from Brandeis University in 1971, and rose to become director of the NIH's Bureau of Health Planning and Resource Development in 1976. In 1978, frustrated with government civil service regulations, Buzz turned out to be as unpredictable as his father—he resigned. His father dryly commented at the time, "Harry found out he couldn't fire those he didn't want to hire, so he decided to fire himself."[4]

Buzz subsequently became a high-level official of the Blue Cross and Blue Shield Association, a major national health care organization. Buzz retired at the end of 1999 to teach, consult, and concentrate on his golf game. The couple has three grown children, including a son named Harry P. Cain III, and eight grandchildren including Harry P. Cain IV, who lives in Atlanta.[5] An exceptional amateur golfer like his father, Harry Cain II still plays in regional tournaments. Buzz once said that the most relaxed, enjoyable times he ever had with his father were on the golf course. "Somehow my golf prowess was important to him, and he liked to see it. He also loved the fact that it took me many years to actually beat him, even though I had become much the better golfer, for at least five years, before I won."[6]

Marlyce "Candy" Cain married Robert Paul Tingstad on July 19, 1961, and still lives in Lakewood, south of Tacoma. The couple has three sons. As a young mother, Candy taught preschool and attended college part-time, often one class per term, ultimately graduating from the University of Puget Sound in 1979 with a degree in education. After graduation, Candy taught child development as an instructor in the Home and Family Life Department at Bates Technical College in Tacoma. At the same time, she earned a master's degree in human development from Pacific Oaks College in Pasadena, California. Candy retired in 2003 and fills her time with volunteer work, keeping track of her ten grandchildren, and travelling with her husband, Bob.[7]

Harry's stepson, David William Hein, born to Bonnie and Lee Hein in 1934, grew up in Tacoma, attended the University of Washington, and graduated with a degree in physics. He married Barbara Kathryn Holm in 1967, and the couple had two children. David Hein worked as an engineer, designing aircraft instruments and electronic controls for mechanical systems for the same company, ultimately becoming Honeywell after a series of mergers, for forty years. His wife, Barbara, originally an elementary school teacher, later became politically active, co-chairing the incorporation committee for the City of Rancho Palos Verdes, California, and later serving as both a city councilmember and mayor. The couple moved to Tucson in 1984, where Barbara became the Republican Party chairman for their state legislative district. Her motivation may have resulted from a comment Harry Cain once made to her to the effect that women were no good at politics. The couple is now retired and living in Tucson, Arizona.[8]

Epilogue

HARRY CAIN ALWAYS had a knack for being in the right place at the right time. As a result, he worked with and for some of the most famous Americans of the twentieth century.

Being on the winning side, all of Harry's military commanders in World War II returned home to relative fame and fortune. The old cavalryman, Major General Kenyon A. Joyce, who had joined the army as a trooper in the Spanish-American War and had been both Mark Clark's and Dwight Eisenhower's commanding officer at Fort Lewis before the war, was appointed to be Deputy President of the Allied Control Commission in Italy where he recruited Harry to serve on his staff. Joyce retired from active service in 1943. He died in 1960 at the age of eighty.

After liberating Rome following the Anzio invasion, General Mark Clark replaced British General Sir Harold R. L. G. Alexander as commander of the 15th Army Group in Italy until the end of the war. Later, he served as the U.S. High Commissioner of Austria and was involved with negotiating the postwar peace treaty with that country. In 1947, Clark returned home and assumed command of the U.S. Sixth Army, headquartered at the Presidio of San Francisco. In 1949, Clark was named commander of all U.S. Army Field Forces. President Truman nominated Clark in 1951 to be the U.S. Ambassador to the Vatican, but his nomination had to be withdrawn following opposition from powerful Texas Senator Tom Connelly and various Protestant groups. Six months later he was named to replace General Matthew Ridgway as commander of all United Nations troops in Korea. After the cease-fire in 1953, Clark returned home to become commandant of the Citadel, the Military College of South Carolina, where he served until 1966. He passed away in 1984. A bridge connecting Camano Island, where he maintained a get-away cabin for many years, to the mainland in Washington State is named for him.

Harry Cain's two military government commanders both completed distinguished military careers. Brigadier General Frank S. McSherry, whom Cain served both in Italy and in London, went on to serve as Eisenhower's Deputy Assistant Chief of Staff at SHAEF and then as the director of SHAEF's Manpower Division for Germany. He retired in December 1946 after more than thirty-nine years of active service. He died at the age of eighty-five in 1977.

The Canadian-born Lieutenant-General Sir Arthur Edward Grassett, Cain's boss at SHAEF in London, had commanded all British troops in China and then in Hong Kong until he was recalled just before the colony was overrun by the Japanese in December 1941. Grassett's previous experience in military government landed him in the job as official spokesman for civil affairs and military government in London, reporting directly to General Dwight Eisenhower. In 1945, he was appointed Lieutenant-Governor and Military Governor of the Bailiwick of Jersey, a British Crown Dependency off the coast of Normandy, where he served until 1953. He died in 1971 at the age of eighty-three.

Following Germany's unconditional surrender, General of the Army Dwight Eisenhower became the military governor of the U.S. Zone of Occupation in Germany. In 1948, Eisenhower returned home to become president of Columbia University in New York City. He was recalled to active military service in December 1950 to become Supreme Commander of the North Atlantic Treaty Organization (NATO) and assumed operational command of all NATO forces in Europe. Eisenhower retired from active military service in May 1952 and returned to Columbia until January 1953. During this period, both major political parties tried to recruit him as their candidate for president. He selected the Republican Party and defeated Adlai Stevenson of Illinois in a landslide, becoming the first Republican president to be elected in nearly twenty-five years.

After Germany's surrender, Mathew Ridgway, now promoted to the rank of Lieutenant General, was transferred to the Pacific to serve under General MacArthur for the final assault on Japan. When the atomic bomb ended the war, Ridgway returned to Europe as the Deputy Supreme Allied Commander. He was given command of the U.S. Eighth Army in Korea in 1950 upon the death of General Walton Walker. After battling the Chinese Communist forces to a standstill in Korea, Ridgway replaced Eisenhower as Supreme Allied Commander at NATO in May 1952. He was named Chief of Staff of the U.S. Army in August 1953 and retired from active duty in May 1955. He outlived Cain, sending a touching note of condolence to Cain's wife Bonnie after his death. Ridgway died in July 1993 at the age of ninety-eight.

BY A QUIRK of fate, Harry Cain arrived on Washington's statewide political scene at roughly the same time as two of the state's most famous and celebrated politicians. Unfortunately for Cain, both of them happened to be Democrats. Cain holds the distinction of being the only man to be defeated by *both* Warren G. Magnuson and Henry M. Jackson for a seat in the U.S. Senate. For a time, it appeared that Cain might pull off a victory against Magnuson in their contest for the open Senate seat in 1944. But, in the end, Cain's inability to campaign in person and Magnuson's great popularity, along with Roosevelt's surprising last-minute comeback in the national presidential election, decided the election for Magnuson.

Warren Grant Magnuson became one of the towering icons of Washington politics, serving as the state's senior senator from 1945 until he was finally defeated at the age of seventy-five in 1980. During his long Senate career, Magnuson served as chairman of the powerful Senate Commerce Committee and became President Pro Tem of the Senate, third in line for the presidency of the United States. Magnuson became one of the most powerful and influential political operators in the modern history of the Senate. While he never lost his New Deal political philosophy, Magnuson believed strongly in political partnerships that benefited his state. He mentored a whole generation of political operatives, business leaders, and successful candidates who serve on to this day. He passed away in 1988.

The man Cain defeated in the U.S. Senate race in 1946, Hugh B. Mitchell, ran again for Congress in 1948, making headlines by calling on President Truman to step aside in the hope that Dwight Eisenhower could be drafted to run as a Democrat. Truman won anyway, as did Mitchell—but by a paper-thin margin. In 1952, Mitchell ran for governor in order to free up the Democratic nomination for the U.S. Senate for Congressman Henry M. "Scoop" Jackson, who then opposed incumbent Harry Cain. Mitchell lost the governor's race to Arthur Langlie in the Eisenhower landslide. He ran for Congress again in 1954 and in 1958 but lost both races amid McCarthy-era charges that he was "left-wing." Mitchell became a successful Seattle businessman and, in 1980, was appointed to the Commission on Wartime Relocation and Internment of Civilians, a group charged with investigating the internment of more than 110,000 Japanese-American citizens and resident aliens and about 900 Aleut Americans during World War II. Mitchell died in 1996 at the age of eighty-nine.[9]

After defeating Cain for re-election in 1952, Henry "Scoop" Jackson never looked back, retaining his Senate seat for the next thirty years. Jackson died in office in 1983 after being re-elected for the fifth time in 1982. Jackson and Magnuson became one of the most effective legislative teams in history, and not only because they served together in the Senate for so long. While there was always a sense of competition between their two staffs, the two men effectively balanced each other's legislative interests and those of their constituents in Washington. Jackson was a traditional New Deal Democrat on most domestic issues, but he was also a determined Cold War anti-Communist. Former Jackson staff members Paul Wolfowitz and Richard Pearle were leaders in what came to be known as the neo-conservative wing of the Republican Party and were architects of America's involvement in both Iraq and Afghanistan. Cain and Jackson shared much in common, and over the years they were able to put the tough 1952 campaign behind them and became good friends.

As we have seen, Harry Cain's two most important mentors in the U.S. Senate were Robert A. Taft of Ohio and Arthur Vandenberg of Michigan. The respected but aloof Taft served as Senate Majority Leader and the philosophical inspiration of the conservative Midwest wing of the Republican Party. Taft lost the Republican nomination for president to Dwight Eisenhower in 1952 and passed away the following year. In 1957, a Senate committee, chaired by future President John F. Kennedy, named Taft as one of the greatest U.S. Senators in history. While Cain held the highest respect for Taft, he most admired Arthur Vandenberg.[10] The reformed isolationist served as the chairman of the Senate Foreign Relations Committee, and Cain often credited his own ability to change his mind on important issues to Vandenberg. Vandenberg died of complications from cancer in 1951.

While Harry Cain was known as a fierce Republican partisan in the Senate, he established at least one lasting relationship with a prominent Democrat that transcended their time together in the Senate. When Hubert Humphrey arrived in the Senate in 1948, he was already one of the four founders, along with Eleanor Roosevelt, Arthur Schlesinger, Jr., and John Kenneth Galbraith, of the liberal Americans for Democratic Action (ADA). It was rare that Humphrey and Cain ever agreed on anything, and yet, they became close personal friends. The two conducted an infrequent, but continuing, correspondence about domestic policy and other political matters during the period that Humphrey served as the Senate Majority Whip, and the two worked unsuccessfully to obtain an appointment for Cain on the Federal Home Loan Bank Board in 1962. Cain later chaired the Florida Citizens for Johnson and Humphrey organization during the 1964 presidential campaign.

Their correspondence continued even after Humphrey became Vice President of the United States in 1964, but Cain became disenchanted with Humphrey's loyalty to Lyndon Johnson during the Viet Nam War. After supporting Nelson Rockefeller in the Republican presidential primary, Cain supported Richard Nixon, rather than Humphrey, for president in 1968. Humphrey returned to the Senate in 1971 and ran for president again in 1972. The revelations about the Watergate break-in and other abuses eliminated Richard Nixon from consideration for reelection as far as Cain was concerned. He ended up supporting his old antagonist, Henry Jackson, over Hubert Humphrey in the 1972 Democratic presidential primary. Humphrey returned to the Senate and served with great honor until cancer ended his career in 1978.

The other U.S. Senator with whom Harry Cain is widely associated is Joseph McCarthy. Cain and McCarthy arrived in the Senate together in 1946 and quickly became close friends. Even after Cain broke ranks with the Wisconsin senator, the two remained friendly, never criticizing each other by name in public. Cain had applauded McCarthy as he attacked the Truman Administration—he agreed with the substance, if not the details, of much of McCarthy's criticism. But by 1955, McCarthy was focusing on a Republican administration instead of a Democratic one, and Cain came to believe that McCarthy's allegations were increasingly irresponsible. By the time that Cain finally broke with McCarthy, his influence was already on the decline. In equal part, McCarthy's problems were the result his own persona and lack of discipline and Eisenhower's behind-the-scenes efforts to limit his arrogance and abuse of power. On June 1, 1954, Vermont Republican Senator George Flanders took the Senate floor to compare McCarthy to Hitler, accusing him of spreading division and confusion. "Were the Junior Senator from Wisconsin in the pay of the Communists he could not have done a better job for them." Ten days later he offered a resolution calling for McCarthy to be removed as chair of his investigations sub-committee and, when that failed to generate adequate traction, introduced another resolution to censure McCarthy for conduct unbecoming a member of the United States Senate. The Senate later changed the language of the final resolution from "censure" to "condemn," but the meaning was clear. In December, the Senate voted to convict McCarthy on two of the forty-six counts brought forward in the resolution. The Senate's action essentially destroyed McCarthy as a political force. He died less than three years later from liver disease at the age of forty-eight.[11]

Harry Cain and Joseph McCarthy were both "outsiders," each in his own way. The two young senators were drawn together by their common interests, their age, and their similar backgrounds, and they became good friends. Their friendship was strong enough to transcend their later intense political differences. Looking back at them now, over a period of sixty years, in which Joe McCarthy is generally seen as one of the great American *bête noirs* of the twentieth century, we may readily wonder why they remained friends. Harry Cain questioned McCarthy's judgment and his politics, but he never questioned their friendship. He maintained it until McCarthy's early death.

McCarthy was gone, but the political movement that bore his name unfortunately lived on—the latest in a long history of anti-alien and anti-radical political repressions. Ellen Schrecker, one of the keenest observers of the McCarthy period, has written that there was not just one but *many* types of McCarthyism—each with its own goals and objectives. These variations of McCarthyism ranged from patriotic groups and right-wing activists who sought to purge textbooks of positive references about the United Nations; to politicians like McCarthy, Nixon, and Cain, who used anti-communism to boost their own careers and the Republican Party; to liberal versions that supported action against Communists but not against non-Communists; to even a left-wing version composed of anti-Stalinist radicals who attacked Communists as traitors to socialism.[12] Joseph McCarthy didn't invent communism. Indeed, he discovered the issue long after Cain and others had used it to further their own political careers. McCarthy's gift was that he used the issue more successfully than anyone else as a means of self-promotion, power, and fear.

The McCarthy era lasted for approximately ten years—from 1946 to 1956—although its repressive influence remained for much longer. Across the nation, liberals of all political hues were accused of being "soft" on communism. By the mid-1950s, 3.5 million Americans—more than 20 percent of the national workforce—were employed under the shadow of some employer-required loyalty program. States, including Washington, mimicked the federal government in creating their own "un-American Activities" investigating committees, so that it was not only the federal government that was looking into people's personal lives but the states and, sometimes, local governments as well. In 1948, the Washington

Epilogue

State Legislature created its own un-American activities committee chaired by Republican Representative Albert F. Canwell. Within a year, his committee was focused on the alleged Communist affiliations of ten University of Washington professors. Three were later dismissed for being Communists. Canwell would later be convicted of libel during the 1962 John Goldmark trial (see Chapter 11).

During the McCarthy era, more than 11,000 Americans were fired from their jobs for suspected disloyalty, often on the flimsiest of evidence.[13] The fear of being investigated potentially opened up other aspects of an individual's life—sexual orientation, personal relationships, financial dealings, or general unorthodoxy—that many would have preferred to have left unopened. The fear of communism evolved into a fear of being different. Over time, "McCarthyism" became a synonym for demagoguery, defamation of character, and political mudslinging.

For every legitimate Communist that was discovered, hundreds of other socialists, ultra-liberals, and non-conformists were attacked by name, and their reputations, their employment, and their lives often ruined. Many thousands of others were quietly forced out of their jobs in education, business, or the media—never formally charged with anything but accused by their peers or by some self-appointed local watchdog group with a past or present indiscretion. Ultimately, over time, the Supreme Court and a Democratic Congress slowly and methodically peeled away the legal mechanisms that had allowed McCarthyism to flourish, while most of the general public increasingly forgot about AGLOSO or the SACB—unless they happened to be one of those hundreds of thousands of Americans whose lives had been negatively impacted by them. Increasingly the nation's attention was drawn to a new battle against foreign Communists in Viet Nam.

FEW PEOPLE DISLIKED Joe McCarthy more than Dwight Eisenhower—with the possible exception of his predecessor, Harry Truman. In 1951, McCarthy had attacked Ike's mentor, General George Marshall, insinuating that he was a traitor. After Eisenhower's election in 1952, McCarthy had tried to block the appointment of Eisenhower's friend and former military chief of staff, Walter Bedell Smith, as Assistant Secretary of State. Eisenhower's advisors recommended that he confront McCarthy directly, as Truman had, but Ike decided on a different strategy. He would just ignore him.

He explained his reasoning in his diary: "I really believe that nothing will be so effective in combating his particular kind of troublemaking as to ignore him. This he cannot stand." [14] He told his White House Chief of Staff, Sherman Adams, that "I will not get down in the gutter with that guy."[15] Another reason for not taking on McCarthy directly was political. Eisenhower had a frail majority in Congress and needed McCarthy's vote in the Senate. It was McCarthy's methods Eisenhower disagreed with, not his goals.[16] The popular Dwight Eisenhower was reelected as president in 1956. Following the completion of his second term, Eisenhower was recommissioned as a General of the Army and retired to his farm near the Gettysburg battlefield in Pennsylvania. He died of heart disease in 1969.

The three Eisenhower associates most closely involved with Cain's "mutiny" were White House Chief of Staff Sherman Adams, Attorney General Herbert Brownell and Maxwell Rabb. Because of Eisenhower's strict and formal staff structure, Adams is generally considered to have been one of the most powerful White House chiefs of staff in the history of the office—including some more recent holders of the position, such as Richard Cheney and Rahm Emanuel. In his memoirs, Adams claimed that his role was limited to managing the White House staff and expediting the urgent business that had to be brought to Eisenhower's attention. "Any power or authority that I exercised while carrying out this appointed task was solely on a 'de facto' basis and, except when I was acting on an explicit directive from the President, my duty and responsibilities were implied rather than stated."[17]

Following Adams's departure, the Eisenhower White House lost focus. Radio talk show host and political commentator Michael Medved, in his book on presidential aides, called *The Shadow President,* repeated a joke that circulated around Washington in the 1950s. Two Democrats were talking, and one said, "Just imagine, what a disaster it would be if Eisenhower died and Nixon became President?" The other replied, "Or even worse, what if Sherman Adams died and Eisenhower became President!"[18] Adams was forced to resign his position in 1958 over a scandal involving the gift of an expensive vicuna coat and an oriental rug from a Boston textile manufacturer who was being investigated for Federal Trade Commission violations. Adams died in his native New Hampshire in 1986.

Herbert Brownell, Jr., served as Eisenhower's Attorney General from 1952 until 1957. While Brownell became the primary target of Harry Cain's wrath over the Justice Department's handling of AGLOSO and other concerns about the government's internal security program, Brownell had a distinguished legal career and was instrumental in several landmark civil rights cases, including *Brown v. Board of Education.* Brownell drafted the legislative proposal that ultimately became the Civil Rights Act of 1957. Eisenhower would have liked to appoint Brownell to the Supreme Court in 1957, and again in 1958, but held back for fear of Southern congressional opposition. Brownell later served in a number of prestigious civic and legal positions, including president of the New York City Bar Association, U.S. Representative to the Permanent Court of Arbitration in The Hague, and Special U.S. Ambassador to Mexico. He died of cancer in 1996.

Maxwell Rabb and Harry Cain had become acquainted during Cain's Senate term, and Rabb was administrative assistant to Massachusetts Senator Henry Cabot Lodge. Although Cain and Lodge did not agree on many issues, the charismatic Rabb, a practicing Jew, was always on friendly terms with a wide circle of people of differing backgrounds and beliefs. Through Lodge, Max Rabb became involved in Eisenhower's 1952 presidential campaign and, after Ike was elected, served as Secretary to the Cabinet, reporting directly to White House Chief of Staff Sherman Adams. Rabb was generally considered to be the administration's point-man on minority and urban affairs. Upon leaving the White House in 1958, Rabb—a Harvard-educated lawyer—entered private practice in New York until he became United States Ambassador to Italy between 1981 and 1989. He died in 2002.

Cain retained a fondness and respect for Dwight Eisenhower all of his life, but his SACB experience had shaken his confidence in the former President as a national leader. In a handwritten comment scrawled on a draft of his son's 1959 college paper, Cain wrote, "It has seemed to me that it was not until after the departure of Governor Adams and Mr. Brownell, and the untimely death of Mr. [John Foster] Dulles that the President began to do his own thinking in important areas where he had not formerly been well informed. At least I think he has been much more 'the President' or 'a President' since the above crutches were no longer available to be leaned on."[19]

WHEN, IN 1953, Harry Cain was appointed to the SACB, it was expected that his would be a safe, non-controversial appointment. Instead, after serving quietly for two years—"listening and learning"—Cain became concerned about the administration's internal security program, and particularly its use of the AGLOSO. After Cain's efforts to change the administration's policies were unsuccessful, he decided to "go public." In an administration forced to defend itself against McCarthy and his followers, Cain's added public criticism was hardly a welcome development. While liberals rejoiced at his apparent change of heart, conservative and even moderate Republicans reacted with surprise and anguish. The administration quietly pushed back against their new critic—questioning his loyalty, his motivation, and the propriety of his speaking out about subjects that were outside his official area of responsibility. In the end, Cain's "mutiny" cost him his job and any reasonable future hope of continuing his political career at the national level.

Harry Cain's public opposition to AGLOSO, and later to the SACB, and the McCarran Act itself, was the most important public service of his long career. Civil liberties historian Robert Justin Goldstein has claimed that the AGLOSO process, not Joseph McCarthy, was the single most important enabler of the McCarthy era.[20] Goldstein is not alone in this view. In his 1952 book, *The Loyalty of Free Men*, Alan Barth called the Attorney General's list "perhaps the most arbitrary and far-reaching power ever exercised by a single public official" in American history.[21] After Cain's departure, AGLOSO remained—unused and moribund—until President Richard Nixon tried to resurrect both it and the SACB in 1971 for use against what the then-current chairman of the SACB referred to as "a number of non-Communist organizations" that "pose a threat to the national security."[22]

At the time, the SACB was being considered for elimination by Congress as a cost-cutting measure. John William Mahan, a lawyer from Montana, who had been appointed as chairman of the SACB by President Lyndon Johnson and then re-appointed by Nixon, was desperately trying to find a new role for the agency that would maintain both it and his job. Mahan recommended that the SACB's mission be redefined by transferring the AGLOSO function from the Justice Department to the SACB. Not surprisingly, this suggestion prompted an extensive internal review of the AGLOSO by Nixon's staffers. Ultimately, a new Executive Order 11605 was developed by Mahan and the FBI and signed by President Nixon on July 2, 1971. The new Executive Order immediately created a firestorm in Congress, which claimed that Nixon was trying to usurp its authority since the SACB had originally been created by Congress as a part of the McCarran Act. Democratic Senator Sam Irvin of North Carolina led the opposition—as he later would the Watergate Hearings—noting with his customary homespun humor that the SACB would be empowered by Nixon's EO "to do one of the things which the Board is set up to keep other people from doing; that is, denying people their rights under Constitution."[23] The matter was made moot in 1972 when Congress refused to provide any more funding for the SACB. On June 4, 1974, Nixon signed another Executive Order that declared that AGLOSO "was abolished and shall not be used for any purpose" in the future.[24]

Almost twenty years earlier, Harry Cain had come to the conclusion that the United States needed to re-examine its definition of internal security. "The way to preserve freedom is to have more of it."[25] That sentiment generally prevailed during the thirty years that followed. Following the bitter Viet Nam era, the nation focused on domestic issues, and internal security became the purview of foreign, rather than domestic, policy. That all changed on September 11, 2001. The psychic shock of the terrorist attacks triggered a wide range of public and governmental reactions that included initiating two new wars in Iraq and Afghanistan and in a host of new initiatives—not all of them well thought-out—aimed at making America more secure. Not surprisingly, some of these initiatives have reopened the divisive fault lines that appear every time that America feels threatened—how to protect the internal security of the nation while ensuring the civil liberties of its people.

The AGLOSO lists and the McCarran Act were both rooted in an honest effort to keep Communists and other subversives out of government and to reduce or eliminate their ability to subvert the nation. Instead, these worthy aims were themselves subverted, as they have been throughout our history, by fear mongering and political posturing. In the aftermath of 9/11, President George W. Bush asked Congress to pass new legislation that would correct the perceived deficiencies in the nation's internal security structure. The result was the USA PATRIOT Act, quickly passed by Congress and signed into law by President Bush on October 26, 2001. The primary focus of the Act was on surveillance and early detection of terrorists, but it also provided the Treasury Department with additional authority to regulate financial transactions—particularly those involving foreign individuals and entities—and broadened the discretion of law enforcement and immigration authorities in detaining and deporting immigrants suspected of terrorist activities.

THE USA PATRIOT Act gives our intelligence services, primarily the FBI and CIA, the right to intercept electronic communication, such as email and cell phone traffic; expands the existing Foreign Intelligence Surveillance Act (FISA) to allow greater surveillance of American citizens, permanent resident aliens, and aliens living within the United States; and increases the government's activity with regard to search warrants. At the time it was passed, a small but influential number of congressmen and senators expressed their concerns about the potential for civil liberties abuses in some of the provisions of the Act, but most of these individuals are no longer in Congress. They were particularly concerned about the dramatic expansion of electronic surveillance on American citizens, so-called "sneak-and-peek" search warrants, and "trap and trace" devices that record or decode electronic communication.[26] These concerns were evident by the inclusion of a sunset clause that would have ended certain provisions in December 2005. However, at that time, most of the questionable provisions were made permanent rather than eliminated or modified. This has led to continued speculation and concern about the level of civil liberties protection afforded American citizens—an issue which Harry Cain would have understood very well.

The basic conflict between the need to make our nation safe and, at the same time, to protect the rights of its citizens has occurred and reoccurred throughout our history. It is occurring now, and it will occur again. The hope is that, while zealots on both sides always make things more difficult, the ultimate balance between these conflicting priorities will be found, over time, through our dynamic system of checks and balances and that as little harm as possible will be done in the meantime.

HARRY CAIN PLAYED a key role in this process during an important time in our history. In doing so, he was sometimes inconsistent, often unpredictable, and generally controversial. Indeed, Cain actively courted controversy when he believed that his position was rooted in his core principles of supporting constitutional rights, limited government, free markets, and civil liberties. For such an idealistic man, these core principles were comforting anchors. However, as a politician, they presented him with often-insurmountable problems. Throughout Harry Cain's life, principle always trumped politics, ultimately leading to the grudging respect and long-term friendship of some of his greatest political adversaries. As a result, Cain was often uncomfortable in both of the major political parties. That accounts for the fact that political labels never seemed to stick successfully with him for very long—the same principle can result in being known as a progressive in one context or liberal in another and a conservative in one instance and a radical in another. Cain once tried to explain this anomaly to a *Seattle Times* film critic, C. J. Skreen, who had written in a review that Cain had been one of the most reactionary of all U.S. Senators. Cain responded that at various times, and for different reasons, he had been known as a progressive, a conservative, a reactionary, a liberal, or as just a publicity-seeker. But he preferred to think of himself as a "political pragmatist," who "from time to time, and for different reasons . . . had been a conservative, a militant, a liberal, a moderate, a purist, a radical and now and again, populist, who had simply done the "best I could' when confronted with situations demanding action."[27]

From an early age, Harry Cain always found a way to be where the action was. He was an early observer of Nazi Germany. He became a dynamic and successful civic booster and managed a major statewide event. He became Tacoma's first modern and most popular mayor. He was a highly decorated army officer who saw war in a half-dozen countries. He was a controversial U.S. Senator and an even more controversial critic of the Eisenhower Administration's internal security program. He started a new life in Florida, where he became a well-known political figure, community leader, and civic activist during the Civil Rights era. Most men would be remembered for accomplishing any *one* of these things. Harry Pulliam Cain accomplished them all.

APPENDIX 1

Radio Address by
Mayor Harry P. Cain

December 7, 1941

GOOD EVENING, TACOMA. This is Harry Cain.

Tragic as the events of this startling day have been, those events during the course of a few short hours, have replaced uncertainty and confused thinking with a certainty of purpose and a desire to have those in authority define clearly our objectives in order that, as a people, each of us will carry his or her full measure of responsibility. The challenge to a survival of decent living has been issued by others and it is for us to prove our contention that America is worth fighting and even slaving for.

For months we have known that some of you were willing to carry out any orders which were and have been given; we have known too that it was useless to appeal to some of you because you were completely convinced that any war could only result from acts of aggression by this country. Tonight our previous conclusions and attitudes are being thrown into discord and as one American community we shall so design our future operations and actions as to include a place for every man and woman, and I have a right to assume that means all of us, who recognize now that our kind of civilization faces a perilous tomorrow.

It isn't my purpose to frighten you for there is little reason for fear and certainly none for hysteria. It is a time for thoughtful thinking and the designing of what it is you will be expected to do. I can't tell you at the minute what you must do but I can tell you that responsible parties will shortly present a program worth taking a second look at.

Tonight a lot of you are likely wondering what steps, if any, Tacoma has taken to anticipate the coming of our immediate emergency. Right here you have cause for reassurance for the efforts, for more than a year, of Tacoma's Home Defense Corps have been progressive and substantial. They have been ready for weeks with plans for the evacuation of the city; they have inventoried every truck and piece of rolling stock situated within the confines of the city limits; at the last count they had enrolled approximately 800 air wardens and their goal of many more was defeated only for the reason that hundreds of normal people couldn't bring themselves to believe that there might ever be a need. Then too, the surface has only been scratched in the field of auxiliary firemen and policemen; those who have had the experience will be able leaders for the many additions which will promptly be added. The Red Cross has a motor corps and other girls have been taught how to wrap and create bandages. There has been a well trained troop of amateur cavalrymen and their abilities can properly be used in a dozen different ways; even to-day, before the news, Bert Bradley was maneuvering with the boats of the independents and the Yacht Club. They have been doing just that for months in preparation for a day when they might be needed. On top of all this some several hundred men have been carefully trained as foot soldiers and officers. Twice or three times a week they have been drilled at the Armory in the theory and practice of discipline and leadership. They are not far from being ready for any job. What Tacoma has in the way of a Home [Defense] Corps is good; what we haven't got are numbers, but an answer to that is not far away and you who listen constitute that answer.

From now on and beginning at 11 o'clock tomorrow morning defense activities in Tacoma will be regulated and governed by Tacoma's Defense Council, an instrument thru which all people will be fully represented. Any opinion or order issued by them will be in reality an expression by the city and as such should be listened to and followed out by every citizen. The job of the Mayor will be to act as chairman; his vice chairman will be the Defense Commissioner – in this instance Mr. Bert Bradley, who has for months been the Commander-in-Chief of the Home Defense Corp. Our police and fire interests will be represented by the Commissioner of Public Safety. The Commissioner of Public Utilities will concern himself, thru the council, with water and light problems.

The following persons are requested to join with me and the above-mentioned in my office tomorrow at 11: Mr. John Taylor of the Veterans; Milton J. Evans of the American Red Cross; Mr. Guy Thompson of the Council of Social Agencies; Mrs. Pratt, President of the Parent Teachers Association; Mr. George Brown, director of the Pierce County Welfare; Mrs. Judson Benton of the Presidents Council; J. J. Kaufman of the Chamber of Commerce; and the following three men from Organized Labor – Mr.

Grover of the American Federation of Labor, Mr. Freeman Cochran of the C. I. O., and Mr. Elmer Cassidy of the Railroad Brotherhoods. These are the persons who will be the charter members of Tacoma's Defense Council and their work begins right now.

May I urge you to reserve all publicly-expressed opinions until the Defense Council has adopted a policy which will govern your actions, and mine. They are stable people and they will have stable reasons for making any request of you.

What's going to happen? Your guess is just about as good as mine. The Japanese, in bombing possessions belonging to these United States, did something most people thought wasn't possible. Will they stop at that or will they continue to strike where they are not expected? If they do, will they disregard the Pacific Coast, and what is more important to us, the shores of Puget Sound? You wouldn't venture a bet on what they might do, would you? Of course not, so let's endeavor to be realistically logical. Were bombs to fall in Tacoma how would you first know and what would you do? Whistles on the Tide Flats would be your air raid warning and what then? Go home and stay there, and by all means get off the streets. Bomb splinters can often be deflected by the side of a house and your basement is a safe refuge unless a direct hit is your burden; then you or anyone else in your company won't be burdened further. I say it just that way because its serious business even if it sounds like the silliest utterance you have ever heard. I believe you must be prepared for anything, even the worst, because if it comes and you continue to refuse to believe, you will be helpless in the face of something you don't understand.

Colonel Walter DeLong, Adjutant General of the State of Washington, has an open phone to the city and he wants you to keep your feet on the ground and yourself off the street if any immediate emergency should arise. Governor Langlie talked to me an hour ago and his concern was for our industrial plants. That responsibility for the moment must be carried by each individual industry for the act of the saboteur might be synchronized to the action of the dive bomber and the latter gave no preliminary notice of what he was going to attempt or do. It isn't necessary to say "wake up," for Pearl Harbor woke you up this morning. If you have a plant, and its operation is important, protect it. How? That must be your immediate concern, for the next twenty four hours constitute a crisis the like of which no people of any present generation have ever seen or dreamed about.

The Japanese as a nation have done that which is criminal and viciously insane and destructive. There will surely be no rest until the Japanese are stopped and prevented from continuing what they have started. But what about those Japanese who have lived for years in this country or those Japanese who assumed American citizenship thru virtue of their having been born here? The days ahead of them are not pleasant but the rest of us must be careful not to make their days unnecessarily unpleasant. Why can't we say to them as we would as we would to any other people living within our cities, "subscribe to our rules and regulations and you will be as one with us." I would suggest one thing further. That they must be ever so careful not to give others cause for suspicion and above all else the Japanese must, in fact, be his brother's keeper. Let's think this over carefully and as intelligent and charitable people. Let's make it as easy as possible on those whose cross, any way you look at it, is going to be brutally heavy. But in fairness to all let us frankly admit that any unfriendly acts, by anyone, are something which better not happen.

There isn't any more to say, at least not tonight. It isn't a happy world but you have no cause for despair. We are all Uncle Sam's children and he will get us out of the present mess if we do what he tells us to do. I'm just the messenger boy between him and you, but a messenger who wants to relay any message in a hurry. Those today have not been good; perhaps those received tomorrow will be better, but you will get them, good or bad.

You better go and get some sleep. A lot of top notch watch dogs will be doing their best for you. The Second Interceptor Command never sleeps and the same thing goes for our flying friends at McChord Field. Then, just a stone's throw away, some thousands of soldiers are anxious to protect you and me. If restful sleep can't be guaranteed by them, nobody can do the job.

Let's use our heads! Let us frown on hysteria! Let us wait for orders which will come from established sources! Let us protect the rights of those Japanese who know so well what it means to be an American! Let us hope that an end will soon come to what was started today! But, above all else, let us determine to drive such ruthlessness from the earth however long it may take.

Address by Colonel Harry P. Cain to Public Officials, Townspeople, and German Prisoners of War, Hagenow, Germany

May 8, 1945

IN THESE OPEN graves lie the emaciated, brutalized bodies of some 200 citizens of many lands. Before they were dragged away from their homes, their livelihoods, to satisfy the insatiable greed and malice; ambition and savagery of the German nation, they were happy and healthy and contented human beings. They were brought to this German soil from Poland, Russia, Czechoslovakia, Holland, Belgium, France, and even from parts of your own German state. They were driven and starved and beaten to slake that unholy thirst of the German war machine. When possessed no longer of the will or ability to work or fight back or live, they were either tortured to death or permitted to slowly die.

What you witness and are a part of in Hagenow today is but a single small example of what can be seen throughout the length and depth or your German Fatherland. Untold numbers of other Allied soldiers and German citizens shudder before similar burial services as you shudder now. The Allies shudder because they never dreamed or visualized that human leadership supported by the masses could so debase itself as to be responsible for results like those who lie in these open graves. You Germans shudder for reasons of your own. Some of you, having been a party to this degradation of mankind, shudder for fear that your guilt will be determined, as in fact it will. Others among you shudder because you let depravity of this character develop while you stood still. The civilized world shudders to find that a part of its society has fallen so low.

That world isn't content to believe that what we are horrified about was the work of any small group of German gangsters, maniacs and fanatics. That world must, as it does, hold the German people responsible for what has taken place within the confines of this nation. Time will prove to what extent the German people recognize the enormity of their crimes and to what extent they will shoulder a full national responsibility for making amends. That any future conduct can eradicate the knowledge and memories of a service like this is a matter in high dispute. If there is a soul within the German nation, it will rise now to make impossible the doing of such future wrongs. If there is not a soul in this German nation, its future is forlorn and totally lacking in hope.

The bodies in these graves came yesterday from Wobbelin. They were buried there in a common grave or lying piled high on the open earth. Bodies from Wobbelin will be buried in Ludwigslust and Schwerin as they are being buried here under the sight of God and true words consecrated by the Protestant, Catholic and Jewish faiths. In death, these bodies are receiving from the Allied Christian hands the decent, humanitarian, and spiritual treatment they didn't receive in life from German hands. As we listen, Allies and Germans alike, let us ask for an understanding which Germany must find if there is to be a future life for her.

In a service last Sunday, held in the German Cathedral of Wismar, two thousand Allied soldiers—the same who had helped beat down and crush your military machine—spoke a prayer aloud that drifted into your German skies—God's skies. "Pray," they said, "for the German people, that they may be rid of the burden of false teaching and one day take their place again among the honorable peoples."

Major Frank Brandstetter of the Commanding General's Staff will now translate into German, word for word, what has just been said in English.

Notes

INTRODUCTION

1. Max Hastings, *Winston's War: Churchill 1940 – 1945* (New York: Alfred A. Knopf, 2010), 97.

2. Harry P. Cain, letter to C. J. Skreen, December 1, 1971, author's collection.

3. Robert Justin Goldstein, "Raising Cain," *Pacific Northwest Quarterly,* 98 no. 2 (Spring 2007): 67.

4. http://www.speaking-tips.com/Eulogies/Neville-Chamberlain-Eulogy.aspx (accessed September 1, 2010).

CHAPTER 1: *Beginnings*

1. "Grace Pulliam," *Louisville Courier*, August 2, 1902.

2. Stuart Welch, "'Surprised,' Says Cain," *Tacoma News Tribune*, March 13, 1940.

3. http://en.wikipedia.org/wiki/Harry_Pulliam (accessed September 9, 2008).

4. Murray Morgan, Rosa Morgan, Rita Happy, *South on the Sound: An Illustrated History of Tacoma and Pierce County* (Woodland Hills, CA: Windsor Publications, 1984), 75–77.

5. Herbert Hunt, *Tacoma: Its History and Its Builders, A Half Century of Activity* (Chicago: S. J. Clarke, 1916), Vol. I, 497–498.

6. Caroline Gallacci and Ron Karabaich, *The City of Destiny and the South Sound* (Carlsbad, CA: Heritage Media, 2001), 54.

7. William H. Baarsma, "A Study of Discussion and Conflict Over Council-Manager Government in Tacoma, Washington and an Analysis of the Impact of that Discussion and Conflict on Governmental Decision-Making in Policy and Administrative Areas" (PhD diss., George Washington University, Washington, D C, 1973), 49–52.

8. Maury Bethea Cain, letter to Elizabeth Doughtie Bethea, July 1, 1970, author's collection.

9. Grace Pulliam Cain, Harry Cain baby book containing handwritten notes and photographs collected by Grace Pulliam Cain, 1906 and 1917, Candy Cain Tingstad collection.

10. Jimmy Chua, MD, e-mail message to the author, November 24, 2009.

11. Grace Pulliam Cain, "The Columbus Light," *American Catholic Historical Society of Philadelphia*, Vol. XXVI (1915), 26, author's collection.

12. James C. Derieux, "'Hurry' Cain Out of the West," *Colliers*, August 13, 1949, 64.

13. http://www.rootsweb.ancestry.com/~orphanhm/washsurr.htm (accessed August 9, 2009).

14. http://www.tarleton.edu/~kjones/gardner.html#50th-Inf (accessed November 1, 2008).

15. Grace Pulliam Cain, "Report by Grace Pulliam Cain," *Confederate Veteran*, 21 (1913): 39.

16. Maury Bethea Cain, letter to Elizabeth Doughtie Bethea, July 1, 1970.

17. "Found Dead in Gas Filled Room," *Tacoma Daily Ledger*, October 23, 1917.

18. Cathy Shockley, e-mail message to the author, August 5, 2009.

19. Derieux, "'Hurry' Cain Out of the West."

20. "From 'Seven Oaks' Reunions," *Miami Herald*, December 22, 1969.

21. Maury Bethea Cain, letter to Elizabeth Doughtie Bethea, July 1, 1970.

22. Harry P. Cain II, e-mail message to author, December 4, 2008.

23. C. Mark Smith, "The Cain 'Mutiny'" (senior history paper, University of Puget Sound, 1961), 8.

24. Harry P. Cain II, e-mail message to author, December 4, 2008.

25. Roderick Crosby, "Senior Class Prophecy," *The Adjutant*, Hill Military Academy, 1924.

26. Maury Bethea Cain, letter to Elizabeth Doughtie Bethea, July 1, 1970.

27. Smith, "The Cain 'Mutiny,'" 8.

28. Harry P. Cain, "Inventing the Future" (speech, Eighth Annual National Institute on Police-Community Relations, Michigan State University, Ann Arbor, MI, May 24, 1962).

29. Arthur Chitty, letter to Harry P. Cain, January 21, 1950, author's collection.

30. Haines Colbert, "Harry Cain: A Man Who Speaks His Mind," *Miami Herald*, September 15, 1963.

CHAPTER 2: *"Hurry" Cain*

1. William and Ellen Hartley, "Harry Cain: The Republican Rebel Who Won't Shut Up," *Pageant Magazine*, October 1965, 114.

2. Harry P. Cain, audiocassette tape interview conducted by Charles Kappes on WNWS Radio, Miami, FL, March 12, 1979, author's collection.

3. Gallacci and Karabaich, *The City of Destiny*, 63.

4. Morris Dickstein, *Dancing in the Dark: A Cultural History of the Great Depression* (New York: W. W. Norton & Company, 2009), 216.

5. Joseph Gordon, Sr., "On a Sunday last September," *The Rotarian*, October 2009, 51.

6. Smith, "The Cain 'Mutiny,'" 9.

7. Ibid.

8. Harry P. Cain II, "A Case Study of Former Senator Harry P. Cain as Critic of the Eisenhower Administration's Internal Security Program in the Years 1955–1956," draft of master's thesis, University of Washington, 1959, 4. (The paper was based on the senior Cain's answers to a series of written questions on various aspects of his public life provided by his son earlier in 1959. The final draft, dated December 7, 1959, is in the Harry P. Cain II collection and contains handwritten notes commenting on the previously provided answers and other comments.)

9. John McCallum, *Six Roads from Abilene: Some Personal Recollections of Edgar Eisenhower* (Seattle: Wood & Reber, Inc., 1960), 107.

10. Harry P. Cain (report to the Washington State Bankers Association Public Relations and Education Committee, April 21, 1938. Washington State Historical Society Archives, Tacoma, MS-55, Record Series 1, Box 1, Folder 3).

11. Douglass Cater, "Senator Cain: Washington Hamlet," *The Reporter*, September 2, 1952.

12. Robert Heilman, "The Amazing Harry Cain," *Seattle Times* Sunday supplement, June 18, 1944.

13. Ibid.

14. Candy Cain Tingstad, personal communication, December 15, 2008.

15. Candy Cain Tingstad, e-mail to the author, December, 14, 2008.

16. Candy Cain Tingstad, personal communication, December 4, 2008.

17. Heilman, "The Amazing Harry Cain."

18. Ibid.

19. Harry P. Cain, "European Trip Journal," September 7, 1935, Harry P. Cain II collection.

20. Harry P. Cain, "European Trip Journal," September 13, 1935.

21. Harry P. Cain, "European Trip Journal," September 12, 1935.

22. Harry P. Cain, "European Trip Journal," September 19–26, 1935.

23. Harry P. Cain, "European Trip Journal," September 29, 1935.

24. Harry P. Cain, "European Trip Journal," October 6, 1935.

25. Harry P. Cain, "European Trip Journal," November 2, 1935.

26. Harry P. Cain, "European Trip Journal," October 4, 1935.

27. Harry P. Cain, completed but unsigned Personnel Placement Questionnaire used to apply for service in the U.S. Army, n. d., Washington State Historical Society Archives, Tacoma, Record Series 4, MS-55, Box 2, Folder 58.

28. Colbert, "Harry Cain: A Man Who Speaks His Mind."

29. Harry P. Cain, "One's Individual Responsibility" (speech before the American Municipal Association, Chicago, October 21, 1942), author's collection.

30. "Cain Tells Spokane C.C. About His Trip to Europe," *Tacoma Times*, December 30, 1942.

31. G. W. Cain II, letter to Harry P. Cain, November 18, 1935, Candy Cain Tingstad collection.

32. Heilman, "The Amazing Harry Cain."

33. Harry P. Cain, handwritten note in the margin of a draft of his son's master's thesis. See note 8.

34. Max Hastings, *Winston's War: Churchill, 1940 – 1945*, (New York, Alfred A. Knopf, 2010), 84.

35. Ibid.

36. Roscoe A. Smith, letter to Harry P. Cain, June 29, 1937, Washington State Historical Society Archives, Tacoma, MS-55, Box 2, Folder 37.

37. Harry P. Cain and Niles Trammell, series of letters between the two, January 4 and May 9, 1938, Washington State Historical Society Archives, Tacoma, MS-55, Box 1, Folder 5.

38. Harry P. Cain, letter to Henry Booth Cain, May 13, 1937, Washington State Historical Society Archives, Tacoma, Record Series 2, MS-55, Box 1, Folder 8.

39. Maury Bethea Cain, letter to Elizabeth Doughtie Bethea, July 1, 1970, author's collection.

40. George William Cain III, telegram to Harry P. Cain, June 17, 1937, Washington State Historical Society Archives, Tacoma, MS-55, Record Series 2, Box 1, Folder 4.

41. "He's A Human Hurricane," *Tacoma Times*, July 24, 1939.

42. Harry P. Cain, memorandum to the board and supporters of the Golden Jubilee Celebration, September 15, 1939, author's collection.

43. Ibid.

44. "5 Warships Due in July," *Tacoma News Tribune*, June 9, 1939.

45. "Here's Full Program for Tacoma's Jubilee," *Tacoma News Tribune*, July 10, 1939.

46. "He's A Human Hurricane," *Tacoma Times*, July 24, 1939.

47. Harry P. Cain, audiocassette tape interview by Kappes.

48. Ibid.

49. J. J. Hunter, letter to G. M. Raleigh, October 24, 1939, Washington State Historical Society Archives, Tacoma, MS-55, Record Series 2, Box 1, Folder 8.

50. Harry P. Cain, handwritten speaking notes on 5" x 8" index cards. Washington State Historical Society Archives, Tacoma, MS-55, Record Series 3, Box 2, Folder 32.

51. Ibid.

52. Harry P. Cain, Remarks written for Mayor J. J. Kaufman announcing that he will not run for mayor in 1940, Washington State Historical Society Archives, Tacoma, MS-55, Record Series 3, Box 2, Folder 47.

53. "Cain Opens Campaign on Day He's 34 with 11 Points," *Tacoma Times*, January 11, 1940.

54. George W. Scott, "Arthur B. Langlie: Republican Governor in a Democratic Age," PhD diss., University of Washington, 1971, 37–43.

55. Editorial, "Cain Not Able," *Tacoma Labor Advocate*, February 23, 1940.

56. Harry P. Cain, audiocassette tape interview by Kappes.

57. Harry P. Cain, reel-to-reel tape recording of a luncheon speech to the Tacoma Young Men's Business Club, August 15, 1952.

58. Harry P. Cain, audiocassette tape interview by Kappes.

55. Ibid.

60. Harry P. Cain, radio address, March 11, 1940, Washington State Historical Society Archives, Tacoma, MS-55, Box 1, Record Series 4, Radio Broadcasts, Folder 47.

61. Joy Reese Shaw, "A Death Brought Harry Cain to Life," *Miami Herald*, January, 17, 1960.

62. "Cain, O'Neil Win; Bowl Plan Okehed," *Tacoma Times*, March 13, 1940.

63. "Court Upholds Election of Cain," *Tacoma Times*, June 1, 1940.

64. "Cain Booster of LaGuardia," *Tacoma Times*, April 11, 1940.

CHAPTER 3: *"I've Got a Job to Do!"*

1. George W. Walk, "Fighting Fawcett: A Political Biography of Angelo Vance Fawcett" (master's thesis, Western Washington State College, 1976), 13–14, 137.

2. "Mayor Crosses Bridge," *Tacoma News Tribune*, June 6, 1940.

3. Harry P. Cain, handwritten speaking notes on miscellaneous cards and scraps of paper, n. d., Washington State Historical Society Archives, Tacoma, MS-55, Box 2, Record Series 9: Miscellaneous Items, Folders 56–60.

4. Harry P. Cain, "Being Mayor" Journal, February 15, 1941, Washington State Historical Society Archives, Tacoma, MS-55, Series 3, Box 1, Folder 45.

5. The scripts of 128 regular and several special radio addresses are located at the Washington State Historical Society Archives, Tacoma, MS-55, Box 2, Record Series 4: Radio Broadcasts, 1940–1946, Folders 3–22.

6. "Tacoma to Go Hollywood as 'Tugboat' Greats Say 'Hello,'" *Tacoma Times*, October 18, 1940.

7. "Cain Opens Campaign on Day He's 34 with 11 Points," *Tacoma Times*, January 11, 1940.

8. "Five-Member Commission to Be Named," *Tacoma Times*, August 14, 1940.

9. "Mayor to Be Asked Why," *Tacoma News Tribune*, August 18, 1940.

10. "Three Housing Sites Offered," *Tacoma Times*, December 31, 1940.

11. "Home Guard Corps Set Up For Tacoma," *Tacoma Times*, August 26, 1940.

12. "Tacoma Forms Model Home Defense Corps; Even Has Civilian Navy for Its Harbor," *New York World-Telegram*, October 29, 1940.

13. Harry P. Cain, "Blitzing the Brothels," *Journal of Social Hygiene*, December 1943, 595.

14. Ibid., 597.

15. "Eastwood, Irked Over News Story, Stages Fisticuffs," *Tacoma Times*, December 1, 1940.

16. Derieux, "'Hurry' Cain Out of the West." 64.

17. Gallacci and Karabaich, *The City of Destiny*. 64

18. "Tacomans Shape '20-Year' Plan," *Tacoma Times*, November 15, 1940.

19. Gallacci and Karabaich, *The City of Destiny and the South Sound*, 125.

20. Phillip J. Funigiello, *The Challenge of Urban Liberalism: Federal-City Relations during World War II* (Knoxville: University of Tennessee Press, 1978), 176–177.

21. "Will Rebuild Wrecked Span at Once, State Chief Says," *Tacoma Times*, November 7, 1940.

22. "Army Challenges Eastwood," *Tacoma Times*, February 10, 1941.

23. Harry P. Cain, "Blitzing the Brothels," 598.

24. Harry P. Cain, entry in "Being Mayor" journal, July 22, 1941, Washington State Historical Society Archives, Tacoma, MS-55, Series 3, Box 1, Folder 45.

25. Harry P. Cain, audiocassette tape interview by Kappes.

Notes

26. "Brothels Are Closed," *Tacoma News Tribune*, August 7, 1941.

27. Funigiello, *The Challenge of Urban Liberalism*, 81–82.

28. Ibid., 88.

29. Harry P. Cain, "Being Mayor" Journal, March 4, 1941.

30. "Big Home Project Is Approved," *Tacoma News Tribune*, October 2, 1941.

31. Ronald E. Magden, *Furusato: Tacoma-Pierce County Japanese 1999–1977* (South Puget Sound Day of Remembrance Consortium, 1998), 115; Washington State Historical Society Archives, Tacoma, MS-55, Box 2, Record Series 4: Radio Broadcasts, 1940–1946, Folders 16.

32. Associated Press wire message sent to Harry P. Cain by Radio Station KMO, December 22, 1941, Candy Cain Tingstad collection.

33. Funigiello, *The Challenge of Urban Liberalism*, 48.

34. "First Lady Urges All to Serve," *Tacoma News Tribune*, December 15, 1941.

35. Ibid.

36. Geoffrey R. Stone, *Perilous Times: Free Speech in Wartime* (New York: W. W. Norton, 2004), 296.

37. Jess Giessel, "Harry P. Cain, Part IV," printed copy of Harry Cain Website, no longer active, author's collection.

38. "Harry Cain Candidate," *Tacoma News Tribune*, January 23, 1942.

39. Editorial, "Mayor Cain," *Tacoma News Tribune*, January 28, 1942.

40. Editorial, "Cain Deserved Re-election," *Tacoma Times*, February 25, 1942.

41. Stone, *Perilous Times*, 290.

42. Ibid., 292.

43. Elting E. Morison, *Turmoil and Tradition: A Study of the Life and Times of Henry L. Stimson,* (New York: Francis Parkman Prize Editon, History Book Club, 2003), 547-548.

44. "Alien Problem for Coast Near Solution: Combination of Martial Law and Licensing of All Persons Within Certain Prescribed Areas May Be Adopted," *Tacoma News Tribune*, February 21, 1942.

45. Stone, *Perilous Times*, 295–296.

46. Ibid., 129.

47. "Forbid Enemy Aliens and Japanese to Move Voluntarily after Sunday," *Tacoma Times*, March 26, 1942.

48. Magden, *Furusato,* 135–136.

49. "City Vice War Up to Cain," *Tacoma News Tribune,* April 21, 1942.

50. "Cain Credited for Raids on Gambling Joints," *Tacoma Times*, August 16, 1942.

51. Ralph Smith, "Drastic Charter Changes Recommended by Cain in Report to City Council," *Tacoma Times*, September 16, 1942.

52. "Langseth Upheld 3 to 1," *Tacoma News Tribune*, May 1, 1943.

53. George W. Walk, "Fighting Fawcett," 124–128.

54. Harry P. Cain II, e-mail to the author, January 8, 2009.

55. Harry P. Cain, duplicate copy of Personnel Placement Questionnaire used to apply for service in the U.S. Army, n.d., Washington State Historical Society Archives, Tacoma, Record Series 4, MS-55, Box 2, Folder 58.

56. "Cain Now Major in Army," *Tacoma News Tribune*, May 6, 1943.

57. Editorial, "Harry Cain," *Tacoma Times*, May 7, 1943.

58. "O'Neil in Attack on Cain," *Tacoma News Tribune*, May 11, 1943.

59. Harry P. Cain, script of radio address #128, May 10, 1943. Washington State Historical Society Archives, MS-55, Record Series 4, Box 2, Folder 12.

60. "Goodbye, Good Luck," *Tacoma News Tribune*, May 12, 1943.

61. "Cain Opens Campaign on Day He's 34 with 11 Points," *Tacoma Times*, January 11, 1940.

CHAPTER 4: *"The Sooner Begun, the Sooner Finished."*

1. Editorial, "Harry Cain," *Tacoma Times*, May 7, 1943.

2. Earl F. Ziemke, *The Army in the Occupation of Germany 1944–1946* (Center of Military History, United States Army, Washington, DC, 1990). 64.

3. Heilman, "The Amazing Harry Cain."

4. "Maj. Cain Half Way with Colors Still High," *Tacoma News Tribune and Sunday Ledger*, July 18, 1943.

5. "Maj. Cain on Brief Visit," *Tacoma News Tribune,* August 5, 1943.

6. Sam Angeloff, "Major-Mayor Harry P. Cain Home from Army Training School on 'Surprise' Visit," *Tacoma Times*, August 8, 1943.

7. Harry P. Cain, V-mail letter to Marjorie Cain, n. d., author's collection.

8. Rick Atkinson, *The Day of Battle: The War in Sicily and Italy 1943–1944* (New York: Henry Holt and Company, 2007), 57.

9. Harry P. Cain, V-mail letter to Marjorie Cain, August 26, 1943, author's collection.

10. Ibid.

11. Hastings, *Winston's War*, 309.

12. Atkinson, *The Day of Battle,* 180–182.

13. Carlo D'Este, *World War II in the Mediterranean 1942–1945* (Chapel Hill, NC: Algonquin Books, 1990), 80–81.

14. Ibid., 197–203.

15. Ibid., 103.

16. Hartley and Hartley, "Harry Cain," 115.

17. "Cain Wins War Bout, Downs Malaria Fever," *Tacoma News Tribune*, September 29, 1943.

18. http://www.history.army.mil/books/wwii/salerno/sal-pursuing.htm, 76 (accessed February 16, 2009).

19. Harry P. Cain, letter to Marjorie Cain, October 4, 1943, Candy Cain Tingstad collection.

20. Ibid.

21. "Cain Writes of Work in Italian War Zone," *Tacoma News Tribune*, November 2, 1943.

22. Harry P. Cain, letter to Marjorie Cain, n. d., Candy Cain Tingstad collection.

23. Clay Blair, *Ridgway's Paratroopers: The American Airborne in World War II* (New York: Random House, 1985), 165.

24. Ibid., 250–263.

25. Heilman, "The Amazing Harry Cain."

26. Robert W. Kormer, "The Establishment of the Allied Control Commission," *Military Affairs*, 26, no. 1 (Spring 1949), 20–28.

27. Cater, "Senator Cain: Washington Hamlet," 13.

28. Harry P. Cain, letter to Marjorie Cain, n. d. (probably November 20, 1943), Candy Cain Tingstad collection.

29. Ibid.

30. Atkinson, *The Day of Battle*, 271–275.

31. Harry P. Cain, letter to Marjorie Cain, January 15, 1944, Candy Cain Tingstad collection.

32. Harry P. Cain, "War Journal," January 6, 1944, Candy Cain Tingstad collection.

33. Harry P. Cain, "War Journal," March 16, 1944, Candy Cain Tingstad collection.

34. Ibid.

35. Harry P. Cain, "War Journal," March 21, 1944, Candy Cain Tingstad collection

CHAPTER 5: *"Who Are These Republican Leaders?"*

1. Ziemke, *The U.S. Army in the Occupation of Germany 1944–1946*, 64.

2. Harry P. Cain, "War Journal," April 18, 1944.

3. Ziemke, *The U.S. Army in the Occupation of Germany 1944–1946*, 42–50.

4. Carlo D'Este, *Eisenhower: A Soldier's Life* (New York: Macmillan, 2003), 490.

5. Harry P. Cain, "War Journal," April 18, 1944.

6. Melvin B. Voorhees, "Harry Cain Rides Once More Out of the Past," *Argus Magazine*, no. 49, December 6, 1963, 70.

7. Harry P. Cain, "War Journal," n. d. (but prior to April 27, 1944).

8. Harry P. Cain, "War Journal," April 27, 1944.

9. Harry P. Cain, "War Journal," May 14, 1944.

10. Harry P. Cain, "War Journal," April 27, 1944.

11. Haines Colbert, "Harry Cain: A Man Who Speaks His Mind.

12. Harry P. Cain, "War Journal," April 27, 1944.

13. Smith, "The Cain 'Mutiny,'" 11–12.

14. Harry P. Cain, "War Journal," April 27, 1944.

15. Ibid.

16. Smith, "The Cain 'Mutiny,'" 12.

17. "Cain Will Run for Senate," *Tacoma News Tribune*, May 4, 1944.

18. Harry P. Cain, letter to Marjorie Cain, June 10, 1944, Candy Cain Tingstad collection.

19. "Cain for Senator Clubs Organized," *Kelso Tribune*, June 29, 1944.

20. Harry P. Cain, "War Journal," April 18, 1944.

21. Ibid.

22. Harry P. Cain, letter to Marjorie Cain, June 27, 1944, Candy Cain Tingstad collection.

23. Ibid.

24. Harry P. Cain, "War Journal," April 18, 1944.

25. Shelby Scates, *Warren G. Magnuson and the Shaping of Twentieth Century America* (Seattle: University of Washington Press, 1997), 111.

26. "The Average Voter's Size-Up of Harry P. Cain," Warren G. Magnuson Papers, Special Collections Division, University of Washington Library, Accession 3181-2, Box 55, Folder 1.

27. Heilman, "The Amazing Harry Cain"; "Major Harry Cain Writes of Hunger in Europe," *Seattle Times*, Sunday supplement, June 25, 1944; and "Cain Home a Busy Place," *Seattle Times*, Sunday supplement, October 22, 1944.

28. Warren G. Magnuson campaign ads and endorsements used in the 1944 U.S. Senate race against Harry P. Cain. Warren G. Magnuson Papers, Special Collections Division, University of Washington Library, Accession 3181-2, Box 55, Folder 16.

29. Scates, *Warren G. Magnuson*, 112.

30. Harry P. Cain, letter to Marjorie Cain, August 6, 1944, Candy Cain Tingstad collection.

31. Ibid.

32. Harry P. Cain, letter to Marjorie Cain, September 1, 1944, Candy Cain Tingstad collection.

33. Harry P. Cain, letter to Marjorie Cain, September 22, 1944, Candy Cain Tingstad collection.

34. Colbert, "Harry Cain: A Man Who Speaks His Mind."

35. Harry P. Cain, letter to Marjorie Cain, September 22, 1944, Candy Cain Tingstad collection.

36. Harry P. Cain, letter to Marjorie Cain, October 15, 1944, Candy Cain Tingstad collection.

37. Harry P. Cain, audiocassette tape interview by Kappes.

38. Harry P. Cain, letter to Marjorie Cain, November 9, 1944, Candy Cain Tingstad collection.

39. Harry P. Cain, audiocassette tape interview by Kappes.

40. Harry P. Cain, letter to Marjorie Cain, November 15, 1944, Candy Cain Tingstad collection.

CHAPTER 6: *"The Fur Is Flying."*

1. Harry P. Cain, letter to Marjorie Cain, November 24, 1944, Candy Cain Tingstad collection.

2. Harry P. Cain, letter to Marjorie Cain, November 29, 1944, Candy Cain Tingstad collection.

3. Harry P. Cain, letter to Marjorie Cain, December 9, 1944, Candy Cain Tingstad collection.

4. Ibid.

5. Matthew Ridgway, *Mission Accomplished: A Summary of Military Operations for the XVIII Corps (Airborne) in the European Theater of Operations 1944–1945* (XVIII Airborne Corps, 1945), 5-6.

6. Harry P. Cain, letter to Marjorie Cain, December 19, 1944, Candy Cain Tingstad collection.

7. Harry P. Cain, letter to Marjorie Cain, December 20, 1944, Candy Cain Tingstad collection.

8. Harry P. Cain II, in conversation with the author, November 28, 2008.

9. Ridgway, *Mission Accomplished*, 10.

10. Maj. Gen. Matthew B. Ridgway, Recommendation for Award of the Legion of Merit to Col. Harry P. Cain, May 13, 1945, author's collection.

11. Derieux, "'Hurry' Cain Out of the West." 64.

12. Harry P. Cain, letter to Marjorie Cain, December 29, 1944, Candy Cain Tingstad collection.

13. Lloyd Clark, *Crossing the Rhine: Breaking into Nazi Germany 1944–1945* (New York: Atlantic Monthly Press, 2008), 14.

14. Harry P. Cain, audiocassette tape interview by Kappes.

15. "Cain Made Full Colonel," *Tacoma News Tribune*, April 2, 1945.

16. Blair, *Ridgway's Paratroopers*, 467.

17. Ridgway, Recommendation for Legion of Merit Award.

18. Robert Heilman, "Cain Greeted in Tacoma; Lauds Yanks, Silent on Self," *Seattle Times*, September 17, 1945.

19. Harry P. Cain, letter to Marjorie Cain, May 8, 1945, Candy Cain Tingstad collection.

20. Matthew B. Ridgway, *Soldier: The Memoirs of Matthew B. Ridgway* (New York: Harper & Bros., 1956), 147–148.

21. Howard Klineberg, "Harry Cain's Finest Moment," *Miami News*, March 7, 1979.

22. Harry P. Cain, letter to Marjorie Cain, May 8, 1945, Candy Cain Tingstad collection.

23. Matthew B. Ridgway, letter to Mrs. Harry P. Cain, March 9, 1979, Candy Cain Tingstad collection.

24. Harry P. Cain, letter to Marjorie Cain, May 8, 1945, Candy Cain Tingstad collection.

25. "Cain Saved 10,000 PWs," *Tacoma News Tribune*, October 9, 1952.

26. Harry P. Cain, letter to Marjorie Cain, May 20, 1945, Candy Cain Tingstad collection.

27. http://en.wikipedia.org/wiki/George_Smith_Patton,_Jr. (accessed March 25, 2009).

28. Harry P. Cain, letter to Marjorie Cain, July 1, 1945, Candy Cain Tingstad collection.

29. Harry P. Cain, letter to Marjorie Cain, August 29, 1945, Candy Cain Tingstad collection.

30. "Tacoma's Mayor Home on Furlough," *Tacoma Times*, September 17, 1945.

31. Heilman, "Cain Greeted in Tacoma."

32. "Tacoma's Mayor Home on Furlough."

33. Ibid.

34. "Cain Refuses Comment on Army Offer," *Tacoma News Tribune*, October 5, 1945.

35. Stanley S. Sommer to Harry P. Cain, letter and other materials, Washington State Historical Society Archives, Tacoma, MS-55, Series 3, Box 1, Folder 45.

CHAPTER 7: *"I Wouldn't Trade Places with Any Man."*

1. "Cain Back as City's Mayor," *Tacoma News Tribune*, December 3, 1945.

2. "Cain Won't Seek Re-election; Plans Other Political Steps," *Tacoma Times*, December 10, 1945.

3. Candy Cain Tingstad, in conversation with the author, December 2, 2008.

4. "Campaign in Torrid Climax," *Tacoma News Tribune*, March 12, 1946.

5. "Cain Presides at Quiet City Council Meeting—His Last," *Tacoma Times*, May 31, 1946.

6. "Cain Open to GOP Service," *Tacoma News Tribune*, February 13, 1946,

7. "Cain Enters Senate Race," *Tacoma Times*, April 12, 1946.

8. "Cain Cites 1946 Issue as Return to Freedom," *Seattle Post-Intelligencer*, June 18, 1946.

9. "Cain Gets Big GOP Ovation," *Tacoma News Tribune*, September 22, 1946.

10. "Tacoma Mayor White Hope of Republicans," *Chicago Daily Tribune*, September 12, 1946.

11. "Cain Stand on Labor," *Tacoma News Tribune*, September 27, 1946.

12. Jack Bell, "Cain, Mitchell Follow Party Lines," *Tacoma Ledger*, October 12, 1946.

13. Washington: Raising Cain," *National Affairs Magazine*, October 18, 1946, 25–26.

14. Ashley E. Holden, "Harry Cain, Man of Action," *Spokane Spokesman-Review*, Sunday supplement, October 20, 1946, 3–4.

15. "Harry Cain Blasts New Deal or Its 'Political Quackery,'" *Tacoma Times*, October 22, 1946.

16. George A. Miller, "Must Re-Establish 'Sanity,' Avers Cain," *Tacoma News Tribune*, October 23, 1946.

17. James T. Patterson, *Mr. Republican: A Biography of Robert A. Taft*, (Boston: Houghton Mifflin Company, 1972), 313.

18. "Cain Says Dies Data Withheld," *Tacoma News Tribune*, October 27, 1946.

19. Jack Jarvis, "Cain Rests, Points to New Job Challenge," *Seattle Post-Intelligencer*, November 6, 1946.

20. "Cain Hews Liberal Line," *Tacoma News Tribune*, November 12, 1946.

21. Cater, "Senator Cain, American Hamlet," 15.

22. Smith, "The Cain 'Mutiny,'" 13.

23. Derieux, "'Hurry' Cain Out of the West."

24. "Tollefson, Cain Leaving," *Tacoma News Tribune*, December 27, 1946.

25. Stub Nelson, "First Day as Senator Spent Hard at Work in Train Office," *Seattle Post-Intelligencer*, December 27, 1946.

26. Marjorie Cain, letter to unidentified friends in Tacoma, January 22, 1947, Candy Cain Tingstad collection.

27. Alice Frein Johnson, "Senator Cain Arrives in Capital," *Tacoma Times*, December 30, 1946.

28. Stub Nelson, "Housing at Capital Senator's Big Problem," *Seattle Post-Intelligencer*, December 29, 1946.

29. Ibid.

30. Harry P. Cain II, e-mail to the author, January 31, 2009.

31. http://www.jwstone.com/westchester/history/ (accessed May 16, 2009).

32. Richard S. Kirkendall, *A Global Power: America Since the Age of Roosevelt* (New York: Alfred A. Knopf, second edition 1980), 1.

33. Alonzo L. Hamby, *Man of the People: A Life of Harry S. Truman* (New York: Oxford University Press, 1995), 271.

34. Ibid., 386.

35. Scates, *Warren G. Magnuson*, 132.

36. Ibid.

37. Diagram of the configuration of Senator's desks on the Floor of the U.S. Senate, 80th Congress—First Session, Office of the Senate Historian, author's collection.

38. "Cain Fourth Youngest of New U.S. Senators, *Tacoma News Tribune*, November 12, 1946.

39. Cater, "Senator Cain: Washington Hamlet," 13.

40. Blair, *Ridgway's Paratroopers*, footnote 304.

41. http://www.infoplease.com/t/hist/state-of-the-union/158.html (accessed August 24, 2009).

42. Robert J. Donovan, *Conflict and Crisis: The Presidency of Harry S. Truman, 1945–1948* (New York: W. W. Norton, 1977), 257.

43. Daniel M. Berman, "Cain and the President," *New Republic*, June 25, 1956, 14–15.

44. William Theis, "Cain for Budget Cut of 6 Billion," *New York Journal & American*, February 24, 1947.

45. "The Record of Senator Harry Pulliam Cain, Eightieth Congress, First Session," Henry M. Jackson Papers, Special Collections Division, University of Washington Library, Accession 3560-12, Box 9, Folder 25.

46. Harry P. Cain, audiocassette tape interview by Kappes.

47. Donovan, *Conflict and Crisis,* 258.

48. Harry P. Cain, audiocassette tape interview by Kappes.

49. "The Record of Senator Harry Pulliam Cain, Eightieth Congress, First Session."

50. Cain II, "A Case Study," 8.

51. Cater, "Senator Cain: Washington Hamlet," 15.

52. Patterson, *Mr. Republican,* 316–317.

53. Richard O. Davies, *Housing Reform during the Truman Administration* (Columbia, MO: University of Missouri Press, 1966), 37–39.

54. Cain II, "A Case Study."

55. "Cain Fights Back in Housing 'Beef,'" *Tacoma Times,* July 4, 1947.

56. Cater, "Senator Cain: Washington Hamlet."

57. Editorial, "Ruling a City of Political Serfs," *Washington Evening Star,* June 9, 1947.

58. Harry P. Cain, *Current Biography,* 88–90.

59. Robert P. Patterson, "We Must Have Military Training—Now!" *Saturday Evening Post,* April 26, 1947.

60. *America's Town Meeting of the Air,* compact disk transfer from a 33 rpm record of program of March 6, 1947, featuring Senators Harry P. Cain and Francis J. Myers discussing rent controls, author's collection.

61. Harry P. Cain, letter to Marjorie Cain, October 31, 1947, Candy Cain Tingstad collection.

62. Harry P. Cain, letter to C. J. Skreen, December 9, 1971, author's collection.

63. Patterson, *Mr. Republican,* 365.

64. Smith, "The Cain 'Mutiny,'" 15–16.

CHAPTER 8: *Controversial Decisions*

1. Cater, "Senator Cain, American Hamlet," 13–16.

2. Derieux, "'Hurry' Cain Out of the West," 65.

3. http://www.infoplease.com/t/hist/state-of-the-union/158.html (accessed January 9, 2009).

4. Patterson, *Mr. Republican,* 384.

5. Harry P. Cain, letter to Marjorie Cain, November 12, 1947.

6. Harry P. Cain, "A Report on the European Situation," constituent newsletter, November 21, 1947, author's collection.

7. Hamby, *A Life of Harry S. Truman,* 397.

8. Cain II, "A Case Study," 9.

9.   Voorhees, "Harry Cain Rides Once More Out of the Past," 70.

10.   "Cain's Thumb in Vandenberg Pie and May Pull Out Plum," *Seattle Times*, April 12, 1948.

11.   "Cain Advises GOP to Realize Responsibility," *Christian Science Monitor*, June 23, 1948.

12.   Harry P. Cain, letter to President Harry S. Truman, November 9, 1948, Harry S. Truman Papers, President's Secretary's Files, Chronological Name File Cain, Harry P., Box 236.

13.   Harry S. Truman, letter to Harry P. Cain, November 22, 1948, Harry S. Truman Papers, President's Secretary's Files, Chronological Name File Cain, Harry P., Box 236, Truman Library.

14.   "Senator Cain Says Wife Will Seek Divorce," *Washington Post*, November 19, 1948.

15.   "Cains Plan Divorce!" *Tacoma Times*, November 18, 1948.

16.   William Prochnau and Richard Larsen, *A Certain Democrat: Senator Henry M. Jackson* (Englewood Cliffs, NJ: Prentice Hall, 1972), 120.

17.   "Mrs. Cain Files for Divorce in Tacoma," *Seattle Times*, February 9, 1949.

18.   Harry P. Cain II, e-mail to the author, February 9, 2009.

19.   http://www.infoplease.com/t/hist/state-of-the-union/160.html (accessed January 9, 2009).

20.   "Cain Introduces new Housing Bill in Senate," *Tacoma Times*, February 1, 1949.

21.   Davies, *Housing Reform*, 108.

22.   Richard O. Davies, *Spokesman for the Old Guard: John Bricker and American Politics* (Columbus, OH: Ohio State University Press, 1993), 138.

23.   Smith, "The Cain 'Mutiny,'" 17.

24.   Derieux, "'Hurry' Cain Out of the West," 64.

25.   "Charges Fly in Campaign," *Yakima Daily Republic*, September 10, 1948.

26.   "Wallgren Unfit, Senator Declares," *New York Times*, February 18, 1949.

27.   "Nomination of Mon C. Wallgren to be Chairman of the National Security Resources Board—Statement and letters by Senator Cain," *Congressional Record*, March 3, 1949, 1770–1784.

28.   Monrad C. Wallgren, draft of written response to comments made by Senator Harry P. Cain before the Senate Armed Services Committee, no date, Box 4, "National Security Resources Board and Senator Cain," Mon C. Wallgren Papers, Truman Library.

29.   Monte M. Poen, ed., *Strictly Personal and Confidential: The Letters Harry Truman Never Mailed,* (Columbia, MO: University of Missouri Press, 1999), 80.

30. http://www.presidency.ucsb.edu/ws/index.php?pid=13396, transcript of President Truman's press conference of March 3, 1949 (accessed June 28, 2009).

31. "Cain verses Wallgren," *Newsweek,* March 21, 1949, 22–23.

32. "Cain for 6 ¾ Hours Assails Wallgren," *New York Times,* March 9, 1949.

33. Cain II, "A Case Study," 10–11.

34. Henry M. Jackson Papers, Accession 3560-12, Special Collections, University of Washington Library, Box 12, Folders 2–3.

35. http://www.presidency.ucsb.edu/ws/index.php?pid=13184 (accessed January 21, 2009).

36. Robert A. Caro, *The Years of Lyndon Johnson: Master of the Senate* (New York: Alfred A. Knopf, 2002), 233–255; Leland Olds correspondence files, Washington State Historical Society Archives, Tacoma, MS-99, Box 4, Folders 2–10.

37. Scates, *Warren G. Magnuson,* 163.

38. Smith, "The Cain 'Mutiny,'" 14.

39. "Fall Planting," *TIME Magazine,* October 3, 1949, 10.

40. "Sen. Cain May Quit to Run for Senate," *The Washington Post*, September 25, 1949.

41. "Cain Will Wait and See about Magnuson Race," *Bellingham Herald*, September 26, 1949.

42. Scates, *Warren G. Magnuson,* 146.

43. Ross Cunningham, "Cain's Program Stirs G.O.P. Study on Policy," *Seattle Times*, October 2, 1949.

44. "Cain Won't Run in '50," *Tacoma Ledger*, February 5, 1950.

45. Emily Walker, "A Tribute to Harry," *Tacoma News Tribune*, March 18, 1979.

46. Candy Cain Tingstad, personal communication, February 9, 2009.

47. Derieux, "'Hurry' Cain Out of the West," 63.

48. http://www.time.com/time/magazine/article/0,9171,805109,00.html (accessed January 12, 2009).

49. Ibid.

50. Cater, "Senator Cain, American Hamlet," 16.

CHAPTER 9: *"The Guy in the Sky."*

1. http://janda.org/politxts/State%20of%20Union%20Addresses/1945-52%20Truman/HST50.html (accessed September 7, 2009).

2. Ibid.

3. Davies, *Housing Reform*, 121.

4. http://janda.org/politxts/State%20of%20Union%20Addresses/ 1945-2%20 Truman/ HST50.html (accessed September 7, 2009).

5. "12 Hours, 8 Minutes," *TIME Magazine*, June 19, 1950, 20.

6. Davies, *Housing Reform*, 122.

7. Editorial, "Futile Gabfest," *The Washington Post,* June 12, 1950.

8. Smith, "The Cain 'Mutiny,'" 17.

9. Stub Nelson, "Cain Appeals for Non-Partisan Harmony to Push Basin Program," Seattle Post-Intelligencer, December 31, 1946.

10. Harry P. Cain, "A Study of the Reasons For and Against a Proposed CVA, n. d., Arthur B. Langlie Papers, Special Collections Division, University of Washington Library, Accession 61-1, Box 5, Folder 2.

11. Cater, "Senator Cain, American Hamlet," 13.

12. Cain II, "A Case Study," 12.

13. Derieux, "'Hurry' Cain Out of the West," 64.

14. Ibid., 63.

15. Shaw, "A Death Brought Harry Cain to Life."

16. George W. Scott, "Arthur B. Langlie: Republican Governor in a Democratic Age," PhD diss., University of Washington, 1971. 205.

17. Bill Sloan, *The Darkest Summer* (New York: Simon & Schuster, 2009), 22.

18. Cater, "Senator Cain, American Hamlet," 14.

19. Richard S. Kirkendall, *A Global Power: America Since the Age of Roosevelt* (New York: Alfred A. Knopf, 1973, 1980), 58.

20. Sloan, *The Darkest Summer*, 314.

21. Ibid., 330.

22. Cater, "Senator Cain, American Hamlet," 14.

23. Hamby, *A Life of Harry S. Truman*, 558.

24. "Cain Demands That U.N. Forces Hit Enemy 'With Everything,'" *The Washington Post*, June 25, 1951.

25. "Cain Rushing Draft of MacArthur Report," *Tacoma News Tribune*, July 6, 1951.

26. "U.S. Policy Is Laid to 'Fear of Russia,'" *New York Times*, July 8, 1951.

27. David Nasaw, *The Chief: The Life of William Randolph Hearst* (Boston: Houghton Mifflin Company, 2000), 598.

28. Jim Farber, "Tacoma Welcomes MacArthur," *Tacoma News Tribune*, November 15, 1951.

29. http://www.presidency.ucsb.edu/ws/index.php?pid=14017 (accessed October 22, 2009).

30. Cater, "Senator Cain, American Hamlet," 16.

31. M. Stanton Evans, *Blacklisted by History: The Untold Story of Senator Joe McCarthy* (New York: Crown Forum, 2007), 34.

32. Patterson, *Mr. Republican*, 445.

33. Roy Cohn, *McCarthy* (New York: New American Library, 1968), 1–2.

34. Smith, "The Cain 'Mutiny,'" 20.

35. Patterson, *Mr. Republican*, 446.

36. Evans, *Blacklisted by History*, 34.

37. Ibid., 444.

38. Hamby, *A Life of Harry S. Truman*, 564.

39. Patterson, *Mr. Republican*, 503.

40. Smith, "The Cain 'Mutiny,'" 21.

41. http://www.americanmafia.com/Allan_May_1-10-00.html (accessed November 17, 2008).

42. Cain II, "A Case Study," 16.

43. "Televised Crime Hearings Will Resume; Cain Balks," *Tacoma News Tribune*, August 10, 1951.

44. Smith, "The Cain 'Mutiny,'" 19.

45. Cain II, "A Case Study," 15.

46. Ashley E. Holden, "Political Issues Defined for 1950," *Spokane Spokesman-Review*, October 11, 1950.

47. "Says Spain's Aid Needed," *Tacoma News Tribune*, October 13, 1950.

48. Robert G. Kaufman, *Henry M. Jackson: A Life in Politics* (Seattle: University of Washington Press, 2000), 15.

49. Prochnau and Larsen, *A Certain Democrat*, 104.

50. Kaufman, *Henry M. Jackson*, 64; also "How Cain Is Rated by Those Who Know," Henry M. Jackson Papers, Special Collections Division, University of Washington Library, Accession 3560-12, Box 9, Folders 21–25.

51. "Jackson to Run for Senate Seat," *Everett Herald*, May 31, 1952.

52. Smith, "The Cain 'Mutiny,'" 22.

53. "Cain Talks 73 Pages in Record," *The Washington Post*, June 8, 1952.

54. Harry P. Cain, reel-to-reel tape recording of a speech to the Tacoma Young Men's Business Club, August 15, 1952, author's collection.

55. Harry P. Cain II, e-mail to the author, April 12, 2009.

56. "Cain Calls for World Police," *Tacoma News Tribune*, August 14, 1952.

57. Smith, "The Cain 'Mutiny,'" 22.

58. "Cain Battle for Senate Gets Hot," *Tacoma News Tribune*, October 21, 1952.

59. Cater, "Senator Cain, American Hamlet," 16.

60. http://www.presidency.ucsb.edu/ws/index.php?pid=14226 (accessed September 21, 2009).

61. "Knights and Knaves in Eisenhower's Great Crusade," *New Republic*, June 28, 1952, 15.

62. Ross Cunningham, "State G.O.P. Leaders Try to Close Breach Caused By Langlie-Cain Differences," *Seattle Times*, October 11, 1952.

63. George W. Scott, telephone conversation with the author, January 25, 2010.

64. Prochnau and Larsen, *A Certain Democrat*, 121.

65. Lawrence E. Davies, "Cain Fight Holds Northwest's Eyes," *New York Times*, October 5, 1952.

66. Retain Cain campaign press release, Washington State Historical Society Archives, Tacoma, Series 4, MS-55, Box 2, Folder 23.

67. Prochnau and Larsen, *A Certain Democrat*, 117–118.

68. Harry P. Cain, reel-to-reel tape, recording a statewide radio address, October 3, 1952, author's collection.

69. Editorial, "A Noted Visitor," *Tacoma News Tribune*, September 30, 1952.

70. Harry P. Cain, audiocassette tape interview by Kappes.

71. Kaufman, *Henry M. Jackson*, 69.

72. Prochnau and Larsen, *A Certain Democrat*, 121–124.

73. Cain II, "A Case Study," 14.

74. Ibid.

75. Script of statewide radio broadcast, October 31, 1952, author's collection.

76. Harry P. Cain II, e-mail message to author, February 17, 2009.

77. Jack Bell, "Gen. Eisenhower Piles On Biggest Popular Vote Ever Given a President," *Seattle Times*, November 5, 1952.

78. "No Tears, Says Senator Cain," *Tacoma News Tribune*, November 11, 1952.

79. Smith, "The Cain 'Mutiny,'" 21.

80. Ibid, 22–23.

81. Harry P. Cain, letter to C. J. Skreen, December 9, 1971, author's collection.

82. Harry P. Cain II, e-mail message to author, February 17, 2009.

Notes

CHAPTER 10: *"Can Security and Freedom Live Together?"*

1. Don Shannon, "Pipeline from Washington, D.C.," *Tacoma News Tribune*, April 5, 1953.

2. Don Shannon, "Cain May Get Defense Job," *Tacoma Sunday Ledger*, November 16, 1952.

3. Sherman Adams, *Firsthand Report: The Story of the Eisenhower Administration* (New York: Harper and Brothers, 1961), 77.

4. "Cain Given 3 Job Choices," *Tacoma News Tribune*, April 7, 1953.

5. Warren G. Magnuson, form letters and telegrams responding to constituents opposed to Cain receiving a federal appointment, Warren G. Magnuson Papers, Special Collections, University of Washington Library, Accession 3181-3, Box 150, File 16.

6. Warren G. Magnuson to Solie M. Ringold, Warren G. Magnuson Papers, Special Collections Division, University of Washington Library, Accession 3181-3, Box 150, Folder 16.

7. Harry P. Cain, letter to Edgar Eisenhower, February 17, 1958, Harry P. Cain II collection.

8. L. Edgar Prina, "The Harry Cain 'Mutiny,'" *Collier's*, September 2, 1955, 32.

9. Harry P. Cain, letter to Edgar Eisenhower, February 17, 1958, Harry P. Cain II collection.

10. Ibid.

11. "Cain Before Committee," *Tacoma News Tribune*, April 21, 1953.

12. "Cain Certain to Get Okay of Senators," *Tacoma News Tribune*, April 22, 1953.

13. Richard M. Fried, *Nightmare in Red: The McCarthy Era in Perspective* (New York: Oxford University Press, 1990), 42.

14. Ellen Schrecker, *Many Are the Crimes: McCarthyism in America* (Boston: Little, Brown and Company, 1998), 48–59.

15. Nasaw, *The Chief*, 588.

16. http://www.historycentral.com/documents/hatchact.html (accessed November 23, 2009).

17. Fried, *Nightmare in Red*, 52.

18. Geoffrey R. Stone, *Perilous Times: Free Speech in Wartime* (New York: W. W. Norton, 2004), 245–246.

19. Robert Justin Goldstein, *American Blacklist: The Attorney General's List of Subversive Organizations* (Lawrence, KS: University Press of Kansas, 2008), 25–43.

20. Ibid., 47.

21. Ibid., 49.

22. Christopher Andrew, *Defend the Realm: The Authorized History of MI5* (New York: Alfred A. Knopf, 2009), 368.

23. Stone, *Perilous Times*, 327.

24. Goldstein, *American Blacklist*, 1.

25. Ibid., 62–63.

26. Marc Patenaude, "The McCarran Internal Security Act, 1950–2005: Civil Liberties Versus National Security," (Master of Arts thesis, Louisiana State University, 2006), 31.

27. Robert Justin Goldstein, e-mail to the author, February 2, 2010.

28. Fried, *Nightmare in Red*, 117.

29. Robert Justin Goldstein, telephone conversation with the author, October 19, 2009.

30. Herbert Brownell, *Advising Ike: The Memoirs of Attorney General Herbert Brownell* (Lawrence, KS: University Press of Kansas, 1993), 230.

31. Ibid., 247.

32. Ibid.

33. http://www.archives.gov/federal-register/codification/executive-order/10450.html (accessed October 20, 2009).

34. Cain II, "A Case Study," 26.

35. Alan Barth, *The Loyalty of Free Men* (New York: Viking Press, 1952), 671–672.

36. Andrew, *Defend the Realm*, 395.

37. Prina, "The Harry Cain 'Mutiny,'" 32.

38. Willard Edwards, "The Reformation of Harry Cain," *American Mercury*, October 1955, 40–42.

39. Sherman Adams, *Firsthand Report*, 459.

40. Michael Medved, *The Shadow Presidents: The Secret History of the Chief Executives and Their Top Aides* (New York: Times Books, 1979), 238.

41. Ibid., 317.

42. Adams, *Firsthand Report*, 14.

43. Harry P. Cain as told to Tris Coffin, "I Could Not Remain Silent," *Coronet*, November 1955, 30–31.

44. Prina, "The Harry Cain 'Mutiny,'" 33.

45. Ibid., 34.

46. Cain II, "A Case Study," 24.

47. Prina, "The Harry Cain 'Mutiny,'" 34.

48. Smith, "The Cain 'Mutiny,'" 26–27.

49. Cain II, "A Case Study," 21.

50. Ibid., 23. (This correspondence is missing from Rabb's papers located at the Eisenhower Library.)

51. Prina, "The Harry Cain 'Mutiny,'" 32–33.

52. Cain II, "A Case Study," 25.

53. "U.S. Security System Evils Cited by Cain," *Tacoma News Tribune and Ledger*, January 16, 1955.

54. Ibid.

55. Smith, "The Cain 'Mutiny,'" 29.

56. "Security of the Republic," *New Republic*, January 31, 1955, 6–10; reprinted in *Congressional Record*, 84th Congress, First Session, February 16, 1955, A978-80.

57. Editorial, "Cain Mutiny," *Washington Post*, January 18, 1955.

58. Marquis Childs, "What Cain Raised," *New York Times*, January 21, 1955.

59. Goldstein, "Raising Cain," 67.

60. Prina, "The Harry Cain 'Mutiny,'" 35.

61. Fulton Lewis, Jr., "Left Wing Darling," *Seattle Post-Intelligencer*, June 12, 1955.

62. Edwards, "The Reformation of Harry Cain," 40.

63. http://www.presidency.ucsb.edu/ws/index.php?pid=10321 (accessed September 23, 2009).

64. Prina, "The Harry Cain 'Mutiny,'" 33.

65. "Cain Says His Speeches Roused Ire of Adams," *Washington Star*, August 18, 1955.

66. Cain II, "A Case Study," 28–29.

67. Prina, "The Harry Cain 'Mutiny,'" 33.

68. Ross Cunningham, "Brownell All-Out for Eisenhower Candidacy, *Seattle Times*, June 3, 1955.

69. Prina, "The Harry Cain 'Mutiny,'" 33.

70. "Cain Says His Speeches Roused Ire of Adams."

71. Cain II, "A Case Study," 33.

72. Goldstein, *American Blacklist*, 206.

73. Cain II, "A Case Study," 34.

74. "Cain Defends Use of 5th Amendment," *New York Times*, March 19, 1955; also "Cain Walks Out On McCarthy and Every One Of His Works," *CIO News*, March 28, 1955.

75. Alice Frein Johnson, "Cain Admits Erring in Wallgren Charge," *Seattle Times*, March 23, 1955.

76. "Cain Assails Tagging All Risks as 'Disloyal,'" *Washington Post*, March 28, 1955.

77. "Cain Speech in Spokane Stirs Interest in Stand," *Tacoma News Tribune*, March 23, 1955.

78. "Cain Says His Speeches Roused Ire of Adams."

79. Edwards, "The Reformation of Harry Cain," 41.

80. Cain II, "A Case Study," 13.

81. Ibid., 32.

CHAPTER 11: *The Cain Mutiny*

1. Smith, "The Cain 'Mutiny,'" 47.

2. Goldstein, "Raising Cain," 70.

3. Prina, "The Harry Cain 'Mutiny,'" 33.

4. Cain II, "A Case Study," 37.

5. Prina, "The Harry Cain 'Mutiny,'" 34; also in Cain II, "A Case Study," 40.

6. Cain II, "A Case Study," 40.

7. Prina, "The Harry Cain 'Mutiny,'" 34.

8. Ibid.; also in Cain II, "A Case Study," 40.

9. Cain II, "A Case Study," 43.

10. John B. Oakes, "The Security Issue: A Changing Atmosphere," *New York Times* Magazine, August 14, 1955, 50.

11. Smith, "The Cain 'Mutiny,'" 35.

12. Senate Committee on Post Office and Civil Service, *Administration of the Federal Employees' Security Program*, 84th Congress, First Session, 1955, 44–99.

13. Cain II, "A Case Study," 45.

14. Goldstein, *American Blacklist*, 209.

15. Harry P. Cain, letter to Sherman Adams, June 30, 1955, Box 233, Official file book 1, White House Central Files, Eisenhower Presidential Library; also Cain II, "A Case Study," 46.

16. Cain II, "A Case Study," 48.

17. William Stringer, "Security Ax Strikes Rocks—Opinion Shifts," *Christian Science Monitor*, June 11, 1955.

18. Goldstein, *American Blacklist*, 69.

19. Oakes, "The Security Issue," 52.

20. Edwards, "The Reformation of Harry Cain, 40.

21. Smith, "The Cain 'Mutiny,'" 33–34.

22. Harry P. Cain, "The Blessings of Liberty: Unto the Least of These, Thy Brethren," speech to the Tenth Annual National Conference on Citizenship, Washington, DC, September 19, 1955, Ca (1-3), Box 20, Eisenhower Administration Series: Subseries B. Correspondence, 1953–1958, Papers of Maxwell M. Rabb, 1938–58, 1989; Dwight D. Eisenhower Presidential Library.

23. Ibid.

24. Cain II, "A Case Study," 47.

25. Harry P. Cain, letter to Maxwell M. Rabb, September 28, 1955, Ca (1-3), Box 20, Eisenhower Administration Series: Subseries B. Correspondence, 1953–1958, Papers of Maxwell M. Rabb, 1938–58, 1989; Dwight D. Eisenhower Presidential Library.

26. Stub Nelson, "Republicans Uninterested in Harry Cain," *Seattle Post-Intelligencer*, September 28, 1955.

27. Lawrence E. Davies, "Dispute Over Cain Stirs Home State," *New York Times*, November 21, 1955.

28. Harry P. Cain as told to Tris Coffin, "I Could Not Remain Silent," 30–31.

29. Editorial, "To Clear the Atmosphere of Intolerance and Doubt," *Seattle Times*, October 24, 1955.

30. Goldstein, "Raising Cain," 71.

31. Harry P. Cain as told to Tris Coffin, "I Could Not Remain Silent," 30–31.

32. Ibid.

33. Ibid.

34. Ibid.

35. Ibid.

36. Harry P. Cain, letter to Maxwell M. Rabb, November 3, 1955, Ca (1-3), Box 20, Eisenhower Administration Series: Subseries B. Correspondence, 1953–1958, Papers of Maxwell M. Rabb, 1938–58, 1989; Dwight D. Eisenhower Presidential Library.

37. Harry P. Cain, letter to Maxwell M. Rabb, December 20, 1955, Ca (1-3), Box 20, Eisenhower Administration Series: Subseries B. Correspondence, 1953–1958, Papers of Maxwell M. Rabb, 1938–58, 1989; Dwight D. Eisenhower Presidential Library.

38. Ibid.

39. Cain II, "A Case Study," 56.

40. Prina, "The Harry Cain 'Mutiny,'" 35.

41. www.vlib.us/amdocs/texts/dde1956.htm (accessed July 11, 2009).

42.   Harry P. Cain, speech to the Chicago affiliate of the Americans for Democratic Action on the occasion of the Twelfth Annual Celebration of Independents' Day, January 30, 1956, Ca (1-3), Box 20, Eisenhower Administration Series: Subseries B. Correspondence, 1953–1958, Papers of Maxwell M. Rabb, 1938–58, 1989; Dwight D. Eisenhower Presidential Library.

43.   Ibid.

44.   Harry P. Cain, letter to letter to Maxwell M. Rabb, February 1, 1956, Ca (1-3), Box 20, Eisenhower Administration Series: Subseries B. Correspondence, 1953–1958, Papers of Maxwell M. Rabb, 1938–58, 1989; Dwight D. Eisenhower Presidential Library.

45.   Smith, "The Cain 'Mutiny,'" 38–39.

46.   Harry P. Cain, speech to the New York Civil Liberties Union, February 22, 1956, Ca (1-3), Box 20, Eisenhower Administration Series: Subseries B. Correspondence, 1953–1958, Papers of Maxwell M. Rabb, 1938–58, 1989; Dwight D. Eisenhower Presidential Library.

47.   "Cain Scores 'Remoteness,'" *Tacoma News Tribune*, February 23, 1956.

48.   Harry P. Cain, letter to Maxwell M. Rabb, March 23, 1956, Ca (1-3), Box 20, Eisenhower Administration Series: Subseries B. Correspondence, 1953–1958, Papers of Maxwell M. Rabb, 1938–58, 1989; Dwight D. Eisenhower Presidential Library.

49.   Harry P. Cain, letter to Maxwell M. Rabb, March 9, 1956, Ca (1-3), Box 20, Eisenhower Administration Series: Subseries B. Correspondence, 1953–1958, Papers of Maxwell M. Rabb, 1938–58, 1989; Dwight D. Eisenhower Presidential Library.

50.   Goldstein, *American Blacklist*, 227–228.

51.   Ibid., 230.

52.   Smith, "The Cain 'Mutiny,'" 41.

53.   Harry P. Cain, "The Individual Is of Supreme Importance," speech to the Jewish Labor Committee, National Trade Union Conference on Civil Rights, New York City, May 5, 1956, Candy Cain Tingstad collection.

54.   Ibid.

55.   "DC Papers Give Big Play to Cain Talk," *Tacoma News Tribune*, May 8, 1956.

56.   Cain II, "A Case Study," 69.

57.   Sherman Adams, *Firsthand Report*, 51.

58.   Smith, "The Cain 'Mutiny,'" 43–44.

59.   Ibid., 46.

60.   William H Stringer, "The Washington Scene," *Christian Science Monitor*, May 18, 1956.

61. Ernest K. Lindley, "Of Harry Cain," *Newsweek*, May 28, 1956.

62. "Harry Cain's Future," *Tacoma News Tribune* editorial, May 21, 1956.

63. "Cains Set to Ride Out Party Row, Says Wife," *Tacoma News Tribune*, May 22, 1956.

64. Goldstein, "Raising Cain," 72.

65. Smith, "The Cain 'Mutiny,'" 44.

66. Goldstein, "Raising Cain," 72.

67. http://www.presidency.ucsb.edu/ws/index.php?pid=10498. (accessed September 29, 2009.

68. Goldstein, "Raising Cain," 72.

69. Cain II, "A Case Study," 73.

70. Berman, "Cain and the President," 10–15.

71. Smith, "The Cain 'Mutiny,'" 49.

72. Berman, "Cain and the President," 11.

73. Ibid.

74. Ibid., 12.

75. Ibid., 13.

76. Smith, "The Cain 'Mutiny,'" 56.

77. Alice Frein Johnson, "President Insists On Ending Injustice in Security System – Cain," Seattle Times, June 7, 1956.

78. Cain II, "A Case Study," 77.

79. Smith, "The Cain 'Mutiny,'" 50–51.

80. "Threat of Fascism Said Bigger Than Communism," *Dallas Morning News*, June 13, 1956.

81. "Cain Questions Need of U.S. Loyalty Program," *Los Angeles Times*, June 14, 1956.

82. Cain II, "A Case Study," 81.

83. Cain's Stormy Tenure in SACB Ends August 9," *Washington Star*, July 25, 1956.

84. "Cain Has No Plans to Stay In Politics," *Tacoma News Tribune*, July 26, 1956.

85. Harry P. Cain to Sherman Adams, August 2, 1956, Box 233, Official File Book 1, White House Central Files, Eisenhower Presidential Library.

86. Daniel M. Berman, "Cain Sees Internal Security Act as Curtailment of Free Speech," *The Washington Sunday Star*, September 2, 1956.

87. Jessie Gessler, "Mrs. Harry Cain Wants Family Together Here," *Tacoma News Tribune*, August 5, 1956.

88.   Emily Walker, "Cain Offers Security Data to Stevenson," *Tacoma News Tribune*, August 23, 1956.

89.   Alice Frein Johnson, "Cain to Be Honored by Liberal Groups at Banquet," *Seattle Times*, October 22, 1956.

90.   "In Tribute to Harry P. Cain," collection of messages of support presented at testimonial dinner, National Press Club, Washington, DC, October 23, 1956, Candy Cain Tingstad collection.

91.   Berman, "Cain Sees Internal Security Act as Curtailment of Free Speech"; also in Cain II, "A Case Study," 85; and Smith, "The Cain 'Mutiny,'" 59.

92.   Arthur Miller, *Timebends: A Life* (New York: Grove Press, 1987), 452.

93.   "Miller Told Truth, Says Cain at Trial," *Tacoma News Tribune*, May 23, 1957.

94.   Miller, *Timebends*, 455.

95.   "Trials: The Limits of Political Invective," *TIME Magazine,* January 31, 1964. http://www.time.com/time/magazine/article/0,9171,8971210-1,00.html (accessed February 20, 2010).

96.   William L. Dwyer, *The Goldmark Case: An American Libel Trial* (Seattle: University of Washington Press, 1984), 209–213.

97.   "Cain Refutes Ex-Reds in Goldmark Test," *Tacoma News Tribune*, January 7, 1964.

CHAPTER 12: *An Uncommon Man*

1.   Harry P. Cain, audiocassette tape interview by Kappes.

2.   "Cain Denies Leaving Job," *Tacoma News Tribune*, April 3, 1957.

3.   "Cain Chose to Lecture at Yale U.," *Tacoma News Tribune*, January 29, 1957.

4.   "Cain Out of Divorce Suit," *Tacoma News Tribune*, January 15, 1957.

5.   Harry P. Cain, letter to Edgar Eisenhower, February 17, 1958.

6.   Harry P. Cain, audiocassette tape interview by Kappes.

7.   Ibid.

8.   Ibid.

9.   "Harry Cain Conducts VIP Show on Miami TV," *Tacoma News Tribune*, August 27, 1957.

10.   Emily Walker, "Cain Mines Political Gold in Miami," *Tacoma News Tribune*, February 27, 1958.

11.   Harry P. Cain, memorandum to Joseph H. Walker, November 1, 1970, author's collection.

12.   Candy Cain Tingstad, personal communication, August 22, 2008.

13.   Harry P. Cain II, e-mail to the author, November 26, 2008.

14. Harry P. Cain, "European Trip Journal," September 4, 1935, Harry P. Cain II collection.

15. Emily Walker, "Tacoman Will Marry Cain," *Tacoma News Tribune*, July 18, 1958.

16. Colbert, Haines, "Harry Cain: A Man Who Speaks His Mind," *Miami Herald*, Sunday Supplement, September 15, 1963.

17. Shaw, "A Death Brought Harry Cain to Life."

18. Betsy Buffington, "Bonnie Cain Joins Her Husband by Working for United Fund," *Miami Herald*, January 17, 1960.

19. Ibid.

20. Harry P. Cain, memorandum to Joseph H. Walker.

21. Ibid.

22. Ibid.

23. Harry P. Cain, memorandum to Joseph H. Walker.

24. Morris McLemore, "Intimate View of Florida Politics," *Miami News*, Sunday Supplement, November 25, 1962.

25. "From Campaign Chairman Cain to His Candidate," *Miami Herald*, November 25, 1962.

26. Harry P. Cain, memorandum to Joseph H. Walker.

27. A.B. Herman, letter to Richard Bryce, May 16, 1963, author's collection.

28. Harry P. Cain, letter to Hubert H. Humphrey, June 3, 1963, author's collection.

29. Harry P. Cain, letter to the author, June 7, 1963, author's collection.

30. Joseph McGowan, Jr., "Cain Denies Candidacy, Would Prefer Senate," *Tacoma News Tribune*, November 21, 1963.

31. Harry P. Cain, letter to Ray Bliss, March 10, 1965, author's collection.

32. Harry P. Cain, letter to Marcus Kyle, August 31, 1965, author's collection.

33. Harry P. Cain, letter to the author, August 31, 1965, author's collection.

34. "Senator Cain: South Florida Republican Strategist," *Florida Trend*, October 1963, 12.

35. Harry P. Cain to Senator George Smathers, March 8, 1967, Henry M. Jackson Papers, Special Collections Division, University of Washington Library, Accession 3560-4, Box 3, Folder 34.

36. Senator Henry M. Jackson to Harry P. Cain, March 10, 1967, Henry M. Jackson Papers, Special Collections Division, University of Washington Library, Accession 3560-4, Box 3, Folder 34.

37. Harry P. Cain to Senator Henry M. Jackson, July 25, 1967, Henry M. Jackson Papers, Special Collections Division, University of Washington Library, Accession 3560-4, Box 3, Folder 34.

38. "Republican Governors to Honor Harry Cain, Tour New College," *Miami Beach Sun*," November 30, 1967.

39. Morris McLamore, "Days of Decision for Cain," *Miami News*, March 20, 1968.

40. Harry P. Cain, letter to Joe Gardner, February 29, 1968, author's collection.

41. Harry P. Cain, letter to W. Marvin Watson, March 15, 1968, author's collection.

42. Harry P. Cain to Senator Henry M. Jackson, March 23, 1968, Henry M. Jackson Papers, Special Collections Division, University of Washington Library, Accession 3560-4, Box 3, Folder 34.

43. Ibid.

44. Charles F. Hesser, "Cain Backs Nixon, Collins; Sees HHH as Trapped Man," *Miami News*, October 9, 1968; Harry P. Cain, "Political Statement" press release, October 10, 1968, author's collection.

45. Harry P. Cain letter to Harry P. Cain II, December 1, 1969; also, Harry P. Cain, letter to Joseph H. Walker, November 27, 1969, author's collection.

46. Harry P. Cain, letter to Joseph H. Walker, November 1, 1970.

47. Samuel A. Jacobs, "Jackson, Old Foe Make Up," *Miami Herald*, July 21, 1971.

48. Samuel A. Jacobs, "Harry Cain: Fighting New Foes in Miami," *Seattle Times*, August 4, 1974.

49. Ibid.

50. Harry P. Cain, letter to Candy Cain Tingstad, August 2, 1972, author's collection.

51. Morton Lucoff, "Cain Refuses to Sign Oath; Simon Asks New Pledge," *Miami News*, April 18, 1972.

52. Charles Whited, "Cain Reflects on His Defeat," *Miami Herald*, September 9, 1976.

53. Howard Ferguson, "Harry Cain Happy with Smoking Ban," *Tacoma News Tribune*, November 22, 1974.

54. Harry P. Cain, letter to Candy Cain Tingstad, August 2, 1972, Candy Cain Tingstad collection.

55. Jacobs, "Harry Cain: Fighting New Foes."

56. Howard Ferguson, "An Uncommon Man," *Tacoma News Tribune and Sunday Ledger*, March 13, 1977.

57. Rod Caldwell, "Harry Cain a Winner," *Tacoma News Tribune*, September 14, 1972.

58. Walter Evans, "Whatever Happened to Harry P. Cain?" *Seattle Post Intelligencer*, June 13, 1976.

59. Harry P. Cain, "Campaign Statement" press release, July 6, 1976, author's collection.

60. Whited, "Cain Reflects on His Defeat."

61. Howard Ferguson, "Harry Cain Enjoys His Greatest Night," *Tacoma News Tribune*, December 29, 1977.

62. "Harry Cain Spoke His Mind," *Miami Herald*, March 6, 1979.

63. "Harry P. Cain, 1906–1979," *Tacoma News Tribune*, March 5, 1979.

64. Sara Rimer, *"Friends: Cain Taught Us about Living,"* *Miami Herald*, March 13, 1979.

65. Henry M. Jackson, letter to Candy Cain Tingstad, March 16, 1979, Candy Cain Tingstad collection.

66. Henry King Stanford, Invocation, Memorial Service for Harry P. Cain, March 12, 1979, author's collection.

67. Candy Cain Tingstad, personal communication, July 11, 2008.

EPILOGUE

1. Harry Cain Tower Dedication Program, January 20, 1984, Candy Cain Tingstad collection.

2. "Harry Cain's Ex-Wife to Marry," *Tacoma News Tribune*, August 8, 1978.

3. Ibid.

4. Jack Pyle, "Harry P. Cain II Quits Bureaucracy," *Tacoma News Tribune*, April 26, 1978.

5. Harry P. Cain II, e-mail to the author, June 6, 2009.

6. Pyle, "Harry P. Cain II Quits Bureaucracy."

7. Candy Cain Tingstad, personal communication, November 5, 2008; e-mail to the author, May 5, 2009.

8. David W. Hein, e-mail to the author, June 13, 2009.

9. http://www.historylink.org/index.cfm?DisplayPage=output.cfm&file_id=5667 (accessed March 7, 2009).

10. Harry P. Cain, audiocassette tape interview by Kappes.

11. http://en.wikipedia.org/wiki/Joseph_McCarthy#Censure_and_the_Watkins_Committee (accessed March 7, 2009.

12. Ellen Schrecker, *Many Are the Crimes: McCarthyism in America* (Boston: Little, Brown and Company, 1998), xii.

13. Evans, *Blacklisted by History*, 314.

14. Stephen Ambrose, *Eisenhower: Soldier and President* (New York: Simon & Schuster, 1990), 307–309.

15. Adams, *Firsthand Report*, 135.

16. Ambrose, *Eisenhower*, 309.

17. Adams, *Firsthand Report,* 50.

18. Medved, *The Shadow Presidents*, 238.

19. Ibid., 78.

20. Goldstein, *American Blacklist*, xi.

21. Barth, *The Loyalty of Free Men*, 110.

22. Goldstein, *American Blacklist*, 272.

23. Ibid., 293.

24. Ibid., 319.

25. Berman, "Cain Sees Internal Security Act as Curtailment of Free Speech."

26. Patenaude, "The McCarran Internal Security Act, 1950–2005, 78–79.

27. Harry P. Cain, letter to C. J. Skreen, December 1, 1971, author's collection.

Chronology

1906

January 10 — Harry Pulliam Cain and his twin brother, George William Cain III (known as Bill), are born Nashville, Tennessee.

1910

March — George Cain, Jr., moves to Tacoma and becomes associated with the *West Coast Lumberman*. His family and Tony McChristian, their African American handyman, follow later in the year.

1917

October 22 — George Cain's wife and the twins' mother, Elizabeth Grace Pulliam Cain, commits suicide at her home in Tacoma, Washington.

1920

September — Harry and Bill Cain enter Hill Military Academy, Portland, Oregon.

1924

July 15 — Harry and Bill graduate from HMA. Harry joins the Army Reserve as an enlisted man upon graduation.

1924–1925 — Harry remains in Portland to work as a cub reporter for the now-defunct *Portland News-Telegraph*. Bill Cain enters Oregon Agricultural College to study engineering.

1925

September — Harry Cain enrolls at the University of the South, Sewanee, Tennessee.

1927

April 27 — Harry Cain commissioned as a Second Lieutenant in the U.S. Army Reserve.

1929

June 11	Harry graduates from Sewanee and returns to Tacoma to see his father before moving to New York City to accept work as a reporter for the *New York Times*.
September	Harry is hired by the Tacoma office of the Bank of California, N.A.
October 29	The New York Stock Exchange crashes.

1932

April 3	Harry resigns his commission in the U.S. Army Reserve.

1934

January	Harry is promoted to manager of the Business Development Department of the Bank of California and begins working in the bank's Trust Department.
September 22	Harry marries Marjorie Elloise Dils in Seattle.

1935

May–June	Violent clashes in downtown Tacoma between members of the Northwest Sawmill and Timber Workers Union and police and Washington National Guard culminate in the "Battle of the 11th Street Bridge."
September 4	Harry takes a leave of absence from the bank to take Marjorie on a year-long tour of Europe.
September 16	The couple arrives in Ireland aboard the SS *Manhattan* after a voyage of five days.
September 19–26	Marj and Harry take a week-long honeymoon at St. Andrews in Scotland.
October–January	The couple lives on a shoestring budget In London. Harry attends lectures at the London School of Economics while the couple spends their days with sightseeing, and attending the theater.
November 14	British Parliamentary elections.

1936

February–September	After six months in Great Britain, Harry and Marjorie continue their tour in Germany and the Continent. They attend a rally in Berlin at which Adolf Hitler speaks. Harry discusses the political situation with everyday Germans.
March	German occupation of the Rhineland.
August 1–16	Berlin Summer Olympics.

Chronology

<table>
<tr><td></td><td>September</td><td>Harry and Marjorie return to Tacoma. Harry returns to work at the Bank of California and begins speaking out publicly about the threat posed to world peace by Nazi Germany.</td></tr>
<tr><td>**1937**</td><td></td><td></td></tr>
<tr><td></td><td>September 26</td><td>Harry P. Cain II (known as Buzzy) is born in Tacoma.</td></tr>
<tr><td>**1938**</td><td></td><td></td></tr>
<tr><td></td><td>March</td><td>The House Un-American Activities Committee is created as a special investigative committee by Congress.</td></tr>
<tr><td>**1939**</td><td></td><td></td></tr>
<tr><td></td><td>April 16</td><td>Harry's father, George W. Cain, Jr., dies in Tacoma.</td></tr>
<tr><td></td><td>June</td><td>Harry agrees to manage the Washington Golden Jubilee Celebration, taking another leave of absence (paid, this time) from the bank.</td></tr>
<tr><td></td><td>July 16–23</td><td>The highly successful Washington Golden Jubilee Celebration takes place in Tacoma. Cain's chairmanship catapults him into public consciousness.</td></tr>
<tr><td></td><td>August 2</td><td>Congress passes the Hatch Act that prohibits federal employees from "membership in any political party or organization which advocates the overthrow of our constitutional form of government."</td></tr>
<tr><td></td><td>October 24</td><td>Harry resigns from the Bank of California to run for mayor of Tacoma.</td></tr>
<tr><td></td><td>November 1</td><td>Cain announces his candidacy for mayor of Tacoma.</td></tr>
<tr><td>**1940**</td><td></td><td></td></tr>
<tr><td></td><td>January 11</td><td>Cain formally kicks off his campaign.</td></tr>
<tr><td></td><td>February 28</td><td>Dr. G. B. Kerstetter wins the primary election for mayor of Tacoma. Cain places third behind George Tennent.</td></tr>
<tr><td></td><td>March 8</td><td>Cain is in attendance when Kerstetter dies of a massive stroke during a debate with Tennent before the Young Men's Business Club.</td></tr>
<tr><td></td><td>March 11</td><td>Pierce County Superior Court rules that Cain can replace Kerstetter on ballot.</td></tr>
<tr><td></td><td></td><td>Congress approves "Lend-Lease" aid to Allies.</td></tr>
<tr><td></td><td>March 12</td><td>Cain defeats George Tennent to win the general election for mayor by 1,802 votes in the general election.</td></tr>
<tr><td></td><td>March 22–May 31</td><td>Tennent appeals the election results to the Pierce County Superior Court and then the Washington Supreme Court, losing both appeals.</td></tr>
</table>

June 3	Cain is sworn in as Tacoma's youngest mayor at age thirty-four.
June 19	The Alien Registration Act (known as the Smith Act) is passed by Congress. It resurrects most of the provisions of the 1917 Espionage Act and applies them during peacetime for the first time. It also requires all resident aliens to register with the government and be fingerprinted.
June 30	U.S. Attorney General Francis Biddle establishes the first Attorney General's List of Subversive Organizations (AGLOSO). It contains eleven organizations and no individuals.
July 1–3	Tacoma Narrows Bridge opens. Tacoma Municipal Airport is turned over to the U.S. Army Air Corps as McChord Field.
August	Cain creates a model Home Defense Corps; attracts national publicity for effort.
October 18	Three-theater Tacoma premier of *Tugboat Annie Sails Again*.
September	Citizens' group begins complaining to the Tacoma City Commission about out-of-control prostitution, gambling, and bootlegging in Tacoma, calling for Public Safety Commission Holmes Eastwood's resignation.
November 5	Tacoma selected as one of three cities in the country to participate in special urban planning program.
November 7	Tacoma Narrows Bridge collapses into Puget Sound.
December	Army officials threaten to place Tacoma "off-limits" if prostitution is not cleaned up. Cain quietly works with the U.S. Army to help them frame their demands.

1941

July 25	Cain meets with Tacoma's "madams" to announce the closure of the brothels.
August 1	The *Cape Alva*, the first of many naval and merchant ships built in the months leading up to and during World War Two, is launched at Seattle-Tacoma Shipbuilding in Tacoma.
August	Construction of North Fort Lewis completed, allowing a second full division to be stationed at the post.
September 16	President Roosevelt signs the Selective Service Act, instituting the first peacetime draft in America's history. Mayor Cain becomes the first Tacoman to register for the draft exactly one month later.

Chronology

	December 7	The Japanese attack Pearl Harbor, Hawaii. Cain makes radio address that evening asking citizens to protect the rights of Japanese citizens.
	December 13	Eleanor Roosevelt visits Tacoma and speaks to Japanese-American students.
1942		
	January 18	Cain announces that he will run for another full term as mayor.
	February 18	President Roosevelt signs Executive Order 9066, paving the way for the evacuation and internment of most of the Japanese-Americans living on the West Coast.
	February 24	Cain wins primary election by 14,921 votes, the largest plurality in the history of city elections, making a general election unnecessary.
	March 2	Cain publicly opposes the wholesale evacuation of the Japanese at a Congressional hearing held in Seattle.
	June 4	Battle of Midway.
	August 2	Washington State Patrol raids Tacoma gambling establishments after Cain appeals to Governor Arthur Langlie without notifying his local law enforcement officials.
	November 8	Allies invade North Africa.
1943		
	April 17	State Patrol raids local gambling establishments again, having to pass by off-duty Tacoma police officers in front of the buildings.
	April 20	Cain charges Public Safety Commission Einar Langseth with misconduct and neglect of duty.
	May 1	Formal hearings on Cain's charges before the Tacoma City Commission begin. The Commission votes 3–1 to retain Einar Langseth in office.
	May 5	Cain takes a leave of absence as mayor and is sworn in as a Major in the U.S. Army.
	May 14– August 4	Cain attends the Army's new School of Military Government at the University of Virginia, Charlottesville, Virginia.
	June 5	The Cain's second child, Marlyce (known as Candy), is born in Tacoma.
	July 9	Start of the Allied invasion of Sicily.

August 15	Cain arrives in Algiers, Morocco, and reports to the Civil Affairs Section, 15th Army Group.
September 3–16	
	Invasion of Italy begins with the crossing of the Strait of Messina
September 9	Start of Allied landings at Salerno, south of Naples.
September 15	Cain lands on the beach at Salerno with elements of the 325th Glider Infantry Regiment of the 82nd Airborne Division.
September 29	Italy surrenders.
September 15– November 11	
	Cain is engaged in continuous combat against German forces between Salerno. He is assigned the responsibility for administering twenty-nine towns and cities.
November 11	The Allied Control Commission, responsible for the administration of the Allied-controlled portions of Italy, is established at Brindisi. Cain reports to Major General Kenyon A. Joyce and is assigned responsibility for the Civil Administration and Personal branches of the ACC. Cain is alerted that he will be transferred to London in January 1944.

1944

January 17	Cain is temporarily reassigned to the Rome Area Command, Fifth Army, awaiting reassignment to England.
January 17– May 19	
	Battle for Monte Cassino. Cain observes bombing of the ancient abbey on March 16.
January 22	Allied invasion of Anzio, south of Rome.
March 1–23	Cain, now reassigned to unknown duties in England, travels by convoy from Italy to England.
April 20	Cain is assigned to Civil Affairs (G-5) at SHAEF Headquarters in London, reporting to Brigadier General Frank S. McSherry and British Lieutenant-General Arthur E. Grassett. He is given responsibility for the Psychological Warfare and Public Relations Division.
c. April 25	Cain receives a cable from Marj indicating that Governor Arthur Langlie and others want to recruit him to run for the open U.S. Senate seat as a Republican. Cain agrees.
May 4	Cain's campaign staff back in Tacoma announces his candidacy.

Chronology

June 4	Rome liberated.
June 6	D-Day, the Allied invasion of Normandy.
July 11	Cain wins the Republican nomination for Senate against ten other candidates in the primary election.
August 15	Cain is promoted to Lieutenant Colonel.
August 25	Paris liberated. The XVIII Airborne Corps is activated in England. Cain successfully campaigns to be appointed G-5 (Assistant Chief of Staff for Civil Affairs) of the new Corps, commanded by Major General Matthew Ridgway.
September 14	Cain reports to XVIII Corps headquarters at Ogbourne St. George, Oxfordshire.
September 17–25	Two of the XVIII Corps's airborne divisions, the 82nd and 101st, participate in Operation MARKET GARDEN, the airborne assault on the Maas, Waal, and the Neder Rijn Rivers in Holland. Because he is new to his assignment, Cain remains behind in England.
November 7	Cain loses Washington Senate race to Congressman Warren G. Magnuson in the general election.
December 16–January 25	The Battle of the Bulge. Cain, along with most of the staff of the XVIII Airborne Corps, arrives by air from England on December 18. He writes home a day later to say that "the fur is flying."

1945

January–February	Cain reorganizes Civil Affairs staff of XVIII Airborne Corps in preparation for Operation VARSITY, the massive crossing of the Rhine, scheduled for March, and the following invasion of Germany.
March 16	Cain promoted to full Colonel and awarded Legion of Merit and second Bronze Star by General Ridgeway.
March 24	Cain in action during Operation VARSITY.
April 6–25	Cain and XVIII Airborne Corps take part in the elimination of the "Ruhr Pocket," taking 300,000 prisoners.
April–May	German resistance collapses. Cain is responsible for the welfare of 500,000 refugees and displaced persons.
May 6	Cain wounded in action near Haganow, Germany, one day before the end of hostilities.
May 7	Germany surrenders.

May 8	At the request of General Ridgway, Cain addresses German officials, townspeople, and prisoners of war on the occasion of a public funeral for concentration camp victims.
June 5	Allied Control Council established to administer defeated Germany
July 15	Cain is reassigned back to SHAEF as a Military Field Inspector. He is assigned by Eisenhower and General Lucius Clay to investigate the use of Nazi administrators by General George Patton in Bavaria.
September 5	Cain departs Europe for the United States on the *Queen Mary*.
September 16	Cain arrives back in Tacoma after stopping off in Washington, DC, to talk with former New York Governor Herbert Lehman about a job at the United Nations Relief and Rehabilitation Agency.
November 5	Cain officially discharged from the U.S. Army at Fort Lewis.
December 3	Cain presides over his first city commission meeting in two and one-half years.
December 10	Cain announces that he will not run for reelection as mayor of Tacoma.

1946

February 12	Cain makes what he calls his "first party political speech" to the Thurston County Republican Central Committee.
March 5	Cain accuses Paul Olson, candidate for mayor, of facilitating payoff to Congressman John Coffee.
March 11	Cain and Olson debate Cain's charges in front of 1,600 in "acrimonious debate."
March 12	Olson loses election for mayor to Val Fawcett
April 12	Cain announces that he will challenge incumbent Hugh B. Mitchell for U.S. Senate seat.
July 9	Cain wins Republican primary election.
September 21	Cain chairs Republican Party state convention in Seattle.
October 26	In his final radio address of the election, Cain claims that Congressman Hugh DeLacy is one of the leaders "of the Communist Party's front movement in the United States."
November 5	Cain defeats Mitchell by more than 60,000 votes to be elected to the U.S. Senate.

November 25	President Truman establishes the Temporary Commission on Employee Loyalty to create criteria for barring "disloyal or subversive persons" from government service.
December 26	Mitchell agrees to resign his Senate seat early and Governor Mon Wallgren appoints Cain to fill the vacancy.
December 27	Cain, his family, and his staff leave by train for Washington, DC, arriving, homeless, on December 30.

1947

January 3	Congress convenes, and Cain is sworn in as Washington's junior U.S. Senator. His seniority, and the influence of key Republican leaders, allows Cain to obtain some excellent committee assignments.
January 6	Cain attends President Truman's State of the Union address.
March	Cain leads opposition to extension of public housing and rent controls. Columnist Drew Pearson calls him "America's No. 1 Real Estate Lobbyist."
March 12	President Truman proposes "Truman Doctrine" to contain the Soviet Union in speech to Joint Session of Congress.
March 21	President Truman signs Executive Order 9835, based on the recommendations of the TCEL, to create a new administrative loyalty program for all federal employees. It creates a new Loyalty Review Board (LRB) to provide "guidance" to all federal agencies. The EO greatly expands the Biddle AGLOSO and becomes one of the central influences of the Second Red Scare, generally known as the McCarthy era.
April 26	Cain supports Universal Military Training in *Saturday Evening Post* article.
May–June	Cain supports the passage of the Taft-Hartley Act, which is passed by a wide margin. President Truman vetoes the legislation.
June 23	The Senate overrides President Truman's veto. His votes earn Cain the lasting opposition of organized labor.

1948

| January 7 | President Truman delivers State of the Union message; supports the "Marshall Plan" for European recovery. |
| April 3 | Cain reluctantly votes to approve the Marshall Plan. |

May 6	Cain is one of two votes in opposition to the creation of a 70-Group Air Force, insuring the future opposition of Boeing and its unions.
June 23	Cain speaks to the Republican National Convention meeting in Philadelphia.
September 23	U.S. announces that the Soviet Union has successfully tested an atomic bomb.
November 2	Truman beats Dewey in come-from-behind victory to win term as President of the United States in his own right. The Democrats regain control of Congress.
November 19	Cain announces that he and Marjorie will divorce. They later reconcile.

1949

January 5	President Truman's State of the Union message stresses passage of his domestic agenda.
February 17	Truman nominates former Washington governor and U.S. Senator Monrad C. Wallgren to be chairman of the National Security Resources Board. Cain opposes the nomination in hearings before the Senate Armed Services Committee.
March 8	Cain filibusters Wallgren's nomination in a six-hour, forty-five-minute speech on the Senate floor.
March 10	Seattle detective agency begins a several-month-long investigation into allegations of mental illness in Cain's family. The investigation is instigated and probably funded by Wallgren.
May–June	Cain votes in favor of Republican efforts to end prematurely the Marshall Plan and against the Point Four Program, a measure that provides technological skills and equipment to poor countries. His views are in the minority on both issues.
June	Cain and others successfully oppose the nomination of Leland Olds to be chairman of the Federal Power Commission. Truman appoints Wallgren to the position.
August 29	The Soviet Union explodes its first atomic bomb.
September–November	Cain explores scheme to resign his Senate seat in order to run against Washington's other U.S. Senator, Warren Magnuson, in 1950. Republican moderates, including Governor Langlie, oppose the idea.
October 1	Mao Tse-Tung proclaims the People's Republic of China.

October 6	Cain votes against the 1949 Military Assistance Act that provides Marshall Plan aid to Western Europe and Korea. The measure is passed by Congress and signed by President Truman.
November 3	Cain opposes passage of the Housing Act of 1949, the only major piece of Truman's "Fair Deal" legislation to pass Congress.

1950

January 4	President Truman delivers his fifth State of the Union address, warning of the threat from international communism and calling twice for the passage of legislation creating the Columbia Valley Administration. Cain claims that the program "borders on Communism."
January 21	Alger Hiss is convicted of perjury in connection with spying for the Soviet Union.
February 9	Senator Joseph McCarthy makes his first public accusations of Communists in the State Department.
March 20	*TIME* magazine reporter Frank McNaughton calls Cain one of "The Senate's Most Expendable" members. Cain responds by delivering a two-hour personal attack against McNaughton on the Senate floor.
June 10	Cain filibusters the extension of federal rent controls for twelve hours eight minutes. The Senate passes the legislation anyway.
June 14	Cain is one of only two senators to vote against an extension of Social Security benefits.
June 25	North Korea invades South Korea.
September 12	Congress passes the Internal Security Act of 1950 (McCarran Act). A cornerstone of the Act is the creation of a Subversive Activities Control Board (SACB) with quasi-judicial powers to hold hearings to consider the allegations made by the Justice Department against organizations it considers subversive.
September 15	General MacArthur outflanks the North Koreans with a brilliant amphibious landing at Inchon.
September 22	President Truman decides to veto the McCarran Act. Congress overwhelmingly overrides President's Truman's veto the next day. Cain votes for both the original legislation and to override the veto.
October 25	Communist China intervenes and invades North Korea.
November 29	Cain defends the liberal Anna Rosenberg, who President Truman has nominated to be Assistant Secretary of

Defense, during her confirmation hearings after she is
attached by Senator McCarthy.

1951

January 8	President Truman delivers his first State of the Union message as a wartime president and specifically warns against "the threat of world conquest by Soviet Russia."
January	Cain's primary Senate committee assignment changes from the Banking and Currency Committee to the Armed Services Committee. Nothing more is heard from him about housing.
March 26	In a Senate speech, Cain defends the civil liberties of two Cleveland mobsters charged with contempt of Congress for refusing to testify before the Kefauver Crime Committee.
April 10	President Truman relives MacArthur of command after he repeatedly ignores orders to cease unofficial communications with Republican members of Congress.
April 17	Cain introduces two simultaneous resolutions on the Senate floor. One calls for a declaration of war against China. The second calls for withdrawing all U.S. forces from the Pacific. Both fail.
November 14	Cain welcomes MacArthur during a visit to Tacoma, calling him "the greatest citizen your junior Senator has known."

1952

May 31	Democratic Congressman Henry M. Jackson announces that he will challenge Cain for his U.S. Senate seat.
July 11	Cain addresses the Republican National Convention meeting in Chicago, the first national political convention to be televised.
September 9	Cain wins the Republican primary, but challenger Carl Viking Holman urges his supporters to vote for Jackson.
October 31	Cain delivers final statewide campaign speech during which he calls Jackson a "moral coward" for refusing to debate him in person.
November 4	Jackson defeats Cain for reelection by nearly 134,500 votes in an otherwise Republican landslide election.

1953

January 20	Dwight D. Eisenhower is inaugurated as President of the United States

Chronology

	April 10	Senator Harry Cain is nominated to fill an unfinished vacant term on the Subversive Activities Control Board.
	April 27	Eisenhower signs Executive Order 10450, which greatly expands the grounds upon which a federal employee may be dismissed from federal service to include "security" in addition to "loyalty."
	April 28	Senate votes to confirm Cain's nomination on the SACB.

1954

	October 1953–November 1954	
		Cain is contacted by a succession of federal employees who are caught up in one way or another with the government's loyalty/security program. He looks into the cases at his own expense and as a private citizen and is concerned by what he discovers about the government's actions. Cain expresses his concerns to Maxwell Rabb, an old friend and Secretary to the Cabinet at the White House.

1955

	January 15	Cain decides to speak out publicly about the loyalty/security program at a meeting of the Fifth District Republican Club in Spokane. He releases copies of his critical speech to the Washington, DC, press corps before leaving for Spokane. Liberals applaud the speech, Republicans are surprised, and the White House is shocked by being blindsided by Cain's criticisms.
	January 20	White House Chief of Staff Sherman Adams calls Cain into his office for a dressing down amounting to "unshirted hell." Attorney General Herbert Brownell and other Justice Department officials accuse Cain of being "disloyal."
	March 18	In a speech to the National Civil Liberties Clearing House, Cain calls for the liquidation of the Attorney General's list and criticizes the methods of his old friend Senator Joseph McCarthy without naming him directly.
	March 28	Cain claims on *Meet the Press* that the government should differentiate between employees who are "unreliable" and those who are "disloyal."
	April 1	Cain holds contentious meeting with Attorney General Brownell. Cain agrees to hold off on additional criticism until late May but notes that "I shall then speak about things as they are."
	May 23	Cain delivers a speech entitled "Truth or Consequences" to B'nai B'rith, specifically attacking the validity of the Attorney General's List of Subversive Organizations. He

continues his criticism, speaking on *Face the Nation* on June 5.

August 18 — Cain's rift with the White House is made public in a detailed article in *Collier's* magazine. While others are quoted in the article, the only detailed source of the information must be Cain.

September 19 — Cain speaks to the Tenth National Conference of Citizenship, describing how the Attorney General's list is being used by "states, municipalities and private agents or agencies from coast to coast."

September–October

Cain is in Seattle as the Hearing Officer in a SACB hearing to determine whether the Washington Pension Union is a Communist-front or Communist-action organization. The WPU tries to disqualify Cain for bias, only to be followed by the Justice Department that claims that Cain is biased in favor of the WPU.

November 15 — The Justice Department announces that it is modifying some aspects of its employee loyalty program and that alleged security risks will no longer be suspended without a hearing. A week later, President Eisenhower announces that his administration is making a "sweeping study" of its internal security program.

December 28 — Cain's friend, Maxwell Rabb, tells him that his future is "in dispute and doubt" around the White House.

1956

January 30 — Cain tells the Chicago affiliate of the Americans for Democratic Action that "to me personal liberty belongs to every other citizen in the same way it belongs to me. The safest and only durable way for each of us to protect our personal liberty is to make certain that the other fellow is fully protected in his."

February 22 — Cain describes the history of the AGLOSO to the New York Civil Liberties Union, telling them that the Eisenhower Administration's version permits "resolving doubts in favor of Authority before those doubts have been established to really exist."

March 2 — Deputy Attorney General William Tompkins recommends in an internal Justice Department memorandum that the AGLOSO be abandoned. FBI Director Hoover opposes the suggestion.

April 12 — Cain asks for appointments with both Herbert Brownell and Sherman Adams. Neither responds to his request.

May 5	Determining that he was not getting anywhere through official channels, Cain speaks to the National Trade Union Conference on Civil Rights in a speech entitled "The Individual is of Supreme Importance." In it, he suggests that President Eisenhower "has no real knowledge about how the individual is being treated," and asks, "Have we made more security risks than we have found?"
May 14	Cain writes directly to President Eisenhower, asking for a meeting to determine "some expression of your future wishes with regard to myself."
May 17	With his term scheduled to end at the end of August, Cain makes what he expects to be his swansong speech as a member of the SACB to the Colorado Chapter of the ACLU. He attacks the administration's "numbers game" that suggests that 9,700 federal employees have been weeded out of the federal government as a result of their loyalty-security program.
May 23	President Eisenhower is asked at his presidential news conference if he would meet with Cain if he asked for an appointment. He answers with a terse "yes." Cain immediately asks for an appointment.
June 7	Cain meets with President Eisenhower and White House Counsel Gerald D. Morgan in the Oval Office. That evening, President Eisenhower is stricken with a severe attack of ileitis that nearly kills him, resulting in a several-month-long-period of recovery. The day-to-day activities of the White House are assumed by Sherman Adams.
June 12	Testifying before the Constitutional Rights Subcommittee of the Democratically-controlled Senate Judiciary Committee, Cain tells them that President Eisenhower had "shown deep concern and interest" in his proposals, but that the rights of free men and women had been "mangled in the past."
June 17	Cain writes to President Eisenhower offering his resignation.
June 25	A detailed description of Cain's meeting with Eisenhower appears in *New Republic* magazine.
July 27	Eisenhower accepts Cain's resignation but asks him to stay on until a replacement can be found. Adams follows up with a letter, saying that it will not be necessary to remain past September 1.

	September 2	Now free to speak his mind, Cain calls for the abolition of the McCarran Act and the SACB. "The price we have paid is the abandonment of serious political dissent. America without dissenters might be secure, but it would not be America."
	c. September 8	Cain writes to Adlai Stevenson and Estes Kefauver, offering his services to their Democratic presidential campaign. He receives no response.
	September 10	Cain returns to Tacoma to explore his future prospects. They are not encouraging.
	October 23	A banquet and testimonial dinner is held in Cain's honor at the National Press Club in Washington, DC. More than 350 attend, including many of the individuals whose jobs Cain saved.
	November 6	Dwight D. Eisenhower elected to another term as President of the United States.
1957		
	April 1	Cain agrees to join the First Federal Savings and Loan Association of Miami, first as the host *First Federal Presents*, a half-hour public affairs program he moderated and they sponsored. He would remain with First Federal until 1972.
	May 22	Cain testifies on behalf of Arthur Miller during his contempt of Congress trial before the House Un-American Activities Committee, saying that he did not believe that Miller had been "under the discipline of the Communist Party."
	November	Cain agrees to work full-time for First Federal, becoming its vice president for community relations and the first non-family member of its board of directors.
1958		
	January	Marjorie Cain files for divorce.
	February 4	The Cain's divorce becomes final.
	July 18	Cain marries LaVonne Kneisley, a long-time friend, in Chevy Chase, Maryland.
1959		
	February	Cain is granted a leave of absence from First Federal to become president of Dade County United Fund. The organization is in severe difficulty. Cain serves two year-long terms and is widely recognized for providing the

leadership that saves the organization and leads to its
future success.

1960

November 8   John F. Kennedy elected President of the United States.

1962

January   Cain lobbies his long-time friend Senator Hubert
                    Humphrey for an appointment to the Federal Home
                    Loan Bank Board.

September 29   Cain agrees to manage the congressional campaign of local
                    Republican attorney Robert A. Peterson and generates
                    considerable public attention with the publication of a
                    letter describing the "terms and conditions" under which
                    he will serve, telling Peterson that his campaign has
                    "neither purpose, direction, workers, nor money." Peterson
                    loses the race, as expected, but makes a good showing by
                    local Republican standards.

1963

June 3   In the aftermath of riots in Birmingham, Alabama, Cain
                    writes to Senate Majority Leader Hubert Humphrey,
                    urging him to press President Kennedy to talk to the
                    nation about race relations.

October–November

                    Can fuels speculation that he will challenge Democratic
                    incumbent Senator Spessard Holland in 1964. He resigns
                    from the Dade County Republican Central Committee
                    over their unwillingness to support his candidacy and
                    dissatisfaction with Republican Presidential candidate
                    Barry Goldwater.

1964

January 8   Cain testifies on behalf of former Washington State
                    legislator John Goldmark during his libel trial against
                    four right-wing accusers. Cain testified that the ACLU
                    has never been a Communist-front organization.

September–October

                    Cain agrees to chair the Florida Citizens for Johnson and
                    Humphrey Committee, campaigning in each of Florida's
                    sixty-seven counties for the national Democratic ticket.

November 3   Lyndon B. Johnson defeats Barry Goldwater to become
                    President of the United States.

1965

August   Cain begins to consider a run for the U.S. Senate seat
                    held by George Smathers of Florida, which will become
                    open in 1968. Local Republican leaders continue to work

against Cain's candidacy. He says, "The only way to have any fun as a Republican in these parts is to engage in hassles with other Republicans."

1966–1967   Cain serves as president, chairman, or board member of scores of community social service agencies, rescuing the Dade County Human Relations Board in the same way as he earlier had the United Fund. He is honored by B'nai B'rith, the National Jewish Hospital and Research Center, and the National Conference for Christians and Jews.

1968

March 15   Cain explores the potential for a federal appointment in a letter to Marvin Watson, Special Assistant to President Johnson.

April 2   Cain decides at the last moment not to run for George Smathers's Senate seat. He believes that he can win a general election but cannot overcome Republican opposition in the primary.

May–December

In the aftermath of the assassination of Martin Luther King, major rioting breaks out in Liberty City. Cain helps to establish the Greater Miami Urban Coalition. He later works to attract the all-black Florida Memorial College to Miami, for which he is honored with a banquet in his honor in December.

October–November

As an opponent of the Viet Nam War, Cain announces that he will not support Hubert Humphrey for President. He supports Nelson Rockefeller for the Republican nomination and later, reluctantly, supports Richard Nixon for President.

1970

November 1   Cain raises the issue of his retirement from First Federal Savings in a thirty-two page letter, detailing the strengths and weaknesses of every major social service agency in the Greater Miami area and pleading with First Federal's management to remain deeply involved in the community after his retirement.

Chronology

1972

March–November

Never enthusiastic about Richard Nixon, Cain endorses Democrat Henry M. Jackson, the man who defeated him for reelection to the Senate, for President. Cain and Jackson became close friends during the previous ten years. While Cain does not chair Jackson's Florida campaign, he does campaign with him throughout the state, introducing Jackson at many campaign stops. Cain doesn't publicly support either Richard Nixon or George McGovern for President.

March 14

Miami voters recall four county commissioners on the same day as the Florida primary.

April 18

Initially declining, Cain later agrees to be appointed to the Miami-Dade County Commission after first resigning from First Federal Savings and Loan Association. Once sworn into office, he refuses to sign the County's outdated loyalty oath. A former two-pack-a-day smoker, one of Cain's first actions is to get the Miami-Dade County Commission to agree to an indoor smoking ban.

July 25

Cain is reelected to a four-year term on the Commission.

August 15

Cain officially resigns his position at First Federal Savings to be become a consultant.

1976

July

Increasingly in poor health, Cain decides to run for reelection to the Commission but doesn't campaign. He is defeated by a young union official, William Oliver.

1977

December 28

On his final trip back to Tacoma, Cain is honored as "Man of the Year" at a dinner sponsored by Pierce County's Japanese-American community.

1979

March 3

Harry Cain dies in his sleep at his home in Miami of complications from emphysema.

March 12

Several hundred mourners attend a memorial service for Cain held in Bayfront Park in Miami. Henry King Stanford, President of the University of Miami, quotes Edmund Burke, one of Cain's philosophical mentors, in his eulogy. "Public life is a situation of power and energy; he who trespasses against his duty sleeps upon his watch."

Photo Credits

DETERMINING THE COPYRIGHT holder of sixty-year-old photographs or whether, indeed, there *is* a current copyright holder, is a daunting process. For the most part, I have been able to rely on the large number of photographs still in the possession of the Cain children and on the extensive image collection of the Tacoma Public Library. The rest of the pictures come from a wide variety of sources and some were available from multiple sources.

The largest collection of Cain photographs is located at in the Image Archives of the Tacoma Public Library. A search under the name of "Harry P. Cain" brings forth 248 different images, while a search for "Harry Cain" generates a further 83 images. During his Senate and SACB years, Cain was extensively photographed by the various news wire services. The Associated Press survives, but many pictures from the other wire services, like Acme and INP, which went on to became UPI, are now in the extensive Corbis Images archives. The extensive TIME and LIFE image collection is now available online through Getty Images. Cain's children also had a number of original photographs that they have generously made available to me for this project.

I have attempted as much as possible to determine the identity of the copyright holder or whether the picture was still under copyright to the best of my ability. Any failures in this regard are completely inadvertent and mine alone for which I apologize in advance.

FRONT COVER: 1949 Portrait of Harry P. Cain by Irving Sinclair, Cain Family Collection

FIRST PHOTO SECTION (following page 104)
   1-6. Cain Family Collection

7. Catalogue of the Hill Military Academy 1920-21, p. 10, Oregon Historical Society Research Library

8. Cain Family Collection

9. University Archives and Special Collections, Sewanee: The University of the South

10. Cain Family Collection

11. Tacoma Public Library, Richards Studio Collection (D601-7)

12. Deutsches Bundesarchiv (B_145_Bild-P022061)

13. Tacoma Public Library, Richards Studio Collection (D8628-5)

14. Tacoma Public Library, Richards Studio Collection (D9520-5)

15. Cain Family Collection

16. Tacoma Public Library, Richards Studio Collection (D12757-1)

17. Tacoma Public Library, Richards Studio Collection (D10341-44)

18. Tacoma Public Library, Richards Studio Collection (D12115-14)

19. Tacoma Public Library, Richards Studio Collection (TPL-561)

20. Tacoma Public Library, Richards Studio Collection (D12299-11)

21. Tacoma Public Library, Richards Studio Collection (D12929-22)

22. Tacoma Public Library, Richards Studio Collection (D15642-11)

23. Tacoma Public Library, General Photo Collection (G24.1-066)

24. Tacoma Public Library, Richards Studio Collection (D14469-8)

25. Cain Family Collection

26. U.S. Navy/National Archives

27. Tacoma Public Library, Richards Studio Collection (D10734-1)

28. Michael McSherry Family/Dwight D. Eisenhower Foundation

29. U.S. Army/National Archives

30. Cain Family Collection

31. U.S. Senate Historical Office

32-33. Cain Family Collection

34. U.S. Senate Historical Office

35. Cain Family Collection

Second Photo Section (following page 258).

36. Cain Family Collection

37. ©Bettman/Corbis

38. Washington State Historical Society (Catalog ID# 1959.75.4.1)

Credits

39-40. U.S. Senate Historical Office

41. Cain Family Collection

42. Harry S. Truman Library (59-995)

43. Holt Labor Library

44. ©Bettman/Corbis

45. Associated Press

46. ©Bettman/Corbis

47. Associated Press

48. Tacoma Public Library, Richards Studio Collection (D69043-1A)

49. Tacoma Public Library, Richards Studio Collection (D69576-7)

50. University of Washington Libraries, Special Collections, Jackson for Senator

51. Marquette University Archives

52. Covello & Covello Historical Photo Collection

53. Library of Congress

54. ©Bettman/Corbis

55. TIME and LIFE Pictures/Getty

56. National Park Service/Dwight D. Eisenhower Presidential Library and Museum

57. Associated Press

58. National Park Service/Dwight D. Eisenhower Presidential Library and Museum

59. Associated Press

60-61. Cain Family Collection

62-64. Miami News Collection, History Museum of South Florida

65. Cain Family Collection

68. Author's Collection

69. Miami-Dade County Public Housing Agency

BACK COVER: Author's Photograph by Jack Zinn/Jan Jackson

Selected Bibliography

ALL OF THE sources used in the writing of this book are listed in this Selected Bibliography and noted in the Endnotes. However, I have also listed some additional documents here that I reviewed and found useful but from which I did not directly quote. For those who may be interested in future research on Harry Cain, I would make a few comments about the known resources that are available.

At some point, Cain's wife Marjorie placed a large amount of material in the archives of the Washington State Historical Society in Tacoma. This material consists of two accessions, but both are fragmentary. MS-55 covers the years 1933–1952 and is divided into nine series: Correspondence, Banking, Mayor, Radio Broadcasts, Senator, Speech Materials, Golfing, Photographs, and Miscellaneous Items. Of particular interest in this collection are Cain's personal letters from the 1930s that clearly show the breadth and scope of his personal networking and his efforts at self-promotion, including a wonderful exchange of letters in which Cain tries to convince radio executives at NBC to hire him as a radio commentator. Also included are other materials related to the 1939 Golden Jubilee Celebration as well as handwritten notes, speeches, and other materials from his campaign for mayor in 1940. The collection also contains newspaper clippings, reports, and speeches from his terms as mayor, including a portion of a journal that he kept between February 10 and November 24, 1941. Of particular interest are the original scripts of 128 weekly radio broadcasts and other special radio addresses he wrote as mayor between November 1940 and May 1946. The collection also contains a limited amount of campaign material from his 1946 and 1952 Senate campaigns.

MS-99 covers the period 1946–1952 and contains portions of Cain's incoming and outgoing correspondence files from his Senate office. These are generally organized by federal agency, Congressional committee, or subject. Cain's responses often contain extensive information about the subject at hand. Of particular interest in this collection are the files pertaining to the Columbia Basin Authority, which Cain opposed, and his personal correspondence with Art Burgess, who became his Executive Secretary in 1948.

Harry's daughter, Candy Cain Tingstad, and I have also agreed to donate all of the additional research material used in the preparation of this book to the Society. In that way, most of Cain's known papers and other material will be together in one place.

Fortunately, Cain's children had retained a great deal of information about their father, which they generously shared with me. Candy provided me with eighteen thick scrapbooks that are filled with press clippings and other items from her father's two terms as Tacoma's mayor. Clearly, her father played a key role in selecting the material that was collected for the scrapbooks, but he selected broadly. Candy also provided me with a portion (approximately forty typewritten pages) of a wartime journal and roughly sixty letters that Cain wrote to his wife and friends during World War II. Together, they provide a valuable, if partial, memoir of his experiences during the war. Of particular interest were several phonograph records and reel-to-reel tape recordings of radio and television interviews from the 1940s and 1950s, and in particular from the 1952 Senate campaign, as well as a cassette tape recording of a multi-part radio interview broadcast by a Miami public affairs radio station in 1979. Thankfully, most of these recordings have been able to be saved in digital format. Candy also provided me with a Cain family history written in 1970 by one of Cain's uncles that was very useful in sorting out the Cain family tradition of giving identical first names to members of successive generations, and Harry's remarkable baby book, full of pictures and data, carefully maintained by his young mother until she took her life when the boys were only eleven years old.

Harry's son, Harry P. Cain II, provided further material about his father's high school days at Hill Military Academy in Portland, a portion of a detailed journal that Harry kept during his year-long European trip in 1935–36, and additional copies of speeches, letters, and more photographs. He also provided me with a copy of an unpublished final draft of a graduate-level term paper he wrote while studying for his master's degree in public administration at the University of Washington. The paper provides a detailed look at the "Cain Mutiny" during the period that his father served on the Subversive Activities Control Board and is based on Cain's personal papers and correspondence, now sadly lost. The paper is really quite remarkable. The draft contains the senior Cain's hand-written notes, making corrections and suggestions for the final version. Some of the chapters in this book rely quite heavily on these previously unpublished family sources.

Irving Thomas's granddaughter, Kathy Lyle, provided me with a folder full of clippings and other mementos that her mother had collected detailing the long friendship and political collaboration between her father, Irving Thomas, and Harry Cain that began even before the 1939 Golden Jubilee celebration and extending to the end of Thomas's tenure as Cain's chief of staff in the Senate.

Unfortunately, the location and disposition of the rest of Cain's official papers from his terms as mayor of Tacoma, U.S. Senator, and SACB member, or from his years in Florida are unknown. Letters found in the WSHS files confirm that both the University of Washington and the University of Oregon wrote Cain asking for his papers, but there is no response to these requests.

Cain's service records were obtained from the National Archives. The Library of Congress provided numerous press clippings. Original copies of his major speeches and reprints from *The Congressional Record* were already available from other sources. The Office of the Senate Historian provided several photographs and well as helped me to identify the location of Cain's Senate offices and the specific desks he occupied on the floor of the Senate. The Harry S. Truman Library and Museum houses the Monrad C. Wallgren Papers. They helped me find a number of letters between Cain and Truman, as well as certain letters and photographs that are referenced later in this book and the texts of Truman's State of the Union messages. The Dwight D. Eisenhower Presidential Library and Museum provided me with copies of the correspondence between Cain and Maxwell M. Rabb, a personal friend of Cain's, who served as Secretary to the Cabinet during the period of the "Cain mutiny," as well directed me to Eisenhower's daily schedules and State of the Union messages.

The Special Collections Department at the University of Washington is a wonderful place for researchers into Washington State history. Over the course of a week in early 2010, I was able to sift through many dozens of boxes containing files related to Harry Cain in the papers of Warren G. Magnuson (Accessions 3181-001/025), Hugh B. Mitchell (Accessions 0281-001-1, 0818-001, 0927-001, and 1407-001), Henry M. Jackson (Accessions 3560-1001/034). Although Governor Arthur Langlie's official papers reside at the Washington State Archives in Olympia, Special Collections at the University of Washington has some of his personal papers, which I found very helpful in sorting out the complicated relationship between Cain and Langlie.

While my book represents the first biography devoted exclusively to Harry Cain, he appears in a number of books devoted to other subjects. I would like to single these out from the rest of the books listed in the bibliography. In 1998, Professor Ronald E. Magden published *Furusato*, a history of Pierce County's Japanese-American community that chronicles Cain's extensive relationships with the local Oriental community before World War II and his opposition to the detention and relocation of the local Japanese-Americans from their point of view. Professor Richard O. Davies has written two books that discuss Cain's opposition to public housing and rent controls while a member of the U.S. Senate. His *Housing Reform during the Truman Administration* was published in 1966, and his *Defender of the Old Guard: John Bricker and American Politics* was released in 1993. Arthur Miller's 1987 autobiography, *Timebends: A Life*, provides a sympathetic view of Cain during the time he defended Miller in his contempt of Congress trial. Judge William Dwyer's excellent 1984 book, *The Goldmark Case: An American Libel Trial*, discusses the role that Cain played in the 1965 Goldmark libel trial.

Three excellent political biographies provide glimpses of Cain and his politics from the viewpoint of his opponents. Long-time Seattle political reporter Shelby Scates wrote a highly favorable and very readable account of Senator Warren G. Magnuson's life and political contributions, *Warren G. Magnuson and the Shaping of Twentieth Century America*, in 1997. He almost certainly had access to Magnuson's personal political papers at the University of Washington that are still closed to most researchers. There are two good biographies of Senator Henry M. Jackson. Both contain valuable insights about Cain and the hard-fought 1952 campaign from the perspective of the Jackson camp. The first, *A Certain Democrat: Senator Henry M. Jackson*, was published by William Prochnau and Richard

Larsen in 1972. The second, Robert G Kaufman's, *Henry M. Jackson: A Life in Politics*, was released in 2000.

I have also been privileged to read several unpublished doctoral dissertations in which Harry Cain makes an appearance. Former Washington State legislator George W. Scott wrote his 1971 doctoral dissertation on the three-term Republican governor, Arthur B. Langlie, who had a long and complicated relationship with Cain. I also owe George a debt of gratitude for guiding me through the many resources of the University of Washington Library. Former Tacoma mayor Bill Baarsma's 1973 dissertation at George Washington University deals with the events leading up to the eventual changes in Tacoma's City Charter that finally moved the city from the commission to council-manager form of government. Cain had advocated that change as early as 1938 and continued to support it during his two terms as mayor. Tacoma historian Caroline Gallacci's 1999 dissertation from the University of Washington deals with the history of urban planning in the city of Tacoma, a movement much supported by Cain.

Most of the record of Harry Cain's long public career comes from the newspaper stories and magazine interviews he often worked so hard to generate. Positive or negative, Cain was always "good copy." Because of his prior newspaper experience, Cain understood how the print media worked and genuinely liked most of its working members. The feeling was mostly reciprocal. He understood the importance of a friendly drink; a timely leak, a colorful quote, and—above all—the importance of making members of the press feel important.

During his term in the Senate and on the SACB, Cain was covered by the much more skeptical and often more cynical national press, primarily the *Washington Post*, the *Washington Evening Star,* and the *New York Times*. Their coverage was picked up by the wire services and re-printed in newspapers across the nation. These were joined by the writers and columnists for the major newsmagazines, *TIME* and *Newsweek,* and additional coverage provided by magazines like *Collier's, The Reporter,* and *The Nation*. His activities in Miami were generously covered in the *Miami News* and the *Miami Herald* and by local columnists like Herb Rau, Herb Bergida, and Larry King—yes, *that* Larry King!

All of the online resources I consulted are listed in the Notes, along with the date I accessed them, with one exception. Sometime prior to the beginning of my research on this book, a Tacoma historian, Jess Giessel, developed an extensive Website about Harry Cain with the intent of someday writing a book about him. Health problems intervened, and the site is no longer online. However, Gessel generously provided me with the text of his site, which was the size of an extensive article, organized into chapters, which I consulted from time to time during the writing of this book. Not knowing where to list it below, I am acknowledging it here. It will eventually be among the other research materials donated to the Washington State Historical Society.

Unpublished Sources

Manuscript Collections

Arthur B. Langlie Papers, Special Collections. University of Washington. Seattle, Washington.

C. Mark Smith Collection. In the author's possession. Richland, Washington.

Candy Cain Tingstad Collection. In the custody of Cain's daughter. Lakewood, Washington.

Dwight D. Eisenhower. Presidential Library and Museum. Abilene, Kansas.

Harry P. Cain Papers. Washington State Historical Society. Tacoma, Washington.

Harry P. Cain II Collection. In the custody of Cain's son. Williamsburg, Virginia.

Henry M. Jackson Papers. Special Collections. University of Washington. Seattle, Washington.

Hugh Mitchell Papers. Special Collections. University of Washington. Seattle, Washington.

Library of Congress. Washington, DC.

Monrad C. Wallgren Papers. Harry S. Truman Museum and Library. Independence, Missouri.

National Archives. College Park, Maryland.

Office of the Senate Historian. Washington, DC.

Tacoma Public Library. Tacoma, Washington.

Harry S. Truman Presidential Library and Museum. Independence, Missouri.

Warren G. Magnuson Papers. Special Collections. University of Washington. Seattle, Washington.

Interviews with the Author

Cain, Harry P., date unknown, 1961.

Cain, Harry P. II, November 28, 2008.

Goldstein, Robert Justin, October 19, 2009.

Selected Bibliography

Scott, George W., January 25, 2010

Tingstad, Candy Cain, July 11, 2008; August 22, 2008, November 5, 2008; November 9, 2008, December 2, 2008; December 4, 2008; December 15, 2008.

Letters and e-mails to the Author

Cain, Harry P. II, December 4, 2008; January 8, 2009; January 31, 2009; February 9, 2009; February 17, 2009; April 12, 2009; June 6, 2009; February 6, 2010.

Chua, Jimmy M.D., November 24-25, 2009

Goldstein, Robert Justin, February 2, 2010.

Greenberg, Harvey R., M.D., December 1, 2009; December 2, 2009

Hein, David W., June 13, 2009.

McSherry, James M., August 12 and 14, 2010

Paranada, Kathleen S., M.D., November 24, 2009

Shockley, Cathy, August 5, 2009.

Tingstad, Candy Cain, December 14, 2008; May 5, 2009; November 23, 2009.

York, Brian, M.D., November 25, 2009

Recorded Speeches and Interviews:

America's Town Meeting of the Air: March 6, 1947. George V. Denny, Jr., Moderator; Senator Harry P. Cain (R-Wash.) and Senator Francis J. Myers (D-Penn.). compact disk transfer from a 33 rpm record. Candy Cain Tingstad Collection.

Meet the Press: October 23, 1952. Martha Roundtree, Moderator; Senator Harry P. Cain (R-Wash.) and Senator Robert S. Kerr (D-Okla.). reel-to-reel tape recording. Candy Cain Tingstad Collection.

Harry P. Cain, luncheon address to the Young Men's Business Club, Tacoma, Washington, August 15, 1952. reel-to-reel tape recording. Candy Cain Tingstad Collection.

Harry P. Cain, statewide radio address: October 3, 1952. reel-to-reel tape recording. Candy Cain Tingstad Collection.

Harry P. Cain, interview on KPUG Radio, Bellingham, Washington, October 28, 1952. reel-to-reel tape recording. Candy Cain Tingstad Collection.

Harry P. Cain, interview with Charles Kappes on WNWS Radio, Miami, Florida, March 12, 1979. audiocassette tape recording. Candy Cain Tingstad Collection.

Marjorie Cain, interview on KPUG Radio, Bellingham, Washington, October 28, 1952.

reel-to-reel tape recording. Candy Cain Tingstad Collection.

Other Unpublished Documents:

Baarsma, William Henry. "A Study of Dissension and Conflict over Council-Management government in Tacoma, Washington and an Analysis of the Impact of that Dissention and Conflict on Governmental Decision-Making in Policy and Administrative Areas." PhD diss., George Washington University, 1973.

Cain, Harry P., II. "A Case Study of Former Senator Harry P. Cain as Critic of the Eisenhower Administration's Internal Security Program in the Years 1955–1956." Draft of graduate-level term paper, University of Washington, 1959.

Gallacci, Caroline. "Planning the City of Destiny: An Urban History of Tacoma to 1930." PhD diss., University of Washington, 1999.

Patenaude, Marc. "The McCarran Internal Security Act, 1950–2005: Civil Liberties Versus National Security." Master of Arts thesis, Louisiana State University, 2006.

Smith, C. Mark. "The Cain 'Mutiny.'" Senior history thesis, University of Puget Sound, 1961.

Scott, George W. "Arthur B. Langlie: Republican Governor in a Democratic Age." PhD diss., University of Washington, 1971.

Walk, George W. "Fighting Fawcett: A Political Biography of Angelo Vance Fawcett."

Master of Arts thesis, Western Washington State College, 1976.

PUBLISHED SOURCES

Newspapers and Periodicals

BECAUSE HARRY CAIN was a trained reporter and had a well-developed flair for publicity, he understood the needs of the reporters and newspapermen who covered him and often sought out their company. For the most part, they responded positively because Cain was always good copy. Much of the research for this book was based upon this reporting. The full citation for each newspaper and magazine article appears under the appropriate chapter heading in the Notes section of the book. Not surprisingly, most of these clippings come from the hometown papers where Cain lived and worked. In particular, these include the: *Tacoma News Tribune, Tacoma Times, Seattle Post-Intelligencer, Seattle Times, Washington Post, Washington Evening Star, Miami Herald,* and *Miami Times.*

Wire service reporting, particularly from the Associated Press, was obtained through the data retrieval services of the Library of Congress and other online services. The majority of these clippings originally appeared in the *New York Times, Washington Post,* and *Dallas Morning News.*

Books, Articles, and Congressional Publications

Adams, Sherman. *Firsthand Report: The Story of the Eisenhower Administration.* New York: Harper & Brothers, 1961.

Ambrose, Stephen E. *Eisenhower: Soldier and President.* New York: Simon & Shuster, 1990.

———. *D-Day: The Climactic Battle of World War II.* New York: Simon & Shuster, 1994.

Ambrose, Stephen and Douglas Brinkley, ed. *Witness to America.* New York: Harper Collins Publishers, Inc., 1999.

Andrew, Christopher. *Defend the Realm: The Authorized History of MI5.* New York: Alfred A. Knopf, 2009.

Atkinson, Rick. *The Day of Battle: The War in Sicily and Italy 1943–1944.* New York: Henry Holt & Co., 2007.

Barth, Alan. *The Loyalty of Free Men.* New York: Viking Press, 1952.

Bell, Jonathan. *The Liberal State on Trial.* New York: Columbia University Press, 2004.

Berman, Daniel N. "Cain and the President." *The New Republic,* June 25, 1956: 10-15.

Berner, Richard. *Seattle: 1921–1940: From Boom to Bust.* Philadelphia: Charles Press, 1992.

Blair, Clay. *Ridgway's Paratroopers: The American Airborne in World War II,* New York: Random House, 1985.

Blumenson, Martin. *Mark Clark: The Last of the Great World War II Commanders.* New York: Congdon & Weed, 1984.

Brownell, Herbert with John Burke. *Advising Ike: The Memoirs of Attorney General Herbert Brownell.* Lawrence, KS: University Press of Kansas, 1993.

Cain, Grace Pulliam. The Columbus Light. *American Catholic Historical Society of Philadelphia,* Vol. XXVI (1915): 26.

———. Report by Grace Pulliam Cain. *Confederate Veteran,* 21 (1913): 39.

Cain, Harry P. Blitzing the Brothels. *Journal of Social Hygiene,* December 1943: 594-600.

———. *Current Biography.* New York: H.W. Wilson, 1949: 88-90.

———. Nomination of Mon C. Wallgren to be Chairman of the National Security Resources Board—Statement and letters by Senator Cain. *Congressional Record,* 81st Cong., 1st sess., March 3, 1949: 1770-1784.

———. "Security of the Republic." *New Republic,* January 31, 1955: 6-10;

reprinted in *Congressional Record*, 84th Cong., 1st sess., February 16, 1955, A978-80.

Cain, Harry P. as told to Tris Coffin. "I Could Not Remain Silent." *Coronet*, November 1955: 29-35.

Cain, Stith Malone. *A History of Our Cain Family of Virginia, Alabama and Tennessee*. Whitewater, WI: self-published, 1970.

Caro, Robert A. *The Years of Lyndon Johnson: Master of the Senate*. New York: Alfred A. Knopf, 2002.

Cater, Douglass. "Senator Cain: Washington Hamlet." *The Reporter*, September 2, 1952: 13-16.

Caute, David. *The Great Fear: The Anti-Communist Purge Under the Truman and Eisenhower*. New York: Simon & Shuster, 1978.

Clark, Mark W. *Calculated Risk: The Personal Story of the War in North Africa and Italy*. London: George G. Harrap & Co., Ltd., 1951.

Clark, Lloyd. *Crossing the Rhine: Breaking into Nazi Germany 1944–1945*. New York: Atlantic Monthly Press, 2008.

Cohen, Adam. *Nothing to Fear: FDR's Inner Circle and the Hundred Days that Created Modern America*. New York: The Penguin Press, 2008.

Cohn, Roy. *McCarthy*. New York: The New American Library, 1968.

Coles, Harry L. and Albert K. Weinberg. *Civil Affairs: Soldiers Become Governors*. Washington, DC: Center of Military History, 1992.

Crosby, Roderick, "Senior Class Prophecy." *The Adjutant*, Hill Military Academy, 1924.

Davies, Richard O. *Housing Reform during the Truman Administration*. Columbia, MO: University of Missouri Press, 1966.

———. *Defender of the Old Guard: John Bricker and American Politics*. Columbus, OH: Ohio State University Press, 1993.

D'Este, Carlo. *World War II in the Mediterranean*. Chapel Hill, NC: Algonquin Books, 1990.

———. *Eisenhower: A Soldier's Life*. New York: Henry Holt and Company, 2002.

———. *Warlord: A Life of Winston Churchill at War, 1874–1945*. New York: HarperCollins Publishers, 2008.

Derieux, James C., "'Hurry' Cain Out of the West." *Colliers*, August 13, 1949: 63-65.

Dickstein, Morris. *Dancing in the Dark: A Cultural History of the Great Depression*. New York: W. W. Norton & Company, 2009.

Donovan, Robert J. *Conflict and Crisis: The Presidency of Harry S. Truman, 1945–1948*. New York: W. W. Norton, 1977.

———. *Tumultuous Years: The Presidency of Harry S. Truman, 1949–1953*.

Selected Bibliography

Columbia, MO: University of Missouri Press, 1982.

Dwyer, William. *The Goldmark Case: An American Libel Trial*. Seattle: University of Washington Press, 1984.

Edwards, Willard. "The Reformation of Harry Cain." *American Murcury*, October 1955: 39-44.

Eisenhower, David. *Eisenhower at War 1943–1945*. New York: Random House, 2002.

Eisenhower, John S. D. *General Ike: A Personal Reminiscence*. New York: Free Press, 2003.

Evans, M. Stanton. *Blacklisted by History: The Untold Story of Senator Joseph McCarthy and His Fight against America's Enemies*. New York: Crown Forum, 2007.

Ferrell, Robert H. *Harry S. Truman: A Life*. Columbia, MO: University of Missouri Press, 1994.

———. *The Eisenhower Diaries*. New York: W. W. Norton, 1981.

Fried, Richard M. Nightmare in Red: The McCarthy Era in Perspective. Reprint, New York: Oxford University Press, 1990.

Funigiello, Phillip J. The Challenge of Urban Liberalism: Federal-City Relations during World War II, Knoxville, TN, University of Tennessee Press, 1978.

Gaddis, John Lewis, The United States and the Origins of the Cold War, 1941–1947. New York: Columbia University Press, 1972.

———. Strategies of Containment: A Critical Appraisal of Postwar American National Security Policy. New York: Oxford University Press, 1982.

Gallacci, Caroline, and Ron Karabaich. City of Destiny and the South Sound. Carlsbad, CA: Heritage Media Corp, 2001.

Gawne, Jonathan. Finding Your Father's War: A Practical Guide to Researching and Understanding Service in the World War II U.S. Army. Drexel Hills, PA: Casement, 2006.

Gerdes, Louise I., ed. The 1940s. San Diego, CA: Greenhaven Press, 2000.

Goldstein, Robert Justin. Raising Cain: Senator Harry Cain and His Attack on the Attorney General's List of Subversive Organizations. Pacific Northwest Quarterly, 98 no. 2 (Spring 2007): 64-77.

———. American Blacklist: The Attorney General's List of Subversive Organizations. Lawrence, KS: University Press of Kansas, 2008.

Gordon, Joseph, Sr. "On a Sunday last September." The Rotarian, October 2009: 51.

Halberstam, David. The Coldest Winter: America and the Korean War. New York: Hyperion, 2007.

Hartley, William and Ellen. "Harry Cain: The Republican Rebel Who Won't Shut Up." Pageant Magazine, October 1965: 113-117

Hastings, Max. Winston's War: Churchill 1940–1945. New York: Alfred A. Knopf, 2010.

Hamby, Alonzo L. Man of the People: A Life of Harry S. Truman. New York: Oxford University Press, 1995.

Herman, Arthur. Joseph McCarthy: Re-examining the Senator's Life and Legacy. New York: Simon & Shuster, 2000.

Hopkins, Harry. Spending to Save: The Complete Story of Relief. Seattle: University of Washington Press, 1936. Reprint 1972.

Hunt, Herbert. Tacoma: Its History and Its Builders: A Half Century of Activity. Chicago: S. J. Clarke, 1916.

Japanese-American Citizen League. "The Case of the Nisei: Brief of the Japanese American Citizens' League." Japanese American Citizens' League, 1945.

Kallen, Stuart A., ed. The 1950s. San Diego, CA: Greenhaven Press, 2000.

Kaufman, Robert G. Henry M. Jackson: A Life in Politics. Seattle: University of Washington Press, 2000.

Kennedy, David M. Freedom from Fear: The American People in Depression and War, 1929–1945. New York: Oxford University Press, 1999.

Kirkendall, Richard S. A Global Power: America since the age of Roosevelt, New York: Alfred A. Knopf, 1973.

———. The United States 1929–1945: Years of Crisis and Change. New York: McGraw-Hill, 1974.

Knightlinger, Ted. "The Golden Age of Tacoma Radio." Tacoma News Tribune Magazine Section, October 25, 1970: 14-15.

Kormer, Robert W. "The Establishment of the Allied Control Commission." Military Affairs, 26, no. 1, (Spring 1949): 20-28.

Lasky, Victor. J.F.K.: The Man and the Myth. New York: Macmillan Company, 1963.

Lindley, Ernest K. "Of Harry Cain." Newsweek, May 28, 1956.

Magden, Ronald E. Furusato: Tacoma-Pierce County Japanese 1999–1977. Tacoma, WA: South Puget Sound Day of Remembrance Consortium, 1998.

Magden, Ronald E., ed. To Live in Dignity: Pierce County Labor 1883–1989. Tacoma, WA: Pierce County Central Labor Council, 1989.

Manchester, William. The Glory and the Dream: A Narrative History of America, 1932–1972. Boston: Little, Brown and Company, 1974.

Matusow, Harvey. False Witness. New York: Cameron & Kahn Publishers, 1955.

McCullough, David. Truman. New York: Simon & Schuster, 1982.

McCallum, John. Six Roads from Abilene: Some Personal Recollections of Edgar Eisenhower. Seattle: Wood & Reber, Inc., 1960.

Medved, Michael. The Shadow Presidents: The Secret History of the Chief

Executives and Their Top Aides. New York: Times Books, 1979.

Melley, Timothy. Empire of Conspiracy: The Culture of Paranoia in Postwar America. Ithaca, NY: Cornell University Press, 2000.

Miller, Arthur. Timebends: A Life. New York: Grove Press, 1987.

Miller, Merle. *Plain Speaking: An Oral Biography of Harry S. Truman.* New York: Berkley Books, 1974.

Morgan, Murray, Rosa Morgan, and Rita Happy. *South on the Sound: An Illustrated History of Tacoma and Pierce County.* Woodland Hills, CA: Windsor Publications, 1984.

Morgan, Murray. *Puget's Sound: A Narrative of Early Tacoma and the Southern Sound.* Seattle: University of Washington Press, 1979.

Morison, Elting E. *Turmoil and Tradition: A Story of the Life and Times of Henry L. Stimson.* New York: Francis Parkman Prize Edition, History Book Club, 2003.

Nasaw, David. *The Chief: The Life of William Randolph Hearst.* Boston: Houghton Mifflin Company, 2000.

National Affairs Magazine. "Washington: Raising Cain." October 18, 1946: 25-26.

New Republic. "Knights and Knaves in Eisenhower's Great Crusade." 127:15 (June 28, 1952): 15.

Newsweek. "Cain Verses Wallgren." March 21, 1949: 22-23,

Oakes, John B. "The Security Issue: A Changing Atmosphere." *New York Times Magazine,* August 14, 1952: 9-56.

Olson, Lynne. *Troublesome Young Men: The Rebels Who Brought Churchill to Power and Helped Save England.* New York: Farrar, Straus and Giroux, 2007.

Oshinsky, David M. *A Conspiracy So Impressive: The World of Joe McCarthy.* New York: The Free Press, 1983.

Parmet, Herbert S. *Eisenhower and the American Crusades.* New York: MacMillan, 1972.

Patterson, James. *Mr. Republican, A Biography of Robert A. Taft.* Boston: Houghton Mifflin, 1972.

Patterson, Robert P. "We Must Have Military Training—Now!" *Saturday Evening Post,* April 26, 1947:

Pierce County Labor Centennial Committee. "To Live in Dignity: Pierce County Labor 1883–1989."

Poen, Monte M., ed. *Strictly Personal and Confidential: The Letters Harry Truman Never Mailed.* Columbia, MO: University of Missouri Press, 1999.

Prina, L. Edgar. "The Harry Cain 'Mutiny.'" *Collier's,* September 2, 1955: 32-35.

Prosch, Thomas W. *McCarver and Tacoma.* Seattle: Lowman and Hanford, 1906.

Procnau, William W. and Richard W. Larsen. *A Certain Democrat: Henry M.*

Jackson. Englewood Cliffs, NJ: Prentice-Hall, Inc., 1972.

Ridgway, Matthew B. "Mission Accomplished: A Summary of Military Operations of the XVIII Corps (Airborne) in the European Theatre of Operations, 1944–1945." XVIII Corps (Airborne), 1945: 5-6.

———. *Soldier: Memoirs of Matthew Ridgway*. New York: Harper and Brothers, 1956.

Scates, Shelby. *Maurice Rosenblatt and the Fall of Joseph McCarthy*. Seattle: University of Washington Press, 2006.

———. *Warren G. Magnuson and the Shaping of Twentieth Century America*. Seattle: University of Washington Press, 1997.

Schrecker, Ellen. *Many Are the Crimes: McCarthyism in America*. Boston: Little, Brown and Company, 1998.

Schwantes, Carlos Arnold. *The Pacific Northwest: An Interpretive History*. Lincoln, NE: University of Nebraska Press, 1989.

Sloan, Bill. *The Darkest Summer*. New York: Simon & Schuster, 2009.

Stone, Geoffrey R. *Perilous Times: Free Speech in Wartime*. New York: W. W. Norton, 2004.

TIME Magazine. "Fall Planting." October 3, 1949: 10.

———. "The Senate's Most Expendable." March 20, 1950.

———. http://www.time.com/time/magazine/article/0,9171,805109,00. html. (accessed January 12, 2009).

———. "12 Hours, 8 Minutes." June 19, 1950: 20.

Tomkins, C. David. *Senator Arthur H. Vandenberg: The Evolution of a Modern Republican, 1884–1945*. East Lansing, MI: Michigan State University Press, 1970.

Voorhees, Melvin B. "Harry Cain Rides Once More Out of the Past." *Argus Magazine*, No. 49, December 6, 1963: 70.

Waller, William, ed. *Nashville: 1900–1910*. Nashville, TN: Vanderbilt University Press, 1972.

Weigley, Russell F. *Eisenhower's Lieutenants: The Campaign for France and Germany, 1944–1945*. Bloomington, IN: Indiana University Press, 1981.

Wright, Gwendolyn. *Building the Dream: A Social History of Housing*. New York: Pantheon, 1981.

Zelizer, Julian. *Arsenal of Democracy: The Politics of National Security – From World War II to the War on Terror*. New York: Basic Books, 2010.

Zinn, Howard. *Postwar America: 1945–1971*. Cambridge, MA: South End Press, 2002.

Ziemke, Earl F. *The U.S. Army in the Occupation of Germany 1944–1946*. Washington, DC: Center of Military History, 1975.

Index

Index

Index

Index

Index

Index

Index

Index

Index

Index

About the Type

THE TEXT OF this book is set in MinionPro 11.5/13.8. Minion is the name of a typeface designed by Robert Slimbach in 1990 for Adobe Systems. The name comes from the traditional naming system for type sizes, in which minion is between nonpareil and brevier. It is inspired by late Renaissance-era type. Minion Pro is an update of the original family, released in 2000.

About the Author

A NATIVE OF Tacoma, Washington, C. Mark Smith spent forty years managing economic development organizations at the local, state, and federal level. He is a Fellow Member and Honorary Life Member of the International Economic Development Council and received a Lifetime Achievement Award from Washington Governor Gary Locke in 2004. Apart from his professional career, Smith's other interests have revolved around history, politics, and community service. He is a graduate of the University of Puget Sound and served for eight years as a member of their Board of Trustees. Through his family, he became acquainted with Harry Cain in the 1950s and credits Cain with influencing his own decision to enter public service. Smith lives with his wife, Elsa, in Richland, Washington.